Salem Story engages the story of the Salem witch trials by contrasting an analysis of the surviving primary documentation with the way the events of 1692 have been mythologized by our culture. Resisting the temptation to explain the Salem witch trials in the context of an inclusive but distorting theoretical framework, the book examines a variety of individual motives that converged to precipitate the witch-hunt. *Salem Story* also examines subsequent mythologicizations, such as the scapegoating of the slave Tituba, the sexualizing and age stereotyping of "witches" in popular culture, and attempts to force interpretations of the witch-hunt into paradigms of future generations.

Of the many assumptions about the Salem witch trials, the most persistent is that they were instigated by a circle of hysterical girls. Through an analysis of what actually happened – by perusal of the primary materials with the "close reading" approach of a literary critic – a different picture emerges: one where "hysteria" inappropriately describes the logical, rational strategies of accusation and confession followed by the accusers, males and females alike.

CAMBRIDGE STUDIES IN AMERICAN LITERATURE AND CULTURE

Salem Story

Continued on pages following the index

Salem Story

Reading the Witch Trials of 1692

BERNARD ROSENTHAL

SUNY–Binghamton

CAMBRIDGE
UNIVERSITY PRESS

Published by the Press Syndicate of the University of Cambridge
The Pitt Building, Trumpington Street, Cambridge CB2 1RP
40 West 20th Street, New York, NY 10011-4211, USA
10 Stamford Road, Oakleigh, Melbourne 3166, Australia

First published 1993

Printed in the United States of America

Library of Congress Cataloging-in-Publication Data
Rosenthal, Bernard, 1934–
Salem story : reading the witch trials of 1692 / Bernard Rosenthal
p. cm. – (Cambridge studies in American literature and culture ; #73)
Includes bibliographical references and index.
ISBN 0-521-44061-0 (hardback)
1. Witchcraft – Massachusetts – Salem.
2. Trials (Witchcraft) – Massachusetts – Salem.
3. Salem (Mass.) – Church history.   I. Title.
II. Series : Cambridge studies in American literature and culture ; 73.
BF1576.R67   1994
133.4′3′097445 – dc20   93–609
                                                                           CIP

A catalog record for this book is available from the British Library

ISBN 0-521-44061-0 hardback

In Memory of My Parents
Charles and Gutte Rosenthal

Contents

Acknowledgments

In writing this book I have been fortunate in having the encouragement and intellectual stimulation of many friends, colleagues, and students. If I cannot name everyone who provided assistance, from sending clippings to suggesting sources, I nevertheless can acknowledge some of the people who in one way or another have helped me. Among my students, I express my appreciation to David Callaway, Millie Crandall, Steve Harriman, Sandra Jamieson, Jyan-Lung Lin, Debbie Mitchell, Everett Wilson, as well as to the other students whose enthusiasm helped so much in intangible ways.

Among my colleagues at the State University of New York at Binghamton, I am particularly grateful to Martin Bidney, Norman Burns, Charles Carpenter, Michael Conlon, Mario DiCesare, Carol Fischler, Lucy Nelson, Bruce Norcross, Marcia Poore, Paul Szarmach, and Albert Tricomi. Elsewhere, I am also grateful to Joseph Andriano, Charlene Avallone, Dorothy Burns, Ely Faber, Elizabeth Fox-Genovese, Jennifer Jopp, Mary McCarl, Jane Kamensky, Brian P. Levack, Stephen Nissenbaum, Sasha Nyary, and Jim, Margaret, Colin, and Ruth Swithenbank. For secretarial and technical assistance, I express my appreciation to Bart Anthony, Arlene Nowalk, Lisa Fegley-Schmidt, and Christine Storrs.

I also wish to thank the library staffs at the American Antiquarian Society, Colonial Williamsburg, Cornell University, the Essex Institute, Harvard University, the Practical Bible Training School, and the State University of New York at Binghamton. I especially acknowledge the help of Mary E. Fabiszewski, Jerry Franz, Diane Geraci, Nancy Heywood, William T. La Moy, George McKee, James Mallone, Rachelle Moore, Edward J. Shephard, and Jane E. Ward. I have a special dept to Irene Norton at the Essex Institute for helping me find so much in the collection there and to Thomas Knoles at the American Antiquarian Society for more than once offering me extraordinary assistance.

In addition to helping me in a variety of ways connected with the town of Salem, Joseph Flibbert gave a meticulous reading to the final chapter. Others have also read portions of the manuscript and made valuable suggestions. Kathryn Sklar made incisive comments on the early chapters and, in response to an appeal for help on George Burroughs and the Baptists, Richard Gildrie offered pointed, valuable criticism. Michael G. Hall read most of the manuscript and offered generous encouragement even as he wisely identified stylistic and substantive problems. David L. Greene similarly read most of the manuscript and saved me from a variety of mistakes. He also readily supplied me with much material that would have otherwise been difficult to obtain. I have been overwhelmed by his generosity and by his knowledge.

Throughout this project, I have deeply appreciated the encouragement and support of Nina Baym, Edward H. Davidson, Cathy N. Davidson, Emory Elliott, and William J. Scheick. In addition to helping me in many other ways, William Scheick also read the manuscript with sharp, discerning skill.

For his confidence in this study I express my appreciation to Eric Sundquist, editor of Cambridge Studies in American Literature and Culture. I have also appreciated his high degree of professionalism and judgment. Similarly I have valued the rigorous and helpful copy-editing of Michael Gnat, the general handling of editorial matters by Julie Greenblatt, and the production management of Deborah Menzell at Cambridge University Press. Michael Gnat generously offered assistance well beyond his normal editorial duties, including, with Linda Gnat-Mullin, preparation of the index. I am grateful to both of them.

I have received other kinds of help, including a summer grant from the National Endowment for the Humanities and a research semester from the State University of New York at Binghamton. Most of all, however, I have had the special pleasure of having my children join me in this journey toward understanding the Salem story. My daughter Helen, a professional comedian, and my son Dan, an engineer, read much of the manuscript and helped me to look at it as the general, educated reader might. My daughter Laura, an Assistant Professor of English, gave the manuscript a thorough reading from a scholarly and stylistic perspective. Dan, with the assistance of his wife Rosalind, developed software called "Perfect Professor" to help me find my way through the thousands of notes I had accumulated in a technology I little understood. Near the completion of the book, my grandson James joined us.

My wife, Evelyn, I thank for the many readings of manuscript drafts, for hours I cannot count in exploring the subject of Salem's story with me, for this journey, and for the others we have taken.

Finally, if I have not expressed my appreciation to all who have helped, the omission has been inadvertent; I also offer the disclaimer that whatever mistakes may appear in this book cannot be the fault of any of the people who so generously assisted me.

Introduction

Behind their victims came the afflicted, a guilty and miserable band; villains who had thus avenged themselves on their enemies, and viler wretches, whose cowardice had destroyed their friends; lunatics, whose ravings had chimed in with the madness of the land; and children, who had played a game that the imps of darkness might have envied them, since it disgraced an age, and dipped a people's hands in blood.
– Nathaniel Hawthorne, "Alice Doane's Appeal"[1]

Few topics in American culture have received the broad attention received by the Salem witch trials. The subject of scholarly tomes, films, television shows, folklore, and newspaper cartoons, and the vehicle for countless metaphors of oppression and persecution, Salem has had a powerful hold on American imagination. An event that by some European standards of witchcraft persecutions would be relatively minor in its magnitude has achieved an archetypal status in our own country and in others.

The story begins in the household of the Reverend Samuel Parris, minister of Salem Village in Massachusetts Bay colony. In January or February of 1691 his 9-year-old daughter Betty and his 11-year-old niece, Abigail Williams,[2] began suffering severely, or feigned such suffering – we will never know exactly which. According to the Reverend John Hale, Betty and Abigail

> were bitten and pinched by invisible agents; their arms, necks, and backs turned this way and that way, and returned back again, so as it was impossible for them to do of themselves, and beyond the power of any Epileptick Fits, or natural Disease to effect. Sometimes they were

1

taken dumb, their mouths stopped, their throats choaked, their limbs wracked and tormented so as might move an heart of stone, to sympathize with them . . . . I will not enlarge in the description of their cruel Sufferings, because they were in all things afflicted as bad as John Goodwins Children at Boston, in the year 1689.[3]

The story of the Goodwin children had been well known through Cotton Mather's account in "Memorable Providences," as well as through word of mouth. According to Mather, in 1688 the four Goodwin children were severely afflicted. Mather reports that the children were of such good character that they would not feign such afflictions, nor could they, since "it was perfectly impossible for any Dissimulation of theirs to produce what scores of spectators were amazed at."[4] Fortunately, "about Nine or Ten at Night they alwaies had a Release from their miseries, and ate and slept all night for the most part indifferently well."[5] His subsequent description of their afflictions vividly describe torments comparable to those of Betty and Abigail. We have no similar account as to how well these two ate and slept at night.

In the case of the Goodwin children a woman identified only as Glover was accused of bewitching them and confessed to the charge. She hanged for it. She was not the first in the colony to suffer such a fate: Throughout seventeenth-century New England, numerous charges of affliction by witchcraft had occurred. In most cases, the authorities had responded with skepticism, although from time to time they had been persuaded. In such cases, people convicted of witchcraft were generally executed unless their convictions were reversed. Such executions had been relatively infrequent: More people were executed in the Salem witch trials of 1692 than had previously been executed for witchcraft in the whole history of New England. Moreover, many other past cases had led to acquittal.[6]

When the children in the Parris household displayed their symptoms, they therefore did so in the context of a culture having had much experience with witchcraft cases and having encountered a dramatic one a few years earlier. Additionally, written accounts of similar cases in England, according to Thomas Hutchinson,

> were in New-England, and the conformity between the behavior of Goodwin's children and most of the supposed bewitched at Salem, and the behavior of those in England, is so exact, as to leave no room to doubt the stories had been read by the New England persons themselves, or had been told to them by others who had read them.

However, "this conformity, instead of giving suspicion, was urged in confirmation of the truth of both . . . . "[7] Parris, rationally responding to this family crisis, sought the guidance of other ministers and at least one physician. They offered the "confirmation" that the children suffered from witchcraft.

Against this attack from the invisible world, Parris sought prayer as a defense, but the praying did not stop the afflictions, and soon, according to Hale, "other persons who were of age to be witnesses, were molested by Satan." In response to this spreading affliction, "some of their Village Neighbours complained to the Magistrates at Salem."[8] They accused three women: Tituba, slave of Parris, Sarah Good, and Sarah Osborne. Had matters proceeded in traditional ways, judicial verdicts would have been rendered, guilty or innocent, and the episode would have ended. There was nothing extraordinary about either the charge of witchcraft, the nature of the afflictions, or the judiciary determining the validity of the charges. The new element that occurred in 1692 concerned the spread of charges and the credibility given by the judiciary to claims of a broad conspiracy of witches. Before the episode ended in the following year, at least 156 people had been imprisoned, including nineteen who hanged, one who was pressed to death, and at least four who died in prison.[9] Out of the early examinations and those soon following them an inner logic developed that generated a growing number of accusations and confessions. What should have stopped with the disposition of cases involving three women continued instead until what we now call the Salem witch trials enveloped Massachusetts Bay colony.

Why this radical departure from the past? The most ambitious modern attempt to explain the Salem Village episode appears in *Salem Possessed*,[10] where an old idea is probed with new sophistication and insight. From this perspective, a pattern of village quarrels led to accusations as the community divided along lines of those supporting the embattled minister, Parris, and those opposing him. The argument brilliantly reveals much of the tension and underlying agendas in Salem Village, although the study stops short of inquiring into why the outbreak spread throughout Massachusetts Bay and caught in its net people having nothing to do with the quarrels of that particular village.[11]

A common explanation for the "witchcraft" outbreak spreading beyond Salem Village centers on the political and social turmoil facing the colony, particularly in view of its lack of a charter. That is, the colony's charter had been revoked in 1684, and although Increase Mather was soon expected to arrive with a new one, a situation of instability and anxiety prevailed. In addition to this uncertainty about the charter, itself a symptom of ongoing political disputes with England, were persistent threats from "Indians" (i.e., Native Americans) against the colony and a decline of power among orthodox clergy – all ingredients for broad social instability, providing fertile ground for the discovery of enemies in the invisible world.

This traditional explanation centering on political and social turmoil is plausible but not satisfying: Essentially the same elements existed in 1688 when the Goodwin case occurred, but the colony did not then lose its way on the witchcraft issue. Differences do exist, of course, between what happened to the Goodwin children and what happened in the Parris household, one being the effort made by Cotton Mather in the Goodwin case to keep secret the names of others besides Glover who were similarly accused of witchcraft. Such differences, along with others, come closer to explaining the Salem witch trials, which only make some kind of sense after the examination of multiple causes. Attempts to explain by a single theory what happened in 1692 distort rather than clarify the events of that year, although anyone who offers to adjudicate once and for all the various competing theories about the Salem witch trials should be a soldier rather than a scholar.

Different conclusions about Salem follow from different questions asked about the event and from different methodologies applied to answering those questions. My own interest in the topic began one day in Salem on my way to visit the House of the Seven Gables. I stopped at a gift shop, where a coffee mug caught my attention. Printed on the mug was the image of a woman, or rather the caricature of one: a witch in black on a broom, a black decoration on a white mug. This was the witch of our Halloween images, that wicked woman who had to die before Dorothy could get back to Kansas. Here was the modern icon of the people I had described to my students as victims in the hour or so a semester I had given to the Salem witch trials while touring the colonial backgrounds of American literature. I had accurately taught my students that of the nineteen people hanged – not burned – all had maintained their innocence, and that many people who had confessed had not been executed. Juxtaposing these facts with the image before me, I wondered why our culture had not made Christian martyrs out of these people rather than turning them into images such as Dorothy's nemesis. After all, had they not chosen to die rather than to risk their immortal souls by lying? Perhaps not all of them had had such a noble motive, but surely some of them had. Where were the mugs that showed pictures of them as Christian martyrs? Where was our Robert Bolt, to do for them what he did for Thomas More in *A Man for All Seasons*? Granted, Arthur Miller had written a powerful play, *The Crucible,* but he had hardly created Christian martyrs: Miller's Salem is a region of sexual entanglement and existential nobility. The Salem of 1692 offered the hanging of people who took seriously their Christianity, who could have lived if only they had confessed, but who preferred hanging to lying before their God. It baffled me that they were not in the canon of American saints, at least along with Nathan Hale. I decided to study the issue.

As so often happens, one begins work on a problem by asking the wrong question, as I did here. I found out soon enough that at least some of the victims had indeed been turned into Christian martyrs, particularly during the nineteenth century; I just had not known. Although I had recalled Hawthorne's passing reference in *The Scarlet Letter* to "the martyrdom of the witches,"[12] I had not known or recalled a body of nineteenth-century prose and poetry that had treated them this way. I had read Arthur Miller's play, but I had not read Henry Wadsworth Longfellow's play *Giles Corey of the Salem Farms,* or Mary Wilkins Freeman's *Giles Corey, Yeoman,* a play waiting to be rediscovered. Nor had I been aware that in 1856 J. W. DeForest in his *Witching Times* had created a fictional descendent of Thomas More and sent him to martyrdom at Salem.[13] The question therefore changed from Why were they not Christian martyrs? to How have we variously perceived them? and How and why have we given Salem the place it has in American imagination?

In order to understand the story of Salem, I thought it necessary to review the events of 1692. This, I assumed, would be an easy part of my project, as I had read about the subject and had taught it. I simply needed as a prelude to refresh my memory and clarify some of the puzzling points. This was an extraordinarily innocent beginning, and I certainly did not expect to discover that significant aspects of what I had been taught about Salem were not supported by the evidence that I found. The more I read the original documentation, the more I realized that the story of what actually happened in 1692, as opposed to how the story has been told, would have to drive my own narration. Perhaps along the way I could speculate about why in our culture we are more attracted to witches than to saints, but the heart of my project had become an exploration of the events of 1692. As had others before me, I had found that Salem does not easily let go of those who probe closely into its history.

The core of the information about what happened in 1692 can be found in the impressive three-volume set called *The Salem Witchcraft Papers,* edited in 1977 by Paul Boyer and Stephen Nissenbaum. Boyer and Nissenbaum have copied from and added to the seminal Works Project Administration typescript compiled in 1938 under the general editorship of Archie Frost. Their edition is generally well indexed and conveniently organized alphabetically by the name of each person involved in judicial proceedings. The virtue of this principle of organization is that one need only know the name of the person being investigated to turn to the section where the legal documents pertaining specifically to that individual are conveniently located. The disadvantage, however, is the lack of any chronological organization. If one is interested in, say, Sarah Good, it does not suffice simply to look under the section heading "Sarah Good": Too many references to her appear under the names of other people's cases, and the chronology has to be provided by the investigator. I do not point this out by way of faulting Boyer and Nissenbaum, or Frost. Different organizational strategies serve different ends. For my own purposes I have as a research tool reorganized the documentation into a chronological account that has allowed me to read the story as I would a novel and to explicate it accordingly. This is in large measure the methodology I have chosen to reach my understanding of what happened in 1692. Along the way, I have inevitably reached some differing editorial conclusions, some trivial, some perhaps significant. I will have more to say on this subsequently.

In addition to *The Salem Witchcraft Papers,* other primary documents are especially useful. Some of the writings of the village minister, Samuel Parris, are available to us. We have accounts by contemporaries, including Cotton Mather, Increase Mather, Robert Calef, John Hale, and Deodat Lawson. There is also the two-volume, nineteenth-century work by Charles W. Upham, *Salem Witchcraft* (1867), which, although not documented and therefore necessarily suspect, does reproduce primary texts that are extremely valuable (assuming we can trust Upham's editing, which for the purposes of this study I have done). Boyer and Nissenbaum have also edited a collection of primary material entitled *Salem-Village Witchcraft.*[14] Although other valuable sources exist, to be discussed as the book develops, those mentioned in this paragraph generally contain the most reliable data about what actually happened. Some very unreliable oral history has found its way into numerous accounts, but the primary sources make it relatively easy to cull away the accretions of tradition in the guise of historical fact. I will shortly turn to a dramatic example of this kind of lore.

The search for the story of the Salem witchcraft trials follows at least two major routes. One concerns the question of what happened in Salem Village where the outbreak began, who were the main characters of the story, and what assumptions we should have about them. On the basis of abundant evidence available to us, we can test the validity of competing theories of the initial causes and motivations.

More difficult is the second route. As Richard Weisman has shown in his *Witchcraft, Magic, and Religion in 17th-Century Massachusetts,* allegations of witchcraft in Massachusetts had historically been given little support by clerical and judicial authorities.[15] What sets the Salem episode apart from other outbreaks of "witchcraft" is that for the first and last time in the colonies the authorities actively supported the accusers rather than seeking to suppress them. Although it is true that people had previously been executed or otherwise punished for witchcraft in the colonies, such events were exceptional, sporadic, and limited.

In theory, belief in witchcraft represented an accepted principle within the dominant theology of the day in colonial Massachusetts; in practice, claims of witchcraft were usually regarded with skepticism and perceived as superstitions of the folk. In the Salem witch trials this attitude changed radically, so that the witchcraft charges were supported by the authorities and encouraged to spread to the whole colony. The competing theories as to why the judicial authorities behaved the way they did are not as easy to test as are those related to the immediate outbreak in Salem Village. There is a lot of information enabling us to reach conclusions about why witchcraft accusations proliferated; as to the motives of the authorities, however, we have only tantalizing clues.

Barring the discovery of new information, this part of the story is not fully recoverable; but much can still be pieced together concerning the conduct of the authorities as well as the motives of individuals involved in the cases. In the end, a multiplicity of causes emerges, with insights into them coming from the painstaking examination of the data case by case. As the story of Salem in 1692 unfolds, motivations and explanations come into sharper focus, accentuating such matters as who happened to be in power at a given time, what religious debates and animosities were occurring in the colony, and who was profiting from the trials. Even as these and other matters become clarified, they resist being subsumed under a single, overall theory; but when elements of the narrative are pieced together, they reveal a comprehensible tale dependent neither on hysteria, drugs, nor the practice of witchcraft as understood in 1692. The narrative also assumes the absence of actual witchcraft involving a real devil – a possibility that from time to time will represent the only arguable alternative to the one given.

The Salem witch trials were not inevitable, occurring from some kind of historical necessity: Along the way, the authorities had opportunities to reassess the situation and bring the proceedings to a halt, but a developing logic kept pointing the other way – toward extending the trials, broadening the number of accusations. This expansion is due partly to the encouragement of the authorities and partly to a series of diverse stories, singular situations that do not lend themselves easily to overarching theories.

Thus to create a unified theory explaining the Salem witch trials would

be to distort the event, at times to trivialize it. The search for such a theory has yielded explanations centering on such matters as ergot poisoning,
hysterical girls, covens of witches, and a plethora of other narrative constructions meant to join discrete occurrences to unifying causes. On the
other hand, the events of 1692 are not merely chaotic: The methodological challenge is to find reasonable conclusions, generalizations at times,
that do more than impose one more myth upon the Salem witch trials.
The present volume thus seeks a middle ground between random moments and cohesive events.

Chapter 1 examines the original response of the judiciary to the three
women first accused and how the attitudes of the magistrates set a pattern
that would hold until the episode ended. Chapters 2 and 3 take a look at
the accusers – mythologized as the "girls of Salem" – whose charges fed a
seemingly insatiable desire by the judiciary for the names of more witches.
As will become clear, these accusers were sometimes trapped or coerced
into responding in very calculated ways. Subsequent chapters, some
marked by the date of one or more executions, tell something of the stories of the people caught up in what has become America's huge metaphor
for persecution. The study then comes to the moment when the authorities saw the need to extricate themselves from the proceedings they had
created when they encouraged rather than discouraged witchcraft trials.
Chapter 9 shows, in part, why they had done this, how it came about that
they reversed themselves, and who with courage and imagination found
the way to bring it all to an end.

Unraveling this tale involves coping with problems of narration. The
core text, *The Salem Witchcraft Papers,* transcribes accounts given by people who were not disinterested in shaping perceptions of the unfolding
events. In a couple of cases, "evidence" appearing in the transcriptions
suggests forgery. To complicate matters further, *The Salem Witchcraft Papers* grows from a project where documents were more compiled than edited, and the collection, extraordinarily valuable as it is, suffers from this
lack of thorough editing. Some of the resultant problems are very minor,
but others skew the narrative and obscure information that make the
events of 1692 more accessible. Thus, reading *The Salem Witchcraft Papers*
and assessing the context in which the documents appeared are acts not
only of historical interpretation, but of literary analysis based on close textual examination.

The story that comes down to us from one generation to the next does
not, of course, depend wholly on the documentation in *The Salem Witchcraft Papers* or on other primary sources. Narrative inventions in various
genres occur through the centuries, and the amalgam of myth and history

that emerges tells more about the periods in which the stories have been told than about the Salem witch trials. Yet it remains possible to separate to a large degree these forces of myth and history that compete to claim the past.

With layers of myth culled away, much that is sordid in the story remains; however, there is also much to remind us of the factual basis for some of the misty-eyed, sentimental responses of the nineteenth century in creating a set of heroes and heroines from those who underwent this ordeal. Although our culture has sought to subsume their lives under grand and unified theories, their individual experiences resist such accounts of the story of Massachusetts Bay colony – which, in our mythology, has become Salem's story.

1

Dark Eve

[Elizabeth Parris, wife of the Reverend Samuel Parris,] emerges as a good-hearted woman, simple and ineffectual, who saw her job in Salem Village as a continuing round of errands to and for the wives in the parish. But in her busy effort to bolster her husband's acceptance in the village, she absented herself more and more from home. Into this void, necessarily, moved Tituba, and from Tituba came the tales that excited Abigail and frightened Betty.

– James F. Droney, "The Witches of Salem"[1]

I

In the beginning there was Tituba: a woman who, according to the politics of the early 1960s, gained power because a working mother paid insufficient attention to her family. Although chroniclers of Salem's story vary in their explanations of her presence, Tituba appears in the overwhelming number of narrations as the central figure in the genesis of the witch trials. Her entrance onto the historical stage, in her precipitating role of beginning the witchcraft, receives its modern codification in the account by Charles W. Upham, whose *Salem Witchcraft,* published in 1867,[2] has served as the most influential work in shaping subsequent myth and history related to the Salem witch trials.

Upham offers a speculation that Tituba and her husband John, slaves of the Reverend Samuel Parris of Salem Village, brought with them "the wild and strange superstitions prevalent among their native tribes, materials which, added to the commonly received notions on such subjects, heightened the infatuation of the times, and inflamed still more the imaginations of the credulous." He suggests that they brought with them "systems of demonology" consistent "with ideas and practices developed here." A group consisting primarily of "a circle of young girls" along with these two slaves met regularly in the Parris household, and from these meetings came the strange practices that eventually became defined as witchcraft.[3]

From Upham's association of Tituba and John with the genesis of the witchcraft accusations, a tradition grew that somewhere along the way transformed from speculation to fact. In most accounts, the role of John slips away as Tituba becomes the central, generating figure in the origins of the witch-hunt. No historical evidence supports this role assigned to Tituba, yet its tenacious hold among popularizers and even many scholars remains unshaken.

In one of the most popular modern accounts of what happened at Salem, Marion Starkey's 1949 *The Devil in Massachusetts,* Starkey writes how

> Tituba yielded to the temptation to show the children tricks and spells, fragments of something like voodoo remembered from the Barbados. . . . It is possible that history would never have heard of Abigail and Betty [the two children first afflicted] . . . had they kept Tituba to themselves. But that they could not do. Tituba's fascination was too powerful to be monopolized by two small girls. Thanks to her, the parsonage kitchen presently became a rendezvous for older girls in the neighborhood.

Evoking the metaphor of a "fatal spark," Starkey writes, "It was given Tituba to strike it."[4]

In the realm of major scholars, Paul Boyer and Stephen Nissenbaum similarly use the image of the "spark" in seeing Tituba as one of the precipitating agents in a cluster of causes that led to the Salem witch trials. They link Tituba's "voodoo lore" with "an intense group of adolescent girls" interested "in fortune telling and the occult."[5] Kai Erikson, in his *Wayward Puritans,* insinuates the guilt of Tituba even as he acknowledges that "No one really knows how the witchcraft hysteria began." He then proceeds to explain how

> In early 1692, several girls from the neighborhood began to spend their afternoons in the Parris kitchen with a slave named Tituba, and it was not long before a mysterious sorority of girls, aged between nine and twenty, became regular visitors to the parsonage. We can only speculate what was going on behind the kitchen door, but we know that

Tituba had been brought to Massachusetts from Barbados and enjoyed a reputation in the neighborhood for her skills in the magic arts.[6]

More cautiously approaching the subject, Chadwick Hansen, in his iconoclastic *Witchcraft at Salem,* cites tradition as placing Tituba in the role of assisting in "occult experiments," but raises no questions about the tradition.[7]

We see the story again in Selma and Pamela Williams's *Riding the Night Mare,* as the authors describe how "in the dark of the night [Tituba] gave lessons in chanting and dancing to gain mysterious powers."[8] In 1983 the Essex Institute, with the best library holdings in the world on the subject, published a pamphlet entitled *The Salem Witchcraft Trials.* At first it approaches the Tituba story tentatively, suggesting it as a possibility; but soon the tale possesses the writer, and we read about "Tituba's vivid stories of sorcery and the black arts," which *"doubtless* provided an enthralling if impious outlet for the repressed adolescent feelings and imaginations of the young people" (my emphasis).[9] In present-day Danvers, Massachusetts – previously known as Salem Village, where the outbreak originally occurred – a historical marker with the following inscription stands at the excavation of the Salem Village Parsonage:

> It was in this house in 1692 that Tituba, Rev. Parris' slave, told the girls of the household stories of witchcraft which nurtured the village witchcraft hysteria. . . .[10]

The sin of Tituba is for all posterity to see.

The Tituba myth appeared on television in the PBS film *Three Sovereigns for Sarah: A True Story,*[11] and reappears fairly regularly at Halloween, as in this excerpt from a Gannett newspaper:

> It is a tale fit for a campfire. The winter of 1692 was long and cold in New England. In the Puritan settlement of Salem, townsfolk lived in icy fear, for they believed they were wrestling their new lives from a land that had formerly been the devil's domain. The evil one, they believed, was manifest in the creak of a house, the howl of a wolf, the onset of disease.
>
> In that murky climate of superstition, a group of young girls passed the dreary season by the warm hearth in the house of the Rev. Mr. Samuel Parris. There Tituba, a slave from Barbados, enthralled them with stories of voodoo, of seeing the devil dance round a bonfire. She may have told their fortunes or hypnotized some of the younger girls. . . .[12]

Similarly, the story finds its way into a "Dear Steve" column in the New York *Daily News;* but Tituba's burden also crops up in more middle-brow publications, such as *Newsweek, Smithsonian,* and *Harvard Magazine.*[13] A recent American scholarly work carries the story as fact; in England, Tituba as teller of voodoo tales appears in a book that uses the Salem witch trials metaphorically regarding accusations of child abuse.[14] Why the continuing appeal of this fiction? Archetypally, the story works around the notion of original sin, the telling of evil stories rather than the eating of an apple or the opening of a box. In a land popularly imagined as born in religious freedom, a place of harmony where settlers and "Indians" ate turkey together, the Salem witch trials have served mythically as a national fall, as disruptive to the idyllic myth of America as is the seduction of Eve to the myth of Eden.

That the role of precipitating agent for this American fall should rest upon a woman is consistent with the archetype it perpetuates. That the woman should be dark reflects America's social engagement with the seemingly intractable problem of synthesizing a myth of national harmony with Indian wars and with slavery. The defeated groups in this war of color become merged into an ambiguously pigmented Tituba, at times "Indian" and at times "Negro."

In a valuable survey of the racial representation of Tituba, Chadwick Hansen has shown how this Indian woman emerged over the years as a half Indian, half black person, finally becoming entirely black in the hands of modern writers, from distinguished playwright to distinguished scholar.[15] Although no one race or color consistently defines her, Tituba remains in our mythology as the dark woman, the alien, who enters the Puritan world and plunges it into chaos. The myth of dark Tituba recapitulates with an American tint the myth of original sin, the archetypal tale of the woman as progenitor of evils to come.

Tituba fits easily enough into American stereotypes. On August 6, 1910, at an event memorializing one of the witch-trial victims, Carolus M. Cobb described how Tituba and John taught their knowledge of "Voodooism, or whatever name one chooses to call that form of mimetic magic which is practiced among the negroes of the south. All races of that order of intellegence [*sic*] originate certain forms of magic. . . ."[16] This view of Tituba, generally implicit, finds further explicit representation in Sidney Perley's standard *History of Salem Massachusetts,* published in 1924: "Like the colored race generally, and especially of the tropics, Tituba was a believer in the occult, and delighted in the exploitation of the mysterious and wonderful."[17] While contemporary perpetuators of the Tituba myth deplore such stereotypes, the unexamined roots of their representations unwittingly reside in these older beliefs.

If it remains unnecessary to belabor the racial and gender implications of Tituba as author of sin, the credibility of the actual story warrants a brief consideration in view of its persistence. Inevitably, those who believe that where there is smoke there is fire will be leery of the notion that the role of Tituba was created out of whole cloth: It was by the smoke-and-fire theory, of course, that authorities hanged people in 1692. Could it be true, however, that Tituba actually presided over a circle of girls, telling the stories she is accused of telling, and that the archetype is a coincidence, fortuitous in mythmaking about Salem? Is there a remarkable convergence of myth and history? Not if one follows reasonable rules of evidence: In the enormous quantity of data available for examining the Salem witch trials – in all the court records, in all pretrial and trial testimony (contrary to what various historians claim, some trial records did survive),[18] in all the contemporary accounts of what happened – not a single person suggests that Tituba told stories of witchcraft or voodoo. Not one person hints at it or says anything that could be misconstrued to imply it. When in 1692 Cotton Mather wrote his official version of the trials, "Wonders of the Invisible World," nothing of the tale appeared. When Robert Calef in 1700 published his response to Mather, "More Wonders of the Invisible World," nothing of this story was told. When John Hale gave his account in "A Modest Inquiry into the Nature of Witchcraft,"[19] he offered an account of fortune-telling that future mythologizers associated with Tituba; but Hale himself made no such association. When Thomas Hutchinson published his *History of the Colony and Province of Massachusetts-Bay* in 1764,[20] the work from which the nineteenth-century accounts generally grew, he told nothing of this version of the Tituba story. Not until the nineteenth century does the story flower. At first we see phrases such as "tradition has it that Tituba . . ."; and although this qualification still appears at times, writers more often than not represent the story as true, with tradition transferred to fact.

Tituba did play a role, of course – making lurid claims about witchcraft at her examination and confessing her own guilt – but nothing she said offers a basis for the legend about her that most scholars have related as fact. Nor did her confession represent the turning point in legitimizing the witchcraft claims: This came instead from Sarah Good, the first of the three women to be interrogated in Salem Village on March 1, 1692.

II

The legal phase of the Salem witch trials began on February 29 with warrants for the arrest of Tituba, Sarah Osborne, and Sarah Good, all three from Salem Village. Each was accused of afflicting Betty Parris and

Abigail Williams, whose behavior had evoked memories of the Goodwin children's afflictions. Added to Betty and Abigail, however, were two new names: Ann Putnam, Jr., 12, and Elizabeth Hubbard, probably 17, although sometimes described in court documents as 16 and sometimes as 18.[21] Who among them, if any, originally accused the three women remains unknown; all but Betty Parris became frequent accusers of others. The actual complaint in the warrants of February 29 came from Joseph Hutchinson, Thomas Putnam, Edward Putnam, and Thomas Preston. The men alleged that the afflictions had been occurring for the previous two months.

Elizabeth Hubbard was the niece of a physician, Dr. William Griggs, and lived in his house.[22] Thomas Putnam was the father of Ann; as the witch-hunt expanded, his name was to appear on roughly 10 percent of all warrants identifying a complainer. Edward Putnam was to offer only three other complaints, one against the child of Sarah Good. Thomas Preston made no further recorded complaints; nor did Joseph Hutchinson, although he did subsequently allege that Abigail Williams had stated her comfort with the devil, and he subsequently signed a petition on behalf of another accused woman, Rebecca Nurse. Betty Parris was a witness at the hearings held in early March for the three accused women; thereafter, she probably participated in no further judicial procedures. Ann Putnam, Abigail Williams, and Elizabeth Hubbard were to play major roles in the events that developed.

On March 1, the three accused women were examined on the charges brought against them. Sarah Good soon offered confirmation of witchcraft, since in defending herself she chose to accuse Sarah Osborne of afflicting the accusers. This decision by Sarah Good gave immediate credibility to the charges of witchcraft and set in motion a process that led to her own execution. Of the three women examined on March 1, she was the only one who would die on the gallows. Sarah Osborne died in prison on May 10 (*SWP* III: 954). Tituba spent time in prison and was subsequently released.

Among the audience in the house of Nathaniel Ingersoll, where the examination of Sarah Good was held, were the four individuals named in the warrant as afflicted. The magistrates were John Hathorne and Jonathan Corwin, with Hathorne apparently asking all the questions. His first question set the tone of the examination as accusatory. In subsequent examinations, Hathorne occasionally varied from this beginning, expressing his hope that the person could prove innocence; not so with Sarah Good, nor with most of the people he questioned. "Sarah Good what evil spirit have you familiarity with[?]" Good denied that she had any or that she was in any way hurting the "poor children" who were behaving as if she were tormenting them during the examination (*SWP* II: 356). Halfway through the examination there was still no substantiation from anyone that witchcraft played a role in the behavior of the."afflicted"; but Sarah Good abruptly gave the afflicted the corroboration they needed when she identified Sarah Osborne as their tormentor. The first legal testimony supporting the presence of witchcraft had been made. When Osborne took the stand, she accused no one. Tituba, however, confessed and accused them both.

Sarah Good – at the examination on March 1, in subsequent examinations, and at her trial – was named by a variety of people as an afflicting witch. Among her accusers was her daughter Dorcas. Her husband, William, while not specifically accusing her of witchcraft, offered hostile testimony against her, including an insinuation that she might have a witch mark, where the devil's familiar suckled (*SWP* II: 363). The testimony against Sarah Good at her examination, as well as at her trial at the end of June, would be typical of the patterns developing in other cases. The magistrates would question the accused, and during the questioning those claiming to be afflicted would assert that the person being examined was at that very moment tormenting them. The accused would then be sent to jail and usually put in chains. Subsequently, at a grand jury hearing, or at the trial, depositions would be given against the accused. Charges here came from individuals other than the original accusers, as members of the community came forward to describe real, imagined, or fabricated offenses by the accused. Their testimony seems sometimes honest, sometimes confused, and sometimes conspiratorial.

Among those giving depositions, genuine belief in the demonic powers of the accused often played a part, as it may have in the reports that Sarah Good caused cows to die, as attested by Samuel and Mary Abbey (*SWP* II: 368), Thomas and Sarah Gage (*SWP* II: 369), and Henry Herrick and Jonathan Batchelor (*SWP* II: 375). Their testimony has no element of magic about it; that is, they report no invisible phenomena. A quarrel occurs, cows die around that time, and a correlation is drawn. Yet the dying-cow stories from the Abbeys, the Gages, and Herrick and Batchelor introduce another element that would loom large in the Salem story: They refer to events of the past. Those cows had died two or three years earlier. In some cases, testimony would be based on events happening twenty years before. Such depositions were legally accepted and suggest no particular misconduct on the part of judicial authorities in receiving them; but their unreliability helped build some of Salem's core myths.

Depositional testimony also offers instances of how people seem simply to have been duped. For example, on June 28 William Batten, William Shaw, and his wife Deborah Shaw testified that they had discovered 18-year-old accuser Susannah Sheldon with her hands tied. Unable to loosen the knot, they had had to cut the string that bound her. Susannah Sheldon claimed that the specters of Sarah Good and Lydia Dustin, both then in prison, had tied her up on that occasion and on others, and that when Susannah touched the string that bound her, Sarah Good would bite her. Batten and the Shaws also testified that, invisible to them, a broom had been carried out of the house and put in an apple tree, and that a shirt, a milk tube, and three poles had invisibly been removed from the house to the woods (*SWP* II: 370–1). There seems no reasonable possibility to explain Susannah Sheldon's conduct other than fraud. Hysteria might make her imagine spirits attacking her, but it cannot tie her up in a knot so tight that others need a knife to free her. As for the invisible disappearances, the items had either been removed by spirits or by cooperating conspirators, whether as pranks or for more serious reasons. In this case, it appears as if there were three dupes and at least one accomplice to Susannah Sheldon.

Other kinds of lurid allegations emerged. Constable Joseph Herrick testified (with the corroboration of his wife Mary) that, instructed to bring Sarah Good to the jail at Ipswich, he had placed her under guard in his own home. The three guards informed him in the morning that Sarah Good, barefooted and barelegged, had disappeared from them "for some time" (*SWP* II: 370). Herrick was subsequently informed that on the night of March 1, with Good under guard at his house, she had tormented Elizabeth Hubbard. Samuel Sibley, the man guarding Elizabeth Hubbard, had struck at the spectral Sarah Good, though without seeing or feeling anything: Only accusers being tormented could see their tormentors, a phenomenon called "spectral evidence." Elizabeth Hubbard, according to Herrick's testimony, had assured Sibley that he had struck Sarah Good on the arm. Moreover, Mary Herrick testified that on the morning of March 2 she saw one of Good's arms bloody from around the elbow to the wrist. As with the Susannah Sheldon episode, some combination of conspiracy and gullibility appears to explain the events.

Our choices for accounting for such testimony are fairly limited. If we exclude the possibility that an invisible Sarah Good went after Elizabeth Hubbard and took a blow from Samuel Sibley that caused her arm to bleed, and that this same invisible woman did not have the sense to get out of town, we are left with collusion of some kind or with an astonishing set of coincidences – or with the possibility that Elizabeth Hubbard somehow found out about an injury to Sarah Good's arm and staged an attack that would implicate her. Although hysteria could account for Elizabeth Hubbard seeing apparitions, it could not account for her awareness of Sarah Good's injured arm. A long tradition of popular and scholarly literature has argued for, or assumed, hysteria as offering the broadest explanation of the Salem witch trials; but too much happened that cannot be explained by hysteria.

This does not mean, however, that no hysteria occurred, and often we are forced to choose between hysteria and fraud. Yet one of the odd facts about Salem's story is that although most renditions of it evoke hysterical females reacting in court to imagined specters tormenting them, males frequently give more plausible indications of hysteria, because their behavior often occurs without evidence of the demonstrable fraud of women such as Elizabeth Hubbard or Susannah Sheldon. Such cases usually involve accounts of one-time experiences that might plausibly be explained by hysteria. Thus, on March 5 William Allen and John Hughes testify that on the night of March 1 they saw a beast transform into two or three women who they assumed to be Sarah Good, Sarah Osborne, and Tituba. Other than accusing Sarah Good, Allen's name appears in only one other instance, and this time as a petitioner on behalf of an accused woman, Mary Bradbury. John Hughes makes only one other charge, a claim that on March 2 a great white dog followed him and then disappeared, and that that night in bed he saw a great light and a cat at the foot of his bed.[23] Although this testimony appears with the materials against Sarah Good, Hughes himself makes no charge that she had anything to do with his bedtime experiences. William Allen, on the other hand, says that on March 2 Sarah Good and an unusual light appeared to him in his bedroom. Good sat on his foot, and when he tried to kick her, she and the light disappeared. If the testimony of Allen and Hughes is fraudulent, one cannot infer it clearly as one can in the case of Elizabeth Hubbard or Susannah Sheldon; thus the idea of hysteria is plausible for them in a way that it is not for the two young women.

Behavior by some women, of course, could plausibly be attributed to hysteria, as in the case of Johanna Childin. She claimed that on June 2 Sarah Good and a deceased child of Good appeared to her, with the child accusing its mother of murdering it and with Good admitting the crime and saying she gave the child to the devil. However, such a tale could also simply be a fabrication, and whether Childin's testimony represents hysteria or collusion is difficult to tell: She testified in only one other case, describing the appearance of an apparition confessing murder. Still, as the pattern would develop, men were more likely than women to be one- or two-time reporters of extraordinary phenomena.

If some testimony seems hysterically derived, and other conspiratorial, some simply leaves us guessing about inconsistencies. The testimony of the Herricks and Sarah Good's bloody arm offers the most conspicuous instance of this in the Good case. Elizabeth Hubbard's testimony is consistent with what the Herricks say about Sibley striking Good, but Sibley himself tells a slightly different story. He says that Hubbard had told him that Good was barebreasted – a sight that surely should have evoked some comment in the testimony of Hubbard or the Herricks. Moreover, Sibley says he had hit Good – according to Hubbard, since he could not see what if anything he was hitting – on the back so forcefully that he had almost killed Good: on the *back*, not the arm, as the Herricks and Elizabeth Hubbard reported. Hubbard simply did not offer consistent accounts of her encounter with the invisible world. If her inconsistency troubled others, no evidence of this survives.

III

What was on the mind of John Hathorne and Jonathan Corwin on March 1, 1692, can only be the subject of speculation. Assuming that they believed in witchcraft and that as honest men they sought to determine fairly whether the evidence against the accused women was sufficient to bring them to trial, what might they reasonably infer? Much of the testimony against Sarah Good would be damning if credited, although stories about the killing of cows did not come until later in the proceedings. Similarly, the inconsistency in connection with Sibley's attack on the apparition of Sarah Good appeared in subsequent depositional testimony. Still, in their presence on March 1, Betty Parris, Abigail Williams, Ann Putnam, and Elizabeth Hubbard expressed their claims of great agony, complaining that the women were torturing them.

For these two justices of the peace, assuming them fair and impartial, a moment of truth must have confronted them early in the proceedings. For this we turn to the account of John Hale, a minister whose description of the occurrences at Salem serves as one of the key documents from a contemporary and a participant in the events. Hale, who would eventually criticize the proceedings in general, nevertheless accepted the idea that witchcraft was occurring and that the "Children" were suffering. At one point he refers to "pins invisibly stuck into their flesh."[24] Hale's observation almost certainly refers to Betty Parris and Abigail Williams, whose original behavior precipitated conclusions of witchcraft. His reference is to events before the examination on March 1, but at that examination Sarah Good was accused of hurting the children in the presence of the justices as well as earlier. In other cases, clear evidence exists that accusers were claiming to be tormented by pins being stuck in them and were showing the magistrates the pins. If we may speculate that the pins also appeared in them in the presence of the justices at the examinations of March 1, or that the justices had heard about the pins earlier, Hathorne and Corwin quickly had some limited choices. Pins are visible and tangible: They are stuck in a person or not, and something puts them in the person. The justices had to choose between the accusers having inserted pins in themselves and witches having done the job. In her children's book, *The Witchcraft of Salem Village,* Shirley Jackson highlights these two alternatives and clearly points to fraud.[25] Not so the justices: They opted for witches. If we can understand the decision of Hathorne and Corwin in the context of another era, it is more difficult to understand the views of scholars who believe that the conduct of the children stemmed from hallucinations or hysteria, theories that do not plausibly account for the accusers bringing and using the pins they claimed the witches employed to attack them, as Betty Parris, Abigail Williams, and others maintained. Not having modern psychological theories to assess, Hathorne and Corwin made their decision. When Sarah Osborne's turn came, the mind-set of the judges was evident enough: They had chosen witchcraft as the only plausible alternative to fraud in the matter of pins.

Sarah Osborne came before the judges not simply accused by the four represented in the original complaint, but now by Sarah Good also. The documentation on Sarah Osborne is slim, probably because she never came to trial, dying in prison on May 10. Acknowledging the concept of witchcraft, she denied that she herself was a witch; nor did she implicate any others. Osborne raised the theological point that the devil could take the shape of others, an argument that would persist in the debate against spectral evidence. She also suggested that she herself had been attacked by the devil, a claim that failed to impress the justices.

Because Sarah Osborne was not indicted, a comparison of her case with Sarah Good's comes to a halt, except in striking similarity on two points. As in the case of Good, Osborne's husband gave damaging testimony against his wife, telling the justices that she had not been to church for a year and two months. The other similarity is this issue of church attendance, since Sarah Good also admitted to having missed church regularly. Indeed, it was this lack of church attendance more than any other factor that the women held in common – that and the use of their husbands' testimony against them. Sarah Good was 38, pregnant, and a pauper; Osborne was 60 and a woman with property, though involved in land disputes.[26]

IV

By the time Tituba took the stand, the pattern of examination was in place: A justice would ask a hostile question, such as Why do you hurt the children?, and the accused was presumed guilty from the outset. Attempts at denial led to noisy fits and accusations by those claiming to be afflicted. Sarah Good had already given the accusers legitimacy, but without detailed accounts of how witches conducted their activities. Tituba filled this void in confessing and offering lurid tales about flying on broomsticks and other adventures with compatriot witches. As to their identity, however, she named only Good and Osborne. Nevertheless, her confession, the first in the witchcraft episode, following the claim of Sarah Good that Sarah Osborne was a witch, solidified the credibility of the accusers and their tales.

At the outset of her interrogation, Tituba flatly denied hurting the children or being a witch. Very quickly, though, she shifted her way of answering and told everything and nothing. She said four women had hurt the children, but she named only Good and Osborne. She said the night before she had been at Boston and had seen a tall man, but she named no man. She admitted hurting the children because she had been threatened if she did not, but said she would do it no more. She said a man appeared to her like a hog and a dog and told her to serve him. The dog was black. Then it turned into a man with a yellow bird. Throughout the trials and examinations, reference would be made to this yellow bird. She saw a red rat and a black rat. She said the yellow bird accompanied Sarah Good. She said she saw a thing with two legs, a head like a woman, and wings. Abigail Williams interjected that she also had seen this and had seen it turn into Sarah Osborne, a point Tituba had not made. What else had Tituba seen with Osborne? Tituba, who was giving the examiners whatever they wanted, except for new names, complied. She saw an upright hairy thing with only two legs that was like a man. Had she seen Sarah Good on Elizabeth Hubbard last Saturday? She said she saw a wolf set upon Elizabeth Hubbard. Elizabeth Hubbard then complained about a wolf. Tituba did not stop with that. She said she saw a cat with Good on another occasion. Hathorne switched away from rats and cats and wolves and dogs in search of identifying witches. What clothes does the man wear, he asked her. He wears black clothes, she said. He's a tall man with white hair. "How doth the woman go?" What woman is unclear, but Tituba had no problem with the question. She had a white hood and a black hood and a "tup knot" (*SWP* III: 749). Hathorne wanted to know who was hurting the children at that very moment. Sarah Good, Tituba replied. And who hurts them now, Hathorne wanted to know. Tituba announced that she was now blind, and the questioning stopped.

A second version exists of Tituba's examination on March 1. Some of it repeats the same story, but new ingredients do appear. The night before, as she was washing the room, she had seen four witches, two of whom were Good and Osborne, hurting the children. No one asked her to explain how she had been washing the room if she had been in Boston. The witches, moreover, had threatened to take her to Boston, and had threatened the children with death. The man was with the four women. The three people whom Tituba could not identify were all from Boston. No one asked how she knew this. She saw two cats: one red, and one black and as big as a little dog. What did the cats do? Tituba did not know. Had the cats hurt or threatened her? They had scratched her. What had they wanted of her? They had wanted her to hurt the children. They had forced her to pinch the children. Did the cats suck Tituba? No, she would not let them. She went on different trips by broom with Good and Osborne to pinch Elizabeth Hubbard and Ann Putnam. Good and Osborne told her she had to kill someone, and those two wanted her to kill Ann Putnam last night.

Ann Putnam joined in to affirm Tituba's story, adding that the witches wanted her to cut her own throat, and if she did not Tituba would cut her head off. If Hathorne or Corwin wondered why Ann survived, they were silent on this. The Reverend Parris did ask for more information about the whole matter, but Tituba said she could not tell, because if she did her head would be cut off. Her interrogator asked who had made such threats. The man, Tituba says, along with Good and Osborne. Tituba changed the subject: The previous night Good had come with her yellow bird. The accusers joined in that they too had seen a yellow bird, and Tituba had seen it suck Sarah Good's right hand. Had Tituba ever practiced witchcraft in her own country? Never. Also, Sarah Good has a cat in addition to a yellow bird. What does Osborne have? A thing that is hair all over, with a long nose, a face she cannot describe, two legs; it goes upright and is about three feet tall. Who was the wolf who appeared to Elizabeth Hubbard? Sarah Good. What clothing was the man wearing who appeared to Tituba? Sometimes black clothes and sometimes a "Searge Coat" of another color – a tall man with white hair (*SWP* III: 752). What did the woman wear? Tituba did not know the color. What kind of clothes did she have? Tituba did not know the color. She was asked a third time: What kind of clothes did the woman have? She had a black silk hood with a white silk hood under it, with top knots; a woman she did not know, although she had seen her in Boston. What clothes did the little woman have?

A serge coat and a white cap. The accusers were having fits, and Tituba was asked who was doing it. Sarah Good, and the accusers confirmed it – except for Elizabeth Hubbard, who was in an extreme fit and said they had blinded her.

On March 2, Tituba was examined again in prison. This time she described a green and white bird, but it never caught on: The yellow bird would prevail. She told of a man who had come to her and asked her to serve him. On a Friday morning he had showed her a book. Was it a big book or a little book? The motif of the book would continue throughout the witchcraft episode, the devil looking for a signature of alliance. Tituba did not know the size of the book. She said he would not show it to her; he had had it in his pocket. Nobody asked how he could have showed her a book that he did not show her. Did he make you write your name in the book? Not yet, said Tituba; her mistress had called her into another room. What did the man say you had to do with the book? Write my name in it. Did you? Yes, once I made a mark in the book in red blood. Did he get the blood out of your body? He said he would get it out the next time and gave a pin tied to a stick for the deed to be done later. Did you see other marks in his book? Tituba had seen many. Some red, some yellow. Did he tell you the names? Only two, Sarah Good and Sarah Osborne. How many marks were there? Nine. Did they write their names? They made marks, Tituba answered. She said Good told her she had made her mark, but Osborne would not tell. When did Good tell you? The same day I came here to prison. Did you see the man that morning? Yes, he told me the magistrates were going to examine me, that I was to tell nothing or else my head would be cut off. You say there were nine names; did he tell you the names of the others? No, but he said I would see them next time. What did you see? A man, a dog, a hog, two cats, one black and one red, and the strange monster, the hairy imp with Osborne; the man offered it to me, but I would not have it. Did he show you in the book which marks belonged to Good and Osborne? Yes. Did he tell you the names of the others? No. Did he tell you where the nine lived? Yes. Some in Boston and some in this town.

Tituba held firm. While describing a lurid world of witchcraft, she had resisted broadening the net of accusations. She would produce no new names. In 1700 Robert Calef published his "More Wonders of the Invisible World" and reported there that Tituba's confession had resulted from beatings and other abuse from her master, the Reverend Samuel Parris.[27] In 1692, a woman delegated to search her body for evidence of demonic familiars suckling her found "upon her body the marks of the Devils wounding of her."[28] No one else seems to have been suspected, and Tituba could have little hope of legal protection from abusive treatment. Instead, she would have every reason to follow the advice heard in Ann Petry's fictional depiction of her life. Here, her husband John tells her, "Remember, always remember, the slave must survive. No matter what happens to the master, the slave must survive."[29] Tituba was a survivor. It is hard to imagine that she felt any sense of obligation to the white society she served. She may even have used her plight to take revenge against the society that had enslaved her, as Maryse Condé writes in her stunning novel, *I, Tituba.*[30]

Whether or not she had revenge in mind, however, Tituba answered the questions with a cautious strategy: She has nothing to tell her interrogators, but she knows that she must tell them what they want to hear. So she feels her way. If they ask her something often enough, she complies. She does this in everything except in giving names. Doing so might have produced names they would not accept, and perhaps her troubles would have deepened; with Good and Osborne she was safe. They wanted more witches, she would give them more. She could hide behind the magic properties of the invisible world to play the game as safely as possible. Like Osborne, she told of her own affliction, complaining, as Hale reports, "of her fellow Witches tormenting of her" for having confessed.[31] By shrewdness or by luck, she had discovered the protection to be found in confession and in claims of her own affliction in retaliation for her cooperation. Whatever else we may guess about her, Tituba was not hysterical. Her answers were well measured in response to the questions asked of her in a room containing hostile magistrates, screaming people claiming to be afflicted, and a crowd of villagers watching the event unfold.

What should reasonable men make of such a tale in 1692? Hathorne and Corwin heard Tituba's story at a time when claims of supernatural powers for witches was a contested issue. Fifteen years earlier, John Webster in England had written a devastating critique of supposed witchcraft activity,[32] and in 1692 Shadwell's *The Lancashire Witches* had been produced in England. The play had its controversies, and the witches in it were real; but Shadwell ridiculed witchcraft and wrote scathingly in his note to the reader that if he had not depicted witches as real, he "would have been call'd Atheistical, By a prevailing party who take it that the power of the Devil should be lessened, and attribute more miracles to a silly old Woman, than ever they did to the greatest of Prophets, and by this means the Play might have been Silenced."[33] While this indeed suggests the strength of a party that believed in the powers of witches, it also makes clear the contested nature of the issue. In England enough freedom existed to express such skepticism, as shown by Webster and Shadwell.

Cotton Mather would not have written so obsessively on behalf of the existence of his invisible world if some universal view of the subject had existed. So those commentators on Salem who claim that the events happened in the context of an English-speaking world that accepted without question the notion of witchcraft – and these include most of those who have written on Salem – have simply perpetuated one of the core myths about Salem: that everybody at the time believed in witchcraft or the supernatural power of witches. It was not so.

Still, it was more likely to be so in Massachusetts Bay than in England; but even in the context of their belief in the supernatural power of witches, Hathorne and Corwin had to evaluate Tituba's testimony. The conflicts in it might readily be exposing Tituba as a liar, something reasonably expected from a witch. Why not press her on the contradictions? Had she been in Boston with the witches or had she not? How could she see a book that she had not seen? Possibly the magistrates thought these details were not worth pursuing when what they wanted were names. However, a more complex possibility occurs, one that takes us to the methodological problems of recreating the core events of Salem's story: We may not be reading exactly what Hathorne and Corwin asked, or even exactly what Tituba answered.

The Salem Witchcraft Papers offers two versions of Tituba's testimony on March 1. The first was recorded by Ezekial Cheever. We do not know who recorded the second or who recorded the questioning of Tituba in prison. Possibly it was Samuel Parris, who had committed himself to witchcraft as an explanation for the difficulties in his household. Although in Tituba's case no evidence supports suspicions of fabricated testimony, there is reason for questioning transcripts in some other instances. For example, Elizabeth Hubbard's testimony against Sarah Good is signed with Hubbard's mark (*SWP* II: 373), which turns out to be different from the mark given by her in her testimony against Susannah Martin (*SWP* II: 575). Since people customarily had their own mark, the discrepancy is significant in suggesting that she may not have confirmed the testimony recorded in her name. As we shall see, instances occur where testimony seems simply to have been invented. Fortunately, in spite of the slipperiness of the documentation, plausible decisions as to credibility can be made.

The problem of narration manifests itself in another way. Different people, not necessarily with any attempt to mislead, simply report the events differently. Surviving documentation is often inconsistent, and conclusions often hinge on a best guess. The story of Salem Village's "witch cake" nicely illustrates the issue. Perhaps no other cake in American history has had so much written about it. This was the cake made early in the episode, before matters went to the judiciary, to determine who was bewitching the afflicted children. Generally, various versions of this story can be traced back to two differing accounts, one by the Reverend John Hale and one by Robert Calef. Calef says that a few days before March 11 "Mr. Parriss' Indian Man and Woman made a Cake of Rye Meal, with the Children's Water, and Baked it in the Ashes, and as is said, gave it to the Dog" to discover witchcraft.[34] Calef, of course, was not there, and his "as is said" suggests that the whole account is removed from anyone of whom Calef himself could be sure. His chronology is demonstrably wrong, since other evidence indicates that the cake appeared before the examinations, which began on March 1.

The Reverend John Hale was in closer contact with those who would have reported the incident, such as the Reverend Samuel Parris. Hale himself went to see the afflicted girls before the judicial proceedings began. He tells us that the Indian servant and his wife baked the cake from meal and urine of the afflicted. He also tells us that Tituba confessed that she had been taught how to make the cake by her mistress "in her own coun-try[, who] was a witch," although she herself denied being a witch.[35] At the time, of course, she had not yet been examined; the confession had not yet been elicited.

In 1857, with the publication of the Danvers Church Records, another version came to light. On March 27, the Reverend Samuel Parris, in a church service, publicly chastised a woman in the congregation, Mary Sibley, wife of the man we recall as swinging away at the invisible Sarah Good. According to Parris, the activity in connection with the witch cake unleashed the witchcraft in the community. "Nay it never broke forth to any considerable light, untill Diabolical means was used, by the making of a Cake by my Indian man, who had his direction from this our sister Mary Sibly."[36] Tituba, we notice, is not even mentioned. If we proceed on the notion that Parris was most likely to know the exact details, and Calef least likely to know, Parris's testimony seems safer, particularly because it was publicly stated and easiest to contest. However, the record of this public statement is from Parris's own church records, privately written. Parris is one of the people who would write the records of testimony in the cases, one of the people whose objectivity is certainly suspect. What are we to believe? We are left with best guesses as to what we should credit. Parris was in the best position to know and, in spite of his editorial biases in transcribing testimony, there really seems no good reason for him to be inaccurate here. However, if Parris's account is accurate, Tituba lied to Hale when she said that she had been taught by her mistress in her former country; for if we believe Parris, it was her husband who had been taught, and by a woman in this country. The cuisine was not unknown in the colony. Rossell Hope Robbins writes:

> A contemporary New England almanac gives a recipe: "To cure ague. Take a cake of barley meal and mix it with children's water, bake it, and feed it to the dog. If the dog shakes, you will be cured." Mrs. Sibley may also have hoped that, alternatively, if the dog got sick, the girls would tell who or what afflicted them.[37]

Why would Tituba make up a story about learning this in the Barbados? Perhaps because she told Hale what she thought he wanted to hear. So a story that probably resolves itself as a cake made with a local recipe by John Indian, as he was known, under the direction of Mary Sibley, comes down historically as one made by Tituba using a recipe from the Barbados, with her husband rarely mentioned. As for the dog, mentioned by neither Hale nor Parris, we can only guess, although the New England recipe did call for one.

The secret of Salem will not be unlocked by determining who made the cake, nor by figuring out why the learned ministers seem not to have known a recipe that Mary Sibley knew; but the event offers a useful illustration of the extent to which uncovering what happened in the witchcraft episode becomes a textual problem – one of narration, of weighing competing narratives against each other for their reliability, at getting under the stated texts to the best versions of what might have occurred. To argue for the reliability or unreliability of every passage cited would result in a tome significantly longer than the three-volume *Salem Witchcraft Papers*. Accordingly, this study limits such analysis to selected episodes culled from a close reading of that work.

So we come back for the moment to Hathorne and Corwin hearing the testimony of Tituba, not in the dispassionate way we can analyze it now, but in the context of screaming accusers and terrified observers.

Other magistrates could have been more critical, less inclined to presume guilt as Hathorne clearly was, and as Corwin may have been, although he seems to have let Hathorne do the talking. Furthermore, Hathorne was not taking the traditionally conservative New England approach: Rather than discouraging the naming of others, as Cotton Mather had in the Glover case, Hathorne encouraged it. This radical departure from traditional ways of dealing with witchcraft cases fundamentally set the course for subsequent events.

Of all who faced the judiciary in the witchcraft episode of 1692, only Tituba was indicted through a normal judicial process rather than through a special Court of Oyer and Terminer that was established later in May. On May 9, 1692, she was indicted by a Court of Assize and General Gaol Delivery in Ipswich. No other person in the whole episode was similarly treated within the normal judicial rules. Her indictment reads as follows:

> That Tittapa an Indian Woman Servant to mr Samuel Parris of Salem village in the county of Essex – aforesaid – upon or about the latter end of the yeare 1691 In the Towne of Salem Village afors'd Wickedly & felloniously A Covenant with the Devill did make & Signed the Devills Booke with a marke like A:C by which Wicked Covenanting with the Devill she the Said Tittapa is become A detestable Witch Against the peace of o'r Sov'r lord & lady the King & Queen their Crowne & Dignity & the lawes in that Case made & provided. (*SWP* III: 755)

This charge against Tituba is consistent with a judicial procedure that, if followed in other cases, would have quickly ended the Salem witch trials. That is, unlike all the other indictments, which based the only specific charges on the claims of the accusers being tormented during judicial proceedings by specters that no one else could see, this indictment is based on the traditional evidence of confession, historically regarded as the most dependable and most reliable of all legal methods of finding witches. That is why in the continental witch trials of the Middle Ages people were systematically tortured, as advocated in Europe's infamous *Malleus Maleficarum*. When one confronted the invisible world, confession offered the most trusted evidence of witchcraft.

This is one of the points made by Samuel Willard late in 1692 in *Some Miscelliny [sic] Observations On Our Present Debates Respecting Witchcrafts*. Only two legal grounds exist for conviction in witchcraft cases, Willard argues: One is a free confession by a mentally competent person; the other is testimony by two "humane witnesses" – that is, witnesses offering testimony on natural, human "Senses" as opposed to claimed divine revelation or "upon the Devils Information."[38] Within the law as it existed in 1692, Tituba's confession was "free," and the indictment against her functioned within the legal tradition that Willard cited, including such authorities as Perkins and Bernard.[39]

The authorities in Massachusetts Bay, however, chose to go outside their normal legal system in all cases except that of Tituba's. The authorities also chose to ignore the biblical injunction, "thou shalt not suffer a witch to live,"[40] by keeping alive those people who confessed to witchcraft. The Salem witch trials are unique in the annals of witchcraft trials in Western civilization for their response to the issue of confession. They simply reversed the traditional rules whereby confessing witches were executed: In Salem, only those who did not confess were executed. Why this strange twist, and why the creation of a special court to handle a legal problem that English courts historically had handled – as, indeed, they had handled Tituba?

The answer most generally given as to why the normal judicial proceedings were not used centers on the chaos of Massachusetts Bay resulting from its lack of a charter. Many explanations for the Salem witch trials have focused on this charter issue, either as creating a situation of great uncertainty that led to instability in the colony, or as creating a form of legal limbo where the authority to prosecute witches did not exist. Boyer and Nissenbaum are the most prominent recent exponents of the view that the colony lacked the legal authority to act prior to the new charter, which Increase Mather brought to the colony on May 14, 1692. According to them,

> The basic problem was that while more and more suspected witches and wizards were being arrested, not one trial had yet been held. Indeed, there could be none, for during these months Massachusetts was in the touchy position of being without a legally established government! Eight years earlier, in 1684, its original form of government had been abrogated by the English authorities, and in 1689 the administration with which the King had replaced it was overthrown in a bloodless *coup d'etat*.[41]

There can be no doubt that this legal ambiguity existed. Nevertheless, judicial proceedings were occurring during the period between charters. The courts in cases not related to witchcraft had not gone out of business even though their work was certainly complicated by the ambiguity of the situation. In the witchcraft cases, although there had indeed been no trials before the new charter, there had been plenty of judicial activity. None of the authorities was taking the view that the filled jails were occupied by people put there illegally. Furthermore, there had already been the indictment of Tituba on May 9. The Court of Assize and General Gaol Delivery was functioning in Essex County before the new charter arrived, as were other normal government agencies.[42] The indictment of Tituba, as well as the numerous arrests, offers compelling evidence that the judiciary believed in its legal authority.

Indeed, when in 1689 Massachusetts Bay had found itself in the legally anomalous position of having overthrown Governor Andros and being without a charter, the government in Boston acted decisively to make sure that everyone knew that the laws and the courts would continue no matter what England thought about local authority. As David Konig points out, fourteen men were speedily condemned to death, eight more than the total number of executions between 1689 and the end of King Philip's War in 1676. Konig writes that "the sentences were unprecedented in Massachusetts judicial history. Although probably only two of the men were executed, the provisional government clearly had demonstrated its powers to all who would question them."[43] Why then the delay in 1692 of the trials' commencement until the arrival of Increase Mather?

The answer here is probably found in a conflict between the magistrates who were jailing the people – Bartholomew Gedney along with Hathorne and Corwin – and the governor, who was opposed to proceeding with indictments in the cases. In an apparent test of wills between the judiciary and the governor, Simon Bradstreet resisted bringing people to trial. Behaving in the traditional New England way, the conservative Bradstreet held the line, and he would do so until the end, until Increase Mather came not just with a new charter, but with a new governor, William Phips.

Increase Mather would emerge as one of the great voices for moderation once the trials began, so it is exquisitely ironic that he brought to power the man who tilted the balance away from the old view, who set up a special court that would have on it some of the very men who had been encouraging the arrest of people as witches.[44] Among others, Phips named to the court Jonathan Corwin, Bartholomew Gedney, and John Hathorne.[45] Thus, three of the nine men named to the court had largely precipitated the crisis by their radical treatment of the cases, and had obviously prejudged the accused. Heading the court was William Stoughton, Phips's lieutenant governor, a man who would cling to his belief in the guilt of people as witches and in the rectitude of the court even after a general consensus had been reached that the court had gone wrong. In months to come, Phips would quarrel with the methods of the court – ironically, a court created by Phips to examine matters that Bradstreet had refused to pursue – and with Stoughton in particular. From the outset, the dice were loaded, and Phips had loaded them. His motives in appointing men who knew something about the outbreak, or simply men of good reputation, may have been purely bureaucratic. If he had other motives, they are not apparent.

Tituba's fate had there been no Court of Oyer and Terminer set up by Phips must remain speculative. Under normal circumstances as a confessing witch she would almost certainly have been tried and hanged in a rare Massachusetts Bay execution for witchcraft.[46] Tituba may have been extraordinarily lucky or extraordinarily shrewd in surviving through the new way, confession. Alternatively, she may have survived simply because she was property. According to Joseph B. Felt, on June 1, 1692, at the time of the first trial, Parris sold Tituba to pay her jail fees.[47] The new Court of Oyer and Terminer chose to keep Tituba out of the judicial system.

With Phips's court in place, the witch trials of 1692 became almost inevitable. In a further irony, early in the proceedings Phips left the colony to deal with military affairs. This greatly decreased the power of Increase Mather, who was Phips's patron, to moderate the behavior of the court, and greatly increased that of Stoughton. With Tituba, Sarah Good, and Sarah Osborne in prison, the episode that we call the Salem witch trials had begun. Tituba, the slave who found her way to survival, slipped into mythology as the woman who by her tales brought chaos and death to the New World garden.

2

The girls of Salem

The terrible witchcraft delusion in Salem in 1692 was caused almost entirely by children. But for a half-dozen young girls, those men and women would not have been hung on Gallows Hill. . . .
– W. S. Nevins, *Salem Observer,* August 30, 1890

I

The judgment against the children, rendered at the end of the nineteenth century by Winfield Nevins, carries a set of assumptions continued into the twentieth century and first articulated in its modern form in the eighteenth century by Thomas Hutchinson, who complained that "None of the pretended afflicted were ever brought upon trial for their fraud . . . ."[1] Hutchinson, reflecting a judicial judgment made in 1711, embellished the account and declared that some of the accusers "proved profligate persons, abandoned to all vice, others passed their days in obscurity or contempt."[2] As Hutchinson realized, however, he held a view not universally shared.

The opinion which prevailed in New-England, for many years after this tragedy, that there was something praeternatural in it, and that it was not all the effect of fraud and imposture, proceeded from the reluctance in human nature to reject errors once imbibed. As the principal actors went off the stage, this opinion has gradually lessened, and perhaps it is owing to a respect to the memory of their immediate ancestors, that many do not yet seem to be fully convinced. There are a great number of persons who are willing to suppose the accusers to have been

32

under bodily disorders which affected their imaginations. This is kind and charitable, but seems to be winking the truth out of sight. A little attention must force conviction that the whole was a scene of fraud and imposture, began by young girls, who at first perhaps thought of nothing more than being pitied and indulged, and continued by adult persons, who were afraid of being accused themselves. The one and the other, rather than confess their fraud, suffered the lives of so many innocents to be taken away, through the credulity of judges and juries.[3]

In the centuries to follow, deviations from the terms of Hutchinson's configuration have been simply matters of degree. In popular imagination, the idea of the "praeternatural" persists, while the scholarly parties have continued to divide between some variation of "bodily disorders" and some variation of "fraud," with the twentieth century tending to favor the illness concept, mental or social, and the nineteenth century inclined to agree with Hutchinson.

As Hutchinson makes clear, a medical model for the Salem episode existed from the beginning. The actual diagnosis of Betty Parris and Abigail Williams was made by one or more physicians, who concluded that witchcraft had occurred. As a professional belief in demonology receded, a pre-Freudian assessment of hysteria emerged. Charles Upham, whose *Salem Witchcraft* has served as the foundation of much modern scholarship on the subject, heavily favored the notion of fraud in connection with those he described as "a circle of young girls," a sobriquet that sticks to this day.[4] Upham drew back, however, from wholly discarding a theory of psychological causes in conceding, though with great skepticism, the possibility that "credulity, hallucination, and the delirium of excitement" contributed to the behavior of the girls.[5] Nineteenth-century commentators frequently invoke vague suggestions of mental problems, harking back to the disorders Hutchinson had described.

The twentieth century has pursued medical models more persistently, particularly psychological ones. Echoes of Freud permeate Salem accounts, popular and scholarly. A professor in Alison Lurie's novel *Imaginary Friends* refers to the early accusers as "some neurotic adolescents."[6] Arthur Miller cites "the ravings of a klatch of repressed pubescent girls who, fearing punishment for their implicitly sexual revolt, began convincing themselves that they had been perverted by Satan."[7] The girls, according to the writer of a magazine account, achieved "an esteem and fame . . . that gave them an orgasmic exultation."[8] Another refers to "young girls [who] lived in dread of a spectral rape by the incubus and of giving birth to a demon child."[9] Less exotic, but deeply passionate in his defense of the girls on psychological grounds, was Ernest Caulfield, a physician whose generalization about the affair serves well to exemplify the case for innocence by reason of hysteria:

> One is not obliged to accept the verdict of the popular historians that the children were deceitful, wicked, malicious and dishonest. History has been unkind to them long enough. They were not impostors or pests or frauds; they were not cold-blooded malignant brats. They were sick children in the worst sort of mental distress – living in fear for their very lives and the welfare of their immortal souls. Hysteria was only the outward manifestation of their feeble attempts to escape from their insecure, cruel, depressive Salem Village world – a world thoroughly saturated with the pungent fumes of burning brimstone.[10]

Chadwick Hansen, in his revisionist *Witchcraft at Salem,* where he argues that actual witchcraft occurred at Salem, continues the kind of argument offered by Caulfield: "The behavior of the afflicted persons was not fraudulent but pathological. They were hysterics, and in the clinical rather than the popular sense of that term. These people were not merely overexcited; they were mentally ill."[11] This paradigm essentially prevailed until around 1970 when John Demos broadened consideration of the issue from psychology to sociology, even as he accepted a model of hysteria.[12] Although he was surely not the first to examine the issue in sociological or anthropological terms, he did so with a sophistication unseen before.[13] His work culminated in *Entertaining Satan,*[14] although this particular study is not primarily about Salem. Pursuing the social model, Paul Boyer and Stephen Nissenbaum offered a landmark critique of the community of Salem Village and argued for a social understanding of the witchcraft episode.[15] Richard Weisman in 1984 examined the larger community of Massachusetts as he offered a sociological analysis of witchcraft in the colony and the particular way in which the authorities in 1692 deviated from past responses to witchcraft accusations.[16] Subsequently Carol F. Karlsen published *The Devil in the Shape of a Woman,* in which she studied New England witchcraft in general, as Demos and Weisman had done, and looked for social understandings, particularly as they related to the plight of women in seventeenth-century New England.[17] With the grave risk of oversimplifying the complex arguments of Demos, Boyer and Nissenbaum, Weisman, and Karlsen, we can say that the critique of Salem shifted from an assessment of individual blame to an examination of how social situations led to certain kinds of behavior. This social model remains the dominant one today.[18]

It has not been the only one, however. In 1976, Linnda Caporael offered her theory regarding ergotism, an analysis that argues for hallucinogenic effects resulting from the eating of contaminated rye – a physiological response – as the basis for behavior deemed by others as hysterical: "The girls were often stricken with violent fits that were attributed to torture by apparitions. The spectral evidence of the trials appears to be the hallucinogenic symptoms and perceptual disturbances accompanying ergotism. The convulsions appear to be epileptiform."[19] Such an explanation, though different from the social one, continues the modern tradition of assessing responsibility on some agency external to the individuals involved, whether that agency emerges as a social or medical one. As with the original claims that witches were causing afflictions, such models shift responsibility for the conduct of the accusers away from them.

The Caporael thesis received a devastatingly persuasive rebuttal later in 1976 from Nicholas P. Spanos and Jack Gottlieb. Aside from pointing to a flawed analysis of the social data, Spanos and Gottlieb attacked the argument on scientific grounds, since convulsive ergotism requires a diet deficient in vitamin A, whereas the community had a diet high in this vitamin. Where the vitamin is abundant, ergotism takes the form of "gangrenous rather than convulsive symptoms."[20] Constructions about Salem, however, do not yield easily, and in 1982 in *American Scientist,* Mary K. Matossian reopened the issue of convulsive ergotism. She did so partly through a process of elimination, arguing that earlier theories failed to account for what happened at Salem. Among those she addressed were Spanos and Gottlieb, claiming that fresh examination of the material diminished the strength of their argument. Matossian did not examine the issue of vitamin A, but she did speculate as to why there were no records of visible symptoms of ergotism, such as "livid or jaundiced skin," or a variety of other symptoms associated with the disease, suggesting that they were not reported because such symptoms "were not commonly associated with bewitchment."[21] If she was aware of the observation in 1692 of Thomas Brattle, an accomplished scientist, that the accusers, when not claiming to be attacked by specters, were perfectly healthy and showed no adverse effects from these assaults – or that the judges knew this – she showed no indication.[22]

Matossian's resurrection of the Caporael thesis was soon reported by Walter Sullivan in the *New York Times,*[23] and the thesis still appears sporadically. Indeed, its refutation not withstanding, the Caporael thesis has made its way into at least one college psychology textbook.[24]

In rebutting the ergot thesis, Spanos and Gottlieb seem to lean heavily toward the view of fraud, though couching the argument in psychological terms:

> Rather than ergot poisoning, these descriptions [of the conduct of the accusers] suggest that the afflicted girls were enacting the roles that

would sustain their definition of themselves as bewitched and that would lead to the conviction of the accused.[25]

Without insisting that the conduct of the accusers was fraudulent, they remind their readers "that numerous 16th-century English demoniacs who displayed all the symptoms manifested by the Salem girls later confessed that they had faked these displays."[26] By implication, we are back to Hutchinson.

We are also back to a persistent model of a governing explanation. That is, when Hutchinson argued for fraud, he asserted "that the *whole* was a scene of fraud and imposture" (my emphasis). Conversely, those arguing for, say hysteria, have tended to argue that all the accusers were hysterics. Scholarship at its best, of course, has sought and found finer distinctions in unraveling the story of Salem, and it is in such discriminations that we discover our best chances for exploring the murky, often contradictory world of the Salem episode. The stories of the accusers unfold as individual cases connected by a common phenomenon. Without a doubt, there was fraud among the girls of Salem; without a doubt, there were moments of extraordinary integrity. Nor were all the "girls" girls: When Upham defined a "circle of girls" he left an image so strong, a myth so powerful, that in the face of all evidence, the image stuck. Thus, to take an example from two of the preeminent scholars of Salem, Paul Boyer and Stephen Nissenbaum, we find them making reference in their indispensable three-volume *Salem Witchcraft Papers* to "four afflicted girls not actually accused of witchcraft, but against whom skeptical testimony was directed: Sarah Bibber (or Vibber, as she was often called), Elizabeth Hubbard, Susannah Sheldon, and Abigail Williams" (*SWP* I: 33). Yet this "girl," Sarah Bibber, was 36 years old at the time (*SWP* II: 376).[27]

II

On August 25, 1706, one of these girls edged toward acknowledging fraud. On that day, Ann Putnam, Jr., was received into communion in the church at Salem Village. Then in her mid twenties, she offered a public confession that her actions in 1692 had contributed to the deaths of people she now believed to be innocent; but she pleaded that Satan had deluded her into doing it.

> I desire to be humbled before God for that sad and humbling providence that befell my father's family in the year about '92; that I, then being in my childhood, should, by such a providence of God, be made an instrument for the accusing of several persons of a grievous crime,

whereby their lives were taken away from them, whom now I have
just grounds and good reason to believe they were innocent persons;
and that it was a great delusion of Satan that deceived me in that sad
time, whereby I justly fear I have been instrumental, with others,
though ignorantly and unwittingly, to bring upon myself and this land
the guilt of innocent blood; though what was said or done by me
against any person I can truly and uprightly say, before God and man, I
did it not out of any anger, malice, or ill-will to any person, for I had
no such thing against one of them; but what I did was ignorantly, being deluded by Satan. And particularly, as I was a chief instrument of
accusing of Goodwife Nurse and her two sisters [Mary Easty and Sarah
Cloyce], I desire to lie in the dust, and to be humbled for it, in that I
was a cause, with others, of so sad a calamity to them and their families; for which cause I desire to lie in the dust, and earnestly beg forgiveness of God, and from all those unto whom I have given just cause
of sorrow and offence, whose relations were taken away or accused.[28]

Ann's confession of "ignorantly and unwittingly" being deluded by Satan represented a compromise whereby she exonerated a few of the victims without fully implicating herself. Her words acknowledge that in
some way she had been an instrument of Satan, an individual whose actions led to the shedding of innocent blood. Just what does that mean? If
we discount the notion that "Satan did it," we do not by that act discount
the possibility that Ann Putnam believed that Satan did it through her. So
giving her the benefit of the doubt, we ask the question, Just what did she
think Satan was doing through her?

Her official career as an accuser had begun on February 29, 1692. Between then and September 1692 she actively accused various people of
torturing her and others, as well as of confessing various crimes to her.
These people communicated their information to her through their
"shapes": At an examination of an accused person, Ann would scream that
the shape of that person had left the body and was, invisible to all but her
and other accusers, tormenting her or others. Ann would behave in ways
bizarre enough to convince some of the people that the invisible world
was attacking her. The shapes came at the will of the corporeal person,
and why these accused "witches" would so openly reveal themselves was
a question that the judicial authorities never asked and that Ann Putnam
never explained.

How "unwitting" Ann behaved is suggested in an episode involving
pins, where, as we have seen, little room for ambiguity exists. On May 31
during the questioning of a suspected witch, Elizabeth How, the accusers
complained of various abuses to them from How. Ann reported "a pin

stuck in her hand," unambiguously implying that the shape of Elizabeth How had put it there (*SWP* II: 434).[29] If we discount that possibility, we are left with only two alternatives: Either someone else put the pin in Ann's hand, with or without her consent, or Ann put it there herself.

If, in the heat of the examination of Elizabeth How, a hysterical or simply upset Ann Putnam failed to notice that one of her fellow accusers was sticking pins in her, secretly, before a crowd of people, we might say that such a possibility could exist. However, the notion that others did it becomes less likely when we examine the testimony of her father, Thomas, and her uncle Edward, who maintained that, being with Anne "in & after her fits," they had seen her various afflictions, including "pins thrust into her flesh" (*SWP* II: 602). Such close private witnesses, added to the public witnesses, significantly reduce the possibility that another person was putting pins in Ann without her knowledge of who was doing it.

Assuming for the moment that Ann's mental state was so distraught that she put pins in herself without realizing what she was doing, we have a case of a hysterical girl inflicting self-punishment without the awareness that she was her own tormentor. The problem with this hypothesis is that it does not square with Ann's confession: She knew she had done something wrong, and she blamed the devil. To examine the issue at its simplest level, she was confessing that her bad deeds had truly been hers and were indeed bad. True, it had been the devil's fault, but the deeds were still there. Such a confession only makes sense if we assume that Ann had been responsible for the presence of the pins and was subsequently saying that she had done such a bad thing because the devil had lured her into it.

There is another problem, however, with the notion that Ann did not know what she was doing, since numerous instances occur where Ann had to be cooperating with others. Thus on May 23, to give only one of many examples, Ann and Abigail Williams testified that they were together when they saw the apparition of Mary Easty, who told them she was afflicting another accuser, Mercy Lewis. A private hallucination resulting from hysteria might be plausible; a shared one is less so, though admittedly not inconceivable; but when two people produce pins as evidence and blame the same specter, as Ann and Abigail Williams did on May 10 at the examination of George Jacobs, Sr., it is hard not to suspect full and rational knowledge of what is happening (*SWP* II: 477). Why Ann Putnam was making false claims presents another kind of problem.

III

Ann, of course, was not alone in fabricating specters, as can be inferred from Deodat Lawson, formerly a minister at Salem Village. On

March 24, 1692, Lawson delivered a sermon, entitled "A Brief and True Narrative of Some Remarkable Passages," which treated the witchcraft outbreak then occurring. In early April he published the sermon. Lawson was on the scene when some of the events were happening, and while we may quarrel with his conclusions, there is no reason to doubt what he claims to have seen. Among his most fascinating observations is the following:

> Some of the afflicted, as they were striving in their fits in open court, have (by invisible means) had their wrists bound fast together with a real cord, so as it could hardly be taken off without cutting. Some afflicted have been found with their arms tied, and hanged upon an hook, from whence others have been forced to take them down, that they might not expire in that posture.[30]

Lawson pointed to such events as horrors perpetrated by witches. For him, afflicted persons, hands bound in court or hanging from hooks, clearly denoted the devil at work. Indeed, to be bound as described or to hang from a hook in this way requires either the devil or some human resourcefulness, a plot rationally set: One must go to a great deal of trouble to arrange such spectacles. Whether the "afflicted" worked these shows out among themselves or had help from others cannot be determined; but there is little doubt that such calculated action was deliberately conceived to perpetuate the fraud in which the afflicted were involved, and that theories of hysteria or hallucination cannot account for people being bound, whether on the courtroom floor or on hooks. To the contrary, the very nature of the activities Lawson reports reminds us how calculated the behavior of the "afflicted" was, and we have every reason to ask, How could people make such false and dangerous charges? How much could one possibly gain in return for the terrible cost that was being inflicted? Such elaborate fraud it was, and not even money to be made in return.

Ann's dissembling did not set any precedents in witchcraft history: A few years earlier, for example, John Webster, in his *The Displaying of Supposed Witchcraft,* had cited cases of such fraud, including one by a girl Ann's age, Rachael Pinder, age 11 or 12.[31] We need not go very far back in our own time to find cases of unreliable accusations from children or young people – such as the former congressional page who in 1982 admitted having invented his story of homosexual encounters with some members of Congress. Likewise, when children in Minnesota charged in 1984 "that other children were murdered after being filmed for pornography. . . . [the] authorities decided the children had fabricated the stories."[32] Some retractions may be false, but certainly not all of them. Terrible things do happen to children, but their word is not infallible.

During the seventeenth and eighteenth centuries such fraudulent charges as Ann Putnam's were explainable by the existence of the devil. In the nineteenth century, Herman Melville would use the motif of an unfounded charge to explore in *Billy Budd* what Captain Vere calls, in citing scripture, "the mystery of iniquity" – a mystery Melville had earlier probed in *The Confidence-Man*. There, one of his characters, baffled by a confidence man going to great lengths to commit a fraud for no monetary gain, looks for an answer to such behavior and is answered with a question: "How much money did the devil make by gulling Eve?"[33] The twentieth century has not liked such models, preferring explanations from psychology and sociology; but in speculations on the motives of Ann Putnam in helping send people to their death, original sin may be as useful as psychoanalysis. It is extremely complex to deduce the motives of living people, even when they are examined by the wisest psychiatrists. Though psychohistorians will surely disagree, the dead – especially those who leave such slim records as did Ann Putnam – are beyond our reach for motivational analysis.

Our guesses, of course, are governed by the cultural interests of our day. With the ascendance of Freud, we offered complex models of hysteria. When we learned about hallucinogenic drugs, we discovered ergot. Why not try out our current concern with child abuse? We might note that on June 3, 1692, Ann Putnam, testifying against John Willard, who would hang as a convicted witch, asserted that the apparition of her deceased 6-week-old sister Sarah cried out for vengeance against John Willard for having whipped her to death (*SWP* III: 851). Ann made this claim in open court, and if anyone raised questions as to whether it had been known that Sarah's death had been caused by beating, there is no record of it. Sarah's mother, Ann Putnam, Sr., was herself an accuser in some of the cases, a woman who claimed to see specters. Who could fault one for speculating that she could not come to terms with having killed her own child, that she found some relief in the fantasy world of blaming witches? Ann Jr. may unwittingly have revealed the family secret; she may have responded to the beating death of her sister by lashing out at the community. Children do get abused, and although I would not want to defend the thesis that the behavior of Ann Putnam, Jr., grew from such abuse, broader theories have been developed from less evidence.

I do not claim to know the heart of Ann Putnam, but it is clear that she lied in her accusations of witchcraft. She told us so in her own convoluted way. Others told of their lying in totally unambiguous ways, but Ann's rhetorical flourishes notwithstanding, she had lied from the outset. Moreover, she continued to lie: Of the four original accusers against Sarah

Good, Sarah Osborne, and Tituba, only Ann Putnam and her cousin Mary Walcott, who lived with her, continued the accusations and theatrical performances throughout the hearings and the trials. She continued through the spring, summer, and fall of 1692. Others came and went for reasons that will become clear in ways that Ann Putnam's presence never will be, but she persisted. When the episode was dying out in the Salem Village area, she and Mary Walcott went to Andover and sparked its renewal. Of the twenty judicially executed people, all but three were accused by Ann. It is possible, of course, that she was implicated in their deaths also, but the records are incomplete.

Anne's activity and retraction make her the most visible of the "girls of Salem," but her career as an accuser began in the company of Betty Parris, Abigail Williams, and Elizabeth Hubbard. Of these, Betty Parris may have stayed with the accusers until late March, but she disappears from the scene after that.[34] Abigail Williams appears as an active accuser in March, April, and May, but her activities level off thereafter: She makes one court appearance at the beginning of June, three at the end of July, and none in August and September. Her disappearance from the scene remains unexplained, since the court was active in August and September and there is no obvious reason for the lack of subpoenas for her to testify. In spite of her early departure, she was involved in at least seventeen capital cases. Elizabeth Hubbard remains active throughout the proceedings, being implicated in the deaths of all the executed except three.

Of the four original accusers, then, the two youngest dropped out along the way, and others joined in as the ranks of accusers grew. Most of these others were as old or older than Elizabeth Hubbard. This means that the accusing "girls" in the Salem phase of the episode were predominately young women in their late teens; some, including Ann Putnam, Sr., were in their twenties or thirties.[35] These "girls" were defined at times in legal documents as "singlewomen," although often referred to in the judicial proceedings as "children." In addition to Ann Putnam and Elizabeth Hubbard, the main subsequent accusers were Mercy Lewis, 19, and Mary Walcott, 18, both of whom lived in the Putnam household with Ann. Thus the core group of early accusers comprised three children, Ann, Betty, and Abigail; two young women from the Putnam household, Mercy Lewis and Mary Walcott; and a neighbor, Elizabeth Hubbard, between 16 and 18. They were joined by Ann Putnam, Jr., 18-year-old Susannah Sheldon, and 36-year-old Sarah Bibber, as well as by Tituba's husband, John Indian, whose age is unknown. A married woman, Bathshua Pope, also joined the accusers; her age has not been determined, but she was identified as "Mrs." or "mistress," indicating a high social status.[36] If there was some original group delusion, conspiracy, or disease that led to the outbreak, it was common to the accusers from the Putnam and Parris households in conjunction with Elizabeth Hubbard, Susannah Sheldon, Sarah Bibber, Bathshua Pope, "and an Ancient Woman, named Goodall."[37] Other "girls" would join this group, with neither age nor gender offering a barrier to accusations of affliction.

IV

If the motives of the core group are elusive and finally subject primarily to speculation – although some speculations are a lot better than others – the behavior of those who joined them becomes progressively easier to understand. At the outset, when Tituba, Sarah Good, and Sarah Osborne were accused of hurting Betty Parris, Abigail Williams, Ann Putnam, and Elizabeth Hubbard, the outcome of the case was uncertain if examined in the light of previous witchcraft proceedings in Massachusetts Bay colony. An odds maker could have been forgiven for betting that the matter would end with that first 1692 case and that no one would be executed. According to Richard Weisman, prior to 1692 there had been fifty complaints in Massachusetts for witchcraft, twenty-five indictments, and seven convictions.[38] When Bridget Bishop on June 10 became the first to be executed as a witch in 1692, there was thus no precedent for believing that a number of other executions would follow. However, something different was already happening, in that many people had been imprisoned. Nor could it easily have passed unnoticed that the person singled out for execution had been a woman who had maintained her innocence, whereas jailed confessors were not hanging. To those who knew that confession traditionally offered the strongest evidence of witchcraft, this reversal of precedent must have seemed extraordinary, its incitement to confession powerful. In time, what might only be intuited by the public as a result of the Bridget Bishop case – confess and avoid the gallows – would emerge as a well-understood formula. Even before Bridget Bishop's execution, one of the judges was already being urged to implement a policy of eliciting confession in exchange for an escape from the gallows.[39]

If the connection between confession and survival took until early summer to become clear, another possible connection had begun to appear sooner: Cooperation with the accusers proved salutary. As the pattern emerged, people who had not even been accused joined the ranks of the accusers, the one sure place of security. The dramatic turning point establishing the benefits of cooperation with the accusers occurred on April 19 in the complex case of Mary Warren, the servant of John and Elizabeth

Proctor, and, to a lesser extent, with the examination of Abigail Hobbs on that same day (and of her parents in the next few days). In the story of these days, we see a course set from which there would be no return.

Abigail Hobbs, age 14 and living with her parents, Deliverance and William, was complained against on April 18.[40] Examined on April 19, she immediately confessed. Insufficient information exists to explain why Abigail was named and why she confessed, but her confession brought salutary results. The accusers refrained from feigning torments during the examination, and at its conclusion Mercy Lewis, Abigail Williams, and Ann Putnam said in court that "they were sorry for the condition this poor Abig. Hobbs was in, which compassion they expressed over and over again" (*SWP* II: 409). Whether a deal had been struck whereby Abigail Hobbs would confess in return for support from the accusers, or whether the outburst of compassion was for other reasons, the effects were clear: To win the favor of those with such power required only the act of cooperation with them.

Other lessons emerged from the examination and subsequent indictment of Abigail Hobbs, who went to jail, the compassion of the accusers notwithstanding. Her case revealed that although confession could soften one's fate, it offered no route to freedom: That path, as Mary Warren would discover, required virulent, active participation with the accusers. Another lesson emerged from the case of Abigail Hobbs, however – one that may or may not have been important to her contemporaries, but is significant for those exploring the judicial process of the trials. It is a lesson about indictments.

The lone surviving indictment against Abigail Hobbs is one accusing her of afflicting Mercy Lewis on April 19, the day of Abigail's examination, as well as on other days. The indictments, except for Tituba's and for some coming out of Andover cases, are consistent in accusing a person of afflicting another on the day of the examination, tormenting the accusers with the person's specter. That is, with the few exceptions indicated, *all* the indictments are based on spectral evidence, and almost all specifically refer to the day of the examination.[41] This pattern had already emerged when Abigail was indicted, and the formulaic aspect of the indictment was followed even though it flagrantly contradicted the recorded testimony that the afflicted "were none of them tormented during the whole examination of this accused and confessing person, Abigail Hobbs" (*SWP* II: 409): The indictment, with Mercy Lewis, Mary Walcott, Elizabeth Hubbard, and Ann Putnam as witnesses, affirms that Abigail afflicted Mercy Lewis at the examination.

The contradiction highlights the extent to which the proccedings had become bureaucratized. Regardless of what precipitated an accusation, or what claims followed, an accused person would be indicted for afflicting someone on the day of the accused's examination. If nothing else, this relentless predictability reveals how insignificant actual testimony became during the Salem prosecutions. Witnesses for and against a person, denials, admissions, and all else were merely ritualized exercises in a process that went from accusation to indictment, always (with the few Andover exceptions) on the same grounds: spectral evidence almost invariably on the day of the examination. This held even on days when the specters did not misbehave, as on April 19 at the examination of Abigail Hobbs.

Lessons also emerged from the examination of Abigail's stepmother, Deliverance, on April 22. When Deliverance Hobbs was brought into the courtroom to be examined, the justices had kept her name secret; Mercy Lewis and another accuser, unnamed, were asked to identify her. Since they had presumably cried out against her, the procedure appears to have been designed to test the accuracy of their charges, and, relatively early in the Salem episode, the judiciary might seem by this test to have been working with a semblance of fairness. Mercy and the other accuser failed: Neither could identify Deliverance Hobbs, the person whose specter they had presumably seen; yet the justices, having provided the test, seemed not only unembarrassed but uninterested in the failure of the two to identify her. When Ann Putnam successfully disclosed Deliverance Hobbs's identity, the justices, Hathorne and Corwin, quickly proceeded in the typical line of questioning that assumed the guilt of the accused: "How come you to commit acts of Witchcraft?" (*SWP* II: 419). There are no questions to Mercy Lewis and her companion as to why they could not identify the woman.

Something even stranger happened at the examination of Deliverance Hobbs. From the questioning, it seems clear that she herself had earlier claimed to have been afflicted, to have seen specters. She said she had seen "shapes of severall persons," but when asked to identify them she named only two. One was Sarah Wilds, already implicated by Deliverance Hobbs's stepdaughter Abigail. Astonishingly, though, she identified the other as Mercy Lewis – astonishing because here was a stunning charge being made against one of the primary accusers, here was perhaps an attempt to play the game the other way, to reverse the trick, to do exactly what the accusers did. True, Deliverance Hobbs said it was only Goody Wilds who hurt her and not Mercy Lewis, but how would the judiciary handle this charge?

Up until now it had credited every last allegation of shapes appearing. In response to the claim, the startled Hathorne asked, "What is that?"

(*SWP* II: 420). Here was a crossroads. If the charge stuck, the process would collapse quickly in an array of specter sightings that could never be untangled. Every accused could complain about the shapes of the accusers, and the line between accuser and accused would disintegrate. That day, April 21, Hathorne and Corwin faced what for others might have proved an overwhelming theological problem; but they simply passed over the assertion. Rather than challenge it, they destroyed its potential usefulness to victims of the accusers by simply ignoring it. By their silent response to the allegation of Deliverance Hobbs they made clear that only a chosen set of people had the prerogative of seeing shapes. Deliverance Hobbs had not been chosen in the game of glimpsing at the invisible world, and an early opportunity to unload the dice passed in silence. John Hathorne, the justice of the peace most influential in conducting the examinations, had cast his lot with the accusers and would not enter the theological miasma invited by the charge of the accused Deliverance Hobbs. How emphatically the justices had chosen sides emerges more significantly in the case of Mary Warren.

V

Mary Warren was a young woman of 20. Although her name appears in no legal document prior to her examination on April 19, she had had or feigned fits at earlier hearings.[42] According to Samuel Sibley, on March 24 John Proctor told him that he wished to bring home his "jade" from the judicial proceedings occurring then in Salem Village (*SWP* II: 684). Sibley refers to Mary Warren's earlier fits and to Proctor's success in stopping them by thrashing her. Perhaps because of Proctor's behavior, he and his wife Elizabeth were complained against on April 4 and examined April 11.[43] Although the accusations against the Proctors seem related to a struggle between the accusers and the Proctors over Mary Warren, their arrest did not immediately commit Mary Warren to her future course as an aggressive accuser. Indeed, on April 19 she was brought to court to be examined as a suspected witch after having previously claimed affliction.

The story of Mary Warren has been attractive to commentators on Salem. The servant of John and Elizabeth Proctor, she participated with the other accusers until Proctor threatened to whip her. She then defected from the accusers and was herself accused. Unlike Abigail Williams, who Arthur Miller chose in *The Crucible* for the woman tempting Proctor and then turning on him, Mary was old enough for the role (although nothing implies that she played the part) – a role speculated on in Ann Rinaldi's novel, *A Break with Charity*.[44] Nevertheless, her behavior suggests a sense of loyalty, or perhaps fear, toward the Proctors. By the time she was brought to court, herself accused, the Proctors were already in jail, and there was nothing she could have done for them in any event; but Mary Warren did not know that. She thus faced the court with the thought that their fate, as well as her own, might well hinge on her words. Still, it was only April; Bridget Bishop had not yet been hanged, and the rules were murky as to whether confession offered her an advantage or a disadvantage.

In this context she had to confront on April 19 the charge from Elizabeth Hubbard that she had claimed the accusers "did but dissemble" (*SWP* III: 793). Assuming that Mary had made this claim, this suggests a young woman with a clear enough sense of reality to know fraud when she saw it; yet testimony by four people accused as witches – Edward Bishop, Mary Bishop, Mary Easty, and Mary English – argues for a mentally unstable person. According to these people, while in prison Mary Warren claimed

> that the Majestrates Might as well Examine Keysars Daughter that has Bin distracted Many Yeares And Take Noatice of what Shee Said: as well as any of the Afflicted pe'sons for Said Mary warrin when I was Afflicted I thought I saw the Apparission of A hundred persons: for Shee said hir Head was Distempered that Shee Could not tell what Shee Said, And the Said Mary tould us that when Shee was well Againe Shee Could not Say that Shee saw any of Apparissons at the time Aforesaid. (*SWP* III: 803)

This picture suggests hallucination and tenuous recovery, a recognition of one's own unreliability.

Ironically, each side had a vested interest in establishing the unreliability of Mary Warren: Elizabeth Hubbard and her cohorts needed to discredit anyone who accused them of lying about being attacked by the invisible world, whereas those accused as witches needed to discredit anyone who argued for spectral visitations. Whether Mary at this time feigned her uncertainty or whether she actually drifted in and out of mental stability must remain unknown; but we do know that she offered the authorities an opportunity to probe deeply into the claims of the accusers. For the first time an accuser had defected and claimed fraud: Here was an invitation to examine honestly the credibility of the accusers. The authorities chose not to do so – not then, not later.

On April 19 Mary Warren appeared in Salem Village before John Hathorne and Jonathan Corwin and maintained her innocence. Indeed, when her accusers put on their fits, Mary responded by falling into her own fit. Apparitions were attacking her, she claimed, as the justices watched the spectacle of accusers and accused undergoing fits. Finally, she was removed from the room and another accused person, Bridget Bishop, was brought in, unaware at the time that she would be the first to hang. When Mary was brought back she displayed more fits, but was lucid enough to deny that she had signed the devil's book. Her "fit" behavior continued, and she was sent out for air and brought in again but still could not answer the questions asked because of her "fits." At this point, a technique that would be used in other cases was introduced: Magistrates and ministers spoke privately with Mary Warren. What they said we do not know; Mary's answers, when they returned, remained evasive. In some subsequent private audiences with others, torture was used.

Mary Warren was taken to prison where the questioning continued, probably on April 20. By now, she was confessing and making some accusations. Of particular interest to us, however, was her ability in prison to describe exactly the clothing worn by Giles Corey, whose apparition she claimed afflicted her. Mary's ability to describe Corey's clothing accurately indicates that someone had given the description to her, and that at this point she was with full knowledge "dissembling" (*SWP* III: 796). Mary Warren was now ready for a public presentation, which came at a new examination on April 21; but she still proved an unreliable witness for the magistrates. She answered questions tentatively, confessing as little as she thought she could get away with: When asked whether she had made a mark in the devil's book, she replied she had done so but only with the top of her finger (*SWP* III: 796). She made damning charges against the Proctors, but she would not admit knowing that they were a witch and a wizard. Asked whether she had afflicted the accusers she denied it, but expressed the fear that the devil had used her shape to do it. Mary Warren was put back in prison.

On May 12 she was examined again. She began in her evasive mode. Had she known that the book she had signed was the devil's book? She did not know it at the time, but she knew it now (*SWP* III: 799). Had she ever seen poppets? On April 21 her answer to the same question had been no, and on this day she had earlier denied ever hurting any of the children; but now she slid further into the role sought for her. Once she had seen Elizabeth Proctor make a poppet. Mary had stuck a pin in it. How many more poppets had she seen afterward? None, she said, and then she began naming the people who brought her poppets. When asked how long her master and mistress had been witches – the question was that leading – she said she did not know, but this time she tacitly endorsed the charge. Mary had converted, and as the episode spread she told horror stories of witchcraft and murder. Although her claims were not always fully integrated with those of the other main accusers, Mary Warren became one of the most active and most virulent accusers. She learned to bleed from the mouth, and charged many a person with causing that as well as other atrocities against her. She was free from jail and safe; to protect herself she had only to keep up the show, and so she did through the months that followed. The lesson of Mary Warren was not lost on others.

When two other young women, Sarah Churchill and Margaret Jacobs, were examined within two days of one another (May 9 and 11, respectively), each responded to the logic of Mary Warren's case. Sarah Churchill, the first of the two to be examined, was the servant of George Jacobs, Sr., the grandfather of Margaret Jacobs. A bewildered and frightened young woman of around 17, she never mustered the enthusiasm that Mary Warren found, and seems to have stayed away from the legal system to the extent that it was possible.[45] After her accusation against George Jacobs, Sr., in May, in early June she accused two women, Ann Pudeator and Bridget Bishop. Both these women had earlier been accused, so she simply added to the stories about them. She did not appear in court again until the following September, when her testimony included charges against Alice Parker and Mary Parker, both of whom would be executed;[46] but Sarah Churchill knew that her stories were lies, and at the outset, at least, she suffered from telling them. Her problem was that she did not know how to escape from the logic that had been imposed. The testimony of Sarah Ingersoll seems definitive as to Sarah Churchill's state of mind after her examination on May 9. Apparently, just after that examination Sarah Churchill came crying and wringing her hands to Ingersoll. Upon being asked what troubled her, she said she had belied herself and others in saying she had set her hand to the devil's book. Sarah Ingersoll then said,

> I told her I believed she had set her hand to the [devil's] book. She answered, crying, and said "no, no no, I never did." I asked then what had made her say she did. She answered because they threatened her and told her they would put her into the dungeon and put her along with Mr. Burroughs, and thus several times she followed on up and down telling me that she had undone herself in belying herself and others. I asked her why she didn't tell the truth now. She told me because she had stood out so long in it that now she dare not. She said also that if she told Reverend Nicholas Noyes just once that she had set her hand to the devil's book he would believe her, but if she told the truth and a hundred times said she had not set her hand to the book he would not believe her. (*SWP* I: 211–12)[47]

Although Sarah Churchill opted for safety through fraud, unlike Mary Warren she did not throw herself with abandon into the proceedings. Yet once committed to her story, as she had learned, subsequent denial would not be tolerated. The investment of Hathorne and his fellow magistrates in the rectitude of their actions continued to grow as the days passed and as the witch-hunt became as much an affirmation of the process as a search for witches. She stayed with the script.

For Margaret Jacobs, however, the guilt of false confession proved too strong, and her case offers the most dramatic example of an individual's refusal to go the way of Mary Warren. Examined on May 11, one day before Mary's freeing confessions and accusations, Margaret opted for the route of accusation. The cases of Mary Warren and Sarah Churchill were showing the way.

On May 12 she aimed her charges at Alice Parker, and on May 13 at Salem Village's former minister George Burroughs; she also accused her own grandfather, George Jacobs, Sr., probably around that time. Margaret Jacobs had little stomach for playing the game, however, and her participation did not last long: After May 13, there is no record of an accusation by her. What does survive are two documents that record the extraordinary tale of the 16-year-old individual whose father was in hiding and whose mother was insane and imprisoned.[48] We see in her a reason for some of the sentimentality of the nineteenth century.

One document is a letter written in prison from Margaret to her father; the other is an undated declaration to the court, probably written after September, when similar appeals for mercy by other imprisoned victims were being made. In the letter from prison, dated August 20, 1692 – the day after her grandfather had been executed – she writes of her own expected execution.[49] Having falsely confessed to witchcraft in the first place, when she tried to tell the magistrates that her confession had been dishonest, they refused to credit the truth and instead put her in jail as a witch. She represented living proof that Sarah Churchill knew of what she spoke when she explained to Sarah Ingersoll why she could not tell the truth. Margaret did. In the language of the letter,

> The reason of my Confinement is this, I having, through the Magistrates Threatenings, and my own Vile and Wretched Heart, confessed several things contrary to my Conscience and Knowledg, tho to the Wounding of my own Soul, the Lord pardon me for it; but Oh! the terrors of a wounded Conscience who can bear. But blessed be the Lord, he would not let me go on in my Sins, but in mercy I hope so my Soul would not suffer me to keep it in any longer, but I was forced to confess the truth of all before the Magistrates, who would not believe me, but tis their pleasure to put me in here, and God knows how soon I shall be put to death. Dear Father, let me beg your Prayers to the Lord on my behalf, and send us a Joyful and Happy meeting in Heaven. My Mother poor Woman is very Crazey, and remembers her

kind Love to you, and to Uncle, *viz.* D.A. [Daniel Andrew]. So leaving you to the protection of the Lord, I rest your Dutiful Daughter, Margaret Jacobs. (*SWP* II: 490–1)

In her declaration to the court, she tells of the bargain offered her, one that many another accused person would receive. The coercion she reports comes here not from judicial authorities but from the accusers, who

> told me, if I would not confess, I should be put down into the dungeon and would be hanged, but if I would confess I should have my life; the which did so affright me, with my own vile wicked heart, to save my life; made me make the like confession I did, which confession, may it please the honoured court, is altogether false and untrue. (*SWP* II: 491)

Mary Warren and Margaret Jacobs offer models of opposite polarities as to the choices that an accused young woman might make. As Mary Warren, free from prison, relentlessly accused one person after another of heinous crimes, Margaret Jacobs remained in prison facing death. That the two young women reached their crossroads at approximately the same time offers a guidepost to viewing the episode retrospectively, but for people living at the time the implications were closer, starker, more difficult to assess. Margaret and others had no reason to believe that in the end people as young as she would not go to the gallows: From their perspective, they faced hanging, and one does not often find people with the strength of Margaret Jacobs. It is therefore no surprise that as the equation held, the logic of confession and accusation grew inexorably more powerful. This does not in general represent hysteria, although people were surely agitated and frightened; rather it represents a desperate logic, rational and correct, that the safest way out of the web of accusation was through confession, accusation, or claims of affliction. We do not need to look for exotic theories to explain the behavior of the "girls of Salem" once the rules became clear. Thus, a script emerged in which accused, accuser, and the judiciary had a vested interest: The accusers and the judiciary needed the ritual of confession to legitimize their activities, and the confessors needed the continuation of the ritual to avoid the gallows.

In early May, the three young women reached their respective conclusions, each following a different route; but all three struggled with their consciences, and each made her attempt to tell the truth. In a context where only confession and accusation were received by the authorities as credible, every person confronting the legal system came to learn what behavior was required for survival. After early May, the behavior of confessors and accusers all made sense.

3
Boys and girls together

I use the feminine pronoun here because in Western Civilization the overwhelming majority of witchcraft victims have been women, who are more subject to hysteria than men.   – Chadwick Hansen, 1972[1]

I

The accusations that had begun formally with the legal complaints of February 29 continued steadily through March, April, and May. Then, as if to pause for the trial and execution of Bridget Bishop in early June, the flow of accusations diminished to the point where, after June 4, no warrants for arrest were issued until July 1. By the end of May, seventeen of the twenty people who would be executed were already in prison. July saw relatively little in the way of new accusations until around the middle of the month, at which point the main activity shifted away from Salem Village to Andover.

Although the first Andover accusation had occurred in May against Martha Carrier, July saw a dramatic outpouring of accusations and confessions in Andover. According to Calef, an Andover constable, Joseph Ballard, invited Salem Village accusers to Andover to uncover the cause of his wife's illness.[2] Ann Putnam, Jr., and Mary Walcott came to Andover and continued their accusations of witchcraft. On July 19, the date of five executions, Ballard complained against Mary Lacey, Sr., whose mother, Ann Foster, had been examined on July 15 and had confessed, although not to hurting Ballard's wife.

By the time of Mary Lacey's examination Abigail Williams had quietly dropped out; but Lacey's daughter, 15-year-old Mary Jr., entered the picture as a new and vigorous accuser. Mary Jr. became involved in a now familiar way: Herself accused on the frightening day of July 19, she found herself confronted by the accusations of Mary Warren, the living example of safety through accusation. Briefly proclaiming her innocence, Mary capitulated quickly and confessed, accusing, among others, her mother and grandmother, both of whom were themselves confessors. After confirming them as witches, Mary Jr. pleaded with Mary Warren for forgiveness; this she was granted, "and both fell a weeping Together etc" (*SWP* II: 524). Nothing indicates that she asked similar forgiveness from her mother, or from her grandmother, who died in prison. Mary Lacey, Jr., was no Margaret Jacobs, and the memory of five women hanged offered continual encouragement for Mary to persist in her accusations.

On July 22, Martha Emerson – niece of Martha Carrier, who would go to the gallows on August 19 – was arrested on the basis of accusations by Mary Lacey, Jr., and Mary Warren. During her examination on July 23, the experienced Mary Warren and the apprentice Mary Lacey, Jr., enacted fits in her presence, falling down when she looked at them. Two others, unidentified, also performed. Martha capitulated and confessed, accusing "her Aunt Carrier & good wife Green of Haverill"; but like Margaret Jacobs, Martha Emerson could not sustain the fraud:

> [A]fter ward she Denyed all. & s'd: what she had s'd was in hopes to have favour: & now she could not Deny god: that had keept her from that sin: & after s'd though he slay me I will trust in him. (*SWP* I: 308–9)

Because Martha's case did not come to trial until the following January, when the courts had returned to their normal ways, she survived.

Martha Emerson's courage reveals itself not only in her capacity to withstand the lesson of the executions of July 19, but also in the fact that her father, Roger Toothaker, had died on June 16, imprisoned as a witch. An accusation against one family member imperiled all, and Martha made her decisions in the context of her father's fate. Her mother, Mary Toothaker, was brought in for examination on July 30 and, like Martha, at first denied the accusations but then confessed and accused. At one point she resisted confessing to a charge, "but with the justices Discourse and the help of god it came into her mind" (*SWP* III: 768). God and the justices had worked differently for her than for her daughter, for there is no indication that she ever recanted. Unlike her sister, Martha Carrier, Mary Toothaker escaped the gallows.

On August 2, Mary Post of Rowley was arrested in response to a complaint by Timothy Swan of Andover, Mary Walcott, and Ann Putnam. Swan's name had come to prominence during the examination of the Laceys, and in the weeks to follow his name would appear often as a victim of the invisible world. Although Swan's testimony does not survive, the Reverend John Hale confirms that he gave it, reporting Swan's claim of having suffered greatly from witchcraft.[3] Numerous people would admit to afflicting Swan, and his suffering became one of the most frequently told stories in the confessions that had started to appear routinely.

The warrant for the arrest of Mary Post reveals a significant insight into the way the judicial authorities had been handling the Salem Village complaints. For the first time in the whole episode an indication appears that "according to Law" bond had been posted for making a complaint (*SWP* II: 645). The bond had been posted with Dudley Bradstreet, Justice of the Peace. The previous failure of other justices to require bond reveals how deeply implicated they were in encouraging the proceedings, perhaps to the point of breaking the law. This offers glaring refutation to those who have argued that the judiciary did its best to work within the constraints of judicial norms.[4] Dudley Bradstreet of Andover, in refusing to issue a warrant without the posting of bond, offers the first instance of judicial skepticism during the episode of 1692. According to Calef, Bradstreet subsequently took stronger action, refusing to issue warrants at all, with the result that "he and his Wife were cried out of, himself was (by them) said to have killed Nine persons by Witchcraft, and found it his safest course to make his Escape."[5]

As for Mary Post, whose arrest warrant is so telling, she confessed, accusing Mary Clarke of Haverhill on August 4 but making no further recorded accusations. If Mary Clarke, who was examined that day, confessed, there is no record of it, and it was perhaps her obstinacy that led to the appearance of a flurry of pins: Mary Walcott had one in her arm, Mary Warren one in her throat, and Susannah Sheldon – who vied with Mary Warren for most theatrical performer – four in her hand, albeit she only blamed Mary Clarke for two of them (*SWP* I: 214).

A few days would pass before a new recruit joined the accusers. On August 10 and 11, 22-year-old Elizabeth Johnson, Jr., was examined and confessed to afflicting several people, including two old standbys, Ann Putnam and Mary Walcott, as well as a "singlewoman" named Sarah Phelps. Elizabeth seems to have been accused because she was the granddaughter of the Reverend Francis Dane, who probably opposed the proceedings at this time and certainly did later.[6] How Phelps came to join the accusers is not clear, but she became a reliable one as the episode ran its course. Elizabeth Johnson quickly got into the spirit of things and made a variety of accusations, including the claim that specters threatened to tear her to pieces. She survived the assault and went on to charge that she had been at the meeting of witches where the Reverend George Burroughs and others had plotted to pull down the kingdom of Christ and substitute the devil's in its place. Yet for all her cooperation, Elizabeth Johnson never developed the enthusiasm for accusing that others did. Her only other recorded court appearance occurred on September 8 at the examination of Mary Osgood.

Sarah Phelps, however, joined the accusers more actively. Around August 11, Martha Carrier's 7-year-old daughter, Sarah, who said she had been a witch since she was 6, admitted afflicting Sarah Phelps. So also did her brother, Thomas, probably confessing around the same time. Abigail Faulkner, examined on August 11, was accused of afflicting Sarah Phelps, as was her mother, Elizabeth Johnson, Sr. Others too were accused of afflicting her, including Mary Parker, who went to the gallows for afflicting not only Sarah Phelps but also Ann Putnam and Mary Walcott, suggesting that Sarah Phelps had cooperated with them.

Abigail Faulkner refused to go along, but her children, Abigail Jr., 8, and Dorothy, 10, joined in the accusations. Other accusers surfaced in Andover, although surviving records do not clarify why they joined: These included Martha Sprague,[7] 16, Abigail Martin, 16, and Rose Foster, whose age, though undetermined, seems to have been roughly that of the others. Whatever their reasons for entering, they were to become regular and reliable witnesses and accusers, influential at the end of the episode in bringing new energy to the still-growing core of accusers. Martha Sprague started with the accusation that on August 15 Samuel Wardwell had afflicted her. Wardwell eventually went to the gallows, as did Mary Parker, whom Martha Sprague also accused. Rose Foster, though second only to Martha Sprague in the August and September accusations, testified against none of those eventually executed, and Abigail Martin was implicated in just one capital case, that of Wardwell. The limited relation of these three to capital cases stems from the fact that by the time they took their parts as active accusers, almost everyone was quickly confessing. By this time, the unusual individual who did not play the game generally acted with the full expectation of having chosen the gallows rather than the lie of confession and the apparent safety of prison. The skill of accusers in fabricating assaults from the invisible world had become secondary. To be named was to be punished: The rest was show.

Other names emerged in the list of accusers, overwhelmingly those of people themselves accused, who protected themselves by implicating one or a few others in witchcraft with them. This group, generally but not always made up of older people, took the route that quickly led to prison but not to the gallows: They confessed, then accused as little as necessary to survive, showing no inclination to continue accusing others. Their confessions served to corroborate the reality of witchcraft, a confirmation so necessary to the authorities that the guilt or innocence of any individual seemed trivial relative to proving that witchcraft really did exist and that the process for finding witches was just. Thus when Martha Sprague, Rose Foster, and Abigail Martin named William Barker, Sr., as a witch, as indicated in the warrant for the arrest of him and others on August 25 (*SWP* I: 63), he speedily confessed, told some appropriately acceptable story of his witchcraft activities, named a few people who had already been named – careful not to implicate anyone new – and affirmed "that he has not known or heard of one innocent person taken up & put in prisone" (*SWP* I: 66).

That William Barker followed the pattern of confession and accusation offers one of numerous examples indicating that the girls of Salem were sometimes "boys." On September 1, Barker's son William Jr. confessed and began implicating others; and so the pattern went (*SWP* I: 73–4). If the boys of Salem have not received the same notoriety as the girls, it is not because they refrained from entering into the spirit of accusation. Those males who performed in 1692 did so in the context of an English tradition in which boys and grown men historically had exhibited the same kinds of "hysterical" behavior manifested by Salem's "girls." Our identification of such behavior with girls grows partly from the fact that females more actively engaged in such roles at Salem and partly from gender stereotyping. "Girls" as accusers were not always the norm: In Massachusetts Bay, the Goodwin boys had been involved in the Glover case a few years earlier. Famous English cases of boys behaving in ways that have been described as hysterical in connection with girls include John Smith, exposed as a fraud in 1616; Thomas Darling, who confessed counterfeiting his fits around 1596; William Perry, who confessed to fraud in 1620; and Edmund Robinson, who similarly confessed in 1634.[8]

The close association of Salem with female accusers reasonably enough grows from the fact that the initial and primary claims of affliction by specters came from females. However, it is certain that one male, John Indian, was initially involved and performed actively in at least six cases where the accused went to the gallows, as well as in other cases, including the episode of Mary Warren. The failure of the judiciary to name him in any indictment as a victim no doubt stems from his racial identification, his status as a slave: That explains the omission in 1692. At the same time, his case reminds us of how much the narrators of Salem have been wedded

to those social attitudes that emphasize the culpability of accusing "girls."
It would take a large bibliography indeed to compile a list of all the works
written to explain the bizarre behavior of the female accusers at Salem,
but a very small one to explain that of the males. From notions of female
predispositions toward hysteria to feminist explanations of expected female roles, theories have persistently sought to explain why the strange
behavior was so specific to girls. It is as if John Indian and the other "boys
of Salem" had not been there.

John Indian knew the game and played it well. Among the earliest of
the accusers, he performed his courtroom theatrics against those who had
been accused. He also exercised the same kind of power as the "girl" accusers did, as we see from an anecdote told by Robert Calef in connection
with Edward Bishop, accused of witchcraft. During an examination at
Salem,

> an afflicted Indian was very unruly, whom he [Edward Bishop] under-
> took, and so managed him, that he was very orderly, after which in rid-
> ing home, in company of him and other Accusers, the Indian fell into a
> fit, and clapping hold with his Teeth on the back of the Man that rode
> before him, thereby held himself upon the Horse, but . . . Bishop strik-
> ing him with his stick, the Indian soon recovered, and promised he
> would do so no more; to which Bishop replied, that he doubted not,
> but he could cure them all, with more to the same effect; immediately
> after he was parted from them, he was cried out of. . . .[9]

Bishop's wife, Sarah, was also accused.

Male accusers such as John Indian were, of course, very different from
those who signed legal complaints, served on juries, presided over courts,
and in the highest public offices made decisions that maintained the reign
of terror; but males were at the front line too, telling in court their tales of
the invisible world, accusing with impunity as did the females. That their
story is relatively unknown is not because men did not claim to be afflicted, or because they failed to offer accounts that, if given by women, would
be called hysteria: They did.

II

On May 30, 1692, a 42-year-old man named Samuel Gray testified against Bridget Bishop. According to Gray's testimony, he had awakened one night, fourteen years earlier, to find the house illuminated, as if
candles had been lit. In his room there stood a woman, but she had vanished when he arose. He had checked the door and found it locked. After

unlocking the door, he had looked about him and seen the woman again. "[I]n the name of God," he had challenged, "what doe you come for[?]" But she had vanished again. So he had gone back to his room, locked the door, and slept fitfully. Then something cold had touched his lips, startling him. The child in the cradle then suddenly screeched as if in great pain. The woman had held something between her hands against Gray's mouth and then she disappeared. Hours had passed before Gray could soothe the baby. Until that night, it had been a healthy child. Within a week or so, Gray had seen the woman again, dressed as she had been the night she came to his room. A few months later the child had died. Gray testified that the woman was Bridget Bishop (*SWP* I: 94).

That same day, May 30, 1692, a 36-year-old man named William Stacy also told of an event that had happened fourteen years earlier. Having been ill with smallpox, he had been visited by Bridget Bishop, who had extended unusual sympathy to him in his plight. Upon recovering, he had done some work for her, and she had rewarded him with three pence; but no sooner had he walked for several yards than he had looked in his pocket for the money and found it gone. The next time they met, she had asked him whether his father would be willing to grind her grist at the mill. Stacy had wondered why she asked. She had replied by expressing her fear that he might not because people thought her a witch. Assuring her that his father would grind it, Stacy then had walked for several yards with a small load in his cart. Suddenly the wheels had gotten stuck in the ground. Unable to extricate the cart by himself, Stacy had found help. Once the cart was free, Stacy had gone back to examine the ground where his wheel had sunk in, but he could find no hole. Later in the winter, around midnight, Stacy had felt something pressing hard between his lips against his teeth, something so cold that it awakened him. He had sat up in bed and seen someone at the foot of his bed – either Bridget Bishop or the shape of Bridget Bishop. The room had been as light as in daylight. She had then hopped on the bed and around the room, then gone out, whereupon the room had become dark again. Some time after this, Bridget Bishop had approached him and asked whether it was true that he had been telling of her appearance in his room. He said the story was true, and he challenged her to deny it. She angrily went away without contradicting him, but afterward tormented him. On a dark night in the barn he had been lifted up and thrown against the wall; later he had been thrown down a bank at the end of his house; after he had passed her on another occasion, his horse could not pull a small load up a hill, and "his Gears & tackeing flew in Pieces and the Cart fell downe." Thereafter he had tried with all his might to lift two bushels of corn and failed. There were "other of her Pranks"

too time-consuming to tell, said Stacy; but he did tell of something beyond a prank: the death of his child, Priscilla, two years before his testimony. Normally a healthy child, she had suddenly screeched out and continued crying in an unusual manner for a couple of weeks; then she had
died suffering. Stacy said he truly believed that Bridget Bishop had been
responsible (*SWP* I: 93–4).

On June 2, 1692, 32-year-old John Louder, servant of Susannah Gedney of Salem, testified that seven or eight years earlier he had awakened in
the night with a great weight upon his breast. Looking up, the moon
brightly lighting the room, he had clearly seen Bridget Bishop or her
shape sitting on his stomach. He had tried and failed to free himself. She
had then taken hold of his throat, choking him, and he had lacked the
power to free himself. She had held him that way until almost daylight.
Informed by Louder of what had happened, Mistress Gedney had confronted Bridget Bishop, whose orchard adjoined the Gedney orchard;
Bishop had denied the charge and responded by threatening Louder.
Sometime after that, Louder – at home on the Lord's day and not feeling
well – had seen a black pig running toward him in the room. When he
had gone to kick it, the pig vanished. Then, however, a black thing had
jumped in the window, with a body like a monkey's, feet like a cock's,
and a face more like that of a man than a monkey. If Louder would allow
himself to be ruled by this creature, he had been promised, he would want
for nothing in this world. Louder angrily had tried to seize it, but it had
had no substance. It had then jumped out the window but returned via
the porch, even though the door had been shut. Once Louder chased it
away, he had gone out of the house and seen Bridget Bishop. Unable to
advance, he had returned to the house and saw the creature again. When it
flew at him, Louder had invoked "the whole armor of god," and it had
sprung back. It had then flown over the apple tree, shaking many apples
from it and flinging dust at Louder's stomach; whereupon Louder had
been struck dumb for around three days (*SWP* I: 99–101).[10]

Richard Coman, 32, also told his story on June 2. About eight years
earlier, awake in bed with his sleeping wife, he had seen Bridget Bishop
and two other women, whom he could not identify, come into the room.
He could not explain how they had gotten into the house, since the door
was locked before and after they left. Right after their appearance the light
had gone out and the curtains at the foot of the bed opened, and Bishop
had come onto the bed and lain down upon his "Brest or body." She "soe
oppressed him" that he could neither move nor awaken his wife. The following night they all had come again, this time Bishop taking him by the
throat and almost hauling him out of bed. On Saturday he had brought
help, his kinsman William Coman, and that night William and he had

gotten into bed together, Richard with a sword at the ready. While the two were still awake and talking, the three women had come in again; but when Richard had said to William that "thay be all Come againe" he was struck speechless and immobile (*SWP* I: 102). The three intruders had then grabbed Richard's sword, but he had held on so tightly that they could not get it away; then his speech had returned, and he had called to William, his wife, and to Sarah Phillips, who had been in bed with his wife. Sarah Phillips had responded first, asking, "in the name of God [Goodman] Coman w't is the Matter with you[?]" The intruders had then vanished.

These men claim sightings of people exposing their demonic identities only to their accusers, as do the accusing "girls," and their claims are no more testable by the contemporaries who hear them. Only the accusers themselves can confirm their position on the front lines in the war between the people of God and the devil. It is worth noting that in three out of four of these cases – those of Gray, Louder, and Coman – demonism is routed by uttering God's name.

The story narrated by these men of witch intruders tormenting them in the privacy of their own bedroom is a relatively predictable one. Just as the stories of "girls" claiming affliction by the accused proved predictable, tales told by men about visitations of witches in their homes contained elements that could be filled in without having heard the story: One only had to know that the man was going to tell of what had happened to him one night in bed. The event was normally set well in the past, where the account would not be verifiable. (Even though Coman had had company, no one else had seen what he had.) The intruder would be female, or there would be a female present if more than one specter appeared. The woman would attack the man in bed and lay on him, making it difficult for him to breath. However Freudians might interpret these events, the men had expressed no overt sexual content when they described them.[11]

As it happens, the men of Salem did not invent this story of the un-welcome woman in the bedroom: Reginald Scot, writing in 1584, tells a story, old in his day, of such an intrusion. The priest in the story complains, "There commeth unto mee, almost everie night, a certeine woman, unknowne unto me, and lieth so heavie upon [my] brest, that I cannot fetch my breath, neither have anie power to crie, neither doo my hands serve me to shoove hir awaie, nor my feete to go from hir."[12] Such is the story from the lore of witchcraft, and whether the men invoked it in calculated lies or hallucinated it, the tale was probably the only claim men made at Salem that differed from the kinds of claims that women made. It was a predominantly male story.

Assessing whether these bedroom encounters grew from fraud or hallucination presents a somewhat more difficult problem than does making the same determination in relation to the core accusers. One can fairly easily tell that either specters were putting pins in Ann Putnam, Mary Warren, and others or they were doing it themselves. Likewise, in the case of someone found tied and hanging on a hook, she had either had co-conspirators tie her up and put her on a hook, or witches had done it. Moreover, there are the admissions of fraud by Margaret Jacobs, Sarah Churchill, and Martha Emerson, as well as the often cited claim by one of the "girls" that she accused "for sport[;] they must have some sport" (*SWP* II: 665). Still, however skeptical one may be about stories of wo-men laying on the breasts of men years ago, easy refutations such as those involving pins, hooks, and explicit admissions are harder to come by, and the possibility of hysteria and hallucination remains real – ironically, more so for men having night visitors than for "girls" performing in court. Nevertheless, the case for fraud persists.

In Samuel Gray's case fraud seems certain. According to Calef, Gray made a deathbed confession that revealed his previous accusations "as be-ing wholly groundless."[13] Gray offers the case of a man who had quarreled previously with an accused person and apparently made the accusation for that reason. Whether Stacy, Louder, and Coman also invented their stories cannot so easily be determined; but we do have reason to wonder why women accused of such intrusions years earlier were still on the loose. Did the judiciary really tolerate such behavior? The extraordinary experiences claimed by the men seem to have occurred without any ap-peals to authority for relief. William Stacy, after having found Bridget Bishop hopping across his bed, gives no indication that he complained to the authorities about this demonic intrusion.[14] Similarly, John Louder suf-fered her on his breast, and apparently declined to report that the devil had offered him a pact. Coman too seems to have been negligent in regard to approaching the authorities. One may reasonably wonder whether their stories had been told years before, when the assaults had allegedly taken place, and if not, why. We have reason to suspect that others might have matched Gray's deathbed confession had they chosen to do so.

Other kinds of accusations by men, however, are more testable. In some cases males engaged in courtroom theatrics similar to those employed by females, as in the case of John Indian, whose motive seems clear enough. Early on he saw the fate of his wife, Tituba, and the credibility given to the female accusers. Most of the community had to await the cases of Abigail Hobbs, Mary Warren, Sarah Churchill, and Margaret Jacobs to realize the relative values of accusation, confession, and claims of innocence; but John Indian seems to have grasped the situation early – that is, unless one takes the view that he hallucinated or acted hysterically. The court records on John Indian give few details of what brought him to his performances.

Richard Carrier, another male accuser who engaged in courtroom exhibitions, offers a clearer record. Richard – the 28-year-old son of Martha Carrier, who would hang on August 19 – was arrested on July 21, as was his 16-year-old brother Andrew. They were examined that day along with Mary Lacey, Jr., and her mother, Mary Lacey, Sr. When Richard was brought for examination in response to the accusations of Mary Warren and Mary Lacey, Jr., the 15-year-old Lacey girl seemed relentless in her wish to implicate him and his brother. With an array of accusations, she urged Richard to confess. Then she asserted that Richard had told her he would make a spindle, similar to the one he had used against Timothy Swan, for his brother Andrew, who would afflict Mary Warren and make blood come out of her mouth – something Andrew subsequently had done, said Mary Lacey. When neither Richard nor Andrew would confess, they were both taken to another room, bound hand and foot, and "a Little while after Rich'd was brought In again" (*SWP* II: 527). Just how long "a little while" meant we do not know; but another account of the same affair offers an insight into a less subtle strategy for eliciting confession when an individual refused to accept the logic of confession and avoidance of the gallows. This strategy worked, for when Richard returned he confessed.

What happened is reported by John Proctor in a letter written in Salem prison two days later, July 23, and addressed to a group of ministers. Complaining of imprisonment on the basis of charges from five confessing people, Proctor protests that

> Two of the 5 are (Carriers Sons) Youngmen, who would not confess any thing till they tyed them Neck and Heels till the Blood was ready to come out of their Noses, and 'tis credibly believed and reported this was the occasion of making them confess that they never did, by reason they said one had been a Witch a Month, and another five Weeks, and that their Mother had made them so, who has been confined here this nine Weeks. (*SWP* II: 689–90)[15]

Proctor himself had been in jail since early April and was the father of a son, William, who had received similar treatment:

> My son William Procter, when he was examin'd, because he would not confess that he was Guilty, when he was Innocent, they tyed him Neck and Heels till the Blood gushed out at his Nose, and would have kept him so 24 Hours, if one more Merciful than the rest, had not taken pity on him, and caused him to be unbound. These actions are very like the Popish Cruelties. (*SWP* II: 690)

How many others received this form of persuasion is unclear; nor do we have any indication as to how the ministers responded. There seems little doubt, however, that those conducting the examination of Richard and Andrew Carrier – Bartholomew Gedney, John Hathorne, Jonathan Corwin, and John Higginson – knew of what was happening.

Richard Carrier was brought back first and immediately reminded of his recalcitrance. "Rich'd though you have been Verry Obstinate Yett tel us how long agoe it is Since you ware taken in this Snare" (*SWP* II: 527). Richard confessed, telling of signing the book for a black man, who in a second appearance had come as a yellow bird. Richard had agreed, he confessed, to permit the devil to afflict the initial accusers, other afflicted people in general, and specifically Timothy Swan and Ballard's wife. It was common in these proceedings to indicate that the devil needed the permission of the accused to afflict a victim. Satan was delicate on this point.

Now Richard Carrier was an accuser. Two of those he named could suffer no further harm from his accusations: Sarah Good had been executed two days before (July 19), and Roger Toothaker – who, according to Richard, was afflicting Mary Lacey even as Richard confessed – had earlier died in prison. However, he also accused Martha Toothaker, her mother, Mary Toothaker (Roger's widow), and George Burroughs. More reluctantly, he accused his mother, Martha Carrier: She had, he said, been with him on his witchcraft activities "Somtimes but not often" (*SWP* II: 528). Among those Richard claimed to have afflicted was the Reverend Samuel Parris's wife Elizabeth, as he perhaps confused the mother with the daughter, Betty, also known as Elizabeth (*SWP* II: 529).[16]

Richard had been brought in for questioning alone; after he confessed, the authorities brought in his brother Andrew. Once Richard told Andrew of his confession, Andrew began his own, although he was reluctant to offer names. Stammering as he spoke, apparently from nervousness – others said he did not normally stutter – Andrew admitted that he had signed the devil's book. He also confessed to hurting a child "a little," and Richard said that Andrew had assisted him "a little" in afflicting Timothy Swan (*SWP* I: 530). Andrew seemed to deny even that, saying that since afflicting the child he had only afflicted Mary Warren. Unlike his brother, Andrew refused to implicate his mother. He did admit that when he had his demonic baptism, Richard had been there, along with two others. When asked who they were, Andrew could not remember, but he did name Rebecca Nurse as the person who had handed out the bread and wine at the devil's sacrament. He could not harm Rebecca Nurse, however: Like Sarah Good, implicated by Richard, Rebecca Nurse had been hanged two days earlier.

After his confession, Andrew appears in no other court records, although Proctor's letter indicates that he continued to some extent as an accuser. Richard, however, became an active one. On August 27 at the examination of John Jackson, Sr., Richard was accusing in such company as Ann Putnam, Mary Walcott, Mary Lacey, and Mary Warren, and, along with them, Richard had a fit, put on a show. Jackson insisted that the accusers were "not in their Right mind," but the spectators saw that "the afflicted was much hurt: & Rich'd Carrier was halled almost und'r the bed" (*SWP* II: 467). One did not have to be a "girl" to know the tricks of such performances, and the elder Carrier continued as an active accuser into September. Late to join the crowd, this 28-year-old man performed reliably as the proceedings moved toward their denouement.

Also late in joining was a 16-year-old boy named John DeRich, who made his first recorded courtroom appearance on August 3 in the case of George Jacobs, Sr. He was apparently the nephew of John and Elizabeth Proctor, who had probably been condemned to death by the time he made his first accusations. Moreover, Mary DeRich, probably his mother, and her mother, Sarah Basset, had already been accused.[17] Young relatives of accused witches were likely recruits for the accusers, and DeRich proved an enthusiastic one. According to him two deceased people had appeared and threatened to tear him to pieces if he did not tell Hathorne that George Jacobs had killed them. Jacobs himself had approached DeRich directly: After having pinched, scratched, and bitten him, threatening to destroy him if he did not sign the devil's book, nearly drowning him, and then knocking him down with a staff, on August 3 Jacobs visited DeRich while he was writing his testimony and explained to him that he had been a wizard for forty years (*SWP* II: 486).

Another spirit who visited DeRich was Mary Warren's mother, who told him that Alice Parker and Bridget Bishop had killed her with the help of Giles Corey and John and Elizabeth Proctor. He also asserted that every day since his own affliction had begun – just what date is not clear – Sarah, Joseph, and John Proctor had afflicted him and unsuccessfully tried to get him to sign the devil's book. Additionally, Philip and Mary English afflicted him, and everyone he had accused threatened to tear him to pieces if he refused to sign the book. Moreover, the same was true about three others who had afflicted him: Sarah Pease, Deliverance Hobbs, and Abigail Hobbs. Spicing up the story, he threw in a woman named Mary from Boston, a woman with black clothes, one eye, and a crooked neck. Fortunately, the woman had said she would not afflict him anymore (*SWP* II: 482);[18] unfortunately, she had declined to identify herself. This was not normal: Witches attacking accusers almost always revealed their identity, as John Willard did. According to DeRich in undated testimony, Willard, who hanged on August 19, "diswaded from confession" Margaret Jacobs and Sarah Churchill, thus giving a spectral explanation for the retraction of at least Margaret Jacobs (*SWP* III: 836).[19] If the justices ever wondered why witches so freely offered their identity to their victims, they never raised the issue.

On September 5, the witches were still trying to get DeRich's signature on the contract. Margaret Jacobs, he told the court, who afflicted him that day and had done so many times before, had promised to make him better if he signed the book. If he would not, she had threatened to run a skewer through him and to cut him with a knife bigger than an ordinary one – and, he assured the court, "she hath don worse before" (*SWP* II: 490). On the same day he complained that Giles Corey afflicted him that day and had at other times. Also, around August 20 Corey had told De-Rich that he wanted some platters because he was going to a feast. He had then taken them without permission, returning them about an hour later without comment. DeRich also observed that Sarah Pease had pinched him in the past but had not been around for awhile.

Testimony about the plates may seem trivial and unincriminating, and the court records include numerous other accounts that could be similarly described. Usually, however, such testimony carries more ominous meaning in context. In the case of the platters, DeRich by implication was accusing Corey of having used them for a feast at a gathering of witches. Occasionally one must reach deeply to guess at how a charge could be incriminating. At times it appears as if stories are told almost independent of witchcraft allegations, as if someone did not want to miss participating in the exciting events unfolding. If in our own day we imagine only wild crowds egging on the persecution of witches, we miss the carnival effect of a community joining in a festival of gossip and tall tales. Set against the tragic circumstances in which such stories are told, these narrations – sometimes comic, sometimes elliptical – appear jarringly incongruent. Although female accusers occasionally told these kinds of stories, they were more likely to come from a male. One such story, told by father and son – Isaac Cummings, Jr. and Sr. – suggests how far one might grasp to participate in the festival of finding witches.

It seems that about eight years earlier James How, Jr., had come to the Cummings's house to borrow a horse. How was told of a mare that he could not borrow. The next day, Friday, Isaac Cummings, Sr., had taken the healthy mare for a ride; but on Saturday morning at sunrise the mare had appeared as if it had been ridden and abused. Cummings, seeing the mare looking in sad condition, had taken it to the barn and attempted to feed it; the animal would eat nothing. Concerned, he had sent for his brother-in-law, Thomas Andros, who sought to treat the horse but failed to help it.[20] Eventually, Andros, having diagnosed the problem as a belly-ache, had said he would try one more remedy: He would take a pipe of tobacco, light it, and stick it in the mare's anus. Cummings had objected that this was not legal, but Andros had insisted "it was lawfull for man or beast." Hence Cummings had taken a clean pipe, filled it with tobacco, and lit it. Andros had received the lit pipe and placed it in the horse, whereupon the pipe of tobacco had blazed and burned blue. Alarmed, Cummings had urged a halt to the proceedings, again protesting its illegality; but Andros had said he would do it again,

> which he did and then thar arose a blaze from the pipe of tobaco which seemed to . . . cover the butocks of the said mear[. T]he blaz went up ward towards the roof of the barn and in the roof of the barn thar was a [great] crackling as if the barn [would] have falen or bin burnt which semed so to us which ware with in and some that ware with out. (*SWP* II: 445)

It "Blazed so much that itt was as much as Two persons Could putt itt [out with] both of Their hands" said Isaac Cummings, Jr., referring to the first attempt. The second time it had blazed "more vehemently" (*SWP* II: 446). Isaac Sr. had then successfully insisted that Andros stop, asserting that he would rather lose his mare than his barn. The next day Andros had been summoned again, and what he had done, "I say not" (*SWP* II: 445), reports Cummings. That night, a neighbor named John Hunkins had gone with Cummings to the barn to examine the mare. Hunkins had suggested cutting off a piece of the mare and burning it. Cummings had declined, but said that if the mare were to live to the following morning he would consider such a remedy. The men had then left the barn, and at that moment the horse had fallen and died.[21]

That was the story. No one was accused of witchcraft: The story, related in connection with the case of Elizabeth How, had as its only link to her the visit of James How, Jr., perhaps with the implication that his visit somehow tied her to the mysterious death of the mare. The case of the flatulent horse fueling the flames from the pipe that almost burned down the barn revealed little about the invisible world. What Elizabeth How made of this tale, told on the 27th and 28th of June, we do not know. On July 19, she was executed for witchcraft.

If it seems reasonable to be skeptical of the accounts given by John De-Rich relating to the assaults against him by the invisible world, there is no similar reason to doubt the testimony of Isaac Cummings, Sr. or Jr. While we shall never know whether they believed that Elizabeth How was a witch, we have no reason to rule out the possibility that this kind of testimony came from gullible men who really believed that their experience involved witchcraft, or men who simply could not bear to be left out of the exciting events of the time. Other testimony more unambiguously related to charges of witchcraft came from men and women who in many cases probably sincerely and honestly presented accounts of perceived witchcraft. Such testimony must be distinguished from the courtroom performances or bedroom remembrances of other accusers, male as well as female – Richard Carrier, John Indian, and Samuel Gray as well as Ann Putnam, Mary Lacey, Jr., and Mary Warren – not to mention all the other "girls of Salem."

4

June 10, 1692

What most convinced me [Cotton Mather] of [Bridget Bishop's] guilt
Was finding hidden in her cellar wall
Those poppets made of rags, with headless pins
Stuck into them point outwards, and whereof
She could not give a reasonable account.
  – Henry Wadsworth Longfellow, *Giles Corey of the Salem Farms*[1]

I

When Sir William Phips arrived on May 14, 1692, he seems not to have been fully informed as to the status of the prisoners in jail, prisoners caught between magistrates who wanted them prosecuted and a governor reluctant to do so. Perhaps he heard exaggerated reports about the threats posed by the prisoners and, in response, Calef writes, "the first thing he exerted his Power in, was said to be his giving Orders that Irons should be put upon those in Prison."[2] But at least some, if not all, were already in chains.[3]

One of them was Bridget Bishop, the first person tried and hanged in the Salem witch trials. On May 27 Phips had established a special Court of Oyer and Terminer to try those accused of witchcraft, and on June 2 the court tried Bridget Bishop and sentenced her to death.

Although Massachusetts Bay colony set no precedent in hanging Bridget Bishop for witchcraft, as it did on June 10, it gave spectral evidence an unprecedented status in the judicial process. The indictments against her charged that she had "Tortured Afflicted Pined, Consumed, wasted: &

tormented" her victims (*SWP* I: 87) on April 19, the day of her examination. Although a variety of claims had been made against Bridget Bishop, the death warrant emphasizes only the harm done to the accusers, primarily on the day of her examination, as legal justification for the execution. Bridget Bishop died because the law said that she afflicted Abigail Williams, Ann Putnam, Jr., Mercy Lewis, Mary Walcott (an indictment that does not survive), and Elizabeth Hubbard, described in the death warrant as "Salem Village Singlewomen" (*SWP* I: 109). The only evidence in support of the claim that these five had been hurt by Bridget Bishop came from their own testimony – and that of their cohorts, who also had the gift of seeing specters – that her spirit had attacked them. Although other testimony surely influenced the judges and jurors, the court used only spectral evidence as the legal basis for convicting Bridget Bishop. Except in cases of confession, this precedent would go unbroken in all other convictions. Even in cases involving confession, spectral evidence remained central to the indictments.

In a sequence that proved typical, the judiciary, after examining Bridget Bishop, brought her before a grand jury and then a trial jury.[4] Except for depositional testimony, the details of her trial, and of other trials, must come from inferences rather than from official court summaries. The Reverend Samuel Willard gives some excellent clues in this connection, strongly indicating a close similarity between the trials and the examinations. Accusers could not "give a full and clear Testimony, to the face of the Prisoner at the Barr" because, as the defenders of the trials claimed, "the Witches smite them down with their poisoned Looks."[5] Governor Phips, in subsequently assessing the trials, corroborates Willard's account of the central role of spectral evidence at the trials.

> The Court still proceeded in the same method of trying them, which was by the evidence of the afflicted persons who when they were brought into the Court as soon as the suspected witches looked upon them instantly fell to the ground in strange agonies and grievous torments, but when touched by them . . . they immediately revived and came to themselves . . . [and] made oath that the Prisoner at the Bar did afflict them and that they saw their shape or spectre come from their bodies which put them to such paines and torments. . . .[6]

At her precedent-setting trial, almost certainly without legal counsel, Bridget Bishop thus found herself in the following situation: Accusers confronted her who had previously accused her of having spectrally afflicted them in public on the day of her examination; yet in trying to defend herself against those charges, the same accusers presented her and the court with new fits in response to new assaults by her specter, which only they could see. Added to this, her accusers remained healthy, so Bridget Bishop received her sentence of death for pining, consuming, and wasting a group of accusers who did not manifest symptoms of such affliction and had reputations with some people for bad character. The anomaly of healthy accusers with claimed afflictions did not go unnoticed, as witnessed in Thomas Brattle's letter, dated October 8, 1692:

> Many of these afflicted persons, who have scores of strange fitts in a day, yet in the intervals of time are hale and hearty, robust and lusty, as tho' nothing had afflicted them. I Remember that when the chief Judge gave the first Jury their charge, he told them, that they were not to mind whether the bodies of the said afflicted were really pined and consumed, as was expressed in the inditement; but whether the said afflicted did not suffer from the accused such afflictions as naturally tended to their being pined and consumed, wasted, etc. This, [said he,] is a pining and consuming in the sense of the law. I add not.[7]

But once the jury convicted Bridget Bishop, Stoughton asserted in the death warrant that she actually had pined, consumed, and wasted the accusers; nothing of "tended" appears there (*SWP* I: 109). Whether for these reasons or not, one of the judges, Nathaniel Saltonstall, resigned from the court.[8] It is scarcely surprising that a pause in the proceedings occurred; at the very least, it seemed time to find out what the prominent clergy had to say about the unfolding events. On June 15, five days after the death of Bridget Bishop, some ministers offered their perspective in a document known as "The Return of Several Ministers," for which Cotton Mather claimed authorship.[9] It would become for future historians one of the most commented upon documents in the Salem witch trials.

The ministers opened by acknowledging the reality of witchcraft occurring in the colony and by expressing appreciation for the successes to date in detecting it; but they quickly shifted to a cautionary note, arguing that by placing too much reliance "only upon the Devil's authority . . . a door [could be] opened for a long train of miserable consequences, and Satan [could] get an advantage over us . . . ." The ministers urged great caution, particularly in connection with complaints against people "formerly of an unblemished reputation." They also confronted the issue of the accusers' behavior in court, and urged "that there may be admitted as little as is possible of such noise . . . and that there may nothing be used as a test, for the trial of the suspected, the lawfulness whereof may be doubted among the people of God. . . ." By "test" they referred to such practices as having the accusers approach the accused and finding evidence of guilt when the accusers fell down, unable to reach the accused – allegedly because the specter of the accused prevented the approach of the accusers, or manipulated them in some way. The ministers offered an unequivocal verdict against depending on spectral evidence.

> Presumptions whereupon persons may be committed, and, much more, convictions whereupon persons may be condemned as guilty of witchcrafts, ought certainly to be more considerable than barely the accused person being represented by a specter unto the afflicted, inasmuch as 'tis an undoubted and a notorious thing that a Demon may, by God's permission, appear, even to ill purposes, in the shape of an innocent, yea, and a virtuous man. Nor can we esteem alterations made in the sufferers by a look or touch of the accused to be an infallible evidence of guilt, but frequently liable to be abused by the Devil's legerdemains.[10]

Finally, the ministers made clear that, in resisting the tricks of the devil, the community could put an end to the wave of accusations. This conclusion, of course, did not mean that the search for witches should end; rather, they recommended "unto the Government the speedy and vigorous prosecution of such as have rendered themselves obnoxious, according to the direction given in the laws of God, and the wholesome statutes of the English nation, for the detection of witchcrafts." It was a prescription that precluded the reliance on spectral evidence.

Why, then, did the court not change its ways? At the next trial, on June 30, the justices conducted business as if they had never read the report of the ministers. In one sense, the answer is obvious enough: The judiciary, led by William Stoughton, represented civil authority, and, contrary to contemporary popular stereotypes, New England was not a hegemonic theocracy. Civil authorities had more power than clerical ones. However, that still begs the larger question. The highest authority was Governor Phips, hand picked by Increase Mather. To be sure, he left the colony on military business, but he was still around at least as late as June 25;[11] and in early July, a reprieve, subsequently withdrawn, was given to the convicted Rebecca Nurse by the governor, an act of leniency unlikely to have come from Stoughton.[12] Could it be that Increase Mather exerted less influence on Phips than generally assumed, or that Mather actually supported the proceedings in spite of the "Return of Several Ministers"? The latter was assumed in the nineteenth century by Samuel Drake, when in his history he excused Phips's conduct because of his deep indebtedness to Mather;[13] but as events will show, Increase Mather, enlisting the help of Phips, helped bring the trials to an end, although Drake was not entirely wrong about him.[14]

When the ministers expressed their opposition to the proceedings that led to the hanging of Bridget Bishop, they could reasonably have hoped that the judiciary would heed their advice; but on June 30 the court answered by condemning the five women who would hang on July 19. The rules of the Bridget Bishop trial would stay in force, the ministers notwithstanding. Thus a confrontation occurred, with the struggle over the reprieve of Rebecca Nurse offering the most visible symbol. How it would have come out had Phips stayed in town is unclear, since the tide of influential opinion had not yet fully turned, as it would after the first males hanged in August. Phips, however, went off to the wars well before then, perhaps leaving because fighting Indians seemed less formidable than fighting witchcraft. By the time he returned, the tide of opinion had shifted, and he was there to exercise his power. Mather would eventually have his ally. As of June 10, though, all this existed in an unknown future. The "Return of Several Ministers," drawing lines as it did, proved prophetic but inefficacious: The judiciary proceeded as if nothing had been written.

Bridget Bishop, of course, did not live to hear this debate. Her struggle to survive suffered from her failure to grasp the efficacy of confession. Understanding that one point would have helped her far more than full comprehension of the events that emerged in the days following her death.

Bridget Bishop had faced charges of witchcraft before, more than ten years earlier, and one can infer from the absence of any record of punishment that she had effectively dealt with the charge.[15] As a person experienced in the New England way, she knew that the courts generally had little patience with witchcraft; so no false confessions for Bridget Bishop. At her examination on April 19 she assumed, mistakenly, that her life depended on her denial of the charges. She did not understand that her only chance lay in admitting witchcraft. When Hathorne, in his relentless accusatory questioning, asked her to explain the torments of the afflicted, Bridget Bishop replied that "I am not come here to say I am a witch to take away my life" (*SWP* I: 86). It must have seemed reasonable enough to rely on her past experience in dealing with such an issue. Perhaps, had she had less personal experience with the judiciary, she would have read the situation better and perjured herself. On the other hand, perhaps she already understood yet would not lie to save herself. We do not know.

As the first person to be executed in the Salem witch trials, Bridget Bishop has received plenty of attention from Salem's historians, amateur and professional. She has served as a paradigm of the executed person as social deviant, the outsider who falls prey to a community devouring the eccentrics on its margin. This is a version of Salem's story codified in 1867 by Charles Upham, who in his *Salem Witchcraft* told the story of Bridget Bishop as a singular character, not easily described.

> [She] kept a house of refreshment for travellers, and a shovel-board for the entertainment of her guests, and generally seems to have countenanced amusements and gayeties to an extent that exposed her to some scandal. She is described as wearing "a black cap and a black hat, and a red paragon bodice," bordered and looped with different colors. This would appear to have been rather a showy costume for the times. Her freedom from the austerity of Puritan manners, and disregard of conventional décorum in her conversation and conduct, brought her into disrepute; and the tongue of gossip was generally loosened against her.[16]

Upham had made a mistake. Although he correctly identified Bridget Bishop as a woman who had previously been charged with witchcraft, he conflated two people into one, inaccurately identifying her as living just outside of Salem Village, rather than in Salem where she did live, and of being a rather colorful tavern keeper, which she was not. Upham's mistake was understandable, since the confusion as to her identity actually goes back to 1692, and only some brilliant detective work by David L. Greene in 1981 brought clarity to the matter; still, some scholars have continued to make the misidentification.[17]

We have seen in Chapter 1 how the history of Tituba was invented in the nineteenth century; however, the misidentification of Bridget Bishop – certainly one of the best-known characters in Salem lore and in scholarly accounts – was a contemporary one. It begins with an error made by two of the accusers: Sarah Churchill, a relative novice at the game, and Susannah Sheldon, whom we have met often enough. Their mistake originated in their misunderstanding of testimony from a far more credible source: the Reverend John Hale, whose deposition in the case of Sarah Bishop – arrested with her husband, Edward – has become misidentified as testimony against Bridget Bishop. On May 22, Hale testified

> that about 5 or 6 years ago . . . Christian the wife of John Trask (living in Salem bounds bordering on the abovesaid Beverly) beeing in full communion in o'r Church came to me to [request] that Goodwife Bishop her Neighb'r wife of Edw: Bishop Jun'r might not be permitted to receive the Lords Supper in our church till she had given her the said Trask satisfaction for some offences that were against her. viz because the said Bishop did entertaine people in her house at unseasonable houres in the night to keep drinking and playing at shovel-board whereby discord did arise in other families & young people were in danger to bee corrupted & that the s'd Trask knew these things & had

once gon into the house & fynding some at shovel-board had taken the peices thay played with & thrown them into the fyre & had reprooved the said Bishop for promoting such disorders, But received no satisfaction from her about it.

The dispute continued, with Hale trying to mediate it.

I was oft praying w'th & councelling of Goody Trask before her death and not many days before her end being there shee seemed more rationall & earnestly desired Edw: Bishop might be sent for that shee might make friends with him, I asked her if shee had wronged Edw. Bishop shee said not that shee knew of unless it were in taking his shovel-board pieces when people were at play w'th them & throwing them into the fyre & if she did evill in it she was very sorry for it & desiered he would be friends with her or forgive her. this was the very day before she dyed, or a few days before.

Hale continues by describing "Her distraction (or bewitching)," which led to death by apparent suicide, although he concluded that the wounds were of such a nature that it would not have been possible for her "to mangle her selfe so without some extraordinary work of the devill or witchcraft" (*SWP* I: 95–7). Hale does not name the perpetrator of the witchcraft, who presumably could have been Edward Bishop as easily as Sarah, both having been accused.

After hearing of Hale's testimony regarding "Goodwife Bishop," almost certainly indirectly, Sarah Churchill and Susannah Sheldon, both inventing stories about people they did not know, mistakenly connected her to Bridget Bishop. Because future historians, particularly Charles W. Upham, repeated the mistake, the story of Bridget Bishop as keeper of a disorderly tavern, "shovel-board" and all, has become a basic part of Salem mythology.[18] Her husband – coincidentally, also named Edward – plays no role in the story as told: With women the usual victim of choice, the accusers had left him out of their charges. The other Edward Bishop, Sarah Bishop's husband, is equally uninvolved in the tale, though he had in the past run afoul of the law for illegally selling liquor.[19]

Thus a conflation emerges: A man selling drinks illegally becomes his wife selling drinks; she transforms from Sarah Bishop to Bridget Bishop, misidentified and made legendary as a sole keeper of a disorderly house, keeper of a tavern that may not even have existed;[20] and this conflated woman dresses in the "Red paragon" bodice worn by Bridget Bishop (*SWP* I: 102).

Ironically, as David L. Greene has shown, Hale, whose misunderstood testimony precipitated all the confusion, did not even seem to know the first name of "Goodwife Bishop" at the time the incidents about which he testified occurred: He had misidentified Sarah Bishop in baptismal entries in 1687 and 1689 as "Mary" Bishop.[21] Hale, of course, never refers to "Goodwife Bishop" in his testimony as "Bridget"; nor does he give her any first name. Greene gives powerful supporting evidence to establish the woman in question as Sarah Bishop, although to take the reader through the genealogical intricacies here is unnecessary: It is all in Greene's essay. However, another point that Greene makes requires no complex digging. As he observes, Cotton Mather, in his "Wonders of the Invisible World," "summarizes all the depositions against Bridget [Bishop] except those of the 'afflicted girls' and, significantly, that of his fellow minister, John Hale." Greene's point is that Mather understood that Hale did not have Bridget in mind.[22] Mather had better sources than Sarah Churchill and Susannah Sheldon.

One of the few connections on this subject that Greene does not make appears in another document found in *The Salem Witchcraft Papers*. On April 12 John Hathorne and Jonathan Corwin ordered a group of people to jail. These included Edward Bishop "of Salem Village Husband." The document is torn, and his wife's name is missing; but the next line refers unambiguously to Bridget Bishop, "the wife of Edward Bushop of Salem Sawyer" (*SWP* II: 474). The tavern of narrative fame was in Salem Village or at its edge, depending on which account we read. Bridget Bishop lived in Salem in 1692, not Salem Village or its outskirts, location of the supposedly disorderly house. When she was examined in Salem Village on April 10, she stated that "I never was in this place before" (*SWP* I: 83). Scholars have given all sorts of complex explanations for this remark, which in all likelihood simply stated the truth: She did not know the people of Salem Village, and she did not live in the house of "shovel-board" and other iniquities. Whatever went on in that house, it was Sarah Bishop who lived there.

There is nothing outrageous in this classic mistake, as in the fabricated case of Tituba; but with the mistake now understood, some generalization begs to be made about the conflation of the two Bishop women into one mythic character. One woman, Bridget, offers us red clothing that conflicts with our stereotypes of somber puritans garbed in black. The other, Sarah, offers us a disorderly house. Put a woman in red in charge of a disorderly house, and we have a titillating, sexualized woman.

Understanding what did and did not happen at the Salem witch trials does not hang on the mistake of transforming the quarrelsome and abused Bridget Bishop of Salem into a colorful, unconventional tavern keeper of Salem Village, but its nearly ubiquitous adaptation in historical accounts of the witch trials explains much about the way our culture has wanted to view the event. It has always been attractive to adhere to the model of a tightly knit group lashing out at the alien within, at the marginal person who becomes a romantic vehicle for the drama's setting. Indeed, one of the most frequently cited popular accounts of the events at Salem asserts that Bridget Bishop had been convicted primarily because of her dress, her habits, and the gossip about them.[23] Moreover, it has not hurt cultural fantasies to make Bridget Bishop sexy. Montague Summers, for example, does this by repeating Upham's account, unacknowledged, and then tossing in the word "buxom" to spice up the putative Bridget Bishop.[24]

The case against Bridget Bishop was neither stronger nor weaker than the case against others. Because the accusations against her occurred early in the proceedings, her primary accusers were from the original Salem Village group. These included Mercy Lewis, Abigail Williams, Elizabeth Hubbard, and Ann Putnam, all of whom performed as usual during her examination. Samuel Parris and Thomas Putnam, as they often did, confirmed that they had observed their suffering at other times; Nathaniel Ingersoll agreed. Throughout the witch trials, men often testified to witnessing the afflictions and sufferings of these accusers, although none went so far as to confirm seeing specters attacking them. Parris and Putnam, however, were particularly prominent in noticing afflictions and bearing witness to them in court: Some of the afflicted seemed particularly susceptible to attacks from the invisible world in the presence of these two men.

The case against Bridget Bishop would serve as a model in cases where the accused did not confess. First the afflicted would make their accusations, which would be denied even as the accusers claimed that the accused tortured them in the presence of the court. One or more confessors would subsequently validate the claim of witchcraft; then, various members of the community, with testimony that had no bearing on the actual indictments, would join in by telling of past witchcraft by the accused. The way to the gallows for Bridget Bishop would be the way for others.

We have already seen the joining in of the community in various reports of Bridget Bishop's visits to the bedrooms of men. Another in this group was 18-year-old John Cook, who told of a bedroom attack by her "about five or six yeares agoe" (*SWP* I: 104). Other charges against her included the claim by Samuel Shattuck that in 1680 she had bewitched his child, and that of John and William Bly that seven years before her trial they had found poppets with pins in them in the cellar wall of Bridget Bishop's former house. It is difficult to evaluate the testimony of people regarding incidents that allegedly occurred years earlier. Possibilities range. Shattuck may have sincerely believed that she bewitched his child; yet he would make a similar claim against Alice Parker, who would hang on September 22 (*SWP* II: 635).[25] Thus, either he was prone to believe that witches hurt his child, or he used the same kind of story to express some animosity. The former seems more probable. The story of John and William Bly may also simply be true: A doll may indeed have been found in a wall. It is also possible, of course, that they invented the tale. Events of seven years earlier were not easily confirmed, and nobody in the court, in any case, seemed interested in pursuing the credibility of such stories. Possibly the poppets were in the walls and put there by someone else, since Bridget Bishop no longer lived in the house. Perhaps the poppets did belong to her, whether used for benign or malign purposes. We simply cannot know how to evaluate such testimony, although broad claims have been made from such narrow evidence, as we shall shortly see.

In addition to the testimony of the kind offered by Shattuck and the Blys, there would often be testimony from the accusers independent of charging assault by specter at the examination. In this case, we have the testimony of Susannah Sheldon, whose stories tended to be more sensational than those of the others and whose fraudulent behavior has already been established. Among her other claims, she had Bridget Bishop admitting to having been a witch for twenty years, and making this confession while a snake crept over her shoulder and into her bosom. Susannah continued by reporting that other accused people had joined Bishop in consorting with the devil, and Giles Corey and Bridget Bishop had knelt in prayer before him. Martha Corey, then in prison, had exposed her breasts, received a hairless black pig from the devil, and suckled it on each breast. Bridget Bishop had volunteered to Susannah that she had killed four women. It was a relatively tame story for Susannah Sheldon to tell.

Another element in the case against Bridget Bishop, also part of the pattern in other cases, was the examination of her body for witches marks – "teats" – where the familiars of the devil could suckle. On the morning of June 2, a committee of nine women and a male surgeon examined the bodies of six women: Bridget Bishop, Rebecca Nurse, Elizabeth Proctor, Alice Parker, Susannah Martin, and Sarah Good. All these women were eventually executed, except for Elizabeth Proctor who escaped because of pregnancy. According to the report,

> The first three, Namely: Bishop: Nurse: procter, by dilligent search have discovered apreternathurall Excresence of flesh between the pudendum and Anus much like to Tetts & not usuall in women & much unlike to the other three that hath been searched by us & that they were in all the three women neer the same place. (*SWP* I: 107)

The three remaining women, it seemed, had no telltale marks; but three or four hours later, when the group was examined again, the preternatural teats were gone from the first three women. Susannah Martin, however, exhibited something different in her breasts: Where they had been fresh and full before, they were now limp. The implication was that they had been sucked, though of what, it is hard to say: Not likely milk, since she was at least 67 years old.[26] In any event, the report of sagging breasts signaled a demonic visit. Thus although only four of the women were implicated as a result of the examinations, the two who were apparently exonerated, Sarah Good and Alice Parker, hanged anyway. We need constantly to bear in mind that the executions were always for afflicting the accusers, and only for that, at least as far as the law was concerned.

Something else in the record of this examination of Bridget Bishop and others catches our attention: The names of nine examining women are listed for each of the two examinations. In one case a woman's signature appears with her mark in the morning examination but without her mark in the afternoon examination. Both signatures match, and it remains only slightly puzzling as to why she would put a mark in one instance and not in the other. The puzzle deepens, however, when all the afternoon marks are compared with all the morning marks as they appear in *The Salem Witchcraft Papers:* None of them matches, not a single one (*SWP* I: 107–8). This has to ring alarm bells, since people had their individual marks, and such a discrepancy strongly suggests forgery.[27] An examination of the original manuscript partially resolves the issue, since about half of these transcriptions in *The Salem Witchcraft Papers* are simply inaccurate; in these cases, no discrepancy really exists. In a couple of other cases the condition of the manuscript makes a definite determination difficult.[28] However, in three of the cases a discrepancy is certain, the morning marks clearly differing from those in the afternoon: These are the marks of Elanor Henderson, Alice Pickering, and Jane Woolings. Since the marks of individuals on legal documents did not reflect random scribbling, it seems reasonable to assume that someone other than Henderson, Pickering, and Woolings had made marks for them either in the morning or in the afternoon, or even possibly on both occasions. Just why one might forge the marks of these women is impossible to determine, although the most likely guess is that the women did not go along with one or more of the observations in the report.

We may wonder what possible advantage there could have been in forgery, since convictions would be obtained only on spectral evidence; however, on June 2 the future behavior of the court remained to be seen, and other kinds of evidence might have been thought necessary. Yet why have the incriminating marks of the devil disappear if someone was setting up this testimony? No doubt to show the power of the devil and the women's complicity in his activities: The "teats" come and go as he needs them; the examining women simply had to confirm that the devil or his familiar had made use of them. Such reports of demonic activity must surely have increased the credibility of those claiming that the devil's minions were attacking them, even though evidence from such testimony proved irrelevant to the indictments.

Since the likelihood of forgery makes suspect the conclusions of the examinations, we shall never know what the examining women actually found. As to who was responsible for the tampering, and whether the judiciary knew of it, these are beyond our reach. The signature of the surgeon, J. Barton, appears in the morning and in the afternoon, but it remains unclear whether he personally examined the accused women or simply received the report of the committee of examining women.

Ironically, although the courts did not execute Bridget Bishop because of her poppets in the wall, hopping around in bed, or afflicting someone's child, in the years that followed more than one historian has identified her as a probable witch on the basis of the kind of testimony that never even led to an indictment in 1692. Although popular lore had raised questions about Bridget Bishop, in relatively recent times the case for her witchcraft has been made, not by an eccentric or a popularizer of Salem, but by a serious scholar: Chadwick Hansen, in *Witchcraft at Salem*.[29] To be sure, Hansen is "controversial," as David D. Hall has observed, but he has also been influential.[30] Boyer and Nissenbaum, in their *Salem-Village Witchcraft*, offer the possibility that "the existence of witchcraft cults in New England made possible the Salem-Village outbreak in its particular form," a proposition that they almost certainly would not have made prior to the appearance of Hansen's book.[31] His name and thesis, stated or by implication, often finds its way into popular histories or journalistic pieces, as in the *New York Times* and the *New York Review of Books*.[32] John Demos – perhaps expressing some frustration over the endless quest for fixing blame at Salem, and interpreting Hansen as claiming that "the accused witches themselves are now the chief culprits" – questions whether this and similar debates, with their "partisan terms and moral tone[, are] appropriate to historical scholarship."[33] Yet no matter how frequently the issue of guilt at Salem is posed and reposed, it will not go away; and our understanding of what happened in 1692 will have to be influenced by whether we believe, as Hansen has argued, that some of the accused really were witches. It is a question that the best of our scholars – who surely include Demos – cannot wholly avoid, and one that popular audiences want to embrace. Hansen's thesis must be given a look.

Hansen, of course, does not make the kinds of claims that Montague Summers made: that covens of witches were at work in Salem and conversing with the devil.[34] Rather, he claims that some people in Salem saw themselves as witches and that their contemporaries responded to them accordingly. He also argues that a kind of sympathetic response to such behavior actually made it effective at times.

The argument he presents about Bridget Bishop offers a nice, capsule, case study for exploring the perpetuation of Salem mythologies. First of all, Hansen makes the classic mistake of misidentifying Bridget Bishop, not having yet had the benefit of Greene's discovery. More pertinent to an analysis of Salem myth persistence is his use of testimony claiming that poppets had been found in the cellar of a house in which Bridget Bishop had lived. Hansen attempts to be fair in pointing out that "the evidence was circumstantial – nobody had seen Bridget Bishop stick the pins in the dolls or bury them in the walls." Counterbalancing that in Hansen's argument, however, is Cotton Mather's argument in his official apology for the trials, "Wonders of the Invisible World," that she could not explain their presence. On the basis of this testimony, and on the basis of rumors that she had bewitched her first husband and had been in trouble with the law previously on the issue of witchcraft, Hansen concludes that "[i]t is probable that Bridget Bishop was indeed a practicing witch."[35]

After reaching this conclusion, Hansen adds another piece of evidence based on the testimony of Samuel Shattuck. Shattuck testified that Bridget Bishop had brought him lace to dye, which he had found too short for any practical use. Hansen infers that Shattuck was implying that the lace, too short for human garb, was appropriate "for dressing a witch's doll."[36] Hansen proceeds to tell how, according to Shattuck, a stranger had suggested Shattuck's child was bewitched and offered to help by taking the child to Bridget Bishop: If the child were to scratch Bishop's face and draw blood, says Hansen, it would break the spell. Shattuck, according to Hansen's account, had given the man money to get cider from her, as a further way of breaking the spell. However, Bishop had not only refused to sell the cider, but had also avoided having her face scratched; instead, she had scratched the face of the boy, after which Shattuck claimed that Bridget Bishop further bewitched the boy.

Hansen then turns to the bedroom-visitation testimony, which he attributes to "hysterical hallucinations."[37] He prints appropriate testimony making the claims of the visitations by Richard Coman, Samuel Gray, and John Louder, pointing out that Bishop lied in denying that she knew Louder, her next-door neighbor. Hansen concludes his assessment of the case against Bridget Bishop in the following manner:

> There is, unfortunately, no way of knowing whether Bridget Bishop was actually using charms or spells against Richard Coman, or Samuel

Gray, or John Louder. But their testimony is eloquent evidence of the power which accompanied a reputation for witchcraft. And the dolls, the pieces of lace too short for use, and the scratching of the Shattuck child's face all suggest that Bridget Bishop had consciously sought such power, that she was in fact a witch, as the community believed her to be.[38]

Hansen's belief that the evidence suggests Bridget Bishop "was in fact a witch" stems from the poppets, the lace, and the scratching of the face, as well as from the responses of Coman, Gray, and Louder. This is a scholar's view not simply about how such testimony might have been interpreted in 1692, but how one ought to interpret it in 1969, when his book was published.

The fact that Hansen fails to note the account of Gray's retraction of his charge simply reflects one scholar's failure to probe deeply enough as he moves from Bridget Bishop as a "probable" witch to a woman who "was in fact a witch." Of broader significance, though, is Hansen's use of depositional testimony. While such statements clearly offer us the best first-hand insights into the events at Salem, they require very critical interpretation. Hansen does nicely point out that Coman's testimony about Bridget Bishop's bedroom visits is based on events recalled eight years earlier; but his account of the poppets in the wall neglects to reveal that this was based on an event alleged to have occurred seven years earlier. Such testimony cannot be treated as fact. Two men claimed that seven years earlier they had found poppets in a house in which, at the time, Bridget Bishop no longer lived: This is tenuous evidence indeed.

The matter of the scratching and the lace are difficult to pin down. Why Bridget Bishop was said to have brought small pieces of lace to be dyed can be explained by any number of theories short of witchcraft, although Shattuck no doubt believed that to be the reason, in spite of his assertion "that I could not judge them fit for *any* uce" (*SWP* I: 97; my emphasis). Yet Shattuck's seventeenth-century belief does not translate into good evidence for a supporting twentieth-century analysis. Whether Bridget Bishop even brought such lace depends on the reliability of Shattuck's depositional recounting of an event he said had happened in 1680, twelve years earlier; the account of the boy's being scratched is from the same witness and pertains also to 1680. Also, Hansen notwithstanding, nowhere does Shattuck describe an attempt to scratch Bridget Bishop's face, although he does indicate that an attempt had been made by the stranger to get blood from her. None of these reasonable doubts about the testimony of Shattuck invalidate the possibility that he thought Bridget Bishop was a witch: He may have. He also, as we have seen, asserted that he thought Alice Parker was a witch, bewitching the same child in 1685 (*SWP* II: 635–6).[39] Shattuck was prone to belief in magic and may indeed have believed that Bridget Bishop, as well as Alice Parker, was a witch; but Hansen, in his case against Bridget Bishop, offers no evidence that she preyed on that belief. In all of Hansen's claims about Bridget Bishop, the one that can stand is the assertion that she lied when she said she did not know John Louder, her next-door neighbor in Salem.

Hansen's case against Bridget Bishop focuses attention on the whole problem of depositional evidence, which paradoxically offers the most useful yet most frequently misused evidence of the Salem episode. Because it contains the best collection of primary evidence about the day-to-day events of the Salem episode, depositional testimony has properly been heavily used for insights into what happened. The problem, of course, is that depositional narratives must be read as if possibly interspersed with fiction. The judiciary of 1692 understood the limits of such testimony, and for that reason never incorporated its contents into indictments. Affliction of the accused happened before the eyes of witnesses at the examinations; depositional tales could not be corroborated with the same certainty, particularly as they applied to witchcraft. These limitations, understood in 1692, must be acknowledged today as well.

II

Of Bridget Bishop, David Greene writes, "The demonstration that Edward and Sarah (Wildes) Bishop, rather than Bridget Bishop, ran the illegal inn disproves the main reason suggested by scholars from Upham (1867) to Boyer and Nissenbaum (1974) for community enmity against the first executed witch."[40] Bridget Bishop has appeared as something of a folk heroine in the annals of Salem's story, a spirited, feisty, perhaps lusty woman – an American Wife of Bath, sometimes – who flaunted Puritan mores with a happy public house where drinking and gambling, and insinuated wenching, occurred. Delicately, in the late nineteenth century, Caroline Upham paid tribute to this heroine: "This vigorous, practical person, indifferent to public opinion, does not seem to have been planned by nature for a martyr; but circumstances made her so, and her crown may be just as bright as those worn by her gentler sisters" who also, in innocence, hanged on the gallows – a site that, for many nineteenth-century writers, was a kind of Calvary.[41] Writes Marion Starkey in the twentieth century:

> There had always been talk about the next witch, Bridget Bishop. For one thing she was a flashy dresser; her "red paragon bodice" set her

style, and for best (one does not wear paragon for best) she had a great store of laces. . . . But the real gossip had centered around Bridget's conduct as tavern-keeper. . . . It was an old complaint that she permitted young people to loiter at unseemly hours playing at "shovelboard" and making an uproar that disturbed the sleep of decent neighbours.[42]

Who was this woman, Bridget Bishop, Caroline Upham's spirited martyr, Marion Starkey's flashy tavern keeper, the witch of Chadwick Hansen, and Montague Summers's "buxom" member of the local coven of witches?[43] Her age is uncertain, probably 55–60 in 1692.[44] We know that she was the widow Bridget Wasselbe on July 26, 1666, when she married Thomas Oliver, who had three children by his former wife, at least two of whom had been born in England before 1637. Bridget was young enough to have her own child with Thomas, a daughter, Christian, born in Salem on May 8, 1667. No records of other children from this marriage are extant, and David Greene speculates that she may have been "at the end of her child-bearing period," but this is not certain.[45] The marriage with Thomas was less than idyllic. In January 1670, both Bridget and Thomas Oliver were sentenced, barring payment of a fine, to be whipped for fighting. A neighbor testified that Bridget's face was bloody on one occasion and black-and-blue on others. Thomas Oliver protested that his wife had given him "several blows."[46] We will never know how many beatings this battered woman endured. In January 1678, Bridget Bishop met the law again, this time accused of calling her husband names on the "'Lord's days.'" The authorities saw some misbehavior in him too, so the two were sentenced to stand gagged in the market place, a paper on their heads indicating their offenses. Thomas Oliver's daughter paid the fine of her father, releasing him from the punishment; no record indicates a similar release for Bridget. Her next encounter with the law, February 1680, was for the charge of witchcraft.

Little is known about this case, although no record of a witchcraft conviction survives. Able to post bond, she avoided imprisonment while awaiting trial, and no record of any punishment survives. The charge of witchcraft came from a man described as "Wonn, John Ingerson's Negro," who told a story of frightened horses, the vanishing shape of Bridget Bishop (at the time Bridget Oliver), the appearance of an unknown cat, and mysterious pinchings and pain. Corroboration in connection with the horses came from "John Lambert, Jonathan Pickering, and some youths," who concluded that "the horses were bewitched."[47]

Whether Wonn had a hallucination or invented the image of Bridget as a shape we will never know. What can be determined, however, is that the accusation against her came after her husband had recently died without leaving a will, a situation that Carol Karlsen has demonstrated left New England women vulnerable to charges of witchcraft.[48] Thomas Oliver having died in 1679, Bridget Oliver had been granted administration of the estate on November 28, 1679. The sons of her husband received twenty shillings each, as did her own daughter Christian. Bridget was also ordered to pay her deceased husband's debts, but she was granted permission to sell a ten-acre lot to pay those debts and to provide for herself.[49] Although no court record survives of any punishment against her in the witchcraft case of 1680, she offers the classic case of the vulnerable, propertied woman, however meager that property, most likely to be accused as a witch. When she had her next encounter with the law on a charge of theft, she was again married, this time to a man named Edward Bishop.[50]

In 1687, 66-year-old Thomas Stacy charged her with stealing brass, and she was arrested on December 14, 1687. Her trial was ordered for March 6, on which day her husband and William Reeves posted bond on her behalf. At the trial William Stacy, presumably the same man who would testify against her in 1692, swore that she had stolen the disputed brass. The case was one of Bridget Bishop's word versus that of Thomas and William Stacy. Hearing the case was John Hathorne, who ordered her to jail until "her trial at the next Sessions of the Peace," although the posted bond presumably kept her from prison.[51] There would be no more records of court cases against her until 1692, and the next recorded appearance of Bridget Bishop in court is on April 19, 1692, at her examination, once more before John Hathorne; Jonathan Corwin also served as magistrate. Two other women, Dorcas Hoar and Susannah Martin, who like Bridget Bishop had been earlier accused of witchcraft, were arrested about a week after her examination. Susannah Martin went to her death on July 19, whereas Dorcas Hoar survived through confession. Past witchcraft charges proved dangerous in 1692.[52]

III

Bridget Bishop came to her examination in 1692 with plenty of experience engaging the legal system; but nothing in that experience had prepared her for an examination where she confronted writhing, screaming accusers who had a credibility with the law well beyond what Wonn had. At her examination on April 19, while Corwin sat silently and Hathorne asked the questions, she replied with courtesy and deference – at least at first. When asked about the story that she had bewitched her first husband, she replied "If it please your worship I know nothing of it"

(*SWP* I: 83). That was an appropriate form of response to a judge. Hawthorne, however, hammered away at her with his usual loaded questions. How is it that your specter hurts those in the room, he wanted to know. A baffled woman could only reply, "I am innocent to a Witch. I know not what a Witch is." Then Hathorne wanted to know how she knew that she was not a witch. It was a question that could confound a learned Puritan theologian. She replied at first, "I do not know what you say." Hathorne was relentless. "How can you know, you are no Witch, & yet not know what a Witch is," he asked. Bridget Bishop was baffled, innocent, and angry. She replied with words that Hathorne did not misunderstand. "I am clear: if I were any such person you should know it." In response to which he said, "You may threaten, but you can do no more than you are permitted" (*SWP* I: 84). Why Hathorne was so confident that God would not permit Bridget Bishop to unleash the devil against him is a matter that he apparently took to his grave.

Bridget Bishop, in exasperation and frustration, had lashed out at Hathorne, but whether we find in this outburst the occurrence that brought her first to the gallows remains unknown: Barring new evidence, the chronology of execution must remain a mystery, a subject merely for speculation. Still, it is not totally improbable that an angry and influential Hathorne responded to this threat with the power of the law. The only person in the episode of 1692 who had the gallows to herself, Bridget Bishop never retracted her innocence, and the moral of her death could not have been lost on the community: Of those who had confessed and of those who had not, it was a person from the latter group who had gone to the gallows.

The grounds were carefully stated in the death warrant issued by Lieutenant Governor William Stoughton. Bridget Bishop must die on June 10 for afflicting Abigail Williams, Ann Putnam, Mercy Lewis, Mary Walcott, and Elizabeth Hubbard, all "singlewomen" of Salem Village, on April 19; afflicting them so that "their bodyes were hurt, afflicted pined, consu[med] Wasted and tormented" (*SWP* I: 109). This legal lie about the debilitated state of the "singlewomen" of Salem Village would be heard often.

So the precedent was set, and all subsequent juries that sent people to their deaths did so with the legal qualification that, although the accused had not really done what the indictment indicated, such a legal distinction offered insufficient grounds for acquittal. The juries behaved as instructed. Whether they comprehended the legal charade or not hardly matters: If they did, they saw the consequences of not playing the game. If a person could die for having a spirit afflict a person, when no one but that person could see the affliction, and when the afflicted demonstrated no visible evidence of having been so hurt, surely it would have taken an unusual jury to do anything but proclaim guilt. It is an amazing fact that, on another occasion, this actually happened – but that is for a later look.

For Bridget Bishop the end had come. On Friday, June 10, some time between 8:00 A.M. and noon, she was brought to the gallows and hanged. As with other condemned victims, she had an attainder placed on her estate. When in the years that followed a public consensus developed that a great injustice had occurred, the colony lifted these attainders and offered small financial compensation to the families of those who had brought court action;[53] but no claims appeared on behalf of Bridget Bishop and five others. Thus when, in 1711, the attainders were lifted and the compensation distributed, Bridget Bishop remained in the eyes of the law a convicted witch.[54]

The question of her innocence, and the innocence of others in her legal position, resisted being lost by the passage of time – a long time. Finally, in 1946, the Massachusetts legislature considered a bill to clear the names of the six remaining executed women – Bridget Bishop, Susannah Martin, Alice Parker, Ann Pudeator, Wilmot Reed, and Margaret Scott – though only Ann Pudeator was mentioned by name. All the convicted men and the other convicted women had already been cleared. The bill failed. It was reintroduced in 1950, 1953, and 1954, and again failed. Then in 1957 – once the legislation was shaped to absolve Massachusetts of any legal obligations to the descendants of the victims – the legislature passed a law clearing their names. On August 28, 1957, Governor Foster Furcolo signed the bill into law. The *Boston Herald* had offered this account while the issue had still been in doubt:

> Ralph C. Fitts of Myrtle street, who described himself as the descendant of witch Susanna Martin, of certain jurors and of some witnesses in the Trials, said: "I am very sure they (the victims) would want this bill passed."[55]

But Mr. Fitts may have been wrong, since it was, after all, a very grudging bill. As Chadwick Hansen has pointed out, the bill did not reverse the attainder on any of them, but rather offered "a pious resolution" about the injustices done to them – an outcome that, for Hansen, was appropriate in regard to Bridget Bishop and one other woman in the group whom he deemed a witch.[56] So Bridget Bishop, the first to hang, remains under attainder. Her only temporal compensation, if it is that, is the mythology that has kept some version of her alive in our culture's memory.

5

July 19, 1692

O Christian Martyr
  who for Truth could die
When all about thee
  owned the hideous lie!

The world redeemed
  from Superstition's sway
Is breathing freer
  for thy sake to-day.

Accused of Witchcraft
She declared
"I am innocent and God will
clear my innocency."

Once acquitted yet falsely
condemned She suffered
death July 19, 1692

In loving memory of her
Christian character
even then fully attested by
forty of her neighbors
This monument is erected
July 1885.

>   – John Greenleaf Whittier, inscription on the Rebecca Nurse
>   Monument, Danvers, Massachusetts

Strange things are happening again near the Danvers home of Rebecca Nurse, a victim of the seventeenth century Salem witch trials. Fifteen to twenty youths were seen at the Rebecca Nurse Cemetery chanting and dancing in front of a corn stalk idol decorated with beer cans at approximately 8:30 p.m. on July 10.

– *The Marblehead Messenger*, July 19, 1973[1]

I

On Tuesday, July 19, five women hanged as witches, having been tried late in June and quickly convicted. On July 12 William Stoughton had signed the death warrants of Sarah Good, Rebecca Nurse, Susannah Martin, Sarah Wilds, and Elizabeth How.

At her execution Sarah Good gained a kind of literary immortality when, on the gallows, she uttered her famous defiant response to the Reverend Nicholas Noyes. He, urging her to confess, asserted that she was a witch and knew it. To this she replied, "you are a lyer; I am no more a Witch than you are a Wizard, and if you take away my Life, God will give you Blood to drink."[2] Even here she was cheated, as Nathaniel Hawthorne, who immortalized the event in *The House of the Seven Gables,* gave Sarah Good's defiant words to a fictional man, Matthew Maule.[3] In this dramatic employment of Sarah Good's words, Hawthorne also played on the legend that Nicholas Noyes had indeed choked on his own blood.[4] Less dramatically, Hawthorne gave Sarah Good a bit part as a witch in "Young Goodman Brown," although he knew better than most that only the innocent at Salem died.[5]

Sarah Good has had some other literary treatment in the guise of historical representation. Those who have read even casually in the histories of the Salem witch trials have run across her name and across her history. She appears in her role as the archetypal outsider, the offending, aged, marginal person in a culture that repudiates weak, vulnerable, offensive, old people. With few exceptions the depiction of Sarah Good, in popular culture and by historians, has been pretty consistent. Thomas Hutchinson, the source for many of our assumptions about Salem, described her in 1764 as an "old woman who was bed-rid."[6] Winfield Nevins, the historian, wrote of her in 1892 that she "is said to have been about seventy years of age."[7] Similarly William Nelson Gemmill in 1924 described her as "a distracted, melancholy old woman of nearly seventy years."[8] The prominent sociologist, Kai Erikson, described her in 1966 as an "old crone."[9] Chadwick Hansen in 1969 referred to Sarah Good as an "old [woman] of dubious reputation,"[10] and the distinguished Hawthorne scholar, Arlin

Turner, in 1980 depicted Sarah Good as an "ancient and infirm woman."[11]

Finding examples of this characterization of Sarah Good as an old woman, whether on the printed page or in pictorial representations, is easy and indeed normal in popular descriptions of her. Yet Sarah Good, when examined for witchcraft on March 1, 1692, had a 4- or 5-year-old daughter named Dorcas and was pregnant with another child. She was around 38 when she died.[12] However, there is something more going on here than catching scholars perpetuating an error: What makes the story of Sarah Good's age so remarkable is the proximity in the narratives of her age to the evidence refuting it. In his *Wayward Puritans,* Kai Erikson describes Sarah Good as "a proper hag of a witch if Salem Village had ever seen one" and defines her as "the old crone," though he is aware on this page that she has children and on the next page refers specifically to her 5-year-old daughter, Dorcas.[13] To say that Erikson simply slipped up misses the point, since the matter occurs too often in the writings of others. Chadwick Hansen in *Witchcraft at Salem* refers to Sarah Good as an old woman, but on the next page writes about her "four-year-old daughter," and elsewhere about her "sucking child."[14] Gemmill writes sympathetically of "five year old" Dorcas Good one page after calling Sarah Good nearly 70.[15] Nevins, ascribing the same age to Sarah Good, also refers to Dorcas as "only five years of age."[16] Hutchinson, the first to make the strange connection, describes Dorcas as 4 years old on the same page where he describes her mother as an "old woman who was bed-rid."[17]

Someone writing a book can make a mistake – and inevitably will. One can forget that a contradictory point had been made in an earlier part of the manuscript; but how does a scholar present us with an old woman and her 4- or 5-year-old child on the same page? If it happened once, one might claim a bizarre occurrence. That it happens so often – well beyond the few examples here – requires some speculation as to how this could be. Selma and Pamela Williams in *Riding the Night Mare* observe that "Sarah Good's hard life was reflected in her face. Seventy years old most observers thought her – somehow forgetting she had a daughter, Dorcas, who was only five or six."[18] If that observation is accurate it would explain odd behavior in contemporaries of Sarah Good; it would not explain the repeated research anomaly. Also, we have no good evidence that Sarah Good even looked old. We do know that she smoked a pipe, that she begged, and that many of her neighbors considered her an objectionable person, as did her husband, who testified against her. From such facts, a myth emerges so powerful as to blind writers to their own words. The stereotype of Sarah Good as an old woman prevails over the presence of her small children.

On a rare occasion, as in Arthur Miller's *The Crucible,* a writer confronts the discrepancy. Here, Miller's character Mary Warren excitedly announces, "Goody Good is pregnant!" Elizabeth Proctor responds, "Pregnant! Are they mad? The woman's near to sixty!"[19] But pregnant she was, a fact that obviates the need to speculate as to why Bridget Bishop died before her: The judicial authorities scrupulously protected prenatal life; only after the birth of the child could its mother be hanged. The needs of Sarah Good's other child, Dorcas, mattered less to the authorities. This child, 4 or 5 years old, remained in chains for seven or eight months. Dorcas Good had been declared a witch. At one point she accused her mother, and had she been more precocious she might have become one of the regulars, thus escaping those chains. The baby died in prison before Sarah Good hanged (*SWP* III: 994).

Sarah Good, of course, did not know her future mythic role, and could never have guessed that she would appear one day in a two-page magazine spread, white haired and ancient, publicity provided by the Boston Chamber of Commerce.[20] Pregnant and 38 years old at her examination on March 1, formerly the wife of a man named Daniel Poole, she listened while her current husband, William Good, expressed his fear that she "was a witch or would be one very quickly."[21] Said Good about his wife, "I may say with tears that shee is an enimy to all good" (*SWP* II: 357). Not that she had no value for him, of course, for in 1710 he would petition the court for compensation, money to help him as a result of the harm done "upon the account of supposed Witchcraft" (*SWP* III: 994). However, many people did not distinguish themselves, including Sarah Good: She, in an attempt to protect herself, had accused Sarah Osborne.

After the initial examination, a plentiful supply of witnesses testified against Sarah Good. In April, Deliverance Hobbs, who had become a cooperating confessor, told of Sarah Good's appearance at a demonic sacrament (*SWP* II: 363). Other kinds of witnesses also appeared, including people not necessarily acting from fear of prosecution or from malice, but perhaps from the genuine suspicion of Sarah Good.

Late in June Sarah Good faced the grand jury and the trial court of the Court of Oyer and Terminer. In evidence against her, 45-year-old Samuel Abbey and his 38-year-old wife Mary, Sarah's age, told of how in charity they had let destitute Sarah and William Good live with them but finally had to turn them out, Sarah Good being so spiteful and malicious. That had been two and a half years earlier, and Sarah Good, according to Samuel and Mary, took her vengeance against them in that time. The cattle of the Abbeys drooped in unusual manners and died: seventeen head within two years, not including sheep and hogs. Moreover, had not William Good himself told them, when two of their cows had died within half an hour of one another, that Sarah Good had said she did not care whether they lost all their cattle? Far more damning was the fact that, on the very day of Sarah Good's arrest, one of their cows could not rise alone, although once Sarah Good was in custody the cow behaved as if nothing had been wrong. Also, since leaving the house of the Abbeys, Sarah Good had been cross and malicious to them and their children, and had threatened them and had called them vile names.

Sarah Gage, 40, and her husband, Thomas, offered their testimony, relating how two and a half years before, after not allowing Sarah Good into their house for fear that she had been exposed to smallpox, one of their cows had died. So also, Henry Herrick, 21, and Jonathan Batchelor, 14, told of strange behavior in the family cattle after they had chased Sarah Good from their barn, fearing she would smoke her pipe there and burn it down. Herrick's father had already rejected her request to live in his house (*SWP* II: 375).

There were the regulars, as always. Sarah Bibber, the 36-year-old woman who sometimes joined the group called "children" or "girls," told of her afflictions by Sarah Good, as did Mary Walcott, Abigail Williams, Ann Putnam, and Mercy Lewis.[22] Then there was Joanna Childin, who in this and one other case spoke of apparitions. Childin testified that the apparition of Sarah Good and her last child, deceased, appeared to her, the child accusing the mother of murdering it, Sarah Good's specter offering as explanation for the murder that she could not take care of it. The child told its mother she was a witch, and the mother told the child she had given it to the devil. This and other stories spoke of the demonic ways of Sarah Good.

Notwithstanding all the damning testimony against her, nothing ensured her execution as certainly as did her own simple refusal to admit to guilt. Either she had not learned from the case of Bridget Bishop, or she possessed, under that spiteful and malicious manner so detested by those in the community, a core of integrity that did not allow so easy a way of survival. Whatever her reason, we can only guess.

II

Salem's mythology has given us the hideous old hag, Sarah Good; but mythologies, like the head of Janus, have their other side, and as our culture has created stereotypical loathly ladies it has also given us sainted women from Salem, particularly Rebecca Nurse. She, more than any other victim, emerged in the story of Salem as a Christian martyr. In 1885 the descendants of Rebecca Nurse gathered together at the family homestead in Danvers, Massachusetts, formerly Salem Village, to erect a monument in her honor. They placed it in the cemetery near the house traditionally assumed to be hers, although the surviving home was probably not built until after her death;[23] somewhere on that land, however, Rebecca Nurse had lived. In her honor a poem by John Greenleaf Whittier is inscribed on the monument. The inscription on another monument nearby reads: "This tablet contains the names of those who at the risk of their lives gave written testimony in favor of Rebecca Nurse in 1692." Forty names are listed thereon, a group close to but not identical with the names of thirty-nine people who in 1692 signed a petition attesting to the good life and character of Rebecca Nurse, as well as the absence of any indication of witchcraft (*SWP* II: 592–3).[24] Most who signed the petition seem not to have been troubled by the authorities for their activity on her behalf; but at least one, Daniel Andrew, was accused, and, according to Upham, escaped from the colony.[25] Nathaniel Putnam, Sr., who did not sign the petition but who elsewhere expressed support for Rebecca Nurse, may have received retaliation from the accusers through the accusation against Mary Black, probably his slave.

The undated petition does not call for a reprieve, so it was probably circulated before her death sentence at the end of June. The chances are that it was prepared as evidence for her grand jury hearing at the end of May and the beginning of June, or for her trial, at the end of June. Amid continuing accusations, signing such a petition must have been an act of courage, the lack of retribution notwithstanding.

At a ceremony on July 29, 1892, honoring those forty people who in 1692 "bore witness" on behalf of Rebecca Nurse "at the time of her great peril and need," the Reverend A. P. Putnam preached that her example "shows us how to face the temptations and terrors of the world and keep ourselves pure and blameless, and be patient and persevering, calm and undismayed, Christlike and triumphant."[26] In more recent times, Marion Starkey has written that "[w]ere the Puritans given to canonizing their saints, such a one as Rebecca Nurse would surely in time have been beatified."[27]

As with so many other stories of Salem, this hagiographic image of Rebecca Nurse was shaped by Charles W. Upham, the nineteenth-century chronicler of the Salem witch trials. Upham describes a loving Christian mother who, through God's inscrutable will, bore the terror of accusation and condemnation. Upon her conviction, she was excommunicated from her church, presided over by the Reverend Nicholas Noyes. For Upham, "in our view now, and, as we believe, in the view of God and angels then, she occupied an infinite height above her persecutors. Her mind was serenely fixed upon higher scenes, and filled with a peace which the world could not take away, or its cruel wrongs disturb."[28] The image Upham set in motion has endured, and Rebecca Nurse has remained the icon of the other side of Sarah Good. As Chadwick Hansen writes, "On the gallows she was, in contrast to Sarah Good, a model of Christian behavior."[29]

That Rebecca Nurse should have emerged as the person to personify the martyrdom of the Salem victims suggests little more than the vagaries and chance of mythmaking, perhaps the fact that her descendants came to honor her. Whether she deserves the singular honor of personifying Christian martyrdom at Salem may be debated but, as did others, she did opt for eternal rather than temporal salvation. As a writer for Boston magazine observed in 1962, she "knew that to confess might mean earthly salvation and eternal damnation, and [she] chose earthly damnation and eternal salvation."[30] Various journalists have gravitated to this theme of Christian martyrdom in Salem, but our leading novelists and playwrights have resisted the motif: Christian martyrdom in America has not been interesting to them.

Rebecca Nurse was a sick, elderly woman when accused of witchcraft. At her examination, she affirmed, "I can say before my Eternal father I am innocent, & God will clear my innocency" (*SWP* II: 584); but a man named Henry Kenny announced his affliction upon her appearance, and Ann Putnam's mother, Ann Putnam, Sr., rivaled her daughter in the accusations of Rebecca Nurse's invisible visits to her. She also added the twist usually reserved to male accusers, that of being attacked in bed. Other regulars joined in and, in a deposition to the court on June 2, Joanna Childin, who told of the apparition of Sarah Good, also declared that Rebecca Nurse had appeared to her with the deceased Goodman Harwood, who accused her of killing him. In an undated document, Sarah Holton recalled the story of how Rebecca Nurse had railed against Sarah's husband, Benjamin: The Holton pigs had crossed onto the Nurse property, and Rebecca had asked her son Benjamin to shoot them; thereafter, Benjamin Holton had become ill and died with fits similar to those of the accusers. Oddly, the name of Sarah Holton appears on the petition in support of Rebecca Nurse's character and on the stone at the cemetery honoring those who spoke in her defense. Sarah Holton may have felt pressure to make her charge after she had signed the petition.

As in all cases, of course, such charges were beside the point when it came to the indictments. Even a positive response to a petition from Rebecca Nurse requesting qualified women to examine her for witch marks could have no bearing on the matter of indictment (*SWP* II: 606). She was charged with afflicting Ann Putnam, Jr., Mary Walcott, Elizabeth

Hubbard, and Abigail Williams, all on March 24, the day of her examination. How the court would respond to these spectral accusations remained unknown, since the trials at the end of June represented the first to be held since "The Return of Several Ministers" appeared on June 15.[31] For Rebecca Nurse, it briefly looked as if the decision to hold to the truth would work in temporal as well as in eternal terms, for the jury found her not guilty.

This one time, and only this time under the Court of Oyer and Terminer, a jury had shown the capacity to follow the rules of evidence, to pay attention to what the ministers had said, and to put aside Stoughton's injunction that it was sufficient that the action of the accused "tended" toward pining, consuming, and wasting the accusers. Here was an early and major opportunity to bring Massachusetts Bay colony back to its traditional, conservative approach toward allegations of witchcraft. The ministers had spoken. A jury had listened.

Our knowledge of what happened next depends heavily on the account given by Robert Calef. According to him,

> all the accusers in the Court, and suddenly after all the afflicted out of Court, made an hideous out-cry, to the amazement, not only of the Spectators, but the Court also seemed strangely surprized; one of the Judges exprest himself not satisfied, another of them as he was going off the Bench, said they would have her Indicted anew.[32]

Nothing in what Calef writes suggests the fiction presented as history by writers such as Montague Summers, who perhaps offers a more creative scenario than most, but who is not alone in his embellishments. Summers writes that, when the verdict came,

> the mob broke out into the wildest clamour, yelling with horrid threats that they would pull the house about the judges' ears and tear the jurors to pieces. Benches were smashed, and missiles began to be thrown, when the acquittal was hurriedly withdrawn and sentence of death speedily pronounced.[33]

In this tale remains the fact that the jurors indeed withdrew their acquittal. While assuring the jurors that he would not impose upon them, Stoughton suggested to them that they might not have considered properly a statement made by Rebecca Nurse. According to Calef, this suggestion, along with "the Clamours of the Accusers," persuaded the jury to reconsider the verdict.[34] Note, however, that the judges behaved as they did not because the accusers had intimidated them: When it suited them, the judges readily ignored the accusers, as when in July one accused the Reverend Samuel Willard and was told by the judges that she had made a mistake.[35] A more brazen example occurred at the trial of Sarah Good on

June 30 – also the day of Rebecca Nurse's trial – when an accuser complained of being stabbed in the breast with a knife, part of which had broken off. A young man produced the handle of the knife that went with the incriminating blade, explaining that he had broken it the day before and had thrown away the piece that the accuser now claimed to be the remainder of Sarah Good's weapon. The judges told the accuser not to lie anymore and then proceeded to hear further incriminating testimony from the same person.[36] Had it pleased the judges to ignore the complaints of the accusers against the acquittal of Rebecca Nurse, they would have done so.

Stoughton's observation to the jury concerned a statement by Rebecca Nurse identifying Deliverance Hobbs and her daughter Abigail Hobbs as "one of us."[37] Much has been made of this remark and the response to it. When asked to explain her words, Rebecca Nurse initially failed to do so. Thomas Fisk, foreman of the jury, indicated a few years later that this incident had proved decisive. After the verdict Rebecca Nurse attempted to explain that "one of us" meant fellow prisoners and not fellow witches, and that her "being something hard of hearing, and full of grief" had prevented her from grasping the interpretation placed on her words (*SWP* II: 608). However, no answer would probably have mattered: Stoughton had made it clear enough to the jury as to what verdict must be given. Only after the Court of Oyer and Terminer ended would another verdict of "not guilty" occur. No mob forced a guilty verdict; the judiciary did. To the bitter end, Stoughton fought for the continuation of the witch trials and the executions.

Massachusetts Bay had one more chance to reassess its actions, for Governor Phips granted Rebecca Nurse a reprieve; but Phips, apparently bending to the pressures of those who disapproved of the reprieve, rescinded it. Whether he consulted with his patron, Increase Mather, is unknown. Calef says that a "Salem Gentleman" persuaded the governor to get rid of the reprieve, and what may be implied by that is probably forever out of reach.[38]

The case of Rebecca Nurse had offered a battleground for the contest between those who would return to the traditional New England way of dealing with witchcraft cases and those who sought a radical break from the colony's tradition of restraint on this issue. The latter had won.

III

In more traditional times, Susannah Martin had fared better in the face of witchcraft accusations. One witness, William Browne, 70, referred to a witchcraft charge against her in the early 1660s. According to Browne, Susannah Martin had frightened his wife Elizabeth thirty years before by vanishing from sight upon meeting her. Elizabeth had subsequently been tormented by Susannah Martin's presence and had found relief only after the church appointed a day of humiliation to seek God's help. Later, Elizabeth had testified before a grand jury, after which Susannah Martin had threatened her. As of about two months later, Elizabeth Browne had not been a rational woman. Two physicians declared that she had been bewitched (*SWP* II: 558–9).

Court records do not confirm this witchcraft case, but on April 13, 1669, Susannah Martin was indeed ordered to jail, unless she posted bond, to be held for trial on suspicion of witchcraft.[39] No record of any conviction against her at that time survives, however, and she is known to have been out of jail a few months later when she had an unrelated legal encounter. Nothing suggests a witchcraft conviction.[40] Thus, when a warrant for her arrest appeared on April 30, 1692, Susannah Martin confronted the situation with a history of at least one previous legal encounter on the subject of witchcraft, and perhaps two.

What may have worked for her in the past, of course, would not work in 1692. Her firm, even defiant response to the charges have made her a figure of admiration by commentators on Salem, and William Carlos Williams singled out her case in his 1925 book, *In the American Grain*.[41] Earlier, Caroline Upham had found her a fit subject for a future literary master:

> When the Shakespeare of the future seeks for characters to people his tragedy from these materials, he could not put into the mouth of Martin more clever speeches than she utters for herself in these records.[42]

Susannah Martin had apparently already appeared as an American heroine in the literature of witchcraft when Upham wrote these words: Whittier, in his "Mabel Martin," presumably had her in mind.

At her examination, Susannah Martin recognized the fraud and had no hesitation in letting the examiners know it. When asked whether she thought the accusers were bewitched, she replied, "No. I do not think they are." Who then was their "Master"? "If they be dealing in the black art, you may know as well as I." She also argued the biblical point that he who appeared in the shape of Samuel, a glorified saint, could appear in anyone's shape.[43] When pressed as to whether she believed the accusers had lied, she replied, "They may lye for ought I know" (*SWP* II: 551). When asked whether she had compassion for their suffering, she stated bluntly, "No, I have none" (*SWP* II: 552). Ann Putnam, Mercy Lewis,

Mary Walcott, Elizabeth Hubbard, Susannah Sheldon, Sarah Bibber, and John Indian performed with enthusiasm, but Susannah Martin held firm. She was a 70-year-old widow, her husband having died six years before.[44] If afraid, she did not seem to show it.

The witnesses in the subsequent proceedings against her told a series of bizarre tales, most set safely far in the past. John Pressey, age 53, described how twenty-four years earlier a light had assaulted him, and he had struck back at it. A little later he had seen Susannah Martin in the same position as the light had been. The next day it had been reported, by whom he does not say, that Susannah Martin was in much pain and needed to have her body swabbed. Pressey also claimed that Major Pike, who in 1692 may have been the person taking this deposition, had chastised Pressey for not telling what had happened sooner so that the body of Susannah Martin could have been examined for evidence of the wounds he had inflicted on her by attacking the light. Pressey claimed that, some years later, Susannah Martin had chastised him and his wife, Mary, with foul language for relating such a story, and had told them that they would never have more than two cows; and from that day on they never had. Mary, 46, joined Pressey in his testimony, confirming all that her husband claimed except for one aspect: Susannah Martin's threat that they would never have more than two cows.

Bernard Peach, 42 or 43 years old, told of Susannah Martin six or seven years earlier having lain on him in bed (*SWP* II: 562), and Robert Downer, 52, told of an experience several years before when a cat had been on him in bed and choked him, the cat appearing after a threat by Susannah Martin (*SWP* II: 572). In other testimony Peach told of an altercation with Susannah's husband, George Martin, about ten years prior, after which a cow had died. Seven or eight years before his testimony, Jarvis Ring had had Susannah Martin on him in bed several times, although she had disappeared whenever anyone had come in response to his summons for help (*SWP* II: 563).

In describing an event unusual because it was so recent, Joseph Ring, 27, told of an adventure the previous September: After a night of drinking, Susannah Martin had ruined the party by turning into a black hog and leaving the house where the libations were occurring; another man and woman had also left, although apparently not as hogs. Ring had found himself mysteriously away from the premises, though finally recognizing the house of a man in Amesbury (*SWP* II: 564). Nor was that the end of his strange encounters: Since the previous April Susannah had stood by his bed and pinched him (*SWP* II: 566). The accumulation of such tales by men – surely suspect, and seemingly not induced by panic – almost suggests the pack behavior of gang rape, the congregation of men assaulting the helpless woman. Perhaps psychologists may speculate as to how similar the motives are.

There were more stories: John Kemball, age 45, told how twenty-three years earlier a dispute with the Martins had been followed by the death of cattle. More ominously, he told of a dispute over a puppy that had preceded a violent assault on him by a black puppy that did not end until Kemball had invoked the name of Christ. The following morning Susannah Martin had told of Kemball having been frightened by puppies, even though Kemball had not told anyone the story (*SWP* II: 567–8). John Allen, age 45, told of losing oxen to Susannah Martin's witchcraft (*SWP* II: 569). Joseph Knight, 40, related how in 1686 Susannah Martin had been walking along with a dog, whom she had then picked up; but, as Knight explains, upon closer inspection it had turned out to be a keg rather than a dog under her arm. Moreover, after he and a friend, Nathaniel Clark, had left her, their horses had been particularly balky. Elizabeth Clark confirmed the testimony, all except the part where her husband said that the keg had been a dog (*SWP* II: 571). Finally, 48-year-old Sarah Atkinson told how eighteen years earlier Susannah Martin had come to her house in Newbury from Amesbury "in an Extraordinary dirty Season." When Sarah had asked Susannah to dry herself by the fire, she had insisted that she was not wet. Nor could Sarah Atkinson find any signs of wetness on Susannah Martin upon inspecting her, though she asserted that she herself would "have been wett up to my knees" (*SWP* II: 578).[45]

There was other testimony, including, of course, the assertions of the accusers. How many of the stories were contrived and how many actually believed by their tellers is impossible to tell. A man may indeed have been attacked by a small dog; a drunk may certainly have believed in the transformations he saw; a woman may in good faith have thought that one should be more muddied after a long walk; and men may indeed have hallucinated about women in bed with them at night. However, the questions that beg asking in most of these stories are Why had they not been reported at the time they happened? and If they had, why had no action been taken? The lack of a historic record makes evident the reality that whatever had occurred in the past – with the possible exception of the Browne witchcraft testimony – had been nothing worth the notice of the judicial system; at least, not before 1692.

IV

Sarah Good, because of her dying epithet against Nicholas Noyes, and Rebecca Nurse, because of her initial acquittal and subsequent honoring by her descendants, figure prominently in the stories of Salem.

Susannah Martin, through the power of her speech, evokes literary remembrances. However, of Sarah Wilds, who hanged with them on July 19, there is little in legend or folklore, nor in the scholarship of Salem. Her story remains embedded in *The Salem Witchcraft Papers*.

On April 21 Hathorne and Corwin issued a warrant, based on a complaint by Thomas Putnam and John Buxton, for the arrest of Sarah Wilds, Nehemiah Abbot, Jr., and several others for afflicting Ann Putnam, Mercy Lewis, and Mary Walcott. As was typical in cases originating with Thomas Putnam and other Salem Village sponsors of the complainers, no bond was posted for the warrants, in contradiction to the law. Buxton's name represents an oddity, since it appears nowhere else in the witchcraft records.

At the examination of this group, a remarkable event occurred: The accusers conceded a mistake in their identification. The 60-year-old Nehemiah Abbot, Jr., had protested his innocence in the face of the standard theatrics of Ann Putnam and Mary Walcott; but for some reason, Mercy Lewis expressed reservations about him as the afflicter. After some discussion the accusers agreed that the specter had looked very much like Abbot but had not been him after all, and he became the only accused person released from an examination as innocent. The accusers expressed ambivalence in a few other cases, but only in this one did they concede an outright mistake. There can be only speculation as to why this occurred. One person in a popular account has argued that Mercy Lewis hedged as a deliberate ploy to establish the integrity and credibility of the accusers.[46] More likely, the accusers had simply disagreed over whether to name him.

Sarah Wilds was examined on April 22, the day of her arrest, having been accused a few days earlier, on April 19, by Abigail Hobbs.[47] Only a fragment of that examination survives, with just the name of Sarah Bibber appearing as one falling into fits in the presence of Sarah Wilds; but the one surviving indictment makes it clear that Ann Putnam, Mary Walcott, and Mercy Lewis were among the accusers. Sarah Bibber proclaimed that she saw Sarah Wilds on a beam. Sarah Wilds politely replied, "I am not guilty Sir" (*SWP* III: 806). She was accused of hurting John Herrick's mother-in-law, Goody Reddington. Testimony of an unclear nature came from another man, Captain How. Little else appears in the examination.

Some animosity may have existed between Abigail's mother, Deliverance Hobbs, and Sarah Wilds. Ephraim Wilds, son of Sarah, claimed that as constable of Topsfield he had, as required, arrested William and Deliverance Hobbs, thus leading to a retaliatory accusation by Deliverance against his mother. This would not explain the original charge by Abigail, which occurred before the arrest of her mother, but it could conceivably have been a factor in the accusation against her by Deliverance Hobbs, who on April 22 at her own examination claimed that the shape of Sarah Wilds had previously "tore me almost to peices" (*SWP* II: 420).

The main testimony against Sarah Wilds, however, revolved around an old controversy with Mary Reddington (*SWP* III: 808).[48] John Wilds, husband of Sarah, described his past threat to sue John and Mary Reddington because Mary had accused Sarah Wilds of witchcraft. On July 2 the Reverend John Hale testified that fifteen or sixteen years earlier Mary Reddington had complained to him that Sarah Wilds was bewitching her. He testified that she also had told him of visits from a young man named John, who had told her that his mother-in-law (probably meaning Sarah Wilds as stepmother) was a witch. Hales also said that about twenty years before, a stepson named Jonathan Wilds had behaved in such a way as to create debate over whether he was bewitched or counterfeiting.

Other testimony was provided regarding the Reddington family, including that offered by Zacheus Perkins, the nephew of Sarah Wilds, in support of the claim that John Gould, related to the Reddington family, had been prevented by witchcraft from transporting some hay; the hay he had brought to the cart had fallen to the ground and the cart had tipped over. The most unusual testimony came from 50-year-old Elizabeth Symons, who told of how on the way to visiting Goodwife Reddington she and her mother had run into Sarah Wilds. The mother had argued with Sarah over an incident related to a borrowed scythe, and had been threatened by Sarah Wilds. Elizabeth had responded, according to her testimony, by trembling terribly, and that night in bed she had seen something standing between her and the wall. When she then switched sides of the bed with her husband, she had felt something lying on her, making her unable to move or speak all night. She referred to another incident in which, after being near Sarah Wilds in church, she had had a fit. Like Ann Putnam, Sr., she testified about bedroom visits of the kind usually the province of males — such as that of 21-year-old Humphrey Clark, who had testified that, a year before, a woman he identified as Sarah Wilds had awakened him in his bed.

Yet another charge of past witchcraft appeared. According to the testimony of 48-year-old Mary Gadge, about two years earlier a boy named David Balch had complained of being tormented by witches and identified Sarah Wilds as one of them,

> saying alsoe there was a Confederacy of them & they were then whispering together at his beds feet, and desired Gabriell Hood to strike them: & when he did strike at the place where s'd. Balch said they sate: s'd Balch said that he had struck Goody wiles & she was Gone presently. (*SWP* II: 401)

Given the many stories of invisible appearances, this one offers nothing exceptional; however, it does remind us once more how much the rules had changed in Massachusetts. Assuming the credibility of Mary Gadge, two years earlier a boy had seen specters, just as the "girls" of 1692 had; yet no "witchcraft outbreak" had occurred in response to the claim of a "hysterical" boy. Sarah Wilds, accused of witchcraft in 1676 or 1677 and in 1690, was a free woman when the events of 1692 began; but she did not survive the year in which past suspicions made her a likely choice for the accusers.

V

As John and Joseph Andrews told the story, in 1674 they had broken a scythe while mowing and had gone to the house of John Wilds, Sr., to borrow another one. Over the objections of Sarah Wilds, wife of John Wilds, Sr., they had taken a scythe belonging to her son, John Wilds, Jr. They told how, after leaving, "a litle lad came affter us whose name was" Ephraim Wilds (*SWP* III: 816); he had told them that his mother had warned them to bring it back. The child could not have known, of course, that the memory of this event would be used as testimony against his mother for witchcraft. Nor could he have known that he would grow up to be a constable. On May 31, a month before his mother was tried, Ephraim Wilds, constable for the town of Topsfield, brought in Elizabeth How. She would be tried with his mother and would hang with her.

Elizabeth How was one of the women perceived as a Christian martyr by nineteenth-century chronicler Charles W. Upham. "The bearing of Elizabeth How," writes Upham, "under accusations so cruelly and shamefully fabricated and circulated against her, exhibits one of the most beautiful pictures of a truly forgiving spirit and of Christlike love anywhere to be found."[49] Indeed, according to Upham, "There is no more disgraceful page in our annals than that which details the testimony given at the trial, and records the conviction and execution, of Elizabeth How."[50]

The case against her, however, was actually similar enough in its ingredients to that of other cases. Added to the feigning of fits were tales of farm animals dying, or not giving milk, or otherwise having problems. Also, as with Bridget Bishop, Sarah Wilds, and Susannah Martin, there was a past history of witchcraft accusations.

The record of the examination of Elizabeth How on May 31 is brief, recorded by Samuel Parris. Mercy Lewis, Mary Walcott, Abigail Williams, Mary Warren, Susannah Sheldon, John Indian, and Ann Putnam were present and performing. From one of the questions asked, it appears as if the person who initially accused her came from Ipswich – "Do not you know that one at Ipswitch hath accused you?" (*SWP* II: 434); yet the predictable warrant against her charged affliction of standard accusers, this time Mary Walcott and Abigail Williams, as well as "others" (*SWP* II: 433). This sequence followed the pattern that produced a steady supply of victims: A person would be accused, and the regulars would take up the case, announcing that the named individual afflicted them. At first the accused were known directly by the accusers or by close relatives; but the accusers came routinely to endorse accusations of people unknown to them and, often, to their relatives.

To the charges of her accusers at her examination, Elizabeth How offered her memorable reply: "If it was the last moment I was to live, God knows I am innocent of any thing in this nature" (*SWP* II: 434). However, her prose proved useless at the examination, what with Ann Putnam showing the pin stuck in her hand by the shape of Elizabeth How, or with Mary Warren shouting that she had been pricked. John Indian complained that How was biting him.

What follows, as in other cases, were the adornments to the key charge that a specter – as always, judiciously sparing the authorities, who, if they noticed this, made no comment – was attacking people at the open examination. Aside from adding to the charade, the subsequent testimony revealed the history of a witchcraft allegation against Elizabeth How, a charge that made her vulnerable to public accusation in 1692. Ten years earlier, in 1682, Hannah Perley, 10-year-old daughter of Samuel Perley, then 42, and his wife, then 36, had begun having some kind of fits; these, her father said, had lasted two or three years, the child then dying. According to the Perleys, the fits had started shortly after a falling out between them and James and Elizabeth How. According to this testimony, the child had complained that Elizabeth How was afflicting her day and night. After being chided by her parents for defaming Elizabeth How, she had insisted "that though we would not beleve her now yet you will know it one day" (*SWP* II: 439). The diagnosis of "an evil hand" had also been confirmed by "several doctors" (*SWP* II: 439).

Notwithstanding the Perleys' disclaimer that they had not wanted to defame Elizabeth How, when she wanted to join the church at Ipswich they had objected, informing the congregation of her activities against their daughter. Although Elizabeth How seems to have been prevented from joining the church because of this, there is no indication of judicial action taken against her; not even when, shortly after her rejection by the church, a healthy cow of the Perleys died strangely and unexpectedly – at least as Perley told the story in 1692.

The history of the Perley child's illness and the failed attempt by Elizabeth How to gain admission to the church at Ipswich offered the core segment of the testimony against her. Deborah Perley, 33, recalling a quarrel between her husband Timothy, now 38, and Elizabeth How over some boards – the result of which had been that Deborah and Timothy's cows had not given the usual amount of milk the next morning – proceeded to tell how the afflicted Hannah Perley had come to Elizabeth How's house and been suddenly frightened and thrown into "a dredful fit." The child had blamed Elizabeth How. Yet Deborah Perley had noted that when Hannah was with Elizabeth How "thai were veri loving together" (*SWP* II: 438). Questioned as to why this was so, Hannah maintained that Elizabeth How would otherwise kill her. From the transcription of the testimony it is difficult to tell which disturbed Deborah and Timothy Perley more: the fit of Hannah or the failure of the cows to give milk in proper quantity. The anonymous transcriber seems to have taken it all in with an even hand.

Mary Cummings, 60 years old and wife of Isaac Cummings, Sr. – the man, as we may recall, whose horse almost set the barn on fire after being subjected to the penetration of a pipe – recalled that she had been asked to write some observations about the life and conversation of Elizabeth How in connection with her attempt to enter the church at Ipswich. This seems to have occurred about eight years before her testimony. Events stemming from the controversy over church membership had led for a few days to the disappearance and abuse of a horse owned by Isaac Cummings. The Cummings family was not alone in claiming retribution against a horse resulting from the church-membership dispute: Jacob Foster, about 29, told how his father, who had been instrumental in denying How her church membership, shortly thereafter could not find his horse. When he did find the animal leaning against a tree, it had shown no inclination to move even after Jacob had whipped it; only after he had put his shoulder to the side of the horse and pushed it from the tree would the animal go home with him. He observed that the horse had "lookt as if she had been miserably beaten and a bused" (*SWP* II: 451). Like Mary Cummings, Jacob Foster makes no actual charge of witchcraft regarding the temporarily missing horse.

Closer to the invisible world was the account by Mary Cummings of the strange behavior of Hannah Perley, who had asked Mary if she did not see Elizabeth How going around the wall. Mary Cummings tells how she looked as diligently as possible at the particular area pointed to by the child but could see nothing of Elizabeth How. After being chided by her mother for what she said, Hannah had pointed to the crack through which Elizabeth How had left.

Related to Hannah Perley and the invisible world is the testimony of Joseph Safford, about 60. According to Safford, his wife had feared Elizabeth How as a result of the reports regarding Hannah Perley; but Safford's wife had suddenly taken the side of Elizabeth How after a visit by How. When How had sought to join the Ipswich church, Safford's wife, over the strenuous objections of her husband, had shown great enthusiasm to attend the meeting and defend her; in fact, breaking her promise to him, she had gone. When Elizabeth How was rejected, Safford's wife had "told her though shee wer condemned before men shee was Justefyed befor god." Safford's wife, according to his testimony, had subsequently fallen into "a Raving frenzy" in defense of Elizabeth How, and thence into a trance. Upon coming out of it, she had declared herself mistaken about Elizabeth How, who was a witch, not "a precious saint of god." She had become afflicted by the apparition of Elizabeth How after seeing How appear through a crevice, something "she knew no good person could do" (*SWP* II: 452).

Safford added another element to his testimony at the trial of Elizabeth How on June 30: One morning, after his wife had turned against How, he had heard her shrieking in her room, exclaiming that the "evill one" was present in the form of two large shapes that soon went out the window. She had identified them as Elizabeth How and "goode ollever," now the executed Bridget Bishop (*SWP* II: 452). Safford testified that he had told his wife that she had never seen Goody Oliver. She agreed, but indicated that the specter had represented herself as the Goody Oliver of Salem who had hurt William Stacy.

It is not clear whether the Saffords had known of Bridget Bishop's supposed affliction of William Stacy at the time this incident allegedly occurred – about eight years earlier – or had only learned of the story from Bishop's trial in 1692. Nevertheless, the linking of the case against How with that against Bishop marked the first time that an executed person's name was invoked as part of a witchcraft case. In the future such linkages would become commonplace, particularly but not exclusively among people who, while confessing to save their lives, wished to limit their accusations. Whether Safford's wife had ever actually complained against Bridget Bishop remains unknown, but it surely seems suspicious that the one companion of Elizabeth How recalled on June 30, 1692, happened to be the woman who had just been executed on June 10. The twin functions of limiting and legitimizing seemed to be operating here.

Most of the remaining testimony in connection with Elizabeth How supported her, although Nehemiah Abbot, Jr., the 60-year-old man earlier exonerated by the accusers, did have some things to say against her. Abbot related that quarrels with Elizabeth How had led to strange things:

specifically, a sick horse and a sick cow, the latter managing to get loose. He had nothing worse to tell. As trivial in its accusation, though no doubt more painful because of the source, was the testimony of Elizabeth How's brother-in-law, John How, about 50. He testified that she had become angry when he refused to escort her to the examination; soon after, a sow of his had died under circumstances that persuaded him it had been bewitched. Moreover, when he had cut off its ear on the advice of a neighbor, his hand had become numb and pained (*SWP* II: 450). All of this he attributed to Elizabeth How.

As in the case of Rebecca Nurse, those who spoke for Elizabeth How had, by historical precedent, no reason to believe that such testimony was dangerous. Yet given the proliferation of accusations, and what must have seemed to be their randomness, it surely took some acts of courage to risk being accused themselves. Still, that courage did exist. Samuel Phillips, a 67-year-old minister from Rowley, described how he and another minister, Edward Payson, had looked into the fits of Hannah Perley and had been assured by the child that Elizabeth How had never afflicted her. Moreover, Phillips affirmed that Hannah's brother Samuel had been telling his sister to accuse Elizabeth How, and that he had rebuked the boy for it. He told how he had observed that it was "noo wonder that the child in har fitts did mention Goodwife How, when her nearest relations were soe frequent in expressing theire suspitions in the childs hearing" (*SWP* II: 442). Joseph Knowlton, 42, told how he had observed Elizabeth How carefully, in view of the accusations against her in connection with the Perley child, and had found her faithful, honest, and willing and eager to forgive those who accused her. His wife, Mary, 32, confirmed his testimony, and Elizabeth How's 94-year-old father-in-law described her as a dutiful, Christian wife, especially considerate of her blind husband (*SWP* II: 444). No evidence indicates that the ministers, the Knowltons, or James How, Sr., ran afoul of the law for their testimony. On what principle the accusers withheld their powers in connection with these people remains unverifiable, but there is a pattern: At this stage, as long as their powers were not directly challenged, the accusers generally showed little interest in generating new accusations. The community at large offerred a steady enough supply for them, as the new authorities on witchcraft, to confirm.

On August 27, 1692, over a month after Elizabeth How was hanged, her nephew, John Jackson, Jr., faced his examination for witchcraft. Family lessons had been well learned, and Jackson quickly confessed and told that it was his "Ant How" who four years earlier had bewitched him (*SWP* II: 469). He evaded, as much as he could, implicating his father, who had resisted confession; however, he readily spoke of witchcraft on the part of his dead aunt. Elizabeth How had become convenient for a confessor trying to avoid the horror of substantiating witchcraft accusations against his living father.

There is a postscript to the story of Elizabeth How, as well as to that of three of the other women hanged on July 19: Sarah Good, Rebecca Nurse, and Sarah Wilds. On September 13, 1710, the General Court awarded compensation to the family of Rebecca Nurse in the amount of twenty-five pounds, while the family of Sarah Wilds received fourteen pounds. The largest award of the group executed on July 19 went to William Good: This man, who had testified against his wife, was granted thirty pounds as compensation for her unjust death. Elizabeth How, Rebecca Nurse, Sarah Wilds, and Sarah Good also had their attainders reversed that day. No compensation or reversal of attainder occurred in the case of Susannah Martin.

The manner in which compensation was awarded for Elizabeth How caught the imagination of Charles Upham, as he reveals in an anecdote that Dickens might have loved. On September 9, 1710, the orphaned daughters of Elizabeth and James How, Mary and Abigail How, appealed for compensation for the improper death of their mother. They described how their blind father had gone twice a week to visit his wife in prison, each time escorted by one of the daughters, who had guided him as he carried provisions for her brought with much difficulty. The daughters asked compensation for the money spent on those trips, which, they said, could not have amounted to less than twenty pounds; but because what mattered more was the restoration of Elizabeth How's good name, they asked only for twelve pounds (*SWP* III: 997). On September 13, the General Court awarded them exactly that (*SWP* III: 1013).

To the image of the How girls leading their blind father to their condemned mother, Charles Upham brought the sentimental imagery that so proliferated in nineteenth-century writings. Even a twentieth-century person might succumb to the melodrama of Upham's portrayal:

> The sight of these young women, leading their blind father to comfort and provide for their "honored mother, – as innocent," as they declared her to be, "of the crime charged, as any person in the world," – so faithful and constant in their filial love and duty, relieved the horrors of the scene; and it ought to be held in perpetual remembrance. The shame of that day is not, and will not be, forgotten; neither should its beauty and glory.[51]

A more secular twentieth century, however, has not easily found either beauty or glory in what happened then, whether to Elizabeth How or others. The image of Sarah Good as hag prevails over that of Elizabeth

How as saint. The house associated with Rebecca Nurse, called "the Witch House" in the brochures of present-day Salem, abuts the cemetery with the nineteenth-century memorial inscribed to a sainted Rebecca Nurse; but youths dancing and drinking beer at this marker on the anniversary of her hanging more accurately reflect a contemporary sensibility that prefers memories of witches to memories of saints. In the gift shop of the house memorializing Rebecca Nurse — and it is in gift shops that we learn so much about our culture — souvenirs and books are mainly of the kind suggesting intimations of witchcraft. In the competing mythologies posing witch against saint, the devil's party has seemed more interesting. Blake's Milton was not the only one who tilted that way.

6

August 19, 1692

They protested their innocency as in the presence of the great God, whom forthwith they were to appear before: they wished, and declared their wish, that their blood might be the last innocent blood shed upon that account. With great affection [emotion] they intreated Mr. C. M. [Cotton Mather] to pray with them: they prayed that God would discover what witchcrafts were among us; they forgave their accusers; they spake without reflection on Jury and Judges, for bringing them in guilty, and condemning them: they prayed earnestly for pardon for all other sins, and for an interest in the pretious blood of our dear Redeemer; and seemed to be very sincere, upright, and sensible of their circumstances on all accounts; especially Proctor and Willard, whose whole management of themselves, from the Goal to the Gallows, and whilst at the Gallows, was very affecting and melting to the hearts of some considerable Spectatours, whom I could mention to you: – but they are executed, and so I leave them.   – Thomas Brattle, 1692[1]

It takes nothing away from the integrity of those who in July would not lie to save their lives to observe that a politically very unsophisticated person might conceivably have failed to grasp the equation of confession and safety from the gallows. However, such an oversight a month later seems impossible, so the August victims must have gone to their execution unambiguously choosing not to buy their lives with fraud. Given the probability that the July victims had made the same choice, the distinguishing characteristic between the two groups resided not in their choice but in their gender: Of the five who hanged on August 19, four were men. For the colony, this represented an extraordinary event. No man in Massachusetts Bay had ever hanged for witchcraft before August 19, 1692. Such punishment had always been an exclusively female domain.[2]

How it came that men should hang for a crime culturally associated with women tells us something about a changing agenda in Massachusetts Bay. Not that women ceased to be disproportionately persecuted – that particular miracle of witchcraft had not occurred; but in 1692 other agendas accompanied the misogyny that had historically driven witchcraft persecutions. The credibility of the accusers and the validity of the judiciary's actions required a treatment of men that brought numerous males to face the same choice confronting females: Confess and survive, or do not confess and hang. The hanging of five women in July visibly signified the colony's reversal of its historic response to witchcraft charges, but the August hangings of men more noticeably caught the attention of the elites. Partly, the enormous attention given to the August executions stemmed from the fact that a minister, George Burroughs, was among the group. Burroughs was a special target who would have drawn a crowd even if he were the only man to be hanged; but the presence of three other males punctuated the fact that something profoundly different was happening in Massachusetts Bay.

The August hangings brought a distinguished crowd. Samuel Sewall, the judge who would later publicly ask forgiveness for his role in the trials, recorded in his diary entry for August 19, 1692, the names of some of those present. There was Cotton Mather, which was most unusual: As Kenneth Silverman notes, "Mather rarely travelled and less than half a dozen of his letters are posted outside the city [of Boston]."[3] There too were "Mr. Sims, Hale, Noyes, Chiever, &c." along with "a very great number of Spectators."[4] Sewall's only other entry on a witchcraft execution was in connection with Giles Corey on September 19: Instances involving men caught his interest. On August 19 four men were hanged: George Burroughs, John Proctor, John Willard, and George Jacobs. One woman, Martha Carrier, joined them on the gallows.

I

Of the four men who died on August 19, John Proctor was the first to be caught in the judicial web. Through Arthur Miller's *Crucible* he is known by many as the man who got into witchcraft trouble as a result of an affair with Abigail Williams, whose age Miller changed to accommodate the play. *The Crucible* is an unusually good play, but it ought not to be thought of as a record of the Salem witch trials. The only known love affair that Proctor had in the last year of his life was with his wife Elizabeth, who was first accused of witchcraft on March 28. At that time, however, the unidentified accuser backed off when challenged by a neighbor and claimed, as cited above in Chapter 3, that "she did it for sport[;] they must have some sport" (*SWP* II: 665) – perhaps the most quoted statement in the history of Salem narration.

There was more than "sport" going on, however, and Elizabeth Proctor was formally complained against on April 4, along with Sarah Cloyce, sister of Rebecca Nurse. The complaint against Sarah Cloyce has generally been attributed to her angry conduct in regard to the accusation of witchcraft against her sister.[5] Elizabeth Proctor was probably caught in the net when the accusers took an interest in her through her servant, Mary Warren, perhaps at first as a way of drawing Mary Warren in; but other women named by Mary Warren were hardly confronted by such a collection of dignitaries as the group that came to the examination of Elizabeth Proctor and Sarah Cloyce on April 11. The attraction was Elizabeth's husband John, who on that date became the first man in 1692 to be examined for witchcraft.[6]

This examination immediately posed two conflicting imperatives: On one hand, the authorities had to face departing from the tradition of identifying witchcraft as women's work; on the other, they had to accept the charges of the accusers or else challenge their credibility. Male witchcraft was hard to believe. In the past, men had had sporadic legal trouble over the issue of witchcraft, but rarely had any serious consequences come from such encounters with the law. Still, the colony had never been confronted with a whole network of witches, but rather had dealt with isolated cases in isolated instances – one woman at a time. If a man, especially as solid a citizen as John Proctor, was implicated in this perceived network, the character of the outbreak would prove different not only in scope but in kind. Thus while one imperative said that such a man as Proctor would hardly be a suspect in an emerging collection of people identified as witches, the other argued that the accusers had to be telling the truth or else all other cases adjudicated so far were suspect. John Proctor became the pivot on which this issue turned, and whether Hathorne and Corwin thought they needed assistance to resolve the matter, or whether Deputy Governor Thomas Danforth decided on his own to come to terms with the issue, Danforth showed up on April 11, as did other prominent men: James Russell, Sam Appleton, Samuel Sewall, and Isaac Addington (*SWP* II: 661). For the first time, the chief examiner was someone other than John Hathorne: It was Danforth, who later came to have serious doubts about the judicial proceedings.[7] Presiding over the examinations of April 11, Danforth had the opportunity to shut down Hathorne's juggernaut. He missed the chance.

John Proctor, for whose case Danforth and the others almost certainly came, was not the first to be examined. That portion belonged to Sarah Cloyce, with John Indian confirming that she had hurt him. More significant testimony, a hint of what would follow, came when Danforth asked Abigail Williams whether she had seen a company of witches eating and drinking at Parris's house. Yes, said Abigail, they were having their sacrament. Danforth wanted to know how many attended, and Abigail said forty, with Sarah Good and Sarah Cloyce as deacons. Danforth then asked whether Mary Walcott had seen a white man. She had, one who "made all the witches to tremble" (*SWP* II: 659). Implicitly, this was Proctor, as head of the group; subsequently, such honors would transfer to someone, called a black or dark man, who was master of these women – an ambiguous presence, partly the devil and partly the Reverend George Burroughs.

For now, the questioning focused on John Proctor's wife, Elizabeth, whom John Indian claimed had afflicted him (*SWP* II: 659). Mary Walcott, the first of the "girls" questioned about Elizabeth Proctor, said, "I never saw her so as to be hurt by her"; Mercy Lewis and Ann Putnam responded with silence; Abigail Williams put her hand in her mouth and said nothing. John Indian, whose role tends to be slighted in accounts of Salem because he cannot pass as a "hysterical girl," then made his accusation against Elizabeth Proctor more specific, affirming that she had choked him. The Reverend Parris explained the silence of Abigail and Ann as "by reason of dumbness or other fits"; more likely it was by reason of their uncertainty as to whether they could safely accuse before Danforth as before Hathorne in spite of John Indian's lead. Their hesitation ended when Elizabeth Proctor denied knowing what caused the afflicted to suffer. "I take God in heaven to be my witness," she said, "that I know nothing of it, no more than the child unborn" (*SWP* II: 660). At this point Ann Putnam broke the spell, adding her voice to John Indian's in accusing Elizabeth Proctor, and the others went into fits.

The circumstances under which John Proctor was drawn into the proceedings have traditionally been confused because no warrant for his arrest survives. In a standard account of his appearance, Marion Starkey refers to him as having "come unsummoned to stand by his wife" at her examination on April 11 and having fallen victim that day to the remark of Abigail Williams that "'he can pinch as well as she!'"[8] This description is erroneous, however: The remark Starkey cites as having been made on April 11 was actually made on April 4, and a subsequent accusation against Proctor occurred on April 6. This means that, even though no warrant survives, Proctor had already been accused and was almost certainly expected on April 11.[9] The fact that Proctor had been accused on April 4 and 6 destroys the appealing myth, begun by Charles Upham, of the dutiful husband undone by defending his wife at her examination – although Proctor certainly did stand by her.[10] That Proctor had already been named is presumably why Danforth and the other dignitaries were there, and probably why the examination of April 11 is the only one for which Samuel Sewall recorded his attendance.[11] It was extraordinary to find a man so accused, and the subject of an examination even though he may not yet have been arrested. Such circumstances would be less extraordinary as time went on.

On April 11, after the tempo of activity had risen, after accusations in the midst of fits had come forth against Elizabeth Proctor, the accusers finally took the next step. Ann Putnam and Abigail Williams, during their fits, crossed the gender line and publicly named John Proctor, as Abigail Williams, and perhaps others, had privately named him earlier. The taboo against naming men at examinations had ended. Soon after, "some of the afflicted cried, there is Procter going to take up Mrs. Pope's feet. – And her feet were immediately taken up" (*SWP* II: 660). Presumably, this means that Bathshua Pope raised her feet, although one can only guess. At this point Danforth asked Proctor to explain why her feet behaved the way they did. Proctor responded by protesting his innocence, but Abigail Williams announced that he was going after Mrs. Pope, who "fell into a fit." Danforth's approach, originally mild, became as accusatory as Hathorne's: "You see the devil will deceive you; the children could see what you was going to do before the woman was hurt. I would advise you to repentance, for the devil is bringing you out." Thereafter, Abigail Williams announced that Proctor was now going after Sarah Bibber, who, like Mrs. Pope, was a married, older woman; she too obliged with a fit. Then Benjamin Gould, about 25, told how he had seen John and Elizabeth Proctor, along with others, "in his chamber last Thursday night" (*SWP* II: 660). Gould was a man with a crowded bedroom, receiving visits there from Martha Corey, the Proctors, Sarah Cloyce, Rebecca Nurse, and a woman identified as Goody Griggs. In his troubled chamber also appeared Giles Corey, the second man to be named publicly, although he was not arrested until April 18.[12]

Danforth was new to this world of bedroom visits and other afflictions; Hathorne and Corwin had experience, and ordered the Proctors committed. Before matters would run their course, other members of the Proctor family would be accused, including Elizabeth Proctor's mother, Sarah Basset; Mary DeRich, another daughter of Sarah Basset; and Benjamin, William, and Sarah Proctor, children of John and Elizabeth. Mary Withridge, who would marry Benjamin Proctor in 1694, was also accused, as was her mother, Sarah Buckley.[13] Of the Proctor family only John DeRich became a confessor and accuser.

The testimony marshaled against John Proctor consists primarily of accusations from the regular accusers. There are no stories of dying cows or accounts of events in years gone by. The most comparable item comes from Joseph Bayley, age 44: While journeying with his wife on May 25, he testified, he had seen the Proctors' house and had immediately been struck with a hard blow to his breast and a pain in the stomach. Seeing John Proctor at the window, he had noted this to his wife, but she had seen only a little maid there. Looking again, he had failed to see any maid, only Elizabeth Proctor. Each time they had seen something else. Down the road a little Bayley had been struck speechless and felt another blow to the breast. Then he had seen an unidentified woman coming toward him, a person his wife had not seen. When he had looked again from his horse, he had seen a cow where the woman had been. His journey then continued without further incident, but once home he had suffered for an unspecified period of time some nipping and pinching from an invisible source – "but now through gods goodness to me I am well again" (*SWP* II: 674). Bayley's wife swore to the testimony. His story seems plausible enough if one assumes some kind of jitteriness or panic response to the whole fear of witchcraft, and if one hypothesizes what might have been a panic or heart attack or some other physiological onslaught.

Little else in this case suggests the herd impulse of the accusers against the accused; that Proctor was a male, and the first one at that, may have something to do with this. Subsequently, of course, his name surfaced in a variety of other cases as he became an appropriate target for confessors and others joining accusers. Spectral sightings of John Proctor, as well as of Elizabeth, became plentiful, but there is scant material as to old offenses, remembered or invented. What does survive is the often mentioned account of his personal response to what he clearly believed were feigned fits: Samuel Sibley tells the story of how Proctor announced his intention to fetch his "jade," Mary Warren, who had remained in Salem Village over the night of March 24, the day of Rebecca Nurse's examination; the accusers needed a whipping lest everyone be accused, and he would do his share with Mary Warren. Proctor also suggested hanging the accusers, and told how, when Mary had had her first fits, hard work and the threat of a thrashing had cured her until the next day when, away from home, he could not supervise her (*SWP* II: 683–4).

The indictment against John Proctor for afflicting Mary Warren is the most unusual record of his case. The formulaic charge, citing the pining, consuming, and wasting of a person, refers to March 26 – not April 11, the date of his examination. All other surviving indictments of Proctor have the same formula but are dated April 11. We may therefore speculate that on March 26 Proctor managed to round up Mary Warren and bring her home for her thrashing, thereby offering a powerful affront to the legitimacy of the proceedings that may have led to the unusual indictment.

Proctor received support from within the community, as had some of the other victims of accusation. The men who examined his body for witch marks found none. Thirty-one people signed a petition stating their belief that they had never seen anything in the conduct of John or Elizabeth Proctor to suggest witchcraft, and reminding the Court of Assistants sitting in Boston of the devil's power to impersonate people "& therby abuse Inocents," though, of course, with the permission of God (*SWP* II: 681). They invoked the story of God's permission to the devil to torment Job, and that of Samuel and the Witch of Endor.[14] The Job approach was a novelty, but Samuel and the Witch of Endor had been invoked before.

Proctor, realizing that neither the judiciary nor the local clergy would help him, made his appeal on July 23 to a group of Boston ministers: Increase Mather, James Allen, Joshua Moody, Samuel Willard, and John Bailey.[15] Proctor took the view that the devil was behind the enmity of the accusers, the judges, and the jury; but he offered a secular rather than a theological solution to this situation, recommending that the trials be moved to Boston or, failing that, that the judges be changed. He also urged the ministers to attend the trials in the hope that this could end "the shedding our Innocent Bloods" (*SWP* II: 690). Whether the ministers ever received his plea is unknown. We know of nothing that came of it.

The August executions proceeded, with Elizabeth surviving because of pregnancy. On January 27, 1693, if Sidney Perley is correct, Elizabeth Proctor gave birth to a son, John.[16] Elizabeth Proctor later married again and went on with her life;[17] but that life involved a long legal struggle to regain her estate. On July 20, 1703, in response to a petition by a group of people from Andover, Salem Village, and Topsfield, the attainder against John and Elizabeth Proctor and others was reversed (*SWP* III: 966, 970). This freed Elizabeth to pursue her case, and in an order by Governor Dudley on December 17, 1711, she and her deceased husband were awarded 150 pounds (*SWP* III: 1017). This was by far the largest sum of money authorized that day by Dudley to any of the victims, with the estate of George Jacobs, Sr., coming in second at 79 pounds. The large award for Elizabeth raises some tantalizing possibilities.

In 1696 Elizabeth Proctor, widow, petitioned the court regarding a will of John Proctor's that had disinherited Elizabeth. As she told it,

> in that sad time of darkness before my said husband was executed it is evident som body had Contrived awill and brought it to him to sign wher in his wholl estat is disposed of not having Regard to a contract in wrighting mad with me before mariag with him . . . [and] sinc my husband's death the s'd will is proved and approved by the Judg of probate and by that kind of desposall the wholl estat is disposed of.[18]

Perhaps someone had forced Proctor to sign the will; perhaps someone had forged it; or, as David L. Greene suggests, perhaps Proctor had not included her in his will because "she was under conviction and in the eyes of the law had no legal existence."[19] That he had freely written a will with the intention of disinheriting his wife seems highly improbable, as nothing in the record suggests that John was anything but a responsible husband to his wife. Yet the will did change, and coercion or trickery against him remains plausible. Elizabeth apparently believed that some chicanery had been involved, as we can infer not simply from her statement to that effect but also because she named her newborn son John even after she had been disinherited. This line of speculation suggests that she did not hold her husband responsible for the new will and that she knew its contents at the time of the baby's birth. Her subsequent attempt at redress was hindered by her legal status resulting from her conviction: She was, as she pointed out in 1696, "dead in the law" (*SWP* III: 963).

The authorities, in granting her such a large sum of money, almost certainly believed that she had been wronged in the matter of her estate. Her view that someone "had Contrived" a will for John to sign seems believable, especially since nothing in John Proctor's relation to Elizabeth suggests a man who would disinherit his pregnant wife.[20] Still, we are left with speculation rather than confirmation. The eldest sons of John Proctor, stepsons of Elizabeth, were the beneficiaries of Proctor's new will; but whether they had in some way contributed to Elizabeth's predicament can only be a matter for conjecture. Had Arthur Miller wanted a tale closer to the core of what had happened to the Proctors at Salem, he might have found it in the untold family story behind the will.

We can only guess at what thoughts of unborn child and disinherited wife accompanied Proctor to the gallows, but we do know he did not die with the firmness of purpose so movingly depicted in Miller's *Crucible*. On that day in 1692, John Proctor, age 60, "pleaded very hard . . . for a little respite of time, saying that he was not fit to Die."[21] Though there would be time enough for the courts to settle questions of compensation, no time was allowed John Proctor on August 19. Still, Thomas Brattle tells us that Proctor died with courage and dignity, leaving ambiguous whether Cotton Mather had acceded to the plea of those on the gallows to pray with him. Perhaps he did so.

II

By the time John Willard was examined as a witch on May 18, the idea of accusing men had become a little less extraordinary. Giles Corey had faced the judicial system on April 18 at the beginning of his odyssey toward an unusual death and some fame as a folk hero. On April 22 Nehemiah Abbot, Jr., had made his mark in history through his unique exoneration, and William Hobbs had escaped execution, but not imprisonment, even though he had maintained his innocence at his examination. April 30 had seen the issuance of two pertinent warrants: One for Philip English, a wealthy merchant who would avoid the authorities until his arrest on May 30 and eventually manage to escape from the colony; the other for George Burroughs, whose examination on May 9 drew a host of dignitaries surpassing that present for John Proctor. Thereafter, the accusation or examination of men would no longer be seen as meriting a special crowd. Thomas Farrer had been examined on May 10, but he was not to be tried until the following January, by which time acquittals had become routine. George Jacobs, Sr., whose case is explored below (see §III), had also been examined on May 10; his son, George Jacobs, Jr., had been complained against on May 14, but he had succeeded in fleeing. May 18, the day of John Willard's examination, saw a warrant issued for Roger Toothaker, who would die in prison. As would be demonstrated by the lives of these and other men, the logic of events at Salem now required men to be included as victims in witchcraft cases.

Brattle reports that John Willard died well; yet a part of Willard's story suggests that, despite a great act of heroism, he did not always live so well. The testimony against Willard identifies him as an abusive husband, and it is that motif — excluding, of course, his spectral activities — that tends to define his case.

Willard adamantly denied the charge that he beat his wife, and asked that she be called as a witness to testify to this; no record of her testimony exists. However, one person, Aaron Wey, did testify in response to the urging of Willard, although what he said surely could not have pleased the accused man. "[I]f I must speak I will," said Wey. "I can say you have been very cruel to poor creatures" (*SWP* III: 827). Willard, in appealing to Wey, had turned to one of his relatives – an imprudent decision, since the family generally turned against him.[22] Allegations of Willard's cruelty appear in the testimony of Benjamin Wilkins, an uncle of his wife, Margaret, that "he abused his wife much & broke sticks about her in beating of her." In addition, Peter Prescot claimed that Willard had told him of beating his wife (*SWP* III: 827). If accusatory testimony must be received cautiously, there is no need to go to the extreme of discounting it all. We are not dealing here with spirits coming through cracks in the wall or people riding through the night on sticks. Nor do we have an isolated charge: A pattern of testimony gives credibility to the notion that Willard beat his wife.

There is another side to Willard, however – one that seems inconsistent with the depiction of a cruel man. According to Calef,

> John Willard had been imployed to fetch in several that were accused; but taking dissatisfaction from his being sent, to fetch up some that he had better thoughts of, he declined the Service, and presently after he himself was accused of the same Crime, and that with such vehemency, that they sent after him to apprehend him.[23]

Earlier, Willard had said of accused people, "hang them. they ar all witches" (*SWP* III: 848). Assuming the reliability of this testimony, we see in Willard an extraordinary reversal of position, and just why or where he drew the line remains unknown. Our sense of him is pervaded by the discrepancy between his initial promotion of hangings and his later endangerment of his life by refusing to bring in other victims.

Although he showed conspicuous courage in abandoning his charge to arrest people, and though Brattle says he died well, Willard's abuse of his wife makes it hard for us to elevate him to heroic stature. At the very least, we are reminded again that heroes do not always bear close scrutiny in their private lives. In fact, *two* of the four men on the gallows on August 19 were plausibly accused of wife-beating: The other was the Reverend George Burroughs.

The case against Willard was largely a family affair. The first warrant against him, on May 10, named no one as afflicted and probably referred to Ann Putnam and her friends (*SWP* III: 819); but the second, on May 15, specifically accuses him of witchcraft against Bray Wilkins, his wife's grandfather, and Daniel Wilkins, 17,[24] son of Henry Wilkins, his wife's uncle (*SWP* III: 820). The regular group of accusers, here as elsewhere, tailored their fabrications to the set of assumptions underlying the case. Willard, with experience in how the system worked, had fled after the first warrant, knowing by then that being male offered inadequate protection. On May 18 John Putnam, Jr., Constable of Salem, announced that he had captured the suspect, but Willard had apparently been brought in the day before. He was rushed to an examination on May 18, the sense of urgency developing from an appeal by Marshall George Herrick based on a stated desire to prevent further murders by Willard. The ostensible event was the death on May 16 of Willard's cousin, Daniel Wilkins.

Wilkins is reported to have suffered from May 14 until his death. A physician, "the french Doctor," diagnosed the cause as witchcraft, and on May 16 Mercy Lewis and Mary Walcott declared that they had seen John Willard participating in the killing of Daniel (*SWP* III: 821). A Jury of Inquest, held on May 17, described the corpse of Daniel Wilkins as being bruised, the skin broken in many places, particularly on his throat and one side of his neck, as well as one of his ears. His back was reported to show an injury equivalent to "the bigness of a small awl." The jury concluded "that he dyed an unnatural death by sume cruell hands of witchcraft or diabolicall act" (*SWP* III: 822). It seems not inconceivable that Wilkins could have been beaten to death. Willard, of course, was never indicted for the death of Wilkins, but rather for afflicting the regulars on the day of his examination. Mercy Lewis, Ann Putnam, Abigail Williams, and Elizabeth Hubbard convinced the jury acting on the indictments that they suffered at Willard's hands; but, astonishingly enough, the jury drew the line when it came to accusations for afflicting Susannah Sheldon, who finally ran into a group she could not gull (*SWP* III: 832).

At his examination on May 18, Willard pleaded fear to explain his flight and assured the justices that God would prove his innocence. Beginning with the predictable issue of why he was afflicting those who were putting on their fits, the interrogation then turned to the matter of why he was "murdering and bewitching" his relatives. The testimony here becomes murky, with Willard giving some kind of speech, in response to which he was told, "We do not send for you to preach" (*SWP* III: 824).

The reference to murder presumably refers to the death of Daniel Wilkins, and the bewitching to the case of his wife's grandfather, 81-year-old Bray Wilkins. According to the elder Wilkins, Willard, when first complained against, had come to Bray Wilkins asking that he and others pray for him. Bray had nothing against the idea but could not manage it at the time, and subsequently heard no similar appeals for prayer; however, he came to fear that he had incurred the wrath of his granddaughter's husband. Later, dining in Boston, he had seen Willard and Bray's son, Henry Wilkins, father of Daniel, join the table (*SWP* III: 847). Bray thought Willard had looked at him strangely, resulting in Bray's suddenly becoming ill, unable to eat or to urinate. He had immediately expressed his fear that Willard had caused the difficulties, after which "a Woman accounted skilfull" had examined him and reached a diagnosis not dissimilar to what the French doctor had discovered with the grandson, Daniel: She had blamed "evil persons" (*SWP* III: 847–8). After three or four days, Bray had gone home, still suffering. By this time, Willard was in hiding, and on May 12, while everyone was looking for him, Mercy Lewis had spotted his shape on the belly of Bray Wilkins, who had felt a pain that did not stop until Willard was in chains. His troubles remained, however, since he now could not control the flow of his urine. On July 5 – while Bray Wilkins talked about the Willard case, claiming that an execution would not be the fault of himself or his son Benjamin, but the responsibility "of the afflicted persons, & the jury" – he became severely afflicted, the pain returning and his urine coming out bloody. This condition continued for twenty-four hours (*SWP* III: 848).

No doubt a competent urologist could explain what was happening to Bray Wilkins, and there is no reason to doubt the severity of his situation, its exacerbation by real fears of bewitchment, and the sincerity of his belief in Willard's responsibility for the situation. Despite the severity of his illness, remarkably enough, he lived another ten years, dying on January 1, 1702.[25]

At Willard's examination, after the allusion to the Bray Wilkins affair and the "preaching" of the accused, Benjamin Wilkins introduced the issue of Willard's "unnatural usage to his wife": In the atmosphere of the day, even the battering of a woman had to take on some relation to the spirit world and be called "unnatural." Peter Prescot, however, brought the charge to the mundane world by simply telling "of his beating of his wife" (*SWP* III: 824). Subsequently, Willard was asked to recite the Lord's Prayer, which he failed to do successfully. Although ministers such as Increase Mather would make clear that such a test was not suitable for discovering witches, the justices and the folk put some credence in it. A baffled Willard could not explain why he kept stumbling at the phrases; he insisted on his innocence and, at the end, responded to the advice that he take good counsel and confess. "I desire to take good counsell, but if it was the last time I was to speak, I am innocent" (*SWP* III: 826). He maintained that to his death.

The surviving documents show almost all of the witnesses, other than the regulars, related to Willard. Some focused on the abusive treatment of his wife, as did Lydia Nichols, 46, Margaret Knight, 20, and Thomas Bailey, 36, all related to Willard (*SWP* III: 842, 844). Other charges from the family included more invisible phenomena: Samuel Wilkins, age 19, claimed that he had become afflicted since Willard's imprisonment; that others said bewitchment stopped when a witch was imprisoned seemed not to matter. Samuel also told of being accosted by the specter of the imprisoned Willard, of being chased by a black hat, and of Willard appearing in his bedroom – a favorite haunt of specters, as we know (*SWP* III: 843). Rebecca Wilkins, also 19, similarly told of a spectral affliction by Willard (*SWP* III: 845). Henry Wilkins, 41, told how the troubles leading to the death of his son, Daniel, had occurred, relating that on May 3 Daniel had said that Willard should be hanged; a few days later he had become sick, remaining so until he died. Mercy Lewis, he reported, along with Ann Putnam and Mary Walcott, had told him that they had seen the specter of Willard on his son (*SWP* III: 846).

Ann Putnam, Sr., added her voice against Willard. In a deposition on June 2, she told how the shapes of Samuel Fuller and Lydia Wilkins had come to her bedside threatening to tear her to pieces if she did not tell Hathorne that Willard had murdered them. The shape of John Willard had made an appearance "at the same time," corroborating their charge (*SWP* III: 839). Willard had then told of a string of murders, mostly of people related to the Wilkins family. Samuel Fuller and Lydia Wilkins, or at least their shapes, had made an additional threat; namely, that if Hathorne did not believe them, the two would appear to the magistrate. The matter seems not to have been tested.

In the array of shapely charges and confessions came the accusation that probably brought Ann Putnam, Sr., into the case: that of Willard having killed her 6-week-old daughter, Sarah. Perhaps she went after Willard because, like Daniel Wilkins, Sarah may have been beaten to death;[26] if so, then Willard – by reputation, and probably in fact, a man who brutally beat his wife – became a logical enough candidate to take the blame for the beating death of Sarah Putnam. Better to have spirits as the abusers of children. Other victims named by Ann Putnam, Sr., were primarily identified as someone's child, including "Aron Ways Child & Ben: fullers Child & this deponents Child. Sarah 6 weeks old & Phillips Knights Child . . . & Jonathan Knights Child & 2 of Ezek: Cheevers Children" (*SWP* III: 839). The killing of people's children was much on the mind of Ann Putnam, Sr., one of the few people outside the family who joined in the assault on Willard.

Willard's case, like that of John Proctor, involves no long list of people dredging up old quarrels. No one recounts incidents experienced ten or twenty years earlier. No neighbor accuses John Willard of having killed a cow. Future authors, looking for stories to tell of Salem, could have created myths of a man ennobled for having refused to confess a lie and for having declined to arrest the innocent, a man ideally suited for the stuff of heroes; but there are other kinds of specters, one being the battered Margaret Willard. It is her presence, perhaps, that has mitigated against legends of a heroic John Willard. Regarding him, our literature has generally been silent.

III

When George Jacobs, Sr., was examined on May 10, only two other men, with the possible exception of Thomas Farrer, had similarly been examined: Proctor and Nehemiah Abbot, Jr. Farrer, frequently referred to as "old pharoah," was examined the same day as Jacobs, but it remains unclear as to who went first. If Farrer and Jacobs had anything in common, it was that they were old men. Little survives about Farrer, but his residence in Lynn reminds us that by this time the accusers were looking beyond Salem Village. Farrer survived the Salem witch trials.

Jacobs was less fortunate. Arrested on May 10 with his granddaughter, Margaret, on "high suspition of sundry acts of witchcraft . . . Committed on Sundry persons in Salem to theire great wrong and Injury," he began his journey to the gallows (*SWP* II: 473). No names of the injured are indicated in the warrant, although other warrants against members of the Jacobs family clearly indicate that the injured included the regulars.

His chief accuser at his examination was his servant, Sarah Churchill. The frightened young woman had tried her best to get out of the web of lies, but threats of jail and worse had brought her to participate in the conspiracy. She told how Jacobs had afflicted her, and Mary Walcott quickly confirmed that she had seen the affliction. Jacobs seemed incredulous at the whole performance. He laughed when confronted with the accusation that he had afflicted Abigail Williams, and he asked of the justices, "Your worships all of you do you think this is true?" In apparent exasperation at their gullibility, he uttered his often quoted assertion, "You tax me for a wizard, you may as well tax me for a buzard," and he appealed to their reason by reminding them that the devil can take any shape. To this came the reply, "Not without their consent" – the theology of Stoughton rather than of most ministers in the colony (*SWP* II: 475). Jacobs was, in fact, proposing the sound theology of the day, the same argument that Susannah Martin had proposed a week earlier on May 2; both were ignored. In June the ministers would affirm "that a Demon may, by God's permission, appear, even to ill purposes, in the shape of an innocent, yea, and a virtuous man";[27] but the judiciary, very much concerned with theology as it related to the devil, would for several months follow its own views on demonology.

Did he pray with his family? came the question asked of the servant, Sarah Churchill. She said he only prayed alone. When asked why, Jacobs replied that he could not read. That was an unsatisfactory answer, and Jacobs was then asked to recite the Lord's Prayer. He seems to have known it, but could not say it flawlessly. When Sarah Churchill was questioned in detail about her signing the devil's book brought by the shape of George Jacobs, he vented his incredulousness and his frustration. "Well: burn me, or hang me, I will stand in the truth of Christ, I know nothing of it" (*SWP* II: 476). If Sarah Churchill is to be believed, on another occasion he offered his opinion of her in the often quoted remark that she was a "bitch witch" (*SWP* III: 702); but the authorities showed little interest in his rhetoric, his profession of faith in Christ, or his later fury at Sarah Churchill; what they wanted now was information about his son, George Jacobs, Jr., and his granddaughter, Margaret.

The examination continued the next day, May 11, primarily with accounts by Abigail Williams, Ann Putnam, Mercy Lewis, Elizabeth Hubbard, and Mary Walcott of his afflicting them. Ann Putnam and Abigail Williams had pins in their hands to prove it. The indictments, or at least the two that survive, were for afflicting Mercy Lewis and Mary Walcott on May 11. No record exists of the disposition of the indictment regarding Mary Walcott; the one concerning Mercy Lewis, however, shows that the jury refused to charge him in that case (*SWP* II: 478). A jury showed that it could make some discriminations, as one would with Susannah Sheldon's testimony against Willard a week later; but it was not enough to keep George Jacobs from hanging.

As in the cases of Willard and Proctor, the neighbors of George Jacobs did not rally to tell old stories of his having killed cows: Women seemed more inclined to bovine bewitchment. Like the women, however, he was examined for witch marks, and one was found (*SWP* II: 480). More revelations followed. In early August, Sarah Bibber testified that she had seen Jacobs on the gallows at Bridget Bishop's execution, helped up by "the black man" (*SWP* II: 481). Others among the regulars testified against him, with one of the motifs being that he beat them. The depositions of Mary Walcott and Mary Warren follow word for word on this point: He afflicted "Mary Walcot and beat her with his staffe," they both said (*SWP* II: 481–2). Although most of the surviving testimony against Jacobs comes from the regulars, 16-year-old John DeRich joined in.

The reliable Putnams added their voice, Thomas Putnam and John Putnam, Jr., describing the torments of the afflicted. As usual, the afflicted told of their afflictions. Nothing else appears in the record against Jacobs except a statement by 30-year-old Joseph Flint that is probably true: He testified that on May 11 he had told George Jacobs, Sr., that Jacobs's granddaughter Margaret had confessed.

> Whereupon s'd Jacobs said that She was charged not to confess and then I asked him who charged her not to confess, he then made & stop and at last said that if she were Innocent and yet Confest she would be accessary to her owne death[.] (*SWP* II: 484)

Jacobs had blurted out the truth before realizing how seriously he had implicated himself by unwittingly suggesting a conspiracy with Margaret in league with the devil. Collecting his thoughts, he clarified the point that false confession would lead to the sin of suicide. In telling Margaret not to confess, he presumably had known of pressures on her to do so. In early May, Jacobs did not understand the efficacy of confession. A few months later, when everyone understood it, people regularly urged family members to confess.

Margaret, of course, understood at an early date that confession meant survival, and the story of her confession and retraction has been told earlier in this volume.[28] Charles Upham's account of this story, the one that has most endured, tells of the destitute Margaret Jacobs forced to stay in prison after the episode had ended. Unable to pay her jail fees, she remained there until a generous fisherman named Gammon, presumably a stranger, heard of her plight and paid the fees that led to her release. Eventually, the Jacobs family repaid this kind man.[29] The story is difficult to confirm or refute. David L. Greene has argued against the account, pointing out that, when released in January, she had been in prison for seven months;[30] but Upham is vague enough about the amount of time that Margaret spent in jail before Gammon came to her rescue that the possibility of his helping the destitute Margaret in January endures. More likely, however, is the probability that Upham conflated Margaret's story with that of her mother, Rebecca Jacobs, who was arrested on May 14. No record of her examination survives, but we can infer that it was on May 18 since a surviving, formulaic indictment, here for afflicting Elizabeth Hubbard, mentions that day.[31]

Rebecca Jacobs had some kind of mental difficulty: There is ample testimony describing her as "crazy," an observation never challenged. Margaret describes her that way, and Rebecca's mother, Rebecca Fox, refers to her as "a Woman Craz'd, Distracted & Broken in her mind, & that She has been so these twelve Years & upwards" (*SWP* II: 496). Her husband, George Jr., escaped early on, leaving her and Margaret behind. He did return after the episode ended, and seems to have reintegrated himself into the family. Rebecca had survived, and in his will George left her the bulk of his estate, reserving two cows and four sheep for Margaret, now married.[32] Whether Rebecca Jacobs ever recovered from her mental affliction we do not know; but a surviving document indicates that the disturbed Rebecca languished in jail for want of fees, whether Margaret did or not. In his petition to the General Court in 1710, George relates how he had been forced to flee the country, and he tells how his wife and daughter had been kept in prison, Margaret for seven months, and Rebecca for eleven, well after she had been exonerated (*SWP* III: 997–8).[33] We do not know how many other exonerated people stayed in jail for want of a fee.

On August 20, the day after her grandfather died, Margaret Jacobs wrote her moving letter to her father. It remains a puzzle as to how she communicated with him in exile, and we cannot know for certain that he received the letter, or if he did, how long it took to reach him. The sentimental tale that Upham perpetuated, and that others have followed, is that her grandfather forgave her, changed his will, and wrote her into it. Oddly enough, this tale appears to be true: On August 12, a week before he died, George Jacobs did change his will, adding a bequest of ten pounds for Margaret.[34] As Upham tells it, Margaret probably visited her grandfather the day before his execution and received his forgiveness along with the legacy of ten pounds.[35]

Although the story of Margaret Jacobs has offered richer dramatic possibilities than those found in the story of her grandfather, legends about George Jacobs have probably reached a wider audience. Many from the nineteenth century to the present have discovered him in the 1855 painting by T. H. Matteson. Here, Jacobs, distinguished looking in his courtly red cape, high leather boots, and elegantly trimmed white hair and beard, kneels in dignified supplication before the stern judges in a setting of frenzied, accusing women. At the end of the same decade in which that painting was made, a tradition found its way into print that the body of George Jacobs had been retrieved from the common grave of the executed and brought home.[36] A grave had been opened and the legend emerged that the bones of George Jacobs had been retrieved from it.[37]

It is hard to say why Jacobs, whether in the apocryphal story of his bones or in his representation as a kind of persecuted English lord, proved so interesting to people in the mid nineteenth century when the myths were publicly presented. We may speculate that the veneration of bones owed something to the hagiography of the era, a similar burial tradition having emerged with Rebecca Nurse. Regarding Mary Jacobs, widow of George Jacobs, Sr., no mythologies have emerged. She seems not to have been accused, and remarried on June 26, 1693. Her new husband was John Wilds, whose wife Sarah had hanged on July 19.[38] George Jacobs, Sr., and Sarah Wilds, who died a month apart, had been ordered to jail on the same day, May 12 (*SWP* II: 474).

IV

Only one woman, Martha Carrier, went to the gallows on August 19. That some of the dignitaries who saw her hang would have missed the event if not for the men who shared the gallows with her is probable – even though on July 21 she had been dubbed by Mary Lacey, Jr., as a woman who the devil promised would "be a Queen In hell" (*SWP* II: 523). The epithet would be passed down through the ages once Cotton Mather recorded it in his "Wonders of the Invisible World":

> This Rampant Hag, Martha Carrier, was the Person, of whom the Confessions of the Witches, and of her own Children among the rest, agreed, That the Devil had promised her, she should be Queen of Hell.[39]

Mather, elevating her to a queen among queens, added the embellishment that her children confirmed her special status.

Despite this inauspicious start, Martha Carrier has had a mixed mythicization, ranging from Montague Summers's description of her as "a notorious witch and 'rampant hag,'" apparently liking Mather's characterization of her, to J. W. DeForest's depiction of her in his novel *Witching Times* as a sexually used victim of the Reverend Nicholas Noyes.[40] Yet there is nothing in the surviving record of Martha Carrier's history to suggest the popular nineteenth-century fictional motif of the woman used by the minister, the tale made most famous in *The Scarlet Letter;* nor does anything in her history suggest her as the grand candidate for the queen of witches. Only the rhetorical power of Mary Lacey, Jr., whatever her motive – enhanced by Cotton Mather's turn of a phrase – has given Martha Carrier this strange distinction.

Probably the most scandalous event in her life was her marriage in 1674 to a servant, Thomas Carrier, with whom she had had a child out of wedlock, thereby committing the crime of fornication – an occurrence not uncommon in Massachusetts Bay.[41] She had also had her run-ins with neighbors, but in exploring the lives of people in Massachusetts Bay, it is hard to find anyone who did not. As troubling as anything in her life, however, may have been the accusations of her children, which were real enough even if they did not call her the queen of hell. We cannot know whether Martha Carrier ever learned that the confessions and accusations from her sons Richard and Andrew were elicited by torture and threats; but we can guess that she understood how her 7-year-old daughter, Sarah, would have been intimidated and confused enough by the events around her to implicate her mother by confirming that a cat, identifying itself as Martha Carrier, had carried Sarah along to afflict people when her mother was in prison (*SWP* I: 196). Whether Cotton Mather knew of anything behind the confessions of Martha Carrier's children, we do not know.

Martha Carrier was arrested on May 28, examined on May 31, and tried in early August. The record of the examination is brief and normal enough. Ann Putnam, as she so often did, "complained of a pin stuck in her." Mary Walcott confirmed the sighting by Susannah Sheldon, recovering from a trance, of thirteen ghosts of people Martha Carrier had murdered (*SWP* I: 185). Martha Carrier was as helpless as others in a court where only accusers were officially credited with telling the truth. "It is shamefull," said Martha Carrier, "that you should mind these folks that are out of their wits." The accusers insisted that Martha Carrier saw the thirteen people, whom no one in the room could see. "You lye, I am wronged," she said, but the show proceeded. The accusers feigned unendurable suffering that could be relieved only when Martha Carrier "was ordered away & to be bound hand & foot with all expedition[. T]he afflicted in the mean while almost [were] killed to the great trouble of all spectators Magistrates & others" (*SWP* I: 185). If any of the officials wondered how it was that people whose spirits could crawl through crevices, turn into cats or birds, and defy all natural laws to torment people could be prevented from hurting the accuser by being bound and removed from the room, they left no surviving evidence of their doubts. Hathorne, Corwin, and Gedney appear either as the most unquestioning of men, or as men very little interested in finding answers to questions they might have pondered – or, perhaps, as men who by now knew the real answer.

Another possibility exists as to the strange response of the magistrates to the charade at the examination of Martha Carrier and others, one we find in Samuel Parris's "Meditations for Peace," a sermon delivered before his congregation in November 1694. Seeking peace in a community that by now took for granted that fraud had occurred, Parris sought to explain his role in the proceedings and to seek forgiveness for whatever mistakes he had made. Since he had often transcribed examinations, he asserted in his defense that "As to my writing, it was put upon me by authority; and therein have I been very careful to avoid the wronging of any." But this clearly did not satisfy his opponents, so on April 3, 1695, he added the following:

> I fear that in and through the throng of many things written by me, in the late confusions, there has not been a due exactness always used; and, as I now see the inconveniency of my writing so much on those difficult occasions, so I would lament every error of such writings.[42]

Parris, of course, did not record all the examinations, even if he probably transcribed Martha Carrier's; but, more important, he did record many of them, and his admission of errors in his transcriptions furthers the possibility that the characterizations of the judicial responses, and the responses of those in the examination room generally, could have been distorted. Although the judiciary certainly came down on the side of the accusers, they, or others in the audience, may at times have shown a skepticism not revealed in the documents.

This problem of narration occurs also in depositions taken at proceedings other than the examination, where we have no clear reason to believe that Parris was the transcriber. So, for example, in testimony against Martha Carrier on July 1, Elizabeth Hubbard and Mary Walcott at times repeat each other almost word for word. "I have ben a long time afflected by a woman which tould me hir name was Carrier and that she came from Andevor," says Mary Walcott (*SWP* I: 195); "I have been along time afflected by a woman that tould me hir name was Carrier and that she came from Andevore," says Elizabeth Hubbard. Elizabeth Hubbard asserts "that had not the Honr'd Majestrats Commanded hir to be fast bound I beleve she would have quickly kiled sume of us: and I verily beleve in my hart that martha Carrier is a most dreadful wicth" (*SWP* I: 194); Mary Walcott asserts "that had not the Hon'rd Majestrats Command hir to be bound fast . . . she would have quickly kild sum of us: and I beleve in my heart that Martha carrier is a most dreadfull wicth" (*SWP* I: 195). Such repetition among the accusers is common, and we are left to choose, from two major possibilities, the story we prefer: The first option is that the accusers rehearsed their claims and found an agreed-upon, accurately transcribed language. The second, more probable, alternative is that the transcribers shaped the gist of the accusers' words, whether for a sinister motive or through bureaucratic expediency.

If other testimony in Martha Carrier's case has been manipulated, it is less obvious. On August 3, Benjamin Abbot, 31, and his wife, Sarah, 32, told of a land dispute that had led to harsh words from Martha Carrier. According to him, Carrier had said she would stick as close to him as the bark to a tree and that he would repent of his actions before seven years. She had also threatened to hold his nose close to the grindstone. After that his foot had started to swell, and he had gotten a pain in his side that then developed into a sore. Dr. Prescott had lanced, it "& severall gallons of Corruption did Run out as was Judged & so Continued about six weeks Very bad" (*SWP* I: 189). Abbott unveiled his other torments, explaining that they had stopped with the arrest of Carrier, at which time he had begun to improve immediately. That Martha Carrier had threatened Abbott is plausible enough, as is his worrying about the threat. Nor is there any reason to doubt that he had had ailments – whose symptoms, perhaps, he had stretched a little – that, in retrospect at least, he had attributed to Martha Carrier. Sarah Abbot confirmed all that her husband had said, but added some unusual occurrences with cows, including their appearance coming from the woods with tongues hanging out "in a strange & affrighting manner, & many such things, which we can give noe account of the reason of, unless it should be the effects, of martha Carriers threatenings" (*SWP* I: 190).

Other testimony against Martha Carrier was surely less lurid than, say, that of the earlier witchcraft attributed to Elizabeth How, and nothing in the Carrier case forms a similarly structuring framework for the bulk of allegations. John Roger, 50, told of cow problems seven years earlier. Phoebe Chandler, 12, offered a more terrifying account of being frightened as she walked along by a voice she attributed to Martha Carrier. The voice threatened to poison her, and Phoebe concluded that the threat had been implemented, since a few days later she had had swelling on her hand and face. She had also been troubled with a great weight on her breast and legs. When Richard Carrier had looked at her in church – Martha was by then in jail and Richard had not yet been examined – the hand had begun to hurt again, her stomach had begun to burn, and she had been struck deaf until the last few words of the singing. Her 40-year-old mother, Bridget Chandler, confirmed that Phoebe had "Complained as above is Expressed" (*SWP* I: 192). Allen Toothaker, 22, nephew of Martha Carrier and son of the deceased Roger Toothaker, accused his aunt of having interfered, but unfairly so, in a fight he had had with his cousin, Richard Carrier: She had done it as a specter on his breast, disappearing after he yielded. He also observed that a four-inch wound had healed since his aunt's arrest, and he blamed her for the death of some of his farm animals, who had died "not of any naturall Causes" (*SWP* I: 193). Samuel Preston, 41, told of how two years earlier a quarrel with Martha Carrier had led to the loss of a cow, and to a later threat that he would lose another one, which he had. Confessors and accusers at other examinations and court hearings added various stories about Martha Carrier, but nothing they said makes her appear exceptional among the other accused – except for the sobriquet given her by Mary Lacey, Jr.

After her death on August 19, we hear of her again in a legal proceeding on September 13, 1710, when her husband Thomas asked for financial compensation and the return of her good name. He told without explanation how he had paid the sheriff fifty shillings; how he had paid the prison keeper four pounds and sixteen shillings for the cost of keeping his wife and four children; how he himself had had to provide for them in prison. He asked for seven pounds, six shillings, along with removal of the attainder (*SWP* III: 983-4). On that day a committee of the General Court recommended the reversal of her attainder and the awarding of the money Carrier had requested. That was all for the reputed queen of hell. On the same day, Mary Lacey, Sr., who with her rhetorical daughter had confessed and made up stories and survived, also received a recommendation for the reversal of her attainder, along with an endorsement for eight pounds, ten shillings in compensation (*SWP* III: 1013). Thomas Carrier had not yet received his money as of the following January, but bureaucracy in Massachusetts Bay was sometimes slow; it appears, however, as if he eventually did receive his compensation. The official story of Martha Carrier had ended. Except for Brattle's comment about those on the gallows dying well, we know nothing of her last moments.

One of those who died with her was the man Mary Lacey, Jr., had named as the person who would be Martha's monarchial companion, the king of hell. He was George Burroughs, the main attraction at the hanging, the primary reason why such a distinguished crowd also witnessed the death of Martha Carrier. She died in the company of the greatest prize that the witch-hunters had gained; but it is not likely that such a distinction mattered to Martha Carrier.

7

George Burroughs
and the Mathers

Our Good God is working of Miracles. Five Witches were Lately Executed, impudently demanding of God, a Miraculous Vindication of
their Innocency. Immediately upon this, Our God Miraculously sent in
Five Andover-Witches, who made a most ample, surprising, amazing
Confession, of all their Villainies and declared the Five newly executed
to have been of their Company; discovering many more; but all agreeing in Burroughs being their Ringleader, who, I suppose, this Day receives his Trial at Salem, whither a Vast Concourse of people is gone;
My Father, this morning among the Rest.
                                    – Cotton Mather, Boston, August 5, 1692[1]

I

However the Salem witch trials are remembered today, in 1692
the central episode centered on the Reverend George Burroughs. His case
brought William Stoughton into the proceedings before the Court of
Oyer and Terminer existed, and it enmeshed Increase and Cotton Mather
into positions inconsistent with their stated views on uncovering witchcraft. The search for witches became entwined with otherwise unrelated
theological issues.

At his examination on May 9, George Burroughs drew even more extraordinary attention than had John Proctor when the judiciary crossed
the gender line. After Proctor's examination, the handling of cases had re-
verted to Hathorne, Corwin, and Gedney; but on May 9, Stoughton, accompanied by Samuel Sewall, who would serve with him on the Court of

Oyer and Terminer, showed up to examine Burroughs, a minister exhibiting some objectionable theological conduct unrelated to witchcraft. Regardless of our cultural representations of people at Salem being persecuted for their beliefs, George Burroughs was probably the only person in the whole episode who fits this description.

The first question asked of Burroughs concerned the Lord's Supper. When had he last taken it? Burroughs, former minister of the congregation at Salem Village, answered that it had been so long ago that he could not remember. He conceded that he had been at church in Boston and Charleston where the sacrament had occurred, and he had not participated. When asked about the baptism of his children, he admitted that only the oldest had been baptized (*SWP* I: 153). Although other questions followed, none addressed such extraordinary matters. Here was a practicing minister – hunted down and brought back to Salem from his residence in Wells, Maine – who openly told the Lieutenant Governor of Massachusetts Bay colony that he neither took communion nor baptized his children.[2]

No evidence survives to clarify whether the accusers, or those who supplied them with his name, knew about this religious conduct. His accusation in the first place stemmed from earlier disputes dating to the time (1680–3) when as minister at Salem Village he had incurred the hostility of Ann Putnam's father, Thomas, among others. His former servant, Mercy Lewis, now lived with the Putnams, and whether she joined in the accusations against him because of personal animosity, or simply because she routinely joined in accusations, is hard to say.

An enemy of Thomas Putnam, George Burroughs fell victim to the village quarrels described by Boyer and Nissenbaum in *Salem Possessed*.[3] Yet good reason exists to believe that had Burroughs not engaged in his particular religious behavior, the charges would have been squelched. Ministers had some inherent protection, as we have seen in connection with the charge against Samuel Willard.[4] Francis Dane, a minister much less prominent than Willard, warded off charges of witchcraft even though his family proved vulnerable.[5] The examples of Willard and Dane suggest that Burroughs would have been similarly protected if not for his unorthodox religious behavior. That his conduct came as no surprise to his interrogators is clear from the initial questions addressed to him.

The behavior of Burroughs indicated something more than neglect of duty, suggesting two clear possibilities as to his behavior: one, that he had lost his faith; the other, that he held dissident religious views. The first, apostasy, would have offered unambiguous reason for incurring wrath; the second, dissident views, offers a more complex prospect. In the broad literature of the Salem witch trials, only rarely does one find Burroughs described as a religious dissident.[6] He may have been.

No information survives to explain conclusively the religious behavior of Burroughs, but in 1692 the failure to baptize infants had a very clear connotation in light of an old and lingering controversy with the Baptists. Missing the opportunity to take communion – as Burroughs had in visits to Boston and Charleston – and eschewing the baptism of one's children was behavior traditionally associated with Baptists, who rejected infant baptism and shunned churches that practiced it.

The history of the Puritan controversy with the Baptists was long and complex, but by 1692 the power to suppress Baptist theology had almost completely evaporated. When Governor Phips ordered the arrest of William Milborne on June 25, he did so in response to Milborne's objections to the witchcraft proceedings and not because he happened to be a Baptist minister.[7] Such a ministry was legal in 1692; but legality did not imply Puritan satisfaction with the situation.

Although the Puritans had generally persecuted religious dissenters, the Baptists created an unusually difficult problem for them: In general, they accepted almost everything the Puritans did, sharing their hostility toward Quakers and Catholics and their quarrel with the Anglicans, who created particular complexities because of the colony's connection to England. This made Baptists difficult targets for those who had an easier time gathering public opinion against Catholics, where no explanations for hostility were needed, or against Quakers, who aggressively flaunted their contempt for Puritan theology.

Baptists in England had found that they could peacefully coexist with their fellow Congregationalists, the Puritans, some of whom were writing to influential people in Massachusetts, questioning the persecution of such brethren. The key difference between the Baptists and the Puritans – both of whom were not only Congregationalists but also Calvinists – was on the issue of infant baptism. However, Puritan objections to people challenging their views in favor of infant baptism were not frivolous: Much of the turmoil within the Puritan community had occurred over that very issue. As Perry Miller and others have described over and again, the question of whose infants had the right to baptism and church membership had led to divisive, bitter quarrels within the community and – if the Miller thesis is even partially correct – was an important factor in the decline of Puritan power. Thus to claim that infant baptism contradicted scriptural authority represented more than a quibble. The British Puritans had not made an "errand into the wilderness";[8] it was a lot easier for them to be tolerant of what, in their context, was a relatively small theological point.[9]

Over the years, the Puritans had fought a long and losing battle against this dissenting sect. When in 1692 Increase Mather returned from England to the colony, he brought with him the new charter that required religious toleration, at least as understood in 1692. Although the charter did not go so far as to tolerate Papists, just about every other Christian sect received the protection of the Crown.[10] William Milborne could be arrested for challenging the conduct of the government, but not for opposing infant baptism. Although colonial Puritans had lost the power to stop the erosion of their theological dominance, they could still lash out at a more obscure minister whose conduct may have symbolized their passing dominion. George Burroughs could not be hanged for behaving like a Baptist; no law prevented his hanging as a witch.

Good evidence does not survive to clarify fully the religious views held by Burroughs in 1692, to explain why he did not go to communion or baptize his children; thus the true nature of his beliefs remains a matter of speculation. What is beyond a doubt is that his case introduced the subject of baptism into the court proceedings. Indeed, the word "baptism" does not even appear in any surviving document of the judicial proceedings before the examination of George Burroughs. Afterward, it begins slowly to emerge as a motif, eventually developing as a central part of the fabrications among some of the confessors. These confessions about "Baptism, and mock Sacrament[s]," as Thomas Brattle reported, played a major role in the continuing defense of the proceedings by "the S. G.," the Salem Gentlemen conducting the trials.[11]

On July 21 the baptism story flowered with an accusing Mary Lacey, Jr., weaving her literary spell. After describing Martha Carrier's future role as queen in hell, she was asked to name the future king of hell. She answered, "the Minist'r." No one asked her to identify what minister she had in mind: Everyone knew. The questioner simply asked, "w't kind of Man Is Mr. Burroughs[?]" (*SWP* II: 523). Mary Lacey described him as someone who came at times in his own shape and at times in the form of a cat. Then came the issue of baptism, introduced by her questioner. Had Mary Lacey, Jr., ever been baptized? Yes, she replied. Had the devil asked her to renounce that baptism and to renounce God? Yes, the devil had told her not to keep God's word and to deny her own baptism. He wanted her baptized again, but Mary assured the questioner that she had refused. Had she ever seen anyone baptized by the devil? No, she had not, although she agreed that she had seen the devil's sacrament at the village. Her examiners, Hathorne, Gedney, and Corwin, joined by the minister, John Higginson, were probing the baptism issue here and moving closer to the revelation of an actual baptism by the devil. The search for witches had conflated demonic parody of Christianity with hostility to Baptists. George Burroughs came to symbolize this amalgam.

The questioning continued, with Mary Lacey, Sr., being asked not whether she had been to the baptism at Newberry Falls of an accused woman, Mary Bradbury, but how she had gotten there. That the devil had carried her in his arms is less interesting to us than that she, on July 21, had affirmed that demonic baptisms were occurring. The devil, of course, needed a nice body of water like Newberry Falls: He, like the Baptists, used immersion. He also needed a minister.

In her confession, Mary Lacey, Sr., told how her mother, Ann Foster, herself, and Martha Carrier had ridden toward Salem Village on a pole, which had broken en route. (Whether they had ever reached their destination after this airborne difficulty remains untold.) In her confession Mary Sr. offered a more specific narrative about an incident of three or four years earlier, when she claimed to have seen Mary Bradbury, Elizabeth How, and Rebecca Nurse "Baptised by the old Serpent at newburry falls" (*SWP* II: 514). This the devil did by dipping their heads in the water. Two days before this confession, Elizabeth How and Rebecca Nurse had hanged with nothing of baptism charges in the cases against them.

Later in July, as well as in August and September, others told stories of demonic baptisms. One of the more vivid accounts came on September 1 from 14-year-old Stephen Johnson, who told of having gone for an evening swim in the Shaw Shim River, after coming from work at Benjamin Abbot's. At the river he had seen the devil for the first time, and had been told that he must serve him and be baptized. Having already stripped his clothing for his anticipated swim, Stephen had been picked up and thrown into the river by the devil, who had said the youth must renounce his first baptism. This Stephen said he had done.

The total immersion described by Stephen Johnson was not typical in the baptism accounts. The more common rendition of partial immersion followed the tale of Mary Lacey, Sr., where the head of the initiate was dipped into the water, usually in a ceremony at Five Mile Pond or at Newberry Falls. Although the form of immersion varied, the ritual, differing from the Puritan method of aspersion or sprinkling, always carried with it the innovation that the devil had introduced in July: His newly baptized converts had renounced their former baptism. Baptists, of course, implicitly had to renounce infant baptism, since they denied that such baptism could occur. As Samuel Willard would write in his monumental treatise, *A Compleat Body of Divinity,* "they disown the Baptism of Infants, and will not acknowledge them to be Baptized at all."[12] It requires very little imagination to observe the implied association of the practices of a dissenting sect struggling for legitimacy with practices now attributed to the devil: The Baptists and the devil alike wanted people to renounce that first baptism.

Yet why had there been no such stories earlier? How do we account for the lapse in time between May 9, when Burroughs was asked about the baptism of his children, and July 21, when Mary Lacey, Sr., confirmed that the devil conducted rebaptisms? The answer is probably to be found in the shift that had occurred from Salem Village to Andover, when confessions accelerated with the growing understanding that such cooperation offered safety from the gallows. As this became clearer, the embellishments of the stories grew: The more lurid the account, presumably the more trustworthy the confession. Even the accusers stretched their stories further. The celebrated account of Mercy Lewis, where

> mr Burroughs caried me up to an exceeding high mountain and shewed me all the kingdoms of the earth and tould me that he would give them all to me if I would writ in his book

was not a story told at the time of Burroughs's arrest and examination (*SWP* I: 169). Building on Mary Lacey, Jr.'s creative image of Burroughs as king of hell, Mercy Lewis offered her own variation of the fiction on August 3. By then the underlying narrative of witchcraft in Massachusetts Bay conformed to a newer script required by the developing imperatives of confession and the introduction of the baptism motif. Mercy Lewis's grand tale of a trip to a "high mountain" notwithstanding, the new storytellers took center stage; the original Salem Village accusers became marginal, brought in at appropriate times to confirm their earlier stories, to swear to their previously stated afflictions, or, as in the Burroughs case, to confirm the summoning of witches by him to "a Sacrament."[13] The subject of baptism and Burroughs had reconfigured the narrative landscape.

It had taken time for the significance of what Burroughs had admitted on May 9 to sink in among the growing number of confessors; it then took time, apparently, for those asking the leading questions to decide to elicit such tales. The issue simply simmered until July, when it burst forth in the confessions of the Mary Laceys, mother and daughter, and those who followed them. That the Lacey confessions occurred shortly before the early-August trial of George Burroughs was no coincidence. Burroughs embodied old controversies with the Baptists, and in pursuit of him Cotton Mather embraced the confession of Mary Lacey, Jr., whose theology he utterly rejected.

On July 21, 15-year-old Mary Lacey, Jr., having declared Martha Carrier and George Burroughs as future monarchs of hell, was offering theological support for the judiciary in the debate over spectral evidence. Mary, who by her own admission had knowledge of the devil, denied that he could take a person's shape without that person's consent. Also, he had personally asked her to renounce her baptism and to be baptized again.

Cotton Mather, like most ministers, opposed the view of Mary Lacey, Jr., when it came to spectral evidence. As he stated two days before the hanging of George Burroughs, "It is the opinion generally of all Protestant writers that the devil may thus abuse the innocent"[14] – which was exactly what Mary Lacey said the devil could *not* do. However, the devil was behaving like a Baptist, and Mather, as shown by his letter to John Cotton on August 5, was happy enough to have Lacey as one of the "Five Andover-Witches" whose confessions justified the July 19 executions and implicated a company of witches, with "Burroughs being their Ringleader."[15] A man of great moderation was suddenly applauding a process he had persistently, though cautiously, criticized. The case of George Burroughs was recasting the agenda.

When Mary Lacey, Jr., told her story, the trial of Burroughs was two weeks away, and from that day to the end of the persecutions the tale of baptism became a core part of the story. Confessor after confessor, responding to what their questioners wished to hear, told stories of demonic baptisms with George Burroughs as the devil's chief agent. The backlash against the Baptists made him an exemplary monster and appropriate metaphor for what the orthodox saw as the ungodly religious wave of the future. Burroughs offered an opportunity for the ritual killing of an idea that had prevailed. The judiciary and some of the clergy, who had often been at odds over the proceedings, converged in agreement that George Burroughs needed hanging.

Burroughs, as a dissenting minister, offered so powerful a symbol of lost Puritan power that such moderate and influential ministers as Increase and Cotton Mather lost their way in confronting his case. Both had voiced views, comprehensible in their own day, critical of the proceedings; but both approved of the hanging of George Burroughs on August 19. How Increase felt about Burroughs's gallows companions is unclear, but Cotton, in his enthusiasm, endorsed the hanging of them all. The Mathers's approval was remarkable given their views on the discovery of witches. Just how dramatic a transformation is represented by their position on the Burroughs case may be seen by probing it in light of their stated theology.

On October 3, 1692, propounding views earlier expressed, Increase Mather gave an address that would be published in November as *Cases of Conscience*.[16] It is remarkable in its adherence to some legal principles of justice that would make contemporary civil libertarians respond with enthusiastic approval. Fourteen ministers endorsed this document.[17] As noted by many scholars, Mather's presentation was a significant milestone in bringing into the open the debate over methods of catching witches, and methods to be avoided. General agreement has existed that Mather's address helped bring the episode to an end; yet this agreement requires even greater attention to the paradox of Mather opposing the judicial practices of the court while at the same time approving the conviction of George Burroughs.[18]

Increase Mather was eloquent in endorsing civil-libertarian principles. "It were better," he wrote, "that Ten Suspected Witches should escape, than that one Innocent Person should be Condemned."[19] "It is better," he argued, "that a Guilty Person should be ABSOLVED, than that he should without sufficient ground of Conviction be condemned. I had rather judge a Witch to be an honest woman, than judge an honest woman as a witch."[20] On the matter of the danger of spectral evidence, he offered a powerful injunction:

> This then I Declare and Testify, that to take away the life of any one, meerly because a *Spectre* or Devil, in a Bewitched or Possessed person does accuse them, will bring the Guilt of Innocent Blood on the Land, where such a thing shall be done. Mercy forbid that it should, (and I trust that as it has not, it never will be so) in *New-England*.[21]

Mather had a stake in proving the existence of witches, since their presence refuted the skepticism about the spiritual world that was emerging so forcefully in Europe.[22] He certainly believed in the reality of witchcraft, but that very belief made him aware of how slippery a task it was to identify a witch. Citing Bernard's *A Guide to Grand-Jury-men . . . in Cases of Witchcraft,* Mather noted that the apparition of a person "'is a great suspicion'" but not conclusive for various reasons, including the fact that the devil can impersonate a person innocent of witchcraft – though such impersonation is rare, especially in cases before "Civil Judicatures."[23] Here was a view inconsistent with what the judiciary had been accepting. Had not Mary Lacey, Jr., denied it could happen? The authorities, who had been happy to accept her theological interpretation, were now being reminded of better sources for scriptural exegesis.

If specters were suspect, confession was the surest indication of guilt, an old view going back to Heinrich Kramer and James Sprenger, who, in *The Malleus Maleficarum* (ca. 1486), recommended appropriate means of torture to extract the confessions.[24] Mather, of course, did not echo their recommendation; in fact, he limited the usefulness of confession to self-incrimination. Confessors who accuse others, he said, "are not such Credible Witnesses [as those who accuse themselves], as in a Case of Life and Death is to be desired. It is beyond dispute, that the Devil makes his Witches to dream strange things of themselves and others which are not so."[25] Although Mather had torn apart the legal justification for the executions, he emphasized that he meant no criticism of the judicial authorities, assuring his audience that they were good people who acted wisely. The easy answer to Mather's inconsistency is that anything else was impolitic, and might also appear as an attack on his son, who defended the proceedings in "Wonders of the Invisible World." These reasons, though plausible and probably accurate, are incomplete; for if Increase Mather had condemned the proceedings, he would have had to condemn the result of the only trial he actually attended – that of George Burroughs – and Mather seems to have been quite content with the hanging of that dissident minister.

Having demolished the justification for the executions, Mather offered a postscript that absolved the judiciary, defended his son, and justified the execution of Burroughs:

> Nor is there designed any Reflection on those Worthy Persons who have been concerned in the late Proceedings at Salem. They are wise and good men, and have acted with all Fidelity according to their light, and have out of tenderness declined the doing of some things, which in their own Judgments they were satisfied about. Having therefore so arduous a case before them, Pitty and Prayers rather than Censures are their due. On which Account I am glad that there is Published to the World (by my Son) a Breviate of the Trials ["Wonders of the Invisible World"] of some who were lately Executed, whereby I hope the thinking part of mankind will be satisfied that there was more than that which is called Spectre Evidence for the Conviction of the persons Condemned. I was not my self present at any of the Trials, excepting one, viz that of George Burreughs [sic]; had I been one of his Judges, I could not have acquitted him. For several persons did upon Oath Testify, that they saw him do such things as no man that has not a Devil to be his Familiar could perform. And the Judges affirm that they have not Convicted any one meerly on the account of what Spectres have said, or of what has been Represented to the Eyes or Imaginations of sick bewitched persons.[26]

What evidence did Mather have in mind that conformed to his requirements for discovering witchcraft? The inevitable difficulty of recovering his experience is that court documents in all the cases are incomplete. Still, although much trial documentation remains missing, the traditional notion that no trial documents survived is inaccurate: Some are embedded in

The Salem Witchcraft Papers. The numerous surviving grand-jury depositions from all the cases were in fact used at the trials, as can be seen by
comparing Cotton Mather's narrative accounts, in "Wonders of the Invisible World," with depositional accounts in *The Salem Witchcraft Papers*.
Their similarity, at times word for word, clearly demonstrates that these
grand-jury depositions were part of the trial records.[27] (Depositions in *The
Salem Witchcraft Papers* given on trial dates but not identified as those of
the grand jury appear to have been first presented at those trials.) Thus, in
spite of some lost trial records, surviving documents do give us a reasonably good account of what happened at many of the trials, including that
of George Burroughs, here buttressed by Mather's "Wonders of the Invisible World."[28] Even some posttrial testimony against Burroughs survives.
By examining all the documents pertaining to his case, we can arrive at a
fair estimate of the nature of that case, and thereby evaluate the discrepancy between Increase Mather's principles and his position on Burroughs.

II

When George Burroughs was examined on May 9, Increase
Mather had not yet returned from England with a new charter and new
governor. He and Phips arrived on May 14; by May 27, Phips had set up
a Court of Oyer and Terminer, and the trials soon began. Since trials of
males for witchcraft represented extraordinary events, and since the trial
of a minister in the colony for witchcraft was unprecedented, the judiciary
moved with caution against Burroughs. It could count on a conviction in
court, but winning public opinion offered a more formidable task. While
the colony would readily accept the idea of female witches, the notion of a
male minister as a witch – indeed, as the leader of the coven – would meet
with considerable suspicion, even on the day of Burroughs's execution. To
bring Burroughs to the gallows required time. Between May 9 and August 19 – and even after his hanging – the case was built.

The case that was constructed – presumably without the involvement
of Increase Mather – grew partly from the coaching of witnesses. Such
coaching was something of a novelty at the time Burroughs first met the
legal system; later, it was a commonplace part of the pattern. At the examination of Burroughs on May 9, he was implicated by testimony from
a confessor, Deliverance Hobbs; but at her own examination, where she
had confessed, she had never mentioned his name. Between her examination and his, she had added new names.[29] Her daughter Abigail similarly
shifted her story to accommodate the case against Burroughs. Examined
on April 19, she confessed to witchcraft but, despite lengthy questioning,

made no mention of Burroughs (*SWP* II: 405–9): The only "witches" she named were Sarah Good and Sarah Wild. Examined in prison again the next day, she repeated her accusation of Good and added a "maid" named Judah White who had lived in Casco Bay, as had the Hobbs family and George Burroughs. Whether or not her family had known Burroughs in Maine – there is no evidence – Abigail gave no clue on April 20 that she thought him a witch, even though she confessed that day to having attended the witches' sabbath held in the pasture of the Reverend Samuel Parris. (In tales of others to come, Burroughs would be the man leading such rituals.) Examined yet again in prison on May 12, Abigail responded to questions heavily directed at implicating Burroughs. Although a confessor, Abigail at first denied knowledge of Burroughs as a witch; eventually, however, she obeyed her implicit instructions and named him (*SWP* II: 410–12).

The indictments that eventually emerged were typical. Four survive, and each one accuses Burroughs of tormenting someone on the day of his examination, May 9. Increase Mather attended the trial of Burroughs, so he knew the nature of the formal charges; whether he knew anything of the coaching of Deliverance Hobbs and others remains unknown, but such testimony, in any event, did not meet his criteria. For those criteria to be met – given that Burroughs did not confess – Mather would have to find two credible witnesses observing Burroughs practicing witchcraft. Confessing witches such as Deliverance Hobbs would not do.

The witnesses Increase Mather found "credible" were those who testified to the unnatural strength of George Burroughs. In popular representations of Burroughs going back to *Rachel Dyer* (1828),[30] few writers have failed to comment on his exceptional strength: Cotton Mather had referred to it in "Wonders of the Invisible World,"[31] and through the ages the story stuck. The subject is described for modern readers in Marion Starkey's *The Devil in Massachusetts*, which cites Burroughs's "extraordinary strength and agility," a variation of a tale often told.[32] Whether or not Burroughs was in fact unusually strong is difficult to determine. That he was a man who boasted of his strength, as Chadwick Hansen points out, seems clear; and these boasts "were coming back to haunt him."[33]

The surviving documents show that, with one exception, people did not testify to having actually witnessed his feats of strength. Thus, Samuel Webber, 36, tells how seven or eight years earlier, having heard stories of the strength of Burroughs, he then heard the minister boast to him that he had "put his fingers into the Bung of a Barrell of Malasses and lifted it up, and carryed it Round him and sett it downe againe" (*SWP* I: 160). Webber's testimony, given August 2, was probably part of the trial record, as was that of Simon Willard, 42, and William Wormall, age not indicated, on August 3. Their testimony describes how Burroughs had claimed he could lift a rifle with one hand and hold it, and how he had even described the way he did it; but he had not actually done it for them. Simon Willard, 42, told of how Burroughs had described his feats of strength but had declined to demonstrate them. These testimonies about the strength of Burroughs may indeed be honest and accurate ones, tales describing a man boasting of his strength but failing to demonstrate the achievements. The testimony became the stuff of folklore, and George Burroughs emerged in history as a man of prodigious strength. The only person who claimed actually to have seen Burroughs perform a feat of unusual strength was Thomas Greenslit, 40, who testified that he had seen Burroughs lift a barrel of molasses with two fingers in the bung, and a gun with one finger in its barrel, holding it at arm's length (*SWP* I: 160–1). Greenslit names other witnesses, some or all of them dead – the testimony is ambiguous on this – to corroborate his story. Yet this particular piece of testimony was given on September 15, after Burroughs had been executed and shortly before the execution of Greenslit's condemned mother, Ann Pudeator.[34] If he hoped to save her by offering a deposition against Burroughs, the attempt failed, and Greenslit hardly emerges as a reliable witness. The only confirmable witness giving "credible" evidence about *himself seeing* a presumed act of witchcraft, Greenslit did so with an obvious motive and after the trial attended by Increase Mather.

Mather noted that "several persons did upon Oath Testify, that they saw him do such things as no man that has not a Devil to be his Familiar could perform,"[35] yet no surviving document, except Greenslit's deposition, confirms this.[36] Could Mather have resorted to testimony after the trial? The answer was probably provided by Charles Upham:

> [Increase] Mather makes statements which show that he was privy to the fact, that testimony [in the Burroughs case], subsequently taken, was lodged with the evidence belonging to the case.[37]

The "statements" are, of course, those confirming that he heard witnesses who saw Burroughs perform his feats of strength. Upham is saying that witnesses against Burroughs appeared later. In the case of Greenslit, we know that this is true. Whether Upham had access to documents on this subject other than those surviving in *The Salem Witchcraft Papers* remains unknown; however, no trial record of "credible" witnesses against Burroughs on the issue of his strength survive. We have a record of his boasting, and some testimony after the trial was over.

Other aspects of the trial included routine matters as well as issues pertaining to quarrels particular to the Burroughs case. As in all other cases, issues not addressing the indictments formed much of the testimony. At the trial, Mather probably learned about the physical examination of George Burroughs by four men for evidence of witch marks on his body; it revealed no such marks in a procedure that Mather, in any event, disavowed as appropriate for the finding of witches. Other witnesses told of Burroughs abusing his wife. On August 2, Mary Webber, 53, told how seven or eight years earlier she had been asked by the wife of Burroughs to write to the wife's father in the hope of rescuing her from an abusive husband. Webber testified that Burroughs's wife had told her of a noise in her chamber at night, which "the negro," when called, had said he could not investigate, that something prevented him (*SWP* I: 162). Burroughs had then been called, and something had come from the area of the chimney and run down the stairs with Burroughs following it, "and the negro then s'd it was something like a white calfe" (*SWP* I: 163). Testimony given by Hannah Harris – a 27-year-old former resident of Burroughs's house in Falmouth – in reference to Burroughs's mistreatment of his wife describes abusive behavior but offers no suggestion of witchcraft. Cotton Mather, in his account of the trial, gives more details of family quarrels against Burroughs, including reports of his abusing his wives.[38]

On August 3, some corroboration of testimony occurred when Thomas Putnam, Peter Prescott, and Robert Morell confirmed that they had been present when Ann Putnam, Jr., was being tortured and tempted by the apparition of George Burroughs; but this was spectral evidence at best, and none of the three claimed to have seen the apparition himself. Again, there is nothing here that meets the test of Increase Mather; if anything, testimony from Ann Putnam, Jr., should have invited his skepticism. In a lurid account of a visit from the supposedly murdered previous wives of George Burroughs, Ann told how they had instructed her to report his crimes to the magistrates in the presence of Burroughs, and had threatened possibly to appear if he failed to confess. There is no indication that Increase Mather saw any specters when Burroughs insisted on his innocence.

Others gave their accounts of spectral visits from Burroughs, including Sarah Bibber and Mercy Lewis, Elizabeth Hubbard, Susannah Sheldon, and Mary Walcott. All of these testified on August 3, except perhaps Susannah Sheldon, for whose testimony no date survives. Also on August 3, Elizar Keysar, 45, testified that he, after arguing with Daniel King over the guilt or innocence of Burroughs, had been at the house of the beadle, where Burroughs was being held, and that Burroughs had stared at him. That night Keysar had seen jellylike visions in the chimney, but neither the maid nor his wife had seen them. Keysar concluded "it was some diabolicall apperition" (*SWP* I: 177).

One need not press the issue that the kind of testimony offered against Burroughs was less than adequate for a civil libertarian; but one cannot easily let go of the discrepancy between the rigorous standards of evidence set by Increase Mather and his willingness to embrace the conviction of Burroughs. So we have something of a puzzle: Why did Mather make such an eloquent case against spectral evidence, a case for strict criteria in the discovering of witchcraft, and yet conclude, on the basis of evidence that defied his criteria, that George Burroughs had been tried fairly? How could Mather have believed that he himself could have reached no other conclusion had he been legally judging the case? Lacking the kind of evidence required by his criteria, Mather could only lamely offer an assertion that "the Judges affirm that they have not Convicted any one meerly on the account of what *Spectres* have said, or of what has been Represented to the Eyes or Imaginations of sick bewitched persons."[39] He was grasping at straws, even dropping the pretense that it was the jury members, and not the judges, who were supposed to be doing the convicting.

Outguessing Mather's reasoning in articulating his belief in the guilt of Burroughs raises two competing, though not mutually exclusive, hypotheses. One is that Mather, while deploring the judicial proceedings, was reluctant to attack the distinguished judiciary conducting them. These were his friends and professional associates, with him among the most powerful people in the colony. None of Mather's comments, no matter how damning, ever faults the individuals who implemented the proceedings. He had the untenable task of faulting the process while asserting the wisdom of those who conducted it. Indeed, when the witch trials ended, he damned the prosecution and justified the prosecutors. The other hypothesis is that the hostility to the theological force symbolized in Burroughs was enough to overcome his legal scruples. Mather had been out of the country when George Burroughs, hauled in from Maine, was arrested and examined, but he would learn who had fallen into the judicial net, and would be forced to choose between his passion for judicial due process and his distaste for religious dissidents – in spite of his having assured the Queen of England that he tolerated them.[40]

III

Like his father, Cotton Mather had to trade off uneasiness with the proceedings versus support for action against George Burroughs. His principles for discovering and dealing with witchcraft were generally quite inconsistent with his passionate insistence on Burroughs as a justly condemned witch.

Cotton Mather, as all historians know, was not the monster reflected in the image of our contemporary accounts of the Salem witch trials. As a cultural archetype, he has served the role of personifying a demented, witch-hunting, Puritan culture. None of this is fair to him, although his egocentric and inflated estimate of his own value to the devil invites such caricature. Mather had concluded that the devil's attack on the colony represented a tactical response to his own spiritual efforts – a view, he felt, that others supported:

> Before I made any such Reflection myself, I heard this Reflection made by *others*, who were more considerate; That this Assault of the *evil Angels* upon the Countrey, was intended by Hell, as a particular Defiance, unto *my* poor Endeavours, to bring the Souls of men unto *Heaven.*[41]

Subsequently, in 1693, after most people in the colony wanted to forget the embarrassment of the whole episode, Mather continued his personal war with the devil and his battle to persuade people of witchcraft's continuing menace. In September of that year he records in his diary that he journeyed to Salem to gather material on, among other things, the late witchcraft so that he could record it for posterity.

> But I had one singular Unhappiness, which befel mee in this Journey. I had largely written three Discourses, which I designed both to *preach* at Salem, and hereafter to *print*. These *Notes,* were before the Sabbath, *stolen* from mee, with such Circumstances, that I am somewhat satisfied, The Spectres, or Agents in the *invisible World,* were the *Robbers.*[42]

A woman claiming to be possessed, Margaret Rule, told him that the notes would reappear, and they did, having been dropped on the streets of Lynn; they showed up in good order in Mather's hands on October 5.[43] The Margaret Rule story represents a separate episode that reveals both Cotton Mather's scrupulousness in wanting to prevent another outburst and his continued, faithful belief in the war with demonic spirits.

In 1692 Cotton Mather deeply believed in the reality of witchcraft and in the reality of a continuing war between the demonic forces and the people of God – the latter often led, in his own mind, by himself. Because in this slippery war one always risked being gulled by the devil, Mather believed in the need for exquisite caution, and he made no secret of the necessity for restraint lest the devil succeed in leading God's people to evil ways, including the shedding of innocent blood. To address the problem of witchcraft, Mather had suggested that "the *possessed* People, might bee scattered far asunder," offering to take in six of them himself to "see whether without more bitter methods, *Prayer* with *Fasting* would not putt an End" to the afflictions.[44] How vigorously Mather pursued this idea is unknown. Had it been accepted, we probably would not have had the Salem witch trials.

Although the circumstances under which Mather made this offer are unclear, his message of caution, as reflected in "The Return of Several Ministers," is unmistakable; but in the letter from Mather to John Foster on August 17, where no issue of collective authorship arises, we see dramatically Mather's alternatives to the methods of the court. In the letter, he unambiguously asserts that spectral evidence, though perhaps useful in raising suspicions, is insufficient for conviction: Any suspicions raised require confirmation by other evidence. Mather also recommends that if the judges have any doubts at all about the evidence against any of the convicted, they should give them reprieves; moreover, bail should be set "for people accused only by the invisible tormentors of the poor sufferers and not blemished by any further grounds of suspicion against them." Mather also offers in this letter the intriguing suggestion that a person whose specter torments someone could be taken out of the colony. Such action "would cleanse the land of witchcrafts, and yet also prevent the shedding of innocent blood, whereof some are so apprehensive of hazard." Mather even indicates that he would accept such punishment if his shape were to afflict someone.[45]

Cotton Mather concludes his letter by evoking a witchcraft episode in Suffolk in 1645 where "a famous Divine or two" addressed the court. One, Mr. Fariclough, after first establishing the reality of witchcraft, proceeded to show the evils of convicting people "upon Defective Evidence." The sermon succeeded and the episode ended with the result that "none were Condemned, who could bee saved without an Express Breach of the Law. . . ." Though it may have been that "some Guilty did Escape, yett the troubles of those places, were, I think Extinguished."[46] Cotton Mather shared the view of his father that it was better for some guilty to escape if this saved the shedding of innocent blood. If Mather eventually destroyed his reputation for posterity by writing his apology for the trials, "Wonders of the Invisible World," he had stood for and articulated views during the proceedings that, if followed, would have ended the trials. Yet he violated those views in his response to George Burroughs, on whose death he insisted. The account of Cotton Mather on horseback, preventing the crowd from rescuing Burroughs from the gallows, presents the most memorable description Robert Calef offered of the Salem executions. Although the account has been questioned by some distinguished scholars, the likelihood of its accuracy remains particularly strong.[47] No friend of Cotton Mather, Calef is a credible reporter here, not in spite of the hostility between him and Mather, but because of it. That is, Mather did not hesitate to repudiate Calef's charges or even to threaten him for false ones as he saw them; but he never complained about the account Calef gave of his role at the execution of Burroughs on August 19. On no other day did Mather come to an execution.

In Calef's description, Burroughs was taken to the gallows in a cart along with others. On the ladder, he spoke to the crowd, proclaimed his innocence, and prayed, ending his prayer with the Lord's Prayer, which "was so well worded, and uttered with such composedness, and such (at least seeming) fervency of Spirit, as was very affecting, and drew Tears from many (so that it seemed to some, that the Spectators would hinder the Execution)." According to Calef, the accusers, those who saw specters, announced that "the black Man stood and dictated to" Burroughs. Cotton Mather, "mounted upon a Horse, addressed himself to the People, partly to declare, that [Burroughs] was no ordained Minister, and partly to possess the People of his guilt; saying, That the Devil has often been transformed into an Angel of Light; and this did somewhat appease the People, and the Executions went on."[48] Samuel Sewall, who does not mention the part of Mather on his horse, does note in his diary on August 19 that "Mr. Mather says they all [Burroughs, Carrier, Jacobs, Proctor, and Willard] died by a Righteous sentence. Mr. Burrough [*sic*] by his Speech, Prayer, protestation of his Innocence, did much move unthinking persons, which occasions their speaking hardly concerning his being executed." If he drew the same inference about Cotton Mather stopping the crowd – "a very great number of Spectators," according to Sewall – he is silent on the matter.[49]

In sorting out the implications of what Calef attributes to Mather's conduct at the execution of Burroughs, the glaring accusation of Burroughs as "no ordained Minister" confronts us. In addressing the issue of the ordination of Burroughs, Mather evoked an old accusation against the failure of Baptists to ordain their ministers properly.[50] According to William McLoughlin, "The ordination of a minister had always been a touchy point in Puritan polity, and while in theory this right lay with the church members, the practice was otherwise." McLoughlin points out that by 1692 "a proper ordination required the presence and approbation of the ministers of neighboring churches."[51] At the simplest level, therefore, Mather told his audience that Burroughs really lacked proper credentials as a minister; however, a deeper debate lay behind the remark, for the question centered not on whether Burroughs was impersonating a minister, but rather his behaving like a dissident. A proper minister in 1692 needed the kind of ordination Mather had in mind; a dissident minister did not. A proper minister also did not pass up communion or neglect baptism, points implicit in Mather's subsequent condemnation of Burroughs in "Wonders of the Invisible World," where he pointed to "G. B's Antipathy to Prayer and the other Ordinances of God."[52] Whether the audience on August 19 fully appreciated Mather's attempted appeal to his version of Puritan orthodoxy, or whether the crowd missed the theological point, is probably not terribly important; what matters is that Mather welcomed the opportunity to make an example of Burroughs.[53] Did he not have a nice equation? A dissident minister in an alliance with the devil?

To confront this menace, this George Burroughs, Mather had to defy his own principles on witch finding, not only shutting his eyes to the reliance on spectral evidence that he deplored, but completely reversing himself on the efficacy of the Lord's Prayer in catching witches. Although his father rejected such a test – the notion that a witch could not properly recite the Lord's Prayer – Cotton had shown no such compunctions of his own. In his account of the Goodwin case in "Memorable Providences," he had stressed the inability of the woman accused of bewitching the children to recite the Lord's Prayer.[54] In other words, during the Goodwin episode in 1688, and in his published account in 1689, Mather had found such a test efficacious – and not just in this case, but "upon two more" as well.

In 1692, he still approved the idea. In his letter to one of the judges, John Richards, dated May 31 – just before the trial and execution of Bridget Bishop – Mather offered broad advice, including this on the Lord's Prayer:

> I should not be unwilling that an experiment be made whether accused parties can repeat the Lord's Prayer, or those other systems of Christianity which, it seems, the devils often make the witches unable to repeat without ridiculous depravations or amputations. The danger of this experiment will be taken away if you make no evidence of it, but only put it to the use I mention, which is that of confounding the lisping witches to give a reason why they cannot, even with prompting, repeat those heavenly composures.[55]

Burroughs was not confounded, and at his execution Mather lost interest in the test. He had found the local commander of the evil army, and he wanted him hanged. Like father like son: Cotton Mather, cautious and moderate in the whole witchcraft episode, had other criteria when it came to George Burroughs.

Of the advice in Mather's letter to Richards, Perry Miller has written, "Had the court heeded his recommendation, there would have been no executions; if, having made it, he had thereafter kept his mouth shut, he would be a hero today."[56] Perhaps, but how could Cotton Mather have been silent on August 19 when George Burroughs hanged? Father and son, Increase and Cotton, had spoken in terms, comprehensible in their own day, critical of the proceedings, and each had declined opportunities to name specific people as justly executed witches – at least until the hangings of August 19, when they both agreed that George Burroughs was justly hanged. Cotton threw in the others who also died that day: Holding the crowd at bay on his horse, he could scarcely have advocated discriminations of guilt and innocence among those about to die. Cotton Mather had chosen the imperative of establishing the guilt of Burroughs over the caution he had earlier advised.

Burroughs died that day, but Cotton Mather kept his story alive for posterity – a slanted version to be sure. Mather, who had written so often and so eloquently on strategies other than hanging for ending witchcraft in the colony, became the man who wrote the official version of the episode, "Wonders of the Invisible World," justifying what had taken place. That his written account could be accepted as accurate was confirmed by the approval of the chief justice, William Stoughton, and of an associate justice, Samuel Sewall.[57] Mather's information, of course, was from written records and from interpretations of such men as Stoughton and Sewall rather than from personal observation. He had not attended the trial.

"Wonders of the Invisible World" has been instrumental in offering the popular view of Cotton Mather as a rabid witch-hunter. As we know, that characterization misses his complexity; but there is more than one way to misconstrue what Mather was about in his defense of the trials. Perry Miller, in assessing Mather's role, comments on Robert Calef's charge that Mather "prostituted a magnificent conception of New England's destiny to saving the face of a bigoted court."[58] Mather did indeed defend the court; but he also had a further agenda.

From the nineteen people hanged, and the one pressed to death, Mather selected five cases for presentation. Four of them were women, the normal gender for a witch; but one was a man, George Burroughs, the first case addressed in the book. "Glad should I have been, if I had never known the Name of this man," wrote Mather. "But the Government requiring some Account of his Trial to be Inserted in this Book, it becomes me with all Obedience to submit unto the Order."[59] Pressure centered on explaining the case of George Burroughs: The "Government," as Mather tells us, *required* that a justification of the Burroughs trial be included in "Wonders of the Invisible World." No such requirement is stated for the others about whom Mather wrote in his apology for the court: Bridget Bishop, Susannah Martin, Elizabeth How, and Martha Carrier. Why did

Cotton Mather emphasize his need to write about him? Why had Increase Mather singled Burroughs out in *Cases of Conscience* as the one identified person he would have found guilty? The issue of religious dissent simmered beneath it all.

If Cotton and Increase parted company on how to handle witchcraft trials – the father's disclaimer of a disagreement notwithstanding – both had found themselves pushed by the Burroughs issue from their cautious, judicious approaches to the discovery of witchcraft. The implications were enormous: Before the Burroughs trial, the Mathers and the clergy in general had discreetly pushed to change the methods of the civil authorities, expressing essential differences with the judiciary over the legal response to the witchcraft episode. On August 19, however, Cotton Mather, astride his horse, offered a dramatic, visible, public symbol of the support of the prominent clergy for the trials. To get at Burroughs, he had to condemn all who died that day, just as he had had to declare the appropriateness of the July 19 executions; for had not the confessing witches, such as Mary Lacey, Jr., who confirmed Burroughs as a future king in hell, said that justice had been done at those executions? The credibility of these confessors could not be applied selectively. Wisdom in Cotton Mather yielded to passion. On his horse, he swept back not just the crowd, but a history of his own judgments in fighting the invisible world.

Although Increase Mather does not lend himself to so dramatic a symbolic representation, the issue and its implications are no less similar in his instance. While delicately telling the world of the fatally flawed trials, Increase Mather affirmed that the same system had justly executed George Burroughs. Could it be that, if not for the case of Burroughs, he might have issued his *Cases* sooner? Had he privately approved the conviction of Burroughs and the subsequent execution, sending the signal that the clergy favored the proceedings – even though he knew "that innocent blood was shed"?[60] Perhaps.

On another matter we need not speculate. By publicly endorsing the execution of Burroughs – explicitly legitimizing the claim of Mary Lacey, Jr., that Burroughs headed a satanic congregation – Cotton Mather announced by implication that, although the head of the group was hanging, there still remained an entire demonic congregation with which to reckon. It seems probable that this revealed fact explains why the next set of executions, those on September 22, brought the bloodiest day yet. The price of legitimizing the hanging of Burroughs was the endorsement of everything the court had been doing and the affirmation that there was a lot more of the same yet to be done. The court responded with expanded executions.

George Burroughs, around whom all this swirled, gives no indication of seeing himself in some larger context, as a pivotal case who would accelerate the execution of others. A candidate for martyrdom – as many in the nineteenth century would find him, despite stories of wife abuse – he could not justify his theology as a defense because the court never said his religious views were on trial. At age 40, flawlessly uttering the Lord's Prayer, George Burroughs went to his death a man who had forgiven those who had convicted him, certain in the knowledge of his own innocence. It is unlikely as he stood with the others – including his prophesied queen in hell, Martha Carrier – that he comprehended what must have seemed like an undifferentiating, demonic force that had settled upon the land. If he suspected that his religious conduct had something to do with his execution, he gave no indication.

IV

When novels began to be written in America, George Burroughs soon became the hero of one such early work, John Neal's *Rachel Dyer* (1828). Over the years, Burroughs would have other fictional representations, most notably in Durward Grinstead's novel *Elva* (1929), a neglected Freudian tale that compares interestingly to Miller's later *Crucible* in its sexual emphasis;[61] but of the many stories about Burroughs, none touches so closely on matters hovering around the case as does the rendition by Neal. Judging from plausible testimony we have seen regarding Burroughs's abusive treatment of his wives, the real Burroughs seems to have been not as nice to women as is Neal's hero: The would-be protector of two Quaker women, he appears as the defender of the religiously oppressed, a physically powerful person whose persistent orations on the law and justice turn the novel into something of a legal brief. He is, from the modern point of view at least, arguing on the side of the angels: Eloquent against bigotry and intolerance, challenging superstition and ignorance in connection with religion and witchcraft, he emerges as a martyred hero. He is also a man who lives in two worlds: among the Indian "savages" and among the Salem Puritans.[62]

Neal's characterization of Burroughs as a "half-blood," the product of Indian and white culture, draws on the persistent representation of him in the records and traditions of 1692 as a very dark man.[63] This darkness owes much to the idea of the devil as the "black man"; but it also stems from hints, bare suggestions, that Burroughs was not "racially pure." We have here that early American association of the dark person with the devil, with its racial and metaphysical implications. Although there is no evidence that Burroughs had been anything other than the child of white people, it remains no less interesting that in 1692 hints of racial contamination formed part of the mix in the identification of the most monstrous of witches as perceived by the authorities in power.[64] There is reason to believe that Burroughs was dark complexioned, as suggested in testimony given by Abigail Williams, who referred to him as "a lettell black menester" telling her in specter form of the women he had killed (*SWP* I: 171). That the devil appeared as a "black man" no doubt had something to do with a typology of demonism associated with darkness, but enough references like that by Abigail Williams to his "blackness" suggest that the innuendo of a mixed race at times fell on Burroughs.

Although Neal's tale fictionalizes Burroughs's conduct at his trial, it does correctly represent that the accused minister mounted an aggressive defense. Deodat Lawson tells us that Burroughs "had the liberty of challenging his jurors, before empannelling, according to the statute in that case, and used his liberty in challenging many; yet the jury that were sworn brought him in guilty."[65] Other clues about the trial, tantalizingly inconclusive though they may be, do survive. Hale writes that Burroughs "denied all, yet said he justified the Judges and Jury in Condemning of him; because there were so many positive witnesses against him: But said he dyed by false Witnesses."[66] Cotton Mather tells us that Burroughs presented a paper in court arguing that witches had no power "to Torment other people at a distance."[67] According to Mather the paper was "Transcribed out of Ady," Mather referring to Thomas Ady's *A Candle in the Dark* (1656), reprinted in 1661 as *A Perfect Discovery of Witches;*[68] but what else Burroughs took from Ady, and how much, remains unknown.

As aggressive as Burroughs may have been in his defense, nothing in his examination or trial indicates that he challenged the actual concept of witchcraft. While his views on the limited powers of witches, his treatment of his wives, and perhaps innuendos of a mixed racial background no doubt contributed to some sentiment against him, nothing matched as a central issue the matter of religious dissent – something Neal intuited no matter how fictionalized his version of the event. Another dimension of the case had little to do with Neal's tale: The trial and execution of George Burroughs, carrying the endorsement of powerful ministers, legitimized stories of a coven of witches determined to impose a satanic kingdom in Massachusetts Bay. This legitimacy made inevitable the acceleration of the witch-hunt.

8

September 22, 1692

[W]hat a sad thing it is to see Eight Firebrands of Hell hanging there.
— Reverend Nicholas Noyes, September 22, 1692[1]

The hangings of August 19 had offered fresh confirmation of a conspiracy of witches against the people of God. They also removed the last possibility for ambiguity as to who hanged and who did not: No confessor had yet gone to the gallows. A clear message appeared for those accused of witchcraft: Get out of the colony if possible, or, failing that, confess. Some did manage to escape; those who could not generally opted to save their lives by confession. Some even came to believe, under heavy psychological pressure, that they actually were witches.[2]

From the point of view of those who had insisted on the reality of a witchcraft threat, these confessions justified the prosecutions, and the army of the Lord appeared in good shape; but sociologists know of a syndrome called "the failure of success." As Cotton Mather would record in his *Magnalia Christi Americana* (1702),

> the more there were apprehended, the more were still afflicted by Satan; and the number of confessors increasing, did but increase the number of the accused. . . . [T]hose that were concern'd, grew amaz'd at the number and quality of the persons accus'd, and feared that Satan by his wiles had enwrapped innocent persons under the imputation of [witchcraft].[3]

The explosion of confessions and accusations had created a new and insurmountable problem, comprehensible even to the most fanatical on the court. Among so many confessors, how could the judiciary differentiate between an honest confession from a repentant witch and an admission from a frightened person dishonestly claiming an alliance with the devil and falsely accusing someone else? William Stoughton, head of the court and surely the most obsessive man in his pursuit of witches, was not trying to destroy Massachusetts Bay but to save it. How in the world could one get things in perspective?

In one way the answer was astonishingly simple, as we shall later see in the eloquence of one of the victims: Mary Easty framed the issue with such powerful lucidity that the court actually paid attention – not simply because of her powerful appeal, but because of growing skepticism among numerous respectable and influential citizens. Among other things, Easty appealed to the court to put confessing witches on trial.

In the early stages of the Salem witch trials, confessors were rare and highly valued. Each confession validated a previous act of the court, and to encourage the continuation of confession these people were either freed to join the accusers or not condemned when jailed. By September, however, a strategy that had proved highly effective in accelerating confessions and in exposing the witchcraft conspiracy was crumbling under the weight of its success. As the safety-in-confession concept took hold, more and more people encouraged accused family members to confess; in so doing they came to understand that, if in their case the witchcraft was a fraud, it might also be a fraud in the cases of others. The very confessions that earlier had validated the actions of the court now began to discredit the whole process. Something had to be done, and it was: In September, selected confessors were put on trial.

As if anticipating its diminishing power, the court accelerated the executions to hang as many unrepentant witches as possible before the process collapsed. In September the court executed nine people, including one who was pressed to death instead of hanged. Nearly half of all the people who would hang were executed on September 22; the ratio would have been closer to 50 percent if not for the escape of Mary Bradbury and the last-minute confession of Dorcas Hoar.[4] There were no further executions in the Salem witch trials after September 22.

Executed that day were seven women: Martha Corey, Mary Easty, Alice Parker, Ann Pudeator, Margaret Scott, Wilmot Reed, and Mary Parker. One man, Samuel Wardwell, joined them. In his complex case, we observe a man navigating between the old rules (confessors live) and the new (some confessors are tried), and the place of his conscience in this navigation.

I

The Wardwell case was a family affair: On September 1, Samuel Wardwell, his wife, Sarah, his daughter, Mercy, and his daughter-in-law, Sarah Hawkes, all confessed to witchcraft. Who brought them before the examiners is uncertain, since no formal complaint against them survives. Clearly, they were caught up in the surge of Andover accusations that began when Joseph Ballard of Andover looked to the Salem Village accusers to identify the witches afflicting his wife. By the time the Wardwell family was brought in, however, the main accusers throwing fits were no longer those of Salem Village: A new set included Rose Foster, age unknown, and Martha Sprague, 16. On September 1 four new accusers emerged: Samuel Wardwell, his wife, his daughter, and his daughter-in-law, Sarah Hawkes.

Sarah Hawkes limited her accusations to confirming the witchcraft of the Wardwells and their daughter Mercy and to naming two other males. Mercy Wardwell, age 19, confessed and briefly joined the accusers in the courtroom ritual of affliction by specter.[5] At the examination of Mary Parker the next day, September 2, Mercy joined others at falling down and otherwise acting afflicted in the presence of the accused; but though interested in saving her life, she had no stomach for sending others to their death, and she tried to survive with as little damage to others as possible. At the trial of Mary Parker on September 16, Mercy equivocated. She herself, she confessed, had afflicted Timothy Swan and had seen the shape of Mary Parker also afflicting him, "but I did not certainly know: that s'd parker was a witch" (*SWP* II: 634).

The balancing act for Mercy was more critical in regard to her confessing parents. At her examination, Mercy told a wild story about rejecting a suitor and being faulted by others for doing so, since they said she would never have such a good one again. The suitor had threatened to drown himself, which had troubled Mercy but had not yet led her to change her mind. Eventually he had shown up as a dog, explaining that he was "god & Christ" and that she should serve him. One of his requirements was that she serve the devil and, having been tricked into this, she had proceeded with her servitude;[6] but Mercy insisted that when she had signed the devil's book she had seen no other names there.

Mercy had avoided naming her parents, but she could hardly be a credible accuser without doing so in some fashion; hence she related how, in afflicting Martha Sprague and Rose Foster, "but Never any before," she was accompanied by her parents, along with Sarah Hawkes, and William

Barker, all of whom were confessors (*SWP* III: 781).[7] This was her compromise: Her parents had done some afflicting, but their names had not been in the book.

Mercy also confessed to being baptized again, an admission that was by now almost required of confessors. Only when Mercy made the baptism admission did the accusers express relief from her afflictions. Everyone was following the revised script. Having implicated her parents, who were subsequently sentenced to death, Mercy sought to back off without losing her status as a confessor. On September 15, she confirmed before Justice of the Peace John Higginson what she had said at her examination, but offered a qualification: "Marcy Wardwell owned all the above s'd Examination & Conffession (only s'd she did not know her farther & Mother ware witches" (*SWP* III: 782). Nor could she be sure by September 15 that confession still offered protection; she seems to have gambled, accurately, that it did.

Even the indictment against Mercy Wardwell reflected some movement away from the earlier protocols, since she was here accused of covenanting with the devil by renouncing her former baptism, being baptized by the devil, and becoming a witch. No indictment of her for afflicting a specific person on the day of her examination survives. It is even possible that none of the accusers even claimed that she had previously afflicted them: At her examination, their only problem seemed to be that they could not come near her until she concluded her confession. No one seems to have been particularly vehement about going after her; Mercy Wardwell had quickly done her duty.

So had her mother Sarah, who also confessed on September 1. She too had been baptized by the devil; additionally, she had been at a witch meeting in Salem Village where a minister was present – though, oddly, she did not identify him. Those she did identify were apparently confessors or, in the case of Martha Carrier, already executed.[8] Sarah Wardwell, like her daughter Mercy, sought to accuse as minimally as necessary. Her husband and daughter, she made clear, had only recently become witches. In a repentant appeal, she affirmed her wish "to renounce the Divel & all his works & serve the true Liveing god" (*SWP* III: 792). This bought her time, for her trial was not held until January 1693, when, under new rules, almost everyone was acquitted. When, for some reason, the court convicted Sarah Wardwell and sentenced her to death, Governor Phips reprieved her and the two others also then convicted, reasoning that these three had been convicted on no better evidence than the others who had been acquitted in January. Sarah Wardwell survived.[9]

Her husband did not. On September 1, Wardwell, in a move that he had every right to believe would protect him, confessed to his witchcraft. Except that he did not name his wife or daughter, things seemed routine enough when the 46-year-old Wardwell made his confession. He explained his entrapment by the devil as stemming from his discontents, including failure to get work and rejection in love, the latter twenty years earlier. Some cats and a man describing himself as "a prince of the aire" had promised him a comfortable life and improved social status (*SWP* III: 783). In line with the new imperative, he told how he had renounced his former baptism and had been rebaptized, in his case by immersion. In an unusual twist, Wardwell explained that his contract with the devil would expire when he reached age 60. Meanwhile, Wardwell confessed to having afflicted Martha Sprague, and he implicated Jane Lilly and Mary Taylor, both of whom were examined on September 5. Unlike his daughter, Wardwell did not limit his accusations to confessors; indeed, Jane Lilly refused to confess (*SWP* II: 539).[10]

Wardwell aggressively accused the two women at their examination on September 5, charging them with killing his brother-in-law, William Hooper.[11] All seemed to be proceeding normally, with Wardwell behaving as many others had done. The next step was supposed to be jail and patience while the stubborn people hanged – but something different happened in this case: Confession suddenly lost its efficacy, and Wardwell was put on trial.

The trial that followed – perhaps starting on the 13th but certainly on the 14th – featured testimony about spectral afflictions and accounts of Wardwell having told fortunes, along with a charge by Joseph Ballard suggesting preternatural knowledge of an event on Wardwell's part. One indictment, clearly based on his own confession, accuses him of entering into a covenant with the devil twenty years earlier. A few such indictments had appeared, but it is the remaining one that catches our interest: It charged Wardwell with afflicting Martha Sprague on August 15, two weeks before his examination. After the long pattern of indictments specifically indicating affliction on the day of an examination, this one suggests that the judiciary was backing away, ever so slightly, from its dependence on spectral evidence. That Wardwell was not indicted for behavior on the day of his examination represented an extraordinary shift in procedure by the court.

The details of Wardwell's trial are much less interesting to us than is his response to it. In a transformation invariably attributed to the workings of his conscience, Samuel Wardwell retracted his confession on September 13, thereby guaranteeing his execution, which occurred on September 22. Though it seems likely enough that Wardwell's conscience bothered him, another major factor was at work: Wardwell had come to believe that his confession no longer guaranteed his survival. We see this conclusion in his retraction:

> Sam'll Wardwell: owned: to the grand Inquest: that: the above written: Conffession: was; taken: from his mouth and that he had said it: but: he s'd he belyed: himselfe: he also s'd it was alone one [that is, it was all the same]: he: knew he should dye for it: whether: he ownd it or no. (*SWP* III: 784)

Samuel Wardwell believed he was headed for the gallows in any event.

He probably miscalculated. As late as September 21, Dorcas Hoar, who had maintained her innocence, confessed and received a reprieve. Hoar's case offers a good context for seeing Wardwell's probable miscalculation. Sewall notes that she had been scheduled for execution on the 22nd and that she was the first condemned person to confess.[12] Wardwell had seen the conviction and condemnation of Hoar as well as of other confessors. These were people who believed that they would hang, and Wardwell assumed that he also would hang in spite of his confession. Dorcas Hoar made a better calculation, and Wardwell's hanging served notice that a confessor could be executed. Nineteenth- and twentieth-century chroniclers have made a hero out of Wardwell for ultimately choosing conscience over fraud, and one would have to be mean-spirited to deny him the integrity he gained by choosing to tell the truth; but it remains the case that, from his point of view, the choice was between dying in a lie or dying in the truth. He chose the truth.

Wardwell was not alone in having to reassess his prospects in the context of a suddenly muddied situation. On September 17, of the nine, including Wardwell, who were sentenced to death, there were four confessors: Rebecca Eames, who had confessed in August; Mary Lacey, Sr., and Ann Foster, both of whom had confessed in July; and, remarkably, Abigail Hobbs, who had confessed in April.[13] Mary Lacey, Sr., and Ann Foster were probably selected for trial because they were among the five confessors in July who had received such prominent attention when they had confirmed the demonic baptisms. (Of the other three in that group, Richard Carrier and Mary Lacey, Jr., had won their safety through joining the courtroom performances of the accusers; Andrew Carrier probably escaped because of his youth.) Wardwell and Rebecca Eames, like Mary Lacey, Sr., and Ann Foster, had implicated themselves on the baptism issue. Only Abigail Hobbs seems out of place among the confessors tried, convicted, and condemned on September 17.

Hobbs, as we recall, had under coaching faithfully told her examiners what they wanted to hear about George Burroughs.[14] As of September 7 she was still actively cooperating, accusing Alice Parker of afflicting Mary Warren and Ann Putnam (*SWP* II: 628). Nor was there any last-minute renunciation on her part, as she once more confirmed her confession on September 9 (*SWP* II: 409). Why make an example of Abigail Hobbs?

At first appearance she might have seemed invulnerable. Not only had she cooperated early and continued to cooperate; she had been aggressive in accusing, even warning a resister, Rebecca Eames, that she would hang if she did not confess (*SWP* I: 284). No other person who joined in this kind of vigorous accusation went to trial. What was going on?

Abigail had turned 15 on August 7[15] and was certainly the youngest person tried under the Court of Oyer and Terminer. Although she was cooperative, her relations with the other accusers seemed unstable: Well after her original confession, she was brought in for a new examination on June 29 and confessed to having afflicted Ann Putnam a week earlier (*SWP* II: 413); no doubt there had been some falling out between her and Ann, and probably others. Additionally, testimony indicated her boasting of having sold herself to the devil (*SWP* II: 413, 415); but it was probably another charge that tilted the matter.

In undated testimony, likely from Abigail's trial or grand-jury hearing or both, Margaret Knight, 18, told of an incident that had occurred a year before:

> Abigail Hoobs.and hir mother ware att my fathers house: and Abigail Hoobs said to me Margaritt are you baptized: and I said yes; then said she my mother is not baptized. but said I will baptize hir and immediatly took watter and sprinckeled in hir mothers face and said she did baptized hir in the name of the father son and Holy Ghost[.] (*SWP* II: 415)

The court, coming under heavy criticism in September for not trying confessing witches, took the step of doing so. In fact, it went further, trying an active accuser, the only one ever tried by the Court of Oyer and Terminer. Although it did not go so far as to execute Abigail, the court nevertheless communicated the fact that not even accusers could be certain of their safety. It comes as no surprise that it chose an accuser and confessor at odds with the others but, more important, an accuser implicated in baptismal parody, her youth notwithstanding. In September of 1692, matters relating to baptism were getting a lot of attention.

Three of the four others condemned on September 17 – Margaret Scott, Wilmot Reed, and Mary Parker – were hanged. The remaining woman, Abigail Faulkner, had first been examined on August 11 and had maintained her innocence. On August 30, under further questioning, Abigail Faulkner persisted at first in denying the accusations, but finally offered a qualified admission, which was apparently not accepted as a confession. She escaped hanging because of pregnancy. What became of her six children, who depended on her for support while she was helpless in prison, is not known. Two of them, Dorothy and Abigail Jr., had testified against their mother.

Thus, of the nine condemned on September 17, five individuals escaped the gallows. Four were confessors, and one was pregnant. Of the four who hanged, only Wardwell retracted, making it clear that the court had struck a compromise: Yes, it would try confessors; no, it would not hang them.

Wardwell may in the end have learned too late that confession could at least buy time. The news of Dorcas Hoar's reprieve on the 21st revealed this. Under sentence of death she had confessed and named others; for doing so she received a reprieve of "one months time or more to prepare for death & eternity" (*SWP* II: 404). A waverer, such as Wardwell, may have wanted to enter eternity on better terms. The confessors – Rebecca Eames, Mary Lacey, Ann Foster, and Abigail Hobbs – stuck with their confessions in light of the developments, perhaps having intuited that holding to confession remained the safer course even though it risked unfavorable terms with eternity. Dorcas Hoar, of course, gained more than a month in escaping the gallows altogether.

For Wardwell, it seems unlikely that yet another retraction after the news of Dorcas Hoar's reprieve would have worked. Having miscalculated earlier, he was stuck with his decision. Perhaps he would in any case have wanted no more to do with false confessions. Of his last moments, we have Calef's account:

> Wardwell having formerly confessed himself Guilty, and after denied it, was soon brought upon his Tryal; his former Confession and Spectre Testimony was all that appeared against him. At Execution while he was speaking to the People, protesting his Innocency, the Executioner being at the same time smoaking Tobacco, the smoak coming in his Face, interrupted his Discourse, those Accusers said, the Devil hindred him with smoak.[16]

Of those sentenced to death on September 17 all but one survived. After twenty-one weeks in prison, and at a cost to her son Abraham of four pounds to pay her expenses while she was incarcerated, Ann Foster, grandmother of Mary Lacey, Jr., died in jail, condemned as a witch. Abraham was also charged two pounds, ten shillings to receive the corpse (*SWP* III: 992–3).

II

The Wardwell execution highlights the shifting response of the judiciary to the handling of the witchcraft episode, but it was certainly not the most unusual case to occur in September; nor was Wardwell the first to die that month. The rapid increase in trials that occurred in September was primarily directed, Wardwell's case notwithstanding, toward concluding cases that had lingered through the spring and summer. The confirmation of witchcraft through the spate of confessions led the authorities to bring to trial people who had languished in jail for months. The time for reckoning with the witches had come. One of those was a man named Giles Corey, who, according to Samuel Sewall, was pressed to death on September 19.[17] Three days later his wife, Martha, hanged.

The stories of Giles and Martha Corey are very closely related, but it has been Giles about whom more legends and stories have been told than about any other Salem witch-trial victim (barring the repeated account of Tituba as progenitor of the "witchcraft" events). The trials may have been mainly about women, but the legends of specific individuals, as opposed to faceless witches in Halloween suits, have been mostly about men, and about Giles Corey more than any other. (Only Burroughs comes close.)

Corey's tale begins with the accusation of his wife, Martha, who was complained against on March 19 for afflicting Ann Putnam, Sr., Ann Jr., Mercy Lewis, Abigail Williams, and Elizabeth Hubbard. The accusation against Martha Corey presented the first new case since the original examinations of Sarah Good, Sarah Osborne, and Tituba on March 1. Unlike them, Martha Corey was a church member and therefore a member of the religious elite in Massachusetts Bay. All witchcraft charges were serious, but the charge against a church member was the most serious yet.

On March 21, Martha was examined. Her church membership notwithstanding, Hathorne began the questioning with what would become his standard presumption of guilt. He asked her to tell him at once "why you hurt these persons" (*SWP* I: 248). She insisted on her innocence, asked to pray, and maintained that she was a gospel woman. To which Hathorne responded, "We do not send for you to go to prayer But tell me why you hurt these?" (*SWP* I: 248).

Martha had a strategy, however, and the story of how she tried to outwit the accusers has been retold in almost every narrative of the Salem trials. Her basic plan hinged on the subject of clothing, on something she had learned from the questioning of Tituba on March 1. At that time, Tituba had a great deal of difficulty describing the woman she claimed had afflicted her, and the question of the woman's clothing held a lot of interest. Tituba finally invented a wardrobe for the specter, who remained un-identified. Martha's plan was to show that Ann Putnam's claim of afflic-tion by the specter of Martha Corey could not be credible if the clothing worn by the specter did not match the clothing worn by Martha Corey. It seemed like a shrewd idea.

Martha's strategy comes to us through the account given by Edward Putnam and Ezekial Cheever. As they tell the story, they chose to test the accuracy of Ann's identification by using the clothing test. They testified that on March 12, in response to complaints by Ann Putnam, Jr., they planned to visit Martha Corey and confront her with the charges. First, they queried Ann as to what Martha Corey wore so that they could con-firm her identity as Ann's afflicter; but once Ann knew their intentions, she informed them that Martha Corey had blinded her. Cheever, Putnam, and Ann all knew what had happened at the Tituba examination. Though Ann's sight was affected, her hearing was spared, since Martha spoke to her. First she identified herself as Martha Corey, and then she told Ann that she would remain out of sight until evening, when she would punish her for her behavior. What Putnam and Cheever thought of all this is hard to say, but it does make Ann seem brighter than they were.

The two men paid their call, and Martha Corey raised the issue of clothing. Had Ann told them what Martha had been wearing? They relat-ed how Martha, when told of Ann's story of being blinded, had smiled "as if shee had showed us a pretty trick" (*SWP* I: 261). Martha's triumphant smile of having exposed Ann was taken by Cheever and Putnam as a gloating smile from a witch who had blinded the child to prevent her identification. By knowing of their interest in clothing without their hav-ing told her, Martha was proving herself a witch. That she was simply smart rather than a witch seems not to have occurred to them – at least, not if we assume that they were simply dupes.

However, if Edward Putnam was a dupe, he was a spectacular one, as we see in an account by him of an incident on March 14. Putnam tells how Martha Corey visited the Putnam house, presumably to talk things over, and how Ann complained vigorously of being tortured on the spot, and behaved accordingly. Mercy Lewis was also afflicted, and the two were reported in such distress that Martha Corey was asked to leave; but Mercy Lewis fell into extraordinary fits and, in the evening, as she sat in the chair, she and the chair were drawn feet first toward the fire. Putnam, seeing the potential disaster, lifted her with the help of two others and pre-vented her from going into the fire. Now, this seems more than a Susan-nah Sheldon rope trick. It is highly unlikely that even a very gullible man could be fooled by someone pulling a chair toward the fire, say, with ropes. Either she wiggled herself, and the chair along with her, toward the fire, or some unknown force pulled or pushed her there, or Edward Put-nam's testimony is not credible. He mentions two others as helping to rescue Mercy, but no names appear in the document as corroborating the testimony. Having Mercy Lewis move in a fit toward the fire can be ex-plained psychologically; it takes parapsychology, however, to explain the chair. This leaves open the reasonable possibility that Edward Putnam is not a reliable reporter, that he had an interest in supporting the claims of those charging affliction, and that maybe the story he and Cheever told was not an accurate narration of the sequence.

Whether Martha Corey's plight grew from collusion, coincidence, or serendipity, she was caught on the stand trying to explain how she could have known what the men had asked Ann about the clothing the specter had worn in afflicting her. Hathorne's questioning omitted such issues as whether afflicting shapes ever change clothes. It was all very simple. How could you know, Hathorne asked, that Ann had been asked to tell what clothing you wore? She gave some answer, unrecorded, to which Cheever and Putnam told her not to lie. She tried again, and Cheever called her a liar. Hathorne repeated the question, and at this point, either desperate for a way out or deciding not to shield her source anymore, she placed her trust in Giles Corey and said "My husband told me the others told" (*SWP* I: 249).

The pressure for an answer other than her cleverness was intense, and the one she found seemed safe enough. It was not, after all, a crime for a husband to tell his wife what he had heard in the village. Giles Corey sim-ply needed to confirm her claim. This does not mean Martha would have been cleared, but it was early enough in the proceedings so that Giles had no reason to believe that he would endanger himself by offering such con-firmation, and he might have believed that supporting her testimony could save her. However, assuming accuracy in the transcription, when Hathorne asked Corey, he denied that he had told her, and any chance that Martha had at this early stage of the examinations – any chance that the court's attention could be turned to the real issue of Ann Putnam's fraud – abruptly ended. Giles Corey may simply have told the truth, and Ann Putnam, who did not have the slightest idea what Martha Corey's specter wore, had turned her ignorance into triumph. Her credibility rose with this victory. Martha Corey, having been caught in an apparent lie, lost her composure and offered conflicting explanations that destroyed her credibility. Who knows what might have happened had her husband given another answer.

Giles was not finished with testimony about his wife. On March 24, three days later, he had more to tell than a simple denial of her account. This new testimony, though including no specific charges by him against his wife, had damaging connotations. The previous Saturday he had had difficulty praying until his wife had come to him. The previous week an ox had lain down and would not get up; also, a cat appeared to have died, and his wife had told him to knock it on the head, which he did not do, and the cat got better. Finally, he told how he had watched his wife kneel down as if to pray but heard nothing. As a report of their activities this seems trivial; in the context in which he delivered his narration, it was damning (*SWP* I: 259–60).

Although the motives of Giles Corey are out of reach, the storytellers have generally settled for a version that has Giles as a believer in the early proceedings, caught up in them even to the point of in good conscience turning on his wife before realizing that he had been deceived. At that point he turned against the accusers, who quickly accused him, and he began his journey to martyrdom. The events to follow suggest that the traditional stories about the conversion of Giles Corey may indeed be accurate. For whatever reason, Giles Corey was arrested on April 18 after Ezekial Cheever and John Putnam, Jr., complained against him and others for afflicting Ann Putnam, Mercy Lewis, Abigail Williams, Mary Walcott, and Elizabeth Hubbard. On April 19, Giles Corey was examined for witchcraft.[18] Now he defended his wife.

When Thomas Gould claimed to have heard Corey tell of damning information against his wife, Giles was asked, "What was that you knew against your Wife?" He answered, "Why, that of living to God, and dying to Sin." Whatever betrayal might have occurred earlier was gone. Questioned for information about Martha's possession of ointment when arrested, he claimed that she made it at the direction of one of the accusers, Sarah Bibber. There was some quarrel over who had directed the making of the ointment; but the most intriguing testimony in view of Corey's eventual fate was the charge by John and Sarah Bibber, and by other witnesses, that Giles Corey had threatened himself with suicide. Some relation may have existed between Corey's possible suicidal impulses and the manner in which he chose to die.

Other surviving testimony against Corey reveals little. There are inventions from Ann Putnam, Jr., Mercy Lewis, Sarah Bibber, and Mary Warren. Mary Walcott, Elizabeth Hubbard, and a new accuser, Elizabeth Woodwell, all offering testimony at a Jury of Inquest on September 9. Mercy Lewis affirmed that "I veryly beleve in my heart that Giles Cory is a dreadfull wizzard" (*SWP* I: 242), and Ann Putnam, Sarah Bibber, and Elizabeth Hubbard all expressed that view in almost identical language. Perhaps because repeating such phrases were becoming tedious, the recorder, in transcribing testimony by Benjamin Gould against Corey, simply wrote: "& I doe beleive in my:—" (*SWP* I: 244); finishing the phrase was not necessary. Since these were statements confirming earlier depositions, the new ingredient of baptism did not appear. The old cases went to trial without that element.

An array of other testimony appeared. Mary Warren, always the outsider, did not repeat the incantation of the other accusers, although she made clear that he had afflicted her especially on the day of his examination. The newcomer, Elizabeth Woodwell, told of Giles Corey's roaming shape while he was in prison; Mary Walcott confirmed this. Benjamin Gould, 25, told of a bedroom visit by Giles and Martha, and Susannah Sheldon told a garbled tale, including the claim that Corey's first wife, whom she said he had murdered, had only given him skimmed milk; she does not make clear whether this was proposed as a motive for murder. Elizabeth and Alice Booth told of spectral visits and observed, along with the regulars and in their language, that "we believe in our hearts that Giles Cory is a wizzard" (*SWP* I: 245). Sixteen-year-old John DeRich in September told his story of Corey requesting platters, presumably for a demonic feast;[19] the devil's powers apparently did not extend to providing tableware. DeRich said Corey took the platters, kept them for half an hour, and then returned them. Hannah Small and Martha Adams testified that some platters had indeed been missing, just as John DeRich had said. As was typical in cases against men, nobody accused Corey of killing cows.

While the evidence against Giles Corey proved to be ordinary, the historical response to him has not been so: The nature of his death has generated legends, stories, poems, plays, and songs. Giles Corey was pressed to death, the most widespread explanation being that weights had been piled on him in a vain attempt to elicit a plea of guilty or not guilty.[20] The reason usually given for his stubbornness is that he resisted a plea in order to protect his estate, the point being that if he did not plead he could not be tried and convicted, and thus his estate could not be confiscated. Good cause exists, however, to doubt this traditional interpretation.

First, there is the question of whether he had had the choice to change his mind once the procedure had started. No court verdict survives, but Samuel Sewall refers to the death as an "Execution."[21] Additionally, a letter written by Thomas Putnam to Sewall describes his daughter Ann as claiming "that she should be Pressed to Death, before Giles Cory" – the point being that the outcome seemed to be taken for granted (*SWP* I: 246). Moreover, the traditional view that Corey simply needed to enter a plea to end the ordeal is certainly inconsistent with Calef's claim that he had already entered a plea of "not Guilty to his Indictment." Then, according to this account, Corey refused to "put himself upon Tryal by the Jury."[22] Giles Corey was probably sentenced to death by pressing for refusing to stand trial, and once the process had started nothing he might do could reverse it – except, perhaps, choosing to confess.[23]

The belief that Corey had a choice stems not from simple invention, but from an interpretation of Sewall's diary entry for September 19:

> About noon, at Salem, Giles Corey was press'd to death for standing Mute; much pains was used with him two days, one after another, by the Court and Capt. Gardner of Nantucket who had been of his acquaintance: but all in vain.[24]

The crux of the textual matter rests on whether Gardner pleaded before the process started or after it had begun. Support for the argument of an execution rather than a test of wills appears in a court notation in 1710 in connection with an appeal for restitution: "Giles Corey & Martha his wife Condemnd & Executed, both of Salem" (*SWP* III: 986). The key word here, of course, is "Condemnd."[25]

The idea of Corey attempting to save his estate by refusing to enter a plea hovers around many of the tales and legends connected with him, and from time to time makes its way into a scholarly account of the subject; yet his death appears to have been unrelated to any such attempt. Contemporaries say nothing of estate protection, with Calef claiming instead that Corey refused a trial because of predictable results. The legend of Corey dying to protect his estate is a hypothesis that probably first appeared in the nineteenth century as a hagiography of Salem victims began to emerge. Like so many Salem legends, it received its great impetus from Charles Upham in 1867.[26] Upham, among other things, incorrectly indicates that Corey did not respond to the indictment, and storytellers ever since have followed his version.

It was less the matter of the estate than the sheer image of a man defying the authorities and enduring torture in doing so that launched the literary legend of Giles Corey, receiving its most prestigious attention in 1868 when Henry Wadsworth Longfellow, at the time probably thought of as America's foremost literary figure, published in his *The New-England Tragedies* the play *Giles Corey of the Salem Farms*. Longfellow features the defiance of the system rather than the protection of an estate.

> I will not plead,
> If I deny, I am condemned already,
> In courts where ghosts appear as witnesses,
> And swear men's lives away. If I confess,
> Then I confess a lie, to buy a life
> Which is not life, but only death in life.
> I will not bear false witness against any,
> Not even against myself, whom I count least.

Another character, Gardner, comments, "Ah what a noble character is this!"[27]

In creating his hero, who in the end died for truth, Longfellow conflates legends of George Burroughs with his hero; for example, giving Corey the strength to lift a keg of cider and having this act interpreted as witchcraft. Other features of an emerging Salem myth also appear, including the sexual undertones in his depiction of Bridget Bishop as a lusty lady. The play incorporates a hodgepodge of events drawn from those at Salem. Mary Walcott appears as wasted and consumed, even as Longfellow in his ambivalence argues against the reality of witchcraft. Similarly, Tituba defines herself as a witch and seems to have a witch's powers, although Longfellow wavers by alternately depicting her as demonic and as simply demented. Other incidents also reveal a reality of witchcraft in the text that persistently argues against the claims of the author in repudiating the notion. The play also explores the central drama of the Corey case, his relation to his wife Martha and his betrayal of her. Martha, in the play, is a young woman whose husband fails her before finding his redemption. The play concludes with Cotton Mather, like a Greek chorus, elegiacally condemning what has happened and prophesying the future glory of Corey's memory.

What defeats Longfellow's play, however, is not the matter of fidelity to history, but a problem that would become endemic to stories about Salem: that of proclaiming the injustice of what happened, rejecting the idea of witchcraft, while at the same time keeping the titillation of witchcraft as a central motif. While the play argues against superstitions about witchcraft, events in it suggest the reality of the phenomenon. The play, in this sense, offers a microcosm of a frequent difficulty among artists and scholars to reject the plausibility of actual witchcraft while at the same time finding in Salem a lure of witchcraft to which they in part succumb. John Demos very nicely describes this phenomenon in the preface to his *Entertaining Satan*.

> I suspect that many writers, at one stage or another, feel joined by fate to their particular topics and projects. But when the topic is witchcraft, such feeling grows unusually – albeit "superstitiously" – strong.[28]

Longfellow seemed very much to feel an allegiance to these superstitious feelings about witchcraft and helped shape the myth of Giles Corey that has become embedded in popular American imagination. Corey as character, among his many appearances, shows up in William Carlos Williams's *Tituba's Children* in connection with a "witch-hunt" against communists; in a debate in the Massachusetts legislature, where Representative Buczko refers to him as an Irishman; in a musical by Nicholas Van

Slyck based on *Giles Corey of the Salem Farms;* and even in the sympathetic reading of Longfellow's play by Montague Summers, who found witches in more places than most people do.[29] Though taking liberties with history, Mary Wilkins Freeman has placed him in her powerful, neglected play, *Giles Corey, Yeoman* (1893).[30]

Though Corey has evoked considerable accolades in his literary treatment, he was a man plausibly accused of having years earlier murdered a hired hand. The story of the alleged murder comes to us through Cotton Mather's printing in "Wonders of the Invisible World" of an undated letter to Samuel Sewall from Thomas Putnam.[31] The letter offers an account by Ann Putnam, Jr., to her father of a specter claiming to have been murdered by Corey. Once we get past Ann's standard complaint of being tormented by witches, we have, surprisingly enough, something related to reality: the story of an event occurring seventeen years earlier involving the beating death of a man named Jacob Goodale. Unlike court testimony referring to events long before that could not be confirmed, this charge was easily refuted if false, since it dealt with a verifiable court case. According to Putnam's account, a jury had brought in a charge of murder against Corey, but the court did not act against him. In the letter Putnam suggested the reason for this as an "Enchantment," although he also claimed "it cost him a great deal of Mony to get off" (*SWP* I: 246).[32]

On September 18, 1692, probably the day before his death, Giles Corey was excommunicated on equivocal grounds: The church document describes him as guilty of witchcraft, or, if not, then of killing himself; either reason would suffice.[33] Corey's excommunication had been preceded by that of his wife on September 11. When her minister, Samuel Parris, and a few others visited her in jail to convey the decision, they

> found [her] very obdurate, justifying herself and condemning all that had done any thing to her just discovery or condemnation. Whereupon after a little discourse (for her imperiousness would not suffer much) and after prayer (which she was willing to decline) the dreadful sentence of excommunication was pronounced against her.[34]

On the gallows, "protesting her Innocency, [she] concluded her Life with an Eminent Prayer upon the Ladder." What she had refused to do with Parris, to pray, she freely did at the end. Of Giles Corey's last moments, Calef writes: "[when] his Tongue [was] prest out of his Mouth, the Sheriff with his Cane forced it in again, when he was dying."[35] On October 17, 1711, the attainder against Giles and Martha Corey was removed (*SWP* III: 1015). On December 17 of that year Governor Dudley ordered compensation paid for the death of Giles and Martha Corey in the amount of twenty-one pounds (*SWP* III: 1017). The Coreys had been rehabilitated, although three hundred years would pass from the time of Giles's excommunication to the lifting of it.

III

Mary and Alice Parker were among the eight who hanged on September 22. Although there is no evidence of any connection between them, there has been enough confusion about them that *The Salem Witchcraft Papers* has much of Alice's story tangled with Mary's. Neither one of these women found many chroniclers to carry her tale, to generate myths about her. They died, and their stories, like those of most of the female victims, have been less appealing to the mythmakers than those of such male victims as George Burroughs and Giles Corey.

Too little of Mary Parker's record survives to determine why the authorities so expeditiously hanged this woman caught up late in the Andover phase; we know more about Alice Parker, whose identification as a daughter of Giles Corey has been suggested as a possibility.[36] Whether or not Alice was the daughter of Giles, Elizabeth Booth's testimony of June 30 links Martha Corey to a dispute with a Parker family. On that day Elizabeth, 18, swore under oath that the departed spirit of Thomas Gould, Sr., had appeared to her bearing information: that he had been killed by Martha Corey for having criticized her treatment of the children of Goodman Parker (*SWP* I: 263).

No record survives of who brought charges against Alice Parker, but she was examined on May 12; on May 25 she was probably sent to Boston jail along with Martha Corey and others (*SWP* I: 255). The warrant for the arrest of Alice Parker identifies her as the wife of John Parker of Salem, but gives no indication of who complained against her or who she is accused of afflicting (*SWP* III: 701); but the surviving record of the examination features charges from Mary Warren, who, after some time in prison, was examined again on May 12, the day of Alice Parker's examination. Margaret Jacobs was there too in her brief foray as an accuser.

The charges against Alice Parker at the examination on May 12 included one by Marshall Herrick that she had affirmed the presence of three score witches. According to the transcription, she did not deny having enumerated the number of witches but did not remember how many she had suggested. Possibly she had flirted with confession; but if so, she had backed away, affirming her innocence. Maybe she had wavered when she had seen Mary Warren finally break. Mary Warren, not yet as creative as she would become, connected the death of her mother and the illness of her sister to the failure of her father to mow the grass of Alice Parker. The murder of Mary Warren's mother by Alice Parker, though not specifically indicated by Mary Warren at her examination, was clarified in undated testimony by 16-year-old John DeRich, who had heard it directly from the dead woman (*SWP* II: 482). In September, Mary more specifically related the fate of her mother and sister: Alice Parker "told me she: bewiched my mother & was a caus of her death: also that: she bewiched my sister: Eliz: that is both deaf & dumb" (*SWP* II: 628).

Accusing witches of killing people was already routine, but Mary emphasized a motif at Alice Parker's examination that would flower as the proceedings developed: She told of demonic sacraments in affirming that Alice Parker "was att the Bloody Sacrament in Mr Parris's Pasture" with thirty in attendance (*SWP* II: 624). This reference to "the Bloody Sacrament" evokes a witchcraft mythology more frequently expressed in continental Europe than in England and in the colony. Relative to European tales, witchcraft stories in Salem tend to be less communal and less ritualized. As if practicing an emerging American individualism, Salem witches tended to pop in on people individually or in small groups. Although allusions to communal activities of witches occurred in the early stages, not until the Burroughs case did such stories, particularly those involving baptisms, flourish. In telling so vividly of the "Bloody Sacrament," Mary adumbrated the stories of community that would later mark the narrations of confessors.

The Reverend Nicholas Noyes, a person with more stature in the community than Mary Warren, also went after Alice Parker. Noyes, like Warren, was something of an outsider among his cohort. With such notable examples as Hale and Parris, Noyes was one of the few ministers who encouraged the proceedings, often attending them. He badgered John Alden at his examination on May 31. When Mary Warren, whom Noyes had questioned intensely on April 21 while she wavered, had a pin in her throat at the examination of Mary Clark, Nicholas Noyes was there to take it out, apparently never doubting that the specter of Mary Clark had put it there. He was also at the examination of Abigail Somes on May 13, observing that after a needle had unaccountably been found on her and been taken away, Mary Warren was no longer bitten, though she was then fiercely attacked at the throat. At the examination of Martha Corey on March 19 Noyes made clear his views that she practiced witchcraft, and he, along with Hathorne, rejected her contention that the accusers were distracted. He attended the examination of Mary Taylor on September 5 as she insisted on her innocence before finally breaking and confessing to him and a "Mr Keyzer" (*SWP* III: 742), and with three other ministers he successfully petitioned for Dorcas Hoar's reprieve. At the July 19 executions Sarah Good flung her famous curse at him; at those of August 19, he refused to pray for the unconfessing John Proctor, who had "earnestly requested" it. He was around a lot, and approvingly witnessed the hanging of Alice Parker and the seven others who died on September 22.[37] Our modern stereotype of Cotton Mather as a rabid witch-hunter probably emerged from applying his name to the conduct of Nicholas Noyes, the minister from the town of Salem who accused Alice Parker on May 12.

Regarding the general testimony against Alice Parker, the regulars gave their usual spectral accounts. Martha Dutch, 36, additionally accused her of saying that Dutch's husband would not come home from the sea, and "he died abroad as I sertinly heare" (*SWP* II: 626). John Westgate, 40, claimed that eight years before, during a quarrel between Alice and her husband, Westgate "tooke her husbands part telling of her itt was an unbeseeming thing for her to come after him to the taverne and raile" at her husband.[38] She told him to mind his own business. "Sometimes afterwards" – how long he does not say – he was attacked by a black hog, "which hog I then apprehended was Either the Divell or some Evill thing not a Reall hog, and did then Really Judge or determine in my mind that it was Either Goody parker or by her meenes, and procureing fearing that she is a witch" (*SWP* II: 632–3).

Alice Parker may have had a physiological disorder, as might be inferred from the testimony of John Bullock, upheld by that of Martha Dutch.[39] Bullock describes Alice as having had a fit similar to those she had had in the past. He describes how, the previous January, he and some of the neighbors had thought her dead after such a fit, but "while we were taking of her Cloaths to put her into bed She rises up & laughs in o'r faces" (*SWP* II: 634).

The lengthiest testimony against Alice Parker came from Samuel Shattuck, 41, who had similarly offered lengthy testimony against Bridget Bishop.[40] As in the Bridget Bishop case, where Shattuck recalled an event from twelve years earlier, he here reached back into the past. In this case, he describes the events as having occurred in 1685, and it appears as if Shattuck is describing the same events he had attributed to the witchcraft of Bridget Bishop, and at times in strikingly similar language. He tells how Alice Parker had come to the house and "fauned upon my wife" (*SWP* II: 635), just as he had told how Bridget Bishop had come to his house "in a Smooth flattering maner" (*SWP* I: 97). Shortly after the visit of Alice Parker, the child "w'ch was Supposed to have bin under an ill hand for Severall years before" manifested new, severe symptoms (*SWP* II: 635); these had led to the same old diagnosis of witchcraft, again by a doctor, as well as by others. Yet the new charge of bewitchment recapitulated symptoms described in connection with Bridget Bishop. Testifying against her, Shattuck had said that "this Child hath bin followed w'th grevious fitts as if he would never recover moor: his hed & Eyes drawne aside Soe as if they would never Come to rights moor" (*SWP* I: 99); after Alice Parker's visit, the child's "neck & Eys [were] drawne Soe much aside as if they would never Come to right againe" (*SWP* II: 635). After Bridget Bishop was finished with the child, the Shattucks "p'rceived his understanding decayed" (*SWP* I: 98); the fits induced by Alice Parker "hath taken away his understanding" (*SWP* II: 636).

Just how many women Shattuck blamed for the plight of his child, as he structured his private mythology, we do not know. In each narration, a woman with an evil, ulterior motive comes to his house and behaves in a flattering way. Both accounts include a spurious business transaction: Bridget Bishop had pretended to be interested in making a purchase from him, and Alice Parker had pretended to want to sell him something – chickens in her case. In both tales, a woman threatens to "bring downe" (*SWP* I: 98) or "see the downfall" (*SWP* II: 636) of Shattuck's wife; in each case he had sent someone on an errand, after the visit, to trick the woman, who, in each case, had responded in anger. It is reasonable enough to infer that Shattuck was seeing witches as he grappled with the tragedy of his child's illness; it is less reasonable that the testimony of this bewildered man has actually been used to demonstrate the reality of witchcraft in Salem.[41]

Of Mary Parker, we know almost nothing. She was a widow from Andover, examined on September 2 and charged with afflicting Sarah Phelps, Hannah Bigsby, and Martha Sprague. The usual formula breaks down slightly in that the indictment for afflicting Sarah Phelps is for tormenting her around the end of August, with no specific date being given, while the other two indictments cite September 1. Perhaps records of examination days other than September 2 do not survive; alternatively, these cases may fit the emergence that we have seen of deviation from earlier rigid patterns toward the end of the proceedings.

No indication appears as to the action on the indictment concerning Sarah Phelps, but a true bill is returned in the indictment for afflicting Hannah Bigsby. Of the Salem Village regulars, only Mary Warren's name survives in the records. The show put on by the accusers was routine enough. As usual, Mary Warren outdid the rest: "Mary Warrin in a violent fitt was brought neare haveing a pin run through her hand and blood runeing out of her mouth" (*SWP* II: 632). She also recalled having seen Mary Parker sitting on a beam at an earlier Salem Village examination.

Fourteen-year-old William Barker, Jr., confessed that he, along with Mary Parker and others, had afflicted Martha Sprague. Presumably, the jury did not believe him: The charge against Mary Parker for afflicting Martha Sprague was surprisingly rejected.

The Barker boy's testimony to the grand jury came on September 16, as the credibility of accusers was diminishing. Yet it was Mary Parker's bad luck to have been brought in just in time for the final trials and executions, and to have been treated with such dispatch. Since so little survives in her case, we cannot say with certainty that the baptism issue influenced the expeditious handling of her case; but it is not a bad guess to make.

IV

In the final rush to gather what witches they could, the court also executed Margaret Scott, Ann Pudeator, and Wilmot Reed. As with Mary Parker, little about the case against Margaret Scott survives. Not a single name of the Salem Village accusers appears in the record of the proceedings, nor even the names of the newly prominent Andover ones. Instead, we have only two documents. One comes from a girl or woman named Frances Wycum, who gives testimony as if she were experienced at it. On September 15 she swears that at Margaret Scott's examination on August 5, as well as on earlier occasions, she had been tortured by her. She also offers the ritual statement that she believes in her heart that Margaret Scott is a witch. The only other document is of a statement sworn the same day by Philip and Sarah Nelson that a man who had died had sworn that Margaret Scott had afflicted him for two or three years prior to his death, and that he would never get well as long as she lived. Although the makers of legends forged no stories about her, she was among those whose case the legislature in Massachusetts addressed in 1957 when it cleared the names of six women, although without removing the attainder from them: After her death, no one had made any claims for judicial redress. At her death, she had been 75.[42]

Ann Pudeator, who died with Margaret Scott, was probably also old, "about 70" according to Samuel Drake;[43] but the future would find some mythic rejuvenation for her in the legislative process that had included Margaret Scott. In 1946, when the Massachusetts legislature first considered a bill to clear six women whose attainders from the 1692 convictions had never been lifted, an array of publicity followed. On September 29, 1946, the following appeared in an essay entitled "Still No Vindication for Salem's Comely Witch": "The shade of Ann Pudeator, as comely a witch as ever side-saddled a broomstick, still cries in vain for Massachusetts justice." The article was adorned with an illustration by William Randall of a sexy Ann Pudeator flying a broom.[44] According to Eleanor Early in the *Salem News,* the attempt at vindication had been precipitated by H. Vance Greenslit, who wanted to clear the name of Ann Pudeator, his ancestor. "Supporting the action," according to Early, "and used as part of the hearings, was an hour-long CBS Television show entitled 'Satan in Salem' which highlighted the story of Ann Pudeator."[45] The 1950s, in the age of McCarthy that inspired Arthur Miller to write his *Crucible,* was a decade that saw more than one account of the Salem witch trials.

That Ann Pudeator emerged as a sex symbol was unrelated to anything in her history; instead, it reflected a growing cultural tendency to make witchcraft sexy. This had emerged in the nineteenth century, and perhaps begun earlier, in a language of fiction that referred to attractive women as "bewitching" men, or practicing "witchery." In Nathaniel Hawthorne's *Blithedale Romance,* the image of Zenobia as a "sorceress . . . fair enough to tempt Satan" specifically evokes the Salem trials, as she submits to the judgment of Hollingsworth.[46] The more common motif, however, evokes the chastely seductive woman successfully employing her charms of romantic "witchery" for the men she encounters.[47]

The metaphor of "witch" for the seductive power of women transformed into physical objects of beauty in the Randall illustration, or in movies such as *I Married a Witch,* with Veronica Lake,[48] and the television series "Bewitched" that grew out of it. Once the idea of witchcraft no longer offered a cultural threat, it became the kind of tamed fantasy that could appear in family entertainment, whether in shows such as "Bewitched" or in the cartoon menace of Dorothy's wicked witches in the Oz story.

How "comely" Ann Pudeator was, we do not know. Nothing in this widow's history suggests wickedness, and surviving records do not link her with images of seductiveness. An ordinary victim in an extraordinary episode, Ann Pudeator was arrested on May 12 along with Alice Parker and, like her, fell victim to accusations from the regenerated Mary Warren. Although named in the confession of Sarah Churchill on June 10, no record of an examination appears until July 2. Because it would have been highly unusual for a person to be arrested, accused, and not examined and jailed, the July date suggests that she may have been released and rearrested, a possibility seconded by a vague assertion at the July examination:

> goodwife puddeater: you have: formerly: bin complaynd of: we now further enquire . . . (*SWP* III: 702)

That the accusers may have approached Ann Pudeator with some ambivalence is further suggested by Mary Walcott's refusal at the examination to accuse Ann Pudeator of hurting her, even though she claimed to have seen her shape; otherwise, things seemed in order as the regulars, including Sarah Bibber, made their claims. Additional testimony to emerge in the examination included the charge by Jeremiah Neal that his sick wife had died after Ann Pudeator had visited her, apparently in part to help treat her;[49] as part of his charge, Neal reported that Pudeator had previously threatened his wife. The remaining issue in the examination concerned competing claims over whether Pudeator had kept ointments in her house, as the constable charged. Subsequent documents relate primarily to spectral accounts by the accusers and to the testimony of John Best, Sr., that she afflicted his wife. John Best, Jr., confirmed his father's testimony, adding information about a quarrel over cows. Samuel Pickworth – perhaps related to Mary Pickworth, a performer at the examination of William Proctor on September 17 – told of the time that a woman he "supposed to be ann Pudeatar . . . pasid by me as swifte as if a burd flue by me" (*SWP* III: 708).

What remains of the record of Ann Pudeator is her simple appeal to the court after her condemnation. Unlike the appeal that would come from Mary Easty, Pudeator's made no attempt to grapple with the prevailing judicial logic; rather, she simply and eloquently maintained her innocence and challenged the credibility of her accusers. In her petition, she accused Mary Warren, Sarah Churchill, John Best, Sr. and Jr., and Samuel Pickworth of bearing false witness against her, and reminded the court that "the abovesaid Jno Best hath been formerly whipt and likewise is [recorded] for a Lyar" (*SWP* III: 709). Better arguments than this would be needed, and Ann Pudeator hanged on September 22, emerging as a sexy witch in the 1940s.

The flip side of witch mythology – that of witch as wicked, menacing woman – would settle upon Wilmot Reed. A married woman from Marblehead, her case would have been routine enough if not for the fact that some writers have taken to declaring her in actuality a witch, mythologizing her as demonic just as Ann Pudeator was mythologized as sexy. What makes the case of Wilmot Reed more remarkable, however, is that her transformation came at the hands of a scholar, not a tabloid journalist.

What we have in the case of Wilmot Reed is almost entirely spectral, with accusations by the regulars. She was arrested May 31 and examined that day. Mercy Lewis, Mary Walcott, Abigail Williams, Ann Putnam, Elizabeth Hubbard, John Indian, and Susannah Sheldon were joined by Elizabeth Booth in getting knocked down by the shape of Wilmot Reed and being otherwise abused. Two indictments survive, one for afflicting Elizabeth Booth that day and the other for afflicting Elizabeth Hubbard. Booth seems not to have been very good at conveying her affliction: The jury rejected her indictment. At court on September 14, Mary Warren astonishingly declined to charge Wilmot Reed with afflicting her; however, she did maintain that she had seen her afflict the others on May 31. Along with Mary Walcott, Ann Putnam, Jr., and Elizabeth Hubbard, Putnam expressed her belief that Wilmot Reed was a witch. All used noticeably similar language in making their assertions.

Other than the spectral testimony, the only surviving testimony is a tale told by Charity Pitman, 29, probably on September 14, and supported in whole or in part by two other witnesses on that date. On the basis of Pitman's tale, Chadwick Hansen has argued that Wilmot Reed "clearly practiced witchcraft" and "had for many years been the town witch of Marblehead."[50]

Charity Pitman tells of a quarrel between a "Mrs Syms" and Reed that had occurred five years earlier over some linen allegedly stolen by Martha Laurence, a servant of Reed. According to her testimony, Mrs. Simms had then threatened to go to Salem and get Hathorne to issue a warrant for Martha Laurence. Wilmot Reed had said that, if Mrs. Simms did not go away, "she wished that she might never mingere [urinate], nor cacare [defecate]." According to Charity Pitman, "Mrs Syms was taken with the distemper of the dry Belly-ake, and so continued many moneths during her stay in the Towne, and was not cured whilst she tarryed in the Countrey." Sarah Dodd swore to this with a bit more delicacy, claiming "s'd Redd. wisht s'd Simse might never any wayes ease nature before she did it: & soon aftar; to this deponent's knowledge it fell out with: Mrs Simse: according. s'd Redds wish" (*SWP* III: 717). Ambrose Hale confirmed the affliction of Mrs. Simms. What had happened to her, we do not know. She may indeed have become constipated, or have been frightened by a threat. If she herself believed Wilmot Reed to be a witch, this is indicated by no court record; nor does any record establish that she believed Reed to be responsible for her troubles. Yet by such evidence does a modern scholar declare without qualification that Wilmot Reed was a witch.

V

In 1891, Caroline E. Upham wrote of Mary Easty, 56 years old when she hanged:

> The lofty tone of [her petition] to the Court recalls the perfect spirit of the Prisoner at Calvary, who entreats "Father forgive them, they know not what they do."[51]

If more than one woman received hagiographic status in the nineteenth century, none surpassed in admiration Mary Easty, whose petition to the court, the ministers, and Governor Phips revealed her eloquence and courage in the face of death.

Yet, notwithstanding the equation with Christ, the response of Upham and others to Mary Easty underestimated what Easty achieved politically in her perfectly timed petition. While no single cause can explain the end of the Salem episode, any more than a single cause can explain the beginning, Mary Easty's petition helped open the way to the trials of confessors, which quickly brought the persecutions to an end. This remarkable woman, saying the right thing at the right time, forced an irresistible logic upon the court, upon the governor, and upon the community. She articulated publicly a position offered only privately by others.

The story begins in an ordinary enough way. Mary Easty, the sister of Rebecca Nurse and Sarah Cloyce – all three accused of witchcraft – was examined on April 22, having been formally complained against the previous day.[52] After routine accusations, which she denied, she went to jail. The accusers, however, were not of one mind on Mary Easty, who appears to have had an outstanding reputation in the community. Whether in response to community support, or for other reasons, the accusers, with the exception of Mercy Lewis, began to back off after Mary Easty was jailed in April, going so far as to clear her of afflicting them. With Mercy Lewis the only holdout, the authorities released Mary Easty on May 18.

Mercy, however, was relentless. She quickly went into a fit, described vividly in some of the sworn depositions at the trial of Mary Easty on September 9. Samuel Abby, who in a September deposition tells of Mercy's suffering on May 20, relates how in her torments she told that Mary Easty "said she would kill hir before midnight because she did not cleare hir so as the Rest did" (*SWP* I: 300). That Mary Easty did not make good on the promise seemed not very interesting to the authorities, and is perhaps not very interesting to us. What does catch our attention, though, is that the other accusers capitulated to Mercy Lewis.

According to his account, Samuel Abby had, on the morning of May 20, gone to the house of John Putnam and found Mercy Lewis "on the bed in a sad condition." He was asked to go to the house of Thomas Putnam to get Ann Putnam's help in determining who was tormenting Mercy Lewis. Ann, again willing to be helpful, responded, as did Abigail Williams: Before even reaching Mercy Lewis, both announced an apparition sighting of Mary Easty, along with John Willard and Mary Witheridge. Easty's apparition explained that she was now afflicting Mercy Lewis; but Ann and Abigail also refer to Easty as the same one who had appeared to them "the other day" (*SWP* I: 300). This strongly suggests that they had complained before May 20, and that by the time Mercy Lewis behaved as she did on that date, an agreement had already been reached that the cleared Mary Easty was to be uncleared.

On May 20, the warrant for Mary Easty's arrest indicated that it was for afflicting Ann Putnam, Mercy Lewis, Mary Walcott, and Abigail Williams "yesterday and this present day" (*SWP* I: 287). The four of them were united again, and Mary Easty, after a brief respite, was back in jail and "laid in Irons" (*SWP* I: 301). On May 23, Mary Walcott offered testimony consistent with what Samuel Abby would say at the trial. She said that Mary Easty had told her – for witches in those days could not keep their mouths shut – that she had blinded all the accusers except for Mercy Lewis, since for some reason or other she lacked the power to do so. That, of course, was the reason that only Mercy Lewis had held out against her. Fortunately, Easty in her spectral form had straightened out the whole story for Mary Walcott.

Mary Easty thus met the judiciary for the second time, and she was to stay in jail until her death; but the record suggests some continuing uncertainty on the part of the court as to how to deal with her. This may have been due to the support she received from her minister, Joseph Capen. It appears as if the authorities planned to put her on trial in August, along with Burroughs, Jacobs, Proctor, Willard, and Carrier. Surviving testimony indicates that a Jury of Inquest was held in her case on August 3 and 4, and this was usually preliminary to the trial and an important part of it. The testimony here indicates that Mary Easty had been examined again on May 23, although the record of that examination does not survive; depositions from May 23 do, however, as do references to that date in the August testimony. Mary Walcott refers specifically to her affliction of May 23, the day of Mary Easty's examination, and Sarah Bibber tells how she had been afflicted at Mary Easty's "last examination" (*SWP* I: 296–7). She had also had a bedroom sighting of Easty's shape on an ill man's bed. Mary Warren, Ann Putnam, Jr., and Elizabeth Hubbard joined in. A close reading of the testimony of May 23 again reveals similarity in the language of the accusers, who sometimes make charges with identical words. Except for three vague charges in undated documents, all the evidence against Mary Easty was spectral. One document records the testimony of Samuel Smith, 25, who told how five years earlier he had been "Rude in discorse"; Mary Easty had told him he should not be rude and that he "might Rue it hereafter." Going home that night he had "Received a little blow on my shoulder with I know not what and the stone wall rattleed very much which affrighted me my horse also was affrighted very much but I cannot give the reson of it." He stopped short of directly accusing her. Margaret Reddington, 70, told how three years

earlier, when she had been ill, Mary Easty had offered her food, which she
had rejected as not fit for dogs, whereupon "she vanished a waye" (*SWP*
I: 302). John and Hannah Putnam tell how John "was taken with strange
kinds of fitts" and how their baby had died after John Putnam had reported something about the mother of sisters Rebecca Nurse, Mary
Easty, and Sarah Cloyce (*SWP* II: 601–2).

Mary Easty did not go to trial in August, but whatever protection she
had proved insufficient to hold off the court in September. Except for two
days in May, she was in jail from April 22 until her death on September
22. During this period two petitions came from Mary Easty: one jointly
from her and her sister Sarah Cloyce, and the other individually. The first
is difficult to date, but its suggestion of an imminent trial make it likely to
have originated in September. Sarah, who had been examined in April,
was examined again, apparently on September 9, for afflicting Rebecca
Towne, probably a relative; however, she survived the Court of Oyer and
Terminer, and the case against her was dismissed in January by the grand
jury.[53]

Sarah Cloyce has over the years been the subject of much narration,
most recently in the fictional film *Three Sovereigns for Sarah: A True Story*.[54] The incident precipitating so much historical interest in her occurred,
according to Calef, on April 3: She walked out of a sermon by Parris, upset at his implicit accusation of her sister, Rebecca Nurse, then in jail.[55]
This incident is also alluded to in undated testimony, some time after June
21, by Sarah Stephens and Margery Pasque. They attest that an afflicted
person, Jemima Rea, had mentioned being told by Sarah Cloyce that, after leaving Parris's church, she had gone to "her Master" and signed the
devil's book (*SWP* II: 606). Cloyce was sent to jail in Boston, probably
on April 12 (*SWP* II: 662).[56]

In their joint petition – on or shortly before the day of Mary Easty's
trial, September 9 – the sisters offer an insight into how loaded the trial
proceedings were against women. They complain that "we are neither
able to plead our owne cause, nor is councell alowed to those in our con-
dicion" and appeal to the judges to serve as their counsels (*SWP* I: 302).[57]
Burroughs, as we recall, pled his case, although it remains unclear whether
he received this privilege as a minister, as a male, or as both. No evidence
survives to indicate that anyone else received this privilege, and it seems
unlikely that any woman had a similar opportunity.

In addition to revealing their difficulty in defending themselves under
the court's rules, they disclaimed knowledge of any guilt, and cited those
who would testify under oath to their good character, mentioning "Mr.
Capen the pastour and those of the Towne & Church of Topsfield, who
are ready to say somthing which we hope may be looked upon, as very

considerable in this matter . . ." Finally, they argued that there was only spectral evidence to be weighed against their good character, and that this was "the Testimony of witches, or such as are afflicted, as is supposed, by witches . . . " and lacked legal corroboration (*SWP* I: 303). This third point made clear their skepticism as to the actual affliction of the accusers, and focused on the case as a spectral one. For the first time an accused person addressed directly the issue of weighing the good character of the accused against the spectral charges of the accusers. An issue that had hovered around many of the cases now came unambiguously before the court.

However, it was the individual petition of Mary Easty that converged with other factors to force an end to the persecutions. Oddly, Easty has come into the folklore as helping to persuade people of the flaws in the court in a manner independent of her actual achievement. The connection is through a widespread popular (and sometimes scholarly) account of the trials ending because of the accusers "reaching too high" by naming Mrs. Hale, wife of the minister, John Hale.[58] In this account, the authorities decided to draw the line when such high-ranking people were named. This tale warrants no credence, however: The authorities had already heard and rejected without any noticeable difficulty the accusation against Samuel Willard, and ignored charges against Margaret Thacher of Boston, the mother-in-law of Jonathan Corwin.[59] That John Hale himself may have awakened as a result of the charge against his wife is entirely possible, but a system that had withstood charges against Samuel Willard would hardly buckle at the naming of Hale's wife: Relative to Willard, Hale was not a particularly prominent minister, and in this society Mrs. Hale could hold no more status than her husband. Finally, no actual record of the charge against Mrs. Hale appears until after the Court of Oyer and Terminer had ended on October 29;[60] the connection to her was not made before November 5.

The link between this traditional story and Mary Easty can be found in its original version, told on November 14 by Mary Herrick, 17, to Hale and to the Reverend Joseph Gerrish of Wenham. In her account, Herrick tells of Mrs. Hale afflicting her and appearing with the ghost of Mary Easty, who had come to tell of her wrongful execution and to instruct Herrick to explain her innocence to the Revs. Hale and Gerrish. Herrick also told how Easty had appeared to her just before her execution, declaring that she was innocent and that, before the year ended, Mary Herrick would believe in that innocence.

Mary Herrick was not one of the regular Salem Village accusers nor even one of the later Andover ones. She seems to have entered the picture independently, and insufficient information exists for speculating whether she was delusional or had some rational motive for the story she told. It is not hard to guess, however, why she cast Mary Easty in the role of articulating the case for innocence: By November, Mary Easty could easily personify those who had been falsely accused and unjustifiably executed. Her petition had helped transform public perceptions, and Mary Herrick understandably chose her as the voice from the dead. The woman of Mary Herrick's tale, unlike the woman who presented the petition, sought vengeance rather than Christian charity. Mary Easty's spirit persuaded Herrick of her innocence; Herrick's previous belief in her guilt had been a delusion fostered by the devil.

Ironically, this story comes down to us for its accusation of Mrs. Hale, but Mary Herrick's point was something else: Mrs. Hale was afflicting her because the spirit world wanted to awaken everybody; once Mary Easty's innocence was established, Mrs. Hale would behave. The main thrust of Herrick's story, the need to clear Mary Easty, became lost in the strange legend that the accusation against Mrs. Hale had something to do with ending the Salem witch trials. Mary Herrick, whether from imagining apparitions or from constructing a tale, understood who the important figure in the story was; but however Herrick glossed this tale, Mary Easty's achievement was of this world rather than the next, in her petition rather than her specter.[61]

The exact dating of this petition is uncertain, but it must have been written between September 9, when she was sentenced to death, and September 17, when some confessors were condemned. In her appeal to the governor, the court, and the ministers, Mary Easty bluntly refers to "the wiles and subtility" of her accusers and, recognizing her own innocence, "can not but Judg charitably of others that are going the same way of my selfe if the Lord stepps not mightily in" (*SWP* I: 303). For herself, she did not expect such divine intervention: Her petition is written from the perspective of a person who asks not for temporal mercy, but who pleads that "no more Innocentt blood may be shed" – although the shedding of such blood seems to her inevitable if the court continues in its procedures. Affirming her faith in the good intentions of the court, Mary Easty proceeds to propose two strategies so utterly reasonable that, if the court did indeed consist of men interested in finding witches, her proposals could hardly be ignored:

> I would humbly begg of you that your honors would be plesed to examine theis Aflicted Persons strictly and keepe them apart some time and Likewise to try some of these confessing wichis I being confident there is severall of them has belyed themselves and others as will appeare if not in this wor[l]d I am sure in the world to come whither I am now agoing[.] (*SWP* I: 304)[62]

Mary Easty did not deny the possibility of witchcraft; she did not even say that all of the confessors lied, just "some"; and she proposed the most reasonable of approaches in recommending that the accusers be kept apart. If under such circumstances they could tell the same stories, corroborating their respective experiences with visiting shapes, their accounts would be credible and doubts as to innocent blood being shed would be removed.

That they could never succeed at this trick Mary Easty knew; the real strength of her petition was that it presupposed the good intentions of the court. Why not, after all, try a confessing witch? Everybody in the community knew the biblical injunction that "Thou shalt not suffer a witch to live" (Exodus 22:18); it was why people were being hanged. Moreover, by all the judicial precedents, there was no better evidence than confession. Thus, Mary Easty cast a two-pronged challenge: Affirm the serious intention of discovering the truth by separating accusers before questioning them; and show good faith by trying confessing witches.

At another time, Mary Easty's appeal would have had minimal influence at best; but with the acceleration of confessions, what she urged publicly must surely have been discussed privately. The spectacle of so many people rushing to proclaim their witchcraft reinforced the trepidations of those dismayed by the proceedings. Confessors were either real witches, in which case they needed to be put to death, or were distempered or fraudulent. The ministers had for some time discreetly expressed their skepticism, and as the number of accused increased, more and more influential people raised more and more doubts. Nobody was willing to offer a public attack on the court, but the opposition was there.

As Thomas Brattle indicates in his letter of October 8, some very prominent people "do utterly condemn the said proceedings," and he names among these Simon Bradstreet, Thomas Danforth – the man who began John Proctor on the road to the gallows – Increase Mather, Samuel Willard, and Nathaniel Saltonstall, formerly a judge on the Court of Oyer and Terminer. Brattle also named other former judges, Thomas Graves, Nathaniel Byfield, and Francis Foxcroft, as well as "several of the present Justices." Indeed, he writes that "some of the Boston Justices, were resolved rather to throw up their commissions than be active in disturbing the liberty of their Majesties' subjects, merely on the accusations of these afflicted, possessed children." As for the clergy, he could think of only three ministers, Hale, Noyes, and Parris, who were not "very much dissatisfyed."[63]

For the court in this context to ignore Easty's challenge would be to acknowledge to the critics that the proceedings were fatally flawed – that the hunt was not really for witches after all but for validating the court.

Witches were confessing; do something, said Mary Easty. Stoughton and the court did, and once they did, the game was up: If confessors were going to trial, there remained no incentive to confess; this would lead inevitably to retractions. Wardwell's was the most dramatic no matter how bad the timing; but others followed in safer circumstances, and by the time the January trials came, under new rules, probably all of the confessions had been retracted.

It is untestable whether confessors would have been tried in September had Mary Easty not made her appeal. All we know is that no other person made that public challenge; that once the challenge was made, the court yielded the point; and that once the point was yielded, old confessors began to reconsider and potential new ones pulled back. The impetus given by the Burroughs affair could not overcome the glaring evidence that confessions grew from pragmatism rather than witchcraft. Those who had always understood the weaknesses of the court's intellectual and theological positions had their hand significantly strengthened. To top it all off, Governor Phips returned to the colony; Stoughton was no longer in charge. Support among the influential for the Court of Oyer and Terminer collapsed. On October 3, Increase Mather politely pointed out how flawed the proceedings were, in what would be published as *Cases of Conscience;* this was a few days before Brattle's damning letter. Then, on October 12, Phips made clear in a letter that innocent people had been caught by the court (*SWP* III: 861–3). He stopped the proceedings, and on October 29 ended the Court of Oyer and Terminer. The process of restoring Massachusetts Bay to an orderly colony was underway within a month after Mary Easty publicly framed the issue that left Stoughton and the rest of the court in an untenable position.[64] We do not know how the court responded to her challenge to interrogate accusers individually, eliciting their spectral stories without the possibility of collusion. We simply know that the Court of Oyer and Terminer lost its credibility.

Why none of the other victims posed the issue as she did is hard to say. When John Proctor on July 23 petitioned five ministers, he made much of the fact that people were being accused by confessed witches, but his emphasis was on the fact that two of them, Richard and Andrew Carrier, had been brought to their confessions by torture. Proctor had argued against the reliability of testimony from confessors: Who could trust the word of a witch? Why should we believe that forced confessions were really from witches? It was a different line of reasoning, and he certainly did not want Richard and Andrew tried: He knew they too were victims. No one else had come as close as Proctor did to forcing the issue.

At least, not until Mary Easty, who emerged to articulate the irresistible logic. The nineteenth-century hagiographers honored Easty for a noble death, but simply did not grasp that she had done more than play the role of martyr. Had she made her appeal earlier, it might not have carried much weight; but in the season of rampant confessions and growing doubts among prominent people, Mary Easty said the right thing at the right time. More than anyone else, she dramatized the fatal weakness of judicial dependence upon confessions, some borne of unbearable stress, but most simply contrived. It was she who stripped the emperor's clothing.

In her appeal, she had not asked for her life, and it was not granted to her; so she died. By Calef's account, she deeply moved those who witnessed her death:

> Mary Easty, Sister also to Rebecka Nurse, when she took her last farewell of her Husband, Children and Friends, was, as is reported by them present, as Serious, Religious, Distinct, and Affectionate as could well be exprest, drawing Tears from the Eyes of almost all present.[65]

Nicholas Noyes presumably kept his eyes dry when, at the hanging, he uttered his famous epithet: "what a sad thing it is to see Eight Firebrands of Hell hanging there." Noyes turned an enduring phrase as Mary Easty and seven others died; but her petition helped defeat his cause.

9

Assessing an inextricable storm

I fear (amongst our many other provocations) that God hath a Controversy with us about what was done in the time of the Witchcraft. I fear that innocent blood hath been shed; & that many have had their hands defiled therwith. I believe our Godly Judges did act Conscientiously, according to what they did apprehend then to be sufficient Proof: But since that, have not the Devils impostures appeared? & that most of the Complainers & Accusers were acted by him in giving their testimonies. Be it then that it . . . was done ignorantly. Paul, a Pharisee, persecuted the chu[r]ch of God, shed the blood of Gods saints, & yet obtained mercy, because he did it in ignorance; but how doth he bewaill it, and shame him self for it before God and men afterwards.

– Michael Wigglesworth, 1704[1]

After September 22 there would be sporadic incidents before a new court in January put an end to the witchcraft episode. On October 1, Mary Brown of Reading charged affliction day and night by the shape or person of Sarah Cole of Lynn. On October 3, Mary Warren performed against Cole at her examination, unaccompanied by the old set of accusers (*SWP* I: 227).[2] On November 5, three men complained against Esther Elwell, Abigail Roe, and Rebecca Dike, all from Gloucester, probably after they were identified by accusers brought to Gloucester to repeat what had been achieved in Andover.[3] Later in November new accusations found another kind of response: "[B]y this time the validity of such Accusations being much questioned, they found not that Encouragement they had done elsewhere, and soon withdrew."[4] The credibility of the accusers had ended. In a final orgy of hanging, Massachusetts Bay had dissipated the legitimacy that had fueled the witch-hunt.

The bulk of the arrested people remained in prison before the January trials, although some found freedom. On October 6, 13-year-old John Sawdy, a confessor, was freed on bond, as was Martha Sparks on December 6. Soon, the January trials, under rules that did not depend on spectral evidence, would offer the legal end to the episode, even though acquitted people could not be freed until they paid their jail bills.

Under the new procedures only three people were found guilty; they received a reprieve from Phips. Some prisoners languished in jail because the court had not finished all its work in January and was not to meet again until the spring. A desperate petition from Ipswich prison reveals the plight of elderly women, pregnant women, one woman nursing a child, one having been in irons for half a year, and a few men facing a perilous winter in prison and appealing for bail. Still, although the horror had not stopped and would last into the spring of 1693, the episode had changed from one of active prosecution by the state to a seemingly indifferent bureaucracy processing the remaining victims. People in irons enduring the harsh winter in prison were the residue of the witch-hunt, but the commitment to secure convictions had ended. The traditional skepticism regarding witchcraft charges had reemerged, and the reassessments of what had happened began.

A consensus in Massachusetts Bay quickly developed that something had gone wrong, but no formal inquiries into the nature of those errors occurred. If people began to take for granted that the confessors had invented stories and that the accusers had borne false witness, nobody was judicially punished. A delicate balance emerged between condemning the past and exonerating those who had participated in it. When on October 17, 1711, the General Court reversed attainders, its linguistic legerdemain was a marvel to behold.[5] The reversal document named the star victim of the proceedings, George Burroughs, in its first sentence or title: "An Act to reverse the attainders of George Burroughs and others for Witchcraft"; it included all but five of the executed in the general exoneration, as well as various other people, but insisted that the province had been "Infested with a horrible Witchcraft or possession of devils" (*SWP* III: 1015). Thus the court, in effect, said that the colony had indeed been attacked by unidentified witches who were not the people convicted of the crime. After listing all those whose attainders had been lifted and verbally slapping the accusers by asserting that "some of the principal Accusers and Witnesses in those dark and severe prosecutions have since discovered themselves to be persons of profligate and vicious conversation" (*SWP* III: 1016), the

General Court closed the door on calling to account the judiciary. It asserted "that no Sheriffe, Constable, Goaler or other officer shall be Liable to any prosecution in the Law for anything they then Legally did in the Execution of their respective offices" (*SWP* III: 1016–17). In spite of the qualifying word "legally," this proved as effective for those who had violated the law as would a Presidential pardon in a future age. The matter was over. Massachusetts Bay had decided to put the trials behind it.

By 1711 the episode was not yet being called "the Salem witch trials"; that would come later as posterity metaphorized and mythologized the event, placing it in the town that happened to be where the court sat. In the seventeenth and early eighteenth century, however, the events were conceptualized as a phenomenon that had engaged a whole colony. When in 1764 Thomas Hutchinson referred to the episode, he wrote of "The great noise which the New England witchcrafts made throughout the English dominions."[6] What in its own day came to be regarded by most of those in authority as a discredited event involving discredited, "profligate" people would retain in the future a continuation of that underlying trope of "a horrible Witchcraft" having infested the land.

The "great number" of people who kept believing in some kind of "horrible witchcraft" came to form much of popular opinion in the later centuries. In refined and more sophisticated forms in modern times, elaborate explanations emerged through theories of psychology, biochemistry, and social interaction. All have had in common a powerful impulse to reject what appears as simplistic the view that at the core of the accusations resided simple fraud. For people who read at supermarket counters about two-headed babies from UFOs, the concept of real witchcraft at Salem comes easily. For scholarly advocates of competing modern theories, Hutchinson's view that fraud lay at the center has simply emerged as a quaint simplification to be challenged through sophisticated insight. Still, no explanation, under scrutiny, has held up as well as that understood by Hutchinson, as well as by a lot of people in 1692.

Our historians, on the whole, have patronized the late-seventeenth-century community of Massachusetts Bay. The view put forth by Winfield Nevins in the late nineteenth century has emerged as the most common motif in critiques of the 1692 witch trials: "The mistake which, it seems to me, the majority of the writers on this chapter of our history have made, is that they did not put themselves in the places of the men and women of 1692, but judged by the standard of the latter half of the nineteenth century."[7] This argument, that we must see it from their perspective, carries an implicit codicil that, given their perspective, they could not have seen it the way we smarter moderns can. One modern literary critic, reflecting what has come to be a truism in commentary on the Salem witch trials, writes that "[m]odern readers must be reminded that the execution of nineteen alleged witches in Salem was not the result of barbarity or bigotry; rather, the event can be seen as another chapter in the long history of witchcraft"; or, as Andrew Lang told us in 1907, the witch-hunters were simply of their age.[8] However, though patronized by future commentators, they saw it well enough – better, on the whole, than the theorists who have come to explain what happened to them. To look at it from the perspective of those among them who understood it best, we do well to review the insights of Thomas Brattle, the man who best codified what had come to be the general wisdom among the elites of Massachusetts Bay colony.

Commentators on the episode have tended to see Brattle as some kind of exception. "Apart from such luminaries as Thomas Brattle," writes Richard Weisman, for example, "and possibly a few iconoclasts, the majority of residents in Essex County were as persuaded by the sufferings of the accusers as were the members of the court."[9] Brattle, though, was essentially saying overtly and precisely what had been implicitly said as early as June, when "The Return of Several Ministers" cautiously suggested that the court had gone wrong.

I

Brattle's famous letter is dated October 8. To whom it was addressed is unknown, and it was not published in his lifetime. Certainly it had less to do with ending the trials than did the trying of confessors, Mather's *Cases of Conscience,* or the return of Governor Phips. Its value rests primarily in offering insights into how various people perceived the episode, for the letter reveals as one of its key motifs that Brattle is not a lone voice crying in the wilderness. At the outset, he seeks to disassociate himself from "those men your letter mentions, whom you acknowledge to be men of a factious spirit."[10] That is, Brattle claims to stake out conservative ground. He is one of many who challenge the conduct of the court; unlike others, perhaps referring to William Milborne, he claims not to attack the judiciary, although the letter emerges as a savage indictment of it.[11] He abhors, he says, those who want to question authority, as, obviously, people are doing. He simply wants to take the view that even judges are mortal, and men of lesser wisdom can sometimes find errors in what they do, and men of goodwill, of course, want to correct such errors.

Beyond a reasonable doubt, Brattle is being ingenuous. We see this in his language laced with sarcasm in pointing out the gullibility, or worse, of the judiciary, which he lets us know at the outset was under attack. In response to what he makes of this attack, he offers his observations, which he asserts at the outset will reveal fundamental errors that "palpably pervert the great end of authority and government" (LTB 170). In the course of the letter, he will give important insights into who has the quarrel with the judiciary, people not necessarily "of a factious spirit." Having offered his demurrals, he proceeds to show with devastating insight the flaws in the proceedings judged by *the criteria of his age.*

He begins by describing the examinations, and quickly drops his deference to the judges by pointing to the absurdity of their judging the credibility of the accusers on the basis of their behavior at the examinations. He cites the case of John Alden, where Bartholomew Gedney, having observed that he knew Alden as a good man, changed his opinion because a child came out of a fit at the touch of Alden. "I know a man," he writes sardonically, "that will venture two to one with any Salemite whatever, that let the matter be duly managed, and the afflicted person shall come out of her fitt upon the touch of the most religious hand in Salem" (LTB 170).

The Alden incident is described elsewhere by another writer, who observes that Alden's gaze did not strike down Gedney as it did the accusers.[12] The account reveals the presence of Stoughton at the examination on May 31, presumably because of Alden's prominence and gender, and in Stoughton's presence it reveals an episode of fraud:

> Those Wenches being present, who plaid their jugling tricks, falling down, crying out, and staring in Peoples Faces; the Magistrates demanded of them several times, who it was of all the People in the Room that hurt them? one of these Accusers pointed several times at one Captain Hill, there present, but spake nothing; the same Accuser had a Man standing at her back to hold her up; he stooped down to her Ear, then she cried out, Aldin, Aldin afflicted her; one of the Magistrates asked her if she had ever seen Aldin, she answered no, he asked her how she knew it was Aldin? She said, the Man told her so. (*SWP* I: 52)

One can put a lot of constructions on this episode, but if the account is accurate, we search with difficulty for one that does not support its premise of fraud and the depiction, as Brattle argues, of the judiciary as people who, at best, should have known better.

As Brattle's letter continues, the decorum with which it began fades rapidly, and he begins to refer sarcastically to the "Salem Gentlemen," the justices holding the examinations in Salem, or "S.G." as he comes to call them (LTB 171). He wants to know why, if the witches could knock people over with a look, they do not knock over others besides their accusers. He ridicules at length the whole concept and asserts "that the reasonable part of the world, when acquainted herewith, will laugh at the demonstration, and conclude that the said S.G. are actually possessed, at least, with ignorance and folly" (LTB 172). He singles out for ridicule the Reverend Nicholas Noyes for being so gullible.

Brattle then switches to the subject of the confessors "as they are improperly called." He estimates that about fifty of them are in jail and informs us that he has seen and heard many of them over and over. He asserts his "faith is strong concerning them, that they are deluded, imposed upon, and under the influence of some evill spirit" (LTB 173). Brattle clearly seems to accept the notion that many of the confessors actually believe they are witches, but his "imposed upon" words make clear his awareness of the pressures on people to confess. Yet granting the premise that they are possessed, he asks how the judges can possibly take testimony as credible from people under the influence of the devil. In reply to "many of our good neighbors" who ask how one cannot believe in the confessions, he asserts that they would think otherwise "if they would but duly consider of the premises" (LTB 174).

In the next section of his letter, Brattle enumerates four specific points. First, using the case of Elizabeth Proctor as an example, he argues that the accusers do not distinguish between the shape and the person they accuse of attacking them, a distinction he faults the judges for failing to make. In his second point he attacks the court for allowing confessors to offer evidence, since they are under the influence of the devil. It is his third point, however, that bears special attention, because it reveals that what emerges as obvious to the modern reader of the judicial proceedings was equally obvious to Brattle and the numerous other skeptics:

> Whoever can be an evidence against the prisoner at the bar is ordered to come into Court; and here it scarce ever fails but that evidences, of one nature and another, are brought in, tho', I think, all of them altogether aliene to the matter of inditement; for they none of them do respect witchcraft upon the bodyes of the afflicted, which is the alone matter of charge in the inditement. (LTB 175)

The court records persistently reinforce Brattle's conclusions. The indictments are for purely spectral attacks on the afflicted, and the depositions, if not "all of them," most of them "altogether aliene to the matter of inditement." The judges were allowing the juries to hear and to act on testimony unrelated to the charge.

Commentators on the witch trials have often wanted to remind us that we cannot judge the judiciary by modern civil-libertarian standards, and that is fair enough; but it is also fair to assess the judges by honorable standards of their own day, as Brattle does. One does not need a modern civil libertarian here. The argument that the Puritans were caught in the superstitions of their day will not do for explaining the conduct of the judiciary. It is by *their* standards, not ours, that Brattle points out the flaws in their behavior. Indeed, although Brattle makes no mention of it, as early as August 9 Robert Pike had explained to Judge Jonathan Corwin that evidence for witchcraft required either a confession or two witnesses to the act. These were, of course, the key points that Mather later made in *Cases of Conscience*. Pike, as Mather would, had argued that it is better to let the guilty live than to execute the innocent; and with devastating clarity, he had pointed out the absurdity of people pleading innocent to witchcraft yet choosing to abuse their accusers in open court.[13] One did not have to live in the twentieth century to have such insights; nor were they reserved only to exceptional individuals such as Thomas Brattle, Robert Pike, and Increase Mather. Still, it remains Brattle's letter that best synthesizes for modern readers the seventeenth-century case against the proceedings.

Brattle's fourth point is a minor one, that of objecting to the searches of bodies for witch marks, since all of us have some kind of inexplicable marks on our bodies. Yet even this objection points out that an observer of the late seventeenth century was quite able to ask for precision in definitions, especially with lives at stake. If people were to be accused of having "a preternatural excrescence," Brattle wants to know what is meant by that. "The term is a very general and inclusive term," he objects (LTB 175). Brattle's heart, however, is more in the issue of the indictments and the kinds of testimony used against the accused. Without naming her, he refers to the case of Mary Bradbury, against whom it was deposed on September 9 that butter she sold went bad and that her shape appeared in a storm that followed:

> But what if there were ten thousand evidences of this nature; how do they prove the matter of inditement! And if they do not reach the matter of inditement, then I think it is clear, that the prisoner at the bar is brought in guilty, and condemned, merely from the evidences of the afflicted persons. (LTB 176)

This was, of course, exactly the case, and he ridicules denials by the judges that cases are based on spectral evidence.

Brattle's next major point concerns the issue of how well-connected people manage to escape. He raises some cases, names names, and refers to it as "a very great scandal and stumbling block to many good people," reminding us again that he is not the only person noticing these things, which have been going on for some time (LTB 178). His complaint is not significant simply on its egalitarian grounds: Brattle is making the deepest challenge of all in chiding the judges for not charging some (such as Judge Corwin's mother-in-law, Margaret Thacher) and for not pursuing others who have escaped after being charged (such as Mrs. Nathaniel Cary, Philip English, and John Alden). The fugitives are in New York, as the judges know: Why are they not sent for?, Brattle wants to know. "In other Capitalls [i.e., capital cases] this [extradition] has been practised; why then is it not practised in this case, if really judged to be so heinous as is made for?" (LTB 178–9). Why indeed?

The implicit answer, whether involving corruption or not, is that the authorities themselves do not credit the accusers in these cases. They are by their actions saying that the accusers are not always right. The heart of their case lacks credibility even with them. Brattle's logic is damning. He is saying nothing less than that people are being executed from the testimony of those whom the judges do not always believe. The percentage of the public supporting the court in view of its selective beliefs must remain unknown, but Brattle offers anecdotal evidence of serious objections, particularly when he turns to the practice of people going to the accusers to discover who is a witch:

> I know there are several worthy Gentlemen in Salem, who account this practise as an abomination, have trembled to see the methods of this nature which others have used, and have declared themselves to think the practise to be very evill and corrupt; but all avails little with the abettours of the said practice. (LTB 179)

In relating one such incident, Brattle tells of a person who had gone from Boston with his child to Salem to consult with the accusers as to who afflicted the child. He found his names, returned to Boston, and unsuccessfully sought an arrest warrant. Brattle implicitly reminds us that, had the appeal been made to the Salem justices, the man's chances would have been better. In Boston, however, the response differed: Increase Mather found out what the man had done and "took occasion severely to reprove the said man; asking him whether there was not a God in Boston, that he should go to the Devill in Salem for advice; warning him very seriously against such naughty practices" (LTB 180).

Brattle proceeds to make much of the Andover cases, the conduct of men who broke "their charity with their wives" by urging them to confess and their subsequent realization of their mistake, of men who "grieve

and mourn bitterly" at what they had done in allowing and even participating in "the rude and barbarous" treatment of their wives in eliciting
confessions (LTB 181). These men clearly knew their fraud, they themselves having persuaded their wives to confess falsely. Brattle's critique of
the Andover episode reemphasized one of the sustaining arguments of his
letter: that the judiciary not only countenanced going to the devil for information, but based its cases on such practices as well as on coerced confessions (LTB 189).

Brattle deals with a variety of other matters in the letter, but his main
remaining issue concerns the subject of fraud. First, there is the matter of
the "'afflicted children,'" as Brattle calls them, though not without explaining that he does so as a matter of convention rather than as a matter
of fact, because "there are several young men and women that are afflicted, as well as children" (LTB 185). One of the points he makes concerns
the contradiction between the description in the indictments regarding the
"afflicted children" and their actual state of health. The indictments refer
"to their being pined and consumed, wasted, etc." (LTB 188). It bears repeating that the modern reader of the documents cannot help but notice
the resiliency of these accusers in going through tortures that, whether
caused by the devil, ergot, or hysteria, ought to have broken anybody's
health. Brattle did not miss this resiliency: "Many of these afflicted persons," he observes, are people "who have scores of strange fitts in a day,
yet in the intervals of time are hale and hearty, robust and lusty, as 'tho
nothing had afflicted them" (LTB 187). Though indictment after indictment told how they were pined, consumed, and wasted, they were on the
contrary "hearty, robust and lusty." Even the judges noticed it, but dis-
counted the legal significance of the fact.

Although Brattle clearly believes that the accusers are fraudulent, he
realizes that they are not always the ones generating the accusations. He
calls attention to the fact "[t]hat several persons have been apprehended
purely upon the complaint of these afflicted, to whom the afflicted were
perfect strangers, and had not the least knowledge of imaginable, before
they were apprehended" (LTB 182). The accusers, as Brattle understood,
were often the conduits for the accusations rather than their creators. This
is a tantalizing observation, perhaps suggesting that Brattle knew more
than he writes about the origins of various accusations. If he did, however,
he chose to remain silent on the matter.

The question, however, has persisted among those who, like Brattle, did
not see the cause in specters. Modern studies, such as *Salem Possessed*,[14]
have helped us understand who might be naming people in Salem Village
quarrels and in some cases beyond the community. *The Devil in the Shape*

of a Woman[15] has helped us understand what kind of woman was most likely to be accused. The widely held view in the nineteenth and twentieth centuries that the family of the Putnams sent signals to Ann Jr. is almost certainly accurate; but that family did not know all the named people in Massachusetts Bay, and not everybody matched the profile defined by Karlsen, or fit into the quarrels pointed out by Boyer and Nissenbaum. The orgy of accusations cut across towns and villages and across gender, class, and age. People fed all sorts of names to the accusers, either in sincere belief that a particular person was a witch, or for motives rooted in malice, greed, or the need to justify the proceedings. Yet there was no grand conspirator behind it all; instead, varieties of individuals, for varying motives, responded to the open invitation of the society in which they lived to provide names to those who had been defined as the witchfinders of their day. Still, even without a broad conspiracy, the context of events did "conspire" to produce a continuous supply of fresh names for the accusers. We do not know in how many cases Brattle knew why specific names were supplied to the accusers; but he knew well enough, as did many others in his day, that the accusers often named "perfect strangers."

We have already seen that various prominent citizens, some justices, some former justices, and almost all the clergy opposed the trials. Even if we include Stoughton, himself a former practicing clergyman, names of clergymen in support of the trials are scarce: Brattle mentions only Parris, Noyes, and Hale. Deodat Lawson can be added, and perhaps there were others, but evidence supporting the existence of such clergy is scarce.[16] Certainly there were some who simply did not know what to make of the whole thing, such as the Reverend Henry Gibbs, who recorded in his diary, "Wonders I saw, but how to judge and conclude, I am at a loss."[17] Still, Brattle's generalization that the clergy opposed the proceedings survives scrutiny.

In a dangerous climate, the clergy at times acted with conspicuous courage and integrity in defending accused people. On June 3, Samuel Phillips and Edward Payson, ministers from Rowley, testified in support of Elizabeth How, with Phillips exposing the pressure on an afflicted girl to offer false statements against Elizabeth How. James Allen, minister at Salisbury, testified for Mary Bradbury on September 7. The Reverend William Hubbard of Ipswich on June 20 defended the Christian character of Sarah Buckley, perhaps helping to save her life.[18] On behalf of John and Elizabeth Proctor, John Wise, a minister of Ipswich, wrote and was the first signatory on a petition supporting their innocence.[19] The Reverend Francis Dane of Andover signed a petition, along with fifty-two other people, that vividly describes how confessions were elicited through coercion and the promise of escaping the gallows (*SWP* II: 618–19). Also, Samuel Willard preached cautious sermons against the proceedings.[20] From a greater distance, and toward the end of the episode, four New York ministers rejected the validity of spectral evidence.[21]

Clerical opposition, however, was not sufficient in a colony that existed as a theocracy only in future mythologies. Brattle, quite specific in naming prominent people, such as most clergymen, who opposed the proceedings, turned vague in naming those who supported them, except for stating the obvious – that the court supported its own actions. His finger of accusation points unerringly to the Lieutenant Governor and Chief Judge, William Stoughton. With irony bordering on contempt, he assesses the latter:

> The chief Judge is very zealous in these proceedings, and says, he is very clear as to all that hath as yet been acted by this Court, and, as far as ever I could perceive, is very impatient in hearing any thing that looks another way. I very highly honour and reverence the wisdome and integrity of the said Judge, and hope that this matter shall not diminish my veneration for his honour; however, I cannot but say, my great fear is, that wisdome and counsell are withheld from his honour as to this matter, which yet I look upon not so much as a Judgment to his honour as to this poor land. (LTB 184)

It would oversimplify what happened in Massachusetts Bay in 1692 to lay at Stoughton's feet the whole affair, but there seems little reason to doubt that he, more than anyone else, influenced the judicial course of events.

II

When Governor Phips returned to the colony and ended the reign of Stoughton, he also began the task of constructing his version of the history that had transpired. In a letter dated October 12, 1692, he tells of finding, upon his initial arrival in the colony in May, a "Province miserably harrassed with a most Horrible witchcraft or Possession of Devills." Phips explains how "scores of poor people were taken with preternaturall torments some scalded with brimstone some had pins stuck in their flesh others hurried into the fire and water and some dragged out of their houses and carried over the tops of trees and hills for many Miles together."[22] Whether Phips colored the story to justify his actions to England, or simply repeated what he had heard, is hard to tell. We do have to keep in mind, however, that the letter aimed at justifying his own conduct.

Phips asserts that, in response to what he encountered, and at the request of friends of the afflicted, the Deputy Governor, and many others, he appointed the Court of Oyer and Terminer. The creation of this court represented a public statement on the gravity of the situation rather than on the lack of a legal basis for the normal judicial system to deal with the problem. Turning over the matter to Stoughton, Phips later asserted that he had just about nothing else to do with what happened:

> I was almost the whole time of the proceeding abroad in the service of Their Majesties in the Eastern part of the Country and depended upon the Judgement of the Court as to a right method of proceeding in cases of Witchcraft but when I came home I found many persons in a strange ferment of dissatisfaction which was increased by some hott Spiritts that blew up the flame, but on enquiring into the matter I found that the Devill had taken upon him the name and shape of severall persons who were doubtless inocent. . . .[23]

Phips continues with how he put an end to it.

Certainly Phips offers a self-serving account. One would hardly guess from it that he was on hand at least as late as June 25, when he ordered the arrest of William Milborne; but between then and the July 19 executions he apparently left the colony. His account, no matter how self-serving, remains plausible and probable. Phips, owing his office to Increase Mather, paid serious attention to him when he returned. By October 3, when Mather offered his *Cases of Conscience,* Phips was presumably home. Mather's power had returned.

Whether Phips exaggerates the turmoil of dissent he confronted upon returning is hard to say, but even allowing for that his narrative corroborates Brattle's. Stoughton, however, had been too powerful to stop until Phips returned. Nor did Stoughton give up easily: Even in January, when acquittals were routine and a new court played at the charade of trying people, Stoughton wanted to keep matters serious. There were three condemned to death in the new court, even though their cases were as spectral as the others. Stoughton relentlessly tried to keep the hangings going. Phips writes on February 21, 1693:

> The Deputy Govr. signed a Warrant for their speedy execucion and also of five others who were condemned at the former Court of Oyer and terminer, but considering how the matter had been managed I sent a reprieve whereby the execucion was stopped untill their Maj. pleasure be signified and declared. The Lieut. Gov. upon this occasion was inraged and filled with passionate anger and refused to sitt upon the bench in a Superior Court then held at Charles Towne [conducting witch trials], and indeed hath from the beginning hurried on these matters with great precipitancy. . . .[24]

Regardless of Phips's interest in offering accounts that shifted blame for the colony's catastrophe from him, it remains a fact that most of the court activity occurred in his absence. While there can be no single explanation for the Salem witch trials, we may reasonably assume that something radically different would have happened had Phips stayed home and the obsessive William Stoughton not been in a position of power. Stoughton pursued his cause to the end, and when others later retreated in shame from what they had done, Stoughton held fast. Unlike Ann Putnam, Jr., who would eventually retract, Stoughton would make no concessions that the devil made him do it. No evidence exists that either Ann Putnam or Stoughton sought or achieved financial gain from their witch-hunting; as we shall soon see, however, plausible suspicion on this score hovers about Stoughton. Ann blamed the devil; Stoughton credited God, and never backed off from affirming the rectitude of his conduct. According to Hutchinson,

> [Stoughton, on] being informed of . . . [Sewall's "confession of error"] observed for himself that, when he sat in judgment he had the fear of God before his eyes and gave his opinion according to the best of his understanding; and although it may appear afterwards, that he had been in an error, yet he saw no necessity of a public acknowledgment of it.[25]

Failing to acknowledge the almost monomaniacal role of Stoughton, we fail to understand why the court persisted so relentlessly.

III

Among the charges Phips made against Stoughton in his letter of February 21, he raised a matter having little to do with the invisible world. Stoughton, complained Phips, "by his warrant hath caused the estates, goods and chattles of the executed to be seized and disposed of without my knowledge or consent."[26] Nothing in this charge by Phips indicates that he either accused or exonerated Stoughton of profiting personally from these seizures; but in a very visible world, personal profit was indeed being made, and illegally so, and nothing was being done to stop it.

No evidence exists to indicate that Stoughton had any legal right to authorize the seizure of estates, a point implicit in the complaint by Phips. Although Carol Karlsen asserts that "Massachusetts passed a law at the height of the Salem outbreak providing attainder for 'conjuration, witchcraft and dealing with evil and wicked spirits,'" this legislation did not appear until after the properties had been seized and the episode had essentially passed.[27] The law to which she refers was introduced in October and passed in December;[28] before this, no legislation in 1692 had been passed in Massachusetts Bay to address the matter of witchcraft and its consequences. The law that is the original source of the Karlsen citation provided the death penalty for some forms of witchcraft and lesser penalties for other forms. Its language in part echoes that of the indictments in creating punishments for those guilty of having "wasted, consumed, pined or lamed" victims of witchcraft.

The reason why the General Court saw fit in October to initiate a definition of punishments for witchcraft seems clear enough: In spite of its mention of the death penalty, the new law sought to avoid future executions of innocent people by categorizing witchcraft activities and assigning them different punishments. Thus, the punishment for enchantments, as opposed to dealing with "evil and wicked" spirits, is a year in prison with six hours at the pillory four times in that year. This relatively mild punishment was legislated even for such activity as the destruction of cattle by enchantment; only after a second offense would the death penalty be invoked. Most significantly, however, the law addressed the point Thomas Brattle had made when he argued that the people who had allegedly been pined, consumed, and wasted were in fact quite healthy. The new law put the *intention* to commit such a crime in the lesser category of punishment. Had it been in force earlier, and had the court complied with it, no executions would have occurred because those named as victims in the indictments were not, in fact, pined, consumed, and wasted.

The new law thus discouraged the very actions that had been the foundation of the court's behavior, and it certainly did nothing to legitimize the seizures of property that had occurred. In instigating or allowing these seizures – his degree of complicity is not clear – Stoughton established a context for the appropriation of property on illegal grounds. As George H. Moore has pointed out, attainders occurred in violation of the 1641 *Body of Liberties;*[29] Governor Phips, after he returned, stated unambiguously that Judge Corwin's nephew, George Corwin, had acted illegally.[30]

Whether the limitations set in the *Body of Liberties* were always honored may be argued, but it remains the case that estates in New England had historically not been plundered in witchcraft cases. As Richard Weisman observes about the traditional New England relation to witchcraft, "the absence of any obvious financial incentive such as rights of confiscation of the property of accused witches further inhibited the development of unrestrained discovery methods similar to those employed on the Continent."[31] The appropriation of property during the Salem trials thus reflects another major deviation from traditional New England approaches to witchcraft. As Hutchinson notes, "Traitors and felons might dispose of their estates, real and personal, by will, after sentence, and if they died intestate, distribution was made as in other cases, there being no forfeitures."[32] Thus, the response of the Reverend Michael Wigglesworth in 1704 when he expressed his shock at learning of the financial sufferings of the families of the executed:

> [I]f it be true as I have been often informed, that the families of such as were Condemned for supposed witchcraft, have been ruined by taking away and making havoke of their estates, & Leaving them nothing for their releiff, I believe the whole Country lies under a Curse to this day, and will do, till some effectual course be taken by our honored Governour & Generall Court to make them some amends and reparations.[33]

Here is where George Corwin – age 26, according to Charles Upham – enters the picture.[34] Corwin, sheriff of Essex County, nephew of Jonathan Corwin, and son-in-law of Bartholomew Gedney, was profiting from the plight of the victims; put more bluntly, he was on the take. As his uncle and father-in-law sent people off to jail, George Corwin profited illegally. Although no evidence exists that these relatives conspired with George Corwin, they almost certainly knew of the financial activity; and unless Phips invented his account of Stoughton issuing warrants for seizures, the Lieutenant Governor also certainly knew (*SWP* III: 865).

Matters become more intriguing as we find another relative of Corwin, Wait Winthrop, on the Court of Oyer and Terminer. As is the case for Jonathan Corwin and Bartholomew Gedney, no evidence exists for Winthrop as part of a financial conspiracy; yet Charles Upham, who thought property seizures to be "in conformity with usage and instructions," observed with unintended irony that

> it appears that two of the judges were his uncles, and one his father-in-law. These personal connections may be borne in mind, as affording ground to believe, that, in the discharge of his painful duties, he did not act without advice and suggestions from the highest quarter.[35]

In addition to seizing estates, ostensibly for the king, Corwin also engaged in larceny on a smaller scale. Nor did he necessarily wait for people to die on the gallows before moving in: Calef gives a vivid account of how, while John and Elizabeth Proctor were in prison, the sheriff came to their house, seized their goods, and left no provisions for their children.[36]

Whether before or after their death, however, Corwin seized the estates of Samuel Wardwell and George Jacobs. Condemned males offered inviting targets, since surviving females no longer had spouses to protect them: The unprotected Margaret Jacobs, whose father fled and whose grandfather was hanged, had property seized.[37] Of the executed males, only the estate of Burroughs may have escaped Corwin's grasp, as no record of a seizure in his case survives. The estates of condemned females proved less inviting when male spouses survived.

Still, male presence offered no guarantee of escape from Corwin's grasp: After Nathaniel Cary's wife fled, Corwin seized property from him. At times, Corwin simply blackmailed his victims: John Moulton, for example, describes what happened after his "honerd father and mother Giles Corey & Martha his wife" were accused and imprisoned:

> [A]fter our fathers death the sh'rife thretened to Size our fathers Estate and for feare thar of wee Complied with him and paid him Eleven pound six shillings in monie. . . . (*SWP* III: 985)

The children of Mary Parker of Andover, John and Joseph Parker, tell an even more revealing story in the form of a petition dated November 7, 1692 – a document of particular interest because it reflects a contemporary view of the law's intention and shows some extortion by Corwin. The Parkers tell how "the sherriff of Essex," Corwin, sent an officer to seize the estate of their mother after she had been condemned. He demanded an account of the estate, "pretending it was forfeited to the King." When they said that no estate had been left, "he seised upon our cattell, Corn & hay, to a considerable value; and ordered us to go down to Salem and make an agreement with the sherrife, otherwise the estate would be exposed to sale." The brothers, uncertain of their legal status, did as instructed, and Corwin, after first demanding ten pounds to spare the estate, settled for six. He explained that he had a right to take the property, but as "a kindness" was allowing them the chance "to redeem" the estate (*SWP* II: 636). Apparently, the Parker brothers thought the matter through and decided to petition the governor and other authorities for redress. What the response to the petition was we do not know, but its assumptions make clear that the Parkers took for granted that the law did not allow for the seizure of a condemned person's estate:

> Now if our Mother had left any Estate, we know not of any Law in force in this Province, by which it should be forfeited upon her condemnation; much less can we understand that there is any Justice or reason, for the sherriff to seise upon our Estate. . . . (*SWP* II: 637)

In another incident Corwin may have actually fabricated an escape to justify his extortion: Calef prints a receipt Corwin gave for getting ten pounds from Samuel Bishop, son of Edward and Sarah Bishop, to recover the estate Corwin had seized when Bishop's parents allegedly escaped.[38] Edward Bishop, however, offers a different perspective in 1710, telling how, after he and his wife had been imprisoned, their estate had been seized by the sheriff. He also notes that he and his wife had been in prison for "thirtiey seven wekes" (*SWP* III: 979). Since they were sent to jail on April 22, the approximately thirty-seven weeks would have kept them in prison until the January trials. Thus, to get ten pounds, Corwin seems to have exploited an escape that did not occur. It may be that the children of the Bishops had thought that their parents had successfully fled; but the couple was in prison when Corwin presented his receipt.

What did Corwin do with the assets he took? Even if property seizures had been legal, he would have had no right to appropriate the assets for himself. Although it seems as if none of the monies even legally seized in the late seventeenth century found their way to England,[39] forfeitures, according to the accepted legal authority of the day, belonged to the Crown; those making them could "take nothing for doing their office."[40] Certainly, a sheriff had no authority to take people's estates and simply keep them for himself; yet the case of Philip English reveals Corwin as doing precisely that – unless he shared his loot.

English was among the wealthiest of those accused, and his money no doubt bought him an escape ticket, but he suffered heavy financial loss. In his account of what was taken from him, probably presented in 1710, he minces no words in describing his property as "Embezeld." He claims to have lost over a thousand pounds and to have recovered only sixty pounds and three shillings. It was where he recovered that money that catches our interest: It was "payd Me by the Administrators of George Corwine Late Sherife desesd and the Estate was so seisd & Tackin away Chiefly by the Sherife and his under offisers not withstanding I had given fore thousand pound Bond with Surety att Boston" (*SWP* III: 991). We do not know what share, if any, the officers had in the loot, but the fact that English received money from the estate of Corwin makes it clear enough that some or all had found its way into the sheriff's pocket.[41]

Although judicial corruption does not suffice to explain the Salem witch trials, the motive of financial gain cannot be excluded as part of the whole configuration. An account of the purported judicial ethics of Hathorne and Gedney in another context supports the possibility that these men may have condoned Corwin's behavior and perhaps shared in his gains. We see something of the way these justices worked from an account of an earlier incident unrelated to the witch trials.

> [A Quaker] woman whose oxen had been seized asked the court why. Hathorne answered, "They will be sold, and the money will go to the poor." She observed that the money would most likely go to Mr. Gedney, in whose tavern the court met. Hathorne was reduced to replying, "Would you have us starve while we sit about your business?"[42]

Whether they shared any of the money or not in 1692, at best Hathorne, Gedney, and Jonathan Corwin looked the other way, and Stoughton authorized the seizures in the first place.

George Corwin was not going to be prosecuted whether these justices or Stoughton shared in his gains or not: Too many people would be embarrassed by prosecutions of this sort. Remarkably, not even Governor Phips could enforce his will when he ordered Corwin to return what he had illegally taken from Philip English. In a letter from Phips to Corwin on April 26, 1693, Phips reminded Corwin that on March 2 he had ordered him to produce a list of the stolen goods; he now insisted that "all the Goods . . . seized from . . . English [be] restore[d] . . . unto him . . . ." Phips made clear in his agreement with Philip English that Corwin had "illegally" taken the goods, a considerable quantity, and that he had illegally taken the goods of "others."[43]

Whatever powers Phips had, however, proved insufficient to make Corwin comply, and a subsequent event points to Stoughton as Corwin's powerful ally. On May 15, 1694, a court presided over by Stoughton, who remained powerful long after the witch trials ended, specifically exempted Corwin and his heirs from any liability resulting from his action as sheriff from the time he began that office.[44] Stoughton protected Corwin, and perhaps himself. That Philip English eventually won some money from Corwin's estate reveals that the attempts to protect him were not failsafe. On the whole, however, they were pretty effective: English received little compensation, and Corwin's other victims received less or none.

In the general amnesty of October 17, 1711, everybody was pardoned of wrongdoing. In spite of the Philip English settlement, the general rule held: Nobody – not thieves, not false accusers – was brought to justice for crimes committed against others. To act against such people would require examining everyone's behavior, and it was a lot simpler and safer to let such matters pass in silence, communicating only – as did the judges in 1694 in the case of George Corwin – that those in authority were not to be held accountable.

Ever since Upham maintained that the property seizures were legal, scholars have argued for and against this proposition. The discovery that Phips assumed the seizures to be illegal does not forever settle the matter, and law scholars may yet find a way to reach a definitive decision from a purely legal point of view.[45] However, such legal complexity does not exist in connection with issues of corruption and theft. Whatever conclusion emerges regarding Stoughton's legal authority to order seizures, or regarding the legality and meaning of attainders placed on people, it remains the case that Stoughton and others knew that Corwin was not forwarding the

money to the colony or to the Crown. An untold story lies in the achievement of Stoughton and the court he headed in thwarting the attempt of
Phips to force restitution from George Corwin.

Ironically, the only person who offered some restitution was Samuel
Parris, in whose house it all started. His offer came in the form of a letter
to Jonathan Corwin in January 1693:[46]

> Whereas some [hints] were [tendered] to your honour[s] this day by
> some of our Village that some families in this place had of late [sus-
> tained] some [impairment] in their Estate, tho it is well known my
> own has suffered no little, yet to gratify Neighbours & to attempt the
> gain of amity, this may signify that I shall be willing to make abate-
> ment of [six] pounds of my sallery of the last year expired, & the like
> for this present year.
>
> Yr honours
humble Serv.
Sam: Parris[47]

IV

On January 19, 1694, Samuel Sewall made two observations in
his diary. One was that the kitchen floor had been finished; the other was
that a woman named Mrs. Prout had died, "not without suspicion of
Witchcraft." On January 27, Sewall noted that the hall floor had been finished; he records nothing more on Mrs. Prout.[48] Normalcy had returned,
and one did not fuss over every witchcraft allegation. That had been normal before the Salem trials; it was normal again. There remained only the
need, as Michael Wigglesworth lamented, to come to terms with the controversy between God and His chosen people over what had happened "in
the time of the Witchcraft."

The lamentations and the regrets came in abundance. Overwhelmingly
those who had witnessed the persecutions took no pleasure from them and
mourned their own ignorance and inefficacy in allowing the devil to triumph so successfully over them. Through property compensation and
public acknowledgment, the terrible mistake was conceded, though never
to the point of punishing individuals for their behavior. Whatever blight
they had placed upon the land, the authorities of Massachusetts Bay chose
to define it as a collective sin.

Individuals, however, did throw themselves upon the mercy of God.
The most famous appeal for help came on the fast day of January 14,
1697, when Samuel Sewall, "sensible of the reiterated strokes of God upon himself and family," publicly acknowledged his guilt as a judge in the

Salem witch trials.[49] It was probably on that day also that a document printed by Robert Calef appeared: In it twelve men who had served as jurors expressed the fear that they had "been instrumental with others, tho Ignorantly and unwittingly, to bring upon our selves, and this People of the Lord, the Guilt of Innocent Blood."[50] On the following day, January 15, a tearful Cotton Mather, in the privacy of his diary, recorded his fears that God would punish his family "for my not appearing with *Vigor* enough to stop the proceedings of the Judges, when the Inextricable Storm from the *Invisible World* assaulted the Countrey. . . ." He received "Assurance of the Lord, that Marks of His Indignation should not follow my Family, but that having the *Righteousness* of the Lord Jesus Christ pleading for us, *Goodness* and *Mercy* should follow us, and the signal *Salvation* of the Lord."[51] Jurors, a minister, and a judge had acknowledged their guilt; on August 25, 1706, Ann Putnam, Jr., offered her words of contrition.[52] However many others made private appeals for forgiveness, they, like the secular authorities, left to God the unraveling of the mystery of their conduct.

Explanations were the bailiwick of the future. In all the retractions, no concession ever came that witchcraft had not occurred. Something had gone wrong, true; but the question was how the innocent had been hurt, not whether witches had tormented the land. To the end of their lives, none of the participants whose written record survives drew back from the claim that the colony had been infested with witches. An enduring paradox developed in the immediate assessment of what had transpired: Injustice had been done, with innocent people punished for witchcraft; but the witchcraft itself had been affirmed. It was for later generations to reestablish as witches those who, at the end of the episode, had been exonerated by their persecutors.

Thus, in American mythology, Salem became both the place of martyrdom where superstition had uttered its final gasp, and the domain where witches had roamed. It became the site of Halloween tours, or for the martyrs of Margaret Murray's land inhabited by real witches: "Joan of Arc at one end of the series and the Salem witches at the other died for their Faith, not for their acts."[53] Some, whether for titillation or in compassion, would want to acknowledge as true what those of the late seventeenth century had come to understand was not: that real witches had hanged in 1692. By clinging tenaciously to the legacy left in the episode's aftermath – that of dark and demonic mysteries in Salem, no matter how dressed in scholarly adornments – we sustain in our image of Salem the paradox of affirming witchcraft in a land where witches who did not exist were hunted. We embrace the image of a past invisible world made visible, some-

times in saintly or sexy guise, but more often in demonic adornment, women darkly dressed. "Such unaccountable masses of shades and shadows,"
wrote Herman Melville in *Moby-Dick,* "that at first you almost thought
some ambitious young artist, in the time of the New England hags, had
endeavored to delineate chaos bewitched."[54]

God's controversy with New England notwithstanding, the image of
the hag endures.

10

Salem story

[S]he gives me a little snort in passing, if she'd been born at the right time they would have burned her over in Salem.

— John Updike, "A & P"[1]

I

The New England hag, the American witch, is nationally identified with the town of Salem, Massachusetts. Mention the word "witch" and ask for a community associated with it: Salem will come to mind. The town of Salem has ambivalently accepted this connection, and has struggled between appreciation of tourist dollars and discomfort with its bad reputation stemming from association with persecution and witchcraft.

On Essex Street in Salem, a dramatic representation of the town's response to its history appears in the presence of two buildings across the street from one another. One is the Essex Institute, repository of an extraordinary collection of information on the town of Salem and on history and lore related to the witchcraft episode and various responses to it since. The other is a store, associated with Laurie Cabot, the "official witch of Salem," where information about witchcraft and products related to it are sold. Various controversies within the community have centered on her presence and activities, and enough resistance to her has existed that, when the idea of naming her the official witch of Salem was proposed, the Mayor of Salem and others opposed it. However, in 1977 Governor Michael Dukakis asserted his authority, and Laurie Cabot gained the recognition she had sought for several years.

Laurie Cabot's Salem of 1692 includes real witches who were persecuted for their faith. The past she acknowledges is the world of Margaret Murray's *The God of the Witches*,[2] a community including covert witches caught and punished for practicing their faith. So Salem has both its historical repository and its contemporary minority of witches. The two compete to confirm their respective pasts.

Away from Essex Street, the town's association with witchcraft continues. Witchcraft museums and souvenir items abound, and an article in *The Boston Globe* offers a paragraph that sums up some of the associations:

> The symbol of the witch on a broom stick is all over Salem. The police have witches on their badges, traffic markers have witches and *The Salem Evening News,* has a witch on its masthead.[3]

This story appeared at Halloween time, when one can usually depend on newspaper coverage about Salem and the traditional Halloween celebrations there, called "Haunted Happenings." Other significations that might have been added include the business "Witch City Motors," the high-school football team "The Salem Witches," and bumper stickers on cars reading "Stop by for a Spell." The list of such examples could cover pages.

That Salem inherited this legacy of association with witchcraft may seem normal enough in view of the trials; yet some statistics complicate the matter. Estimates of how many people were actually accused of witchcraft in 1692 vary from scholar to scholar, with Richard Godbeer specifically listing 156 people and others listing fewer. Of the known cases, fewer than 10 percent of those charged came from the town of Salem.[4] Salem became associated with witchcraft because the legal system in Massachusetts Bay colony chose it as the location for the trials and executions – not because the town had a deeper allegiance to the concept of witchcraft than did others in the colony. Neither the initial accusations nor the decision to end the trials originated there. Only years later would the event take its particular mythic form of the "Salem witch trials" as a local event.

The initial outbreak of accusations occurred in Salem Village, now the town of Danvers. Much has been written about the underlying causes in Salem Village leading to the early accusations, and scholars in focusing their attention there have understood that knowing about the community of Salem Village was more important than knowing about the town of Salem. Yet, by Godbeer's data, those accused in Salem Village represented fewer than 20 percent of all the accused. One may quarrel with some of his data, as in his placement of Bridget Bishop as a Salem Village resident, but the picture Godbeer presents pretty accurately represents the aggregate percentages: Fewer than 30 percent of the accused resided in either Salem or Salem Village, although roughly half those executed came from one or the other.

The town of Andover, with about 27 percent of the accused, has some right to claim itself as the community unsurpassed in witch-hunting, but it has not chosen to define itself that way. Nor has Danvers, with a better claim than the town of Salem. In Danvers one finds the home of Rebecca Nurse, described as the "Witch House" in Salem brochures for tourists, although nothing sensational appears to the visitor: One finds instead a quiet cemetery and some monuments honoring Rebecca Nurse and others. Prior to the establishment in 1992 of a monument in Salem commemorating the victims of 1692, the monuments in Danvers represented by far the most visible memorials to the Salem victims; they remain the most visible memorials to those who defended the victims.

In Danvers one also finds historical markers and an aborted archeological dig of the Parris household. There, too, is the marker connecting Tituba to the outbreak's genesis; but nothing comparable to the carnival attractions found in Salem exists in Danvers. No ads appear in Danvers as in Salem to "Raise the Devil in Salem's Witch Dungeon" or to "Relive the famous witch hysteria at the Salem Witch Museum." One does not find, as in Salem, a tourist brochure carrying on its cover the image of an ugly hag of a witch,[5] or other such mementos.

The town of Salem has struggled with its location as the place of witch trials, partly exploiting the tourism and partly looking for redemption. Salem, now comprising about 38,000 people, is a tourist attraction that brings in over a million people a year, 100,000 for the "Haunted Happenings" Halloween celebration alone.[6] The signs welcoming tourists invite them to "Witch City," and a friendly atmosphere prevails as congenial and courteous residents of Salem encounter them. The enthusiasm among the residents to tell the "real" story of the witch trials sometimes seems pervasive.

Yet Salem has inherited the same ambivalence toward the trials reflected in the official assessments shortly after their occurrence. In the middle of the eighteenth century, somebody planted locust trees over the graves of the victims, buried around a half mile from the site of their execution – at least, that is what John Adams records in his diary in August 1766 in describing the trees "as a Memorial of that memorable Victory over the Prince of the Power of the Air."[7] However, as the years passed, the location of the burial site slipped from Salem's memory even as the town promoted itself as "Witch City." Nor did any markers indicate the location of the executions, popularly known as "Witch Hill."

In 1828 Supreme Court Justice Joseph Story thought that "Witch Hill" itself represented an appropriate monument "not to perpetuate our dishonor, but as an affecting, enduring proof of human infirmity; a proof that perfect justice belongs to one judgment-seat only, – that which is linked to the throne of God."[8] Nevertheless, through the years committees have formed or individuals have suggested another kind of monument: a memorial erected in Salem to those persecuted in the witch trials. In 1835 Nathaniel Hawthorne expressed his "regret, that there is nothing on its [Gallows Hill] barren summit, no relic of old, nor lettered stone of later days, to assist the imagination in appealing to the heart."[9]

In 1867 Charles W. Upham passionately urged a monument to the victims:

> When, in some coming day, a sense of justice, appreciation of moral firmness, sympathy for suffering innocence, the diffusion of refined sensibility, a discriminating discernment of what is really worthy of commemoration among men, a rectified taste, a generous public spirit, and gratitude for the light that surrounds and protects us against error, folly, and fanaticism, shall demand the rearing of a suitable monument to the memory of those who in 1692 preferred death to a falsehood, the pedestal for the lofty column will be found ready, reared by the Creator on a foundation that can never be shaken while the globe endures, or worn away by the elements, man, or time – the brow of Witch Hill. On no other spot could such a tribute be more worthily bestowed, or more conspicuously displayed.[10]

In 1892 the Reverend A. P. Putnam cited and endorsed the words of Justice Story, but added that while "Witch Hill"

> tells of man's frailty and injustice and wickedness, it tells, also, of those who died there for truth and for Christ. Some noble shaft should surmount the summit to do honor to their names and the sacrifice they made. . . .[11]

But no monument rises from "Witch Hill" in Salem today, nor does uncontested evidence even exist as to the actual location of the executions.[12]

The quest for monuments to memorialize the Salem witch trials continued. The *Boston Evening Transcript,* probably in 1931, reported a debate in the Salem City Council over whether to appropriate $1,000 for a suitable memorial.[13] In 1963, John Beresford Hatch published a monograph affirming that "net proceeds from the 1st printing of this publication shall be donated to the City of Salem [*sic*] . . . to further implement a fund-raising effort now in progress which will facilitate the erection of a Monument. . . ."[14] On January 26, 1970, the *Boston Herald-Traveler* reported plans for "A memorial to the 19 women [*sic*] who were hanged for witchcraft. . . ." The Salem Witchcraft Memorial Committee, formed in 1970, planned a fund drive for a monument in the hope that such a memorial would "be an enduring reminder" of "generally ordinary people" victimized by superstition and prejudice.[15] James Dodson in 1986 writes of an attempt to create a memorial to the victims of the persecutions, and Anne Driscoll, in 1988, writes of sculptor Yiannis Stefanakis's attempt to donate a statue of Rebecca Nurse, Mary Easty, and Sarah Cloyce, and the attendant controversy.[16]

These and other attempts failed, and the "coming day" envisioned by Charles Upham somehow did not materialize until the three hundredth anniversary of the Salem witch trials. Finally, a monument was built, unveiled in 1991 by Arthur Miller, whose choice symbolized the validation of truth over superstition and bigotry, and dedicated in 1992 by Elie Wiesel, whose presence emphasized the association of Salem with persecution and suffering. However, those who placed the memorial departed from Charles Upham's vision of an edifice at "Witch Hill"; instead, the monument is adjacent to a cemetery near Charter and North Liberty streets, inconspicuously tucked away. A small rectangular park is bordered by stone walls on three sides, with twenty stone "benches," each bearing the name of an executed person. At the entrance, inscribed stones in the ground record claims of innocence by the victims. People leave tokens of remembrance and even of protest at this memorial park. A visitor on November 10, 1992, would have seen a Halloween pumpkin on the bench of Mary Parker and flowers, tokens of remembrance, elsewhere. Against another wall in the memorial park on that day stood a poster bordered by a circle of flowers, a poster protesting the memorial:

> This Memorial was erected without the consultation, approval or permission of the Witches of Salem and it perpetuates a lie. The truth is Witchcraft is neither sin, nor lie, nor wickedness. May the Dead Rest in Peace.
> So Mote It Be.

The competition for claiming Salem's past persists; its identification as "Witch City" endures. The memorial does not change this.

As opposed to Salem wrestling with its identity, the world outside it has a reasonably consistent image of the community. If most people do not know that only a small minority of the witchcraft cases of 1692 occurred in this town, countless individuals associate the town with the ignorance of the past, with persecution rooted in cultural sensibilities now outgrown. If we accept the findings of a Gallup Poll taken in 1990, few people in America today – only 14 percent – believe in the existence of witches, even though 55 percent of the respondents believe in the devil.[17] Nevertheless, the word "witch" conjures the word "Salem."

Although much of the popular literature and media seek to make Salem sexy and entertaining – as ABC-TV did in 1970 in its "Salem Saga" episode of the show "Bewitched" with Elizabeth Montgomery – the prevailing notion of Salem remains that of a metaphor for persecution, a barbaric vestige of medieval Europe that came over with the Puritans. It is this association with medieval Europe that leads people to imagine witches burned at the stake in Salem. No matter how often the mistake is corrected, the popular image of burning witches in Salem remains, because burning evokes the starkest image of ignorance and barbarity that we popularly associate with the superstitions of the past. The burning image of Salem pervades the way we imagine the Salem episode and utilize it metaphorically. Sometimes we add the imagined water test, as the syndicated columnist Joseph Perkins does in protesting the treatment of former Secretary of Defense Caspar Weinberger:

> Right about now, Weinberger must imagine that he has been transported back to the time of the Salem witch trials. The accused were dunked on the bottom of a lake. If they drowned, they were innocent. If they floated to the surface undrowned they were burned at the stake as witches. They couldn't win either way.[18]

More often the image remains focused on burning. When Skip Bayless, sportswriter for the *Dallas Times Herald* complained about restrictions of the National Football League against players celebrating touchdowns by doing a dance, he asked what would be next, "Cornerbacks burned in Salem?"[19] When Jim Borgman of King Features drew his cartoon attacking the Moral Majority, it was a picture of a woman burning at the stake with a crowd of people in Puritan garb running toward her, some with torches. The caption read "A Feminist! . . . A Feminist! . . . Tool of Satan! . . . Burn Her! . . . It is God's Will! . . . ." A sign hovers over the scene reading "Welcome to Salem where resides in virtue the Moral Majority Rev. Cotton Falwell, Gov."[20] When Jim Castelli, bureau chief for the Catholic weekly *Our Sunday Visitor,* wanted to make the point that America at its inception was not "a model Christian society," he reminded his readers that "early Americans burned witches at the stake. . . ."[21] When Cibella Borges protested her suspension from the police force for posing nude in a magazine, she insisted that her action had constituted no crime. "She said she feared 'the trial is just like the New England witch hunt. They've made up their minds that I'm a witch and they want to burn me.'"[22] When Arthur Wade, writing for the tabloid *Weekly World News,* offered his account of the baby born in the north of France who at birth spoke "in the anguished voice of a woman being burned at the stake as a witch," he made it clear that in the infant's former life it had been enflamed in Salem.[23] In his vivid poem, "The Permanence of Witches," Michael Van Walleghen writes of "Salem / where the pale women / burned like leaves," reminiscent perhaps of Walt Whitman's image of "The mother of old, condemn'd for a witch, burnt with dry wood. . . ."[24] At the memorial in Salem on November 10, 1992, there rested on a stone border by the entrance a wreath of flowers with an inscribed ribbon band reading "Never Again the Burnings."

From poets to political commentators, from tabloid journalists to theologians and others, the persistent story of the Salem burnings repeats itself, as Salem's story forms a parable of the state offering up to the flames those who choose to defy its will. Historic scenes of hanging will not blur away mythic images of flames licking at the stake. Burning witches represents a more savage superstition, offers an association with a pre-Enlightenment world of Europe; yet, paradoxically, it keeps us more distant from Thoreau's reminder that we "are generally still a little afraid of the dark, though the witches are all hung, and Christianity and candles have been introduced."[25]

Salem safely accommodates the myth of America as the new Eden, the "brave new world" of *The Tempest,* the land where Europe might begin again and make the world right this time. It does this even though the "purity" of our Puritans has been irretrievably tarnished, even though those who, like John Winthrop, would have built "the good land" and "a Citty upon a Hill" along the way built a society that gave us "Witch Hill."[26] The expected and ordinary in Europe was not supposed to happen in America; that it happened so soon made overwhelmingly apparent that the new society would carry the old flaws. America has dealt with this intrusion into "the good land" by localizing it in the town of Salem and by representing it as European and medieval, the part that should have been left behind but that mistakenly and briefly intruded. Yet the image continues to haunt us, the image of the state persecuting its citizens, our image of not yet being safe from what we sought to escape in Europe. Salem metaphorically remains as our reminder of the Old World within us even as we encase and isolate it, and make it safe.

In defending Salem from the identification of it with ancient barbarities even as he condemned the witch trials, Charles W. Upham presented a defense that unwittingly offers us some insight into why Salem has evolved into its present metaphoric role. Upham referred to another incident in America's past, one that happened in New York City in 1741. He recounts that a rumor had been spread of "a conspiracy . . . among the colored portion of the inhabitants [of New York] to murder the whites." As the false report spread,

> a universal panic, like a conflagration, spread through the whole community; and the results were most frightful. More than one hundred persons were cast into prison. Four white persons and eighteen negroes were hanged. Eleven negroes were burned at the stake, and fifty were transported into slavery. As in the witchcraft prosecutions, a clergyman was among the victims, and perished on the gallows.

For Upham there is a moral in this, one showing "that any people, given over to the power of contagious passion, may be swept by desolation, and plunged into ruin."[27]

Thus, Upham's message is clear: A mob in any age can get out of hand; dangerous, false stories can spread, and only the bulwark of reason protects us from the horrors accompanying such tales. The New York riots and the injustices attending them offered him and his readers confirmation that New England, though it had sinned, had not sinned beyond the norms of humanity gone wrong. The riots confirmed that Salem was not the worst of places: It did not deserve the exclusive image of superstition, ignorance, and reason gone awry.

In constructing the modern myth of Salem, Upham had at the same time to show its enormous horror and to offer an apology and a defense of what had happened there. His Puritan predecessors at the end of the witch trials had acknowledged the horror and explained the action by insisting on the reality of witchcraft having occurred. Upham, like them, saw the horror but found an alternative mitigating factor: Witchcraft had not occurred, but Salem must be forgiven, for its denizens are human and subject to frailties seen in greater magnitude elsewhere, as in the New York episode. Finding sainted people having gone to their unjust death, he embraces their martyrdom and casts the sins of Salem as reflecting the nature of humanity having temporarily lost its way.

In choosing the New York riots of 1741, Upham also tells us something else, giving us a clue as to why Salem has served its metaphoric role. Obscure in our cultural memory, the events of 1741 brought a summer full of jailed people, as in 1692, and twenty-two people to the gallows, as opposed to the nineteen at Salem. It also brought what Salem did not:

people burned to death, thirteen of them. Of the thirty-five people executed, four were white, the others black.[28] All thirteen burned were black.
Why have we mythologized burnings at Salem that did not happen and
relegated to obscurity burnings in New York that did?

To say that "racism" explains this is accurate yet insufficient; something else must go into the equation. Partly, Salem's special place stems
from geographical scope, from being a whole colony rather than a city.
More important, Salem, in the distant past, almost in a never-never land
of magic, offers an imaginative landscape where we may more safely encounter the monsters we conjure. Salem serves our myths better because
the "burnings" occurred in a world no longer with us: Unlike the blacks,
the "witches" are gone. The myth of Salem as something that cannot
happen again, because the age of "witchcraft" has passed, ironically reas-
sures us of our safety from random irrationality by the state even as we
evoke Salem to label acts of persecution. From these quaint old times that
no longer apply to us, we have found our metaphor, no matter how far-
fetched, for injustice and irrationality. With our references to Salem – for
example, the trivialization of the trials in comments about cornerbacks –
we make our present points and tame the past. We create our national
mythology of Salem as if the "burning" could no longer happen. What
Upham remembered about 1741, most of us never knew.

II

Perry Miller has observed that, in the long history of Puritanism,
the Salem witch trials represented a blip of sorts, an event of almost no
significance in the development of the political and religious agendas of
Massachusetts Bay.[29] There is a lot to support that view. We have seen
that Stoughton's behavior certainly did little to hurt his political career,
and the subsequent politics and social behavior of Massachusetts Bay colony for the most part did indeed seem to progress as if the trials had never
happened. Wars with the French and with the Indians continued to hold
paramount interest, and the daily business of farming the land, trading,
and further establishing the fledgling culture that was less than a century
old continued undiverted from its course by the event that had absorbed
the colony's attention for a year.

Yet this blip, as of course Miller knows, had a different effect on future
generations. The Salem witch trials, uninfluential though they may have
been in the years immediately following 1692, have emerged as one of the
major images in American imagination. Any historian could quickly rattle
off a number of events in American history that were rooted in injustice
and caused the death of more than some twenty people; but none could

find an episode of injustice that has similarly shaped our metaphors of persecution or found a city to contain its symbol.

So powerful has this metaphor been that, ironically, it has crossed the ocean back to England and caught the attention of a country with its own long record of witchcraft persecutions. In 1987 in the County of Cleveland, United Kingdom, many children were removed from their homes after allegations against their parents of child sexual abuse. The parents, vehemently expressing their indignation, maintained their innocence; but a local physician, Dr. Marietta Higgs, insisted that, such protestations notwithstanding, the children had been sexually abused. Her case was based in part on evidence of traumas she had uncovered during anal examinations. The community split as the number of accusations increased and as the controversy spread across the country. The story ran frequently in the London papers.

Vociferously defending the parents was the Member of Parliament representing the district, Mr. Stuart Bell. Asserting his anger at what he saw as the injustice of false accusations, Mr. Bell protested the innocence of his constituents and was finally moved to write a book about what had happened. He titled it *When Salem Came to the Boro: The True Story of the Cleveland Child Abuse Cases.* Bell begins his book with a one-sentence paragraph: "The body that turned slowly and sadly in the wind was that of Bridget Bishop, the first of the Salem witches to be hanged."[30] He then proceeds with a brief account of the Salem witch trials. His work is divided into three "books," each with a title taken from something associated with those trials. Salem, for Mr. Bell, becomes the metaphor by which the events in Cleveland can be explained.

Why, one wonders, Salem? England had its own history of witch trials with imprisonments and executions. If England did not have any specific episode involving as many people as at Salem, it suffered from no shortage of witch-hunts. According to Alan Macfarlane, for example, of thirty-six accused women "at the 1645 Essex Assizes . . . nineteen were almost certainly executed, nine died of gaol fever, six were still in prison in 1648, and only one . . . was acquitted and escaped free."[31] The number of deaths are comparable to the Salem witch trials, and perhaps slightly greater. Governor William Phips had sanctioned the actions of the judiciary and the general reign of terror for a few months and then put an end to it; but England's King James had almost single-handedly rescued ignorance from enlightenment by writing a book on witchcraft, having Reginald Scot's intelligent treatise on witchcraft burned, and legitimating witch-hunting in England for almost another hundred years. The overall record of witch-hunting in the colonies is more modest than that of England, yet Mr. Bell went to Salem for his metaphor.

At issue here is no jingoism, no howl of outrage from an American over the indignity of "the pot calling the kettle black." The issue rather is one of curiosity: Why, after all, pick Salem when England offers a rich history of witchcraft persecution? One presumably understands why Americans turn to Salem for a metaphor of persecution: It is our country, our history, and our shame, might be an easy enough response. So why do not the British, such as Mr. Bell, turn to their history? Why has England not mythologized its witchcraft history as we have? True, you can visit Mother Shipton's Cave, where a witch is said to have once been, or you can go to Boscastle Harbour's small witch museum where a little erotica can be observed; but you will look in vain for an attraction in England such as Salem. The country has ignored, for tourists at least, a strong record of persecuting innocent people for witchcraft – not as strong a record as one finds in France, Germany, or Scotland, but one that might have offered its own metaphors. If Bell's use of Salem were a rare event, one might make less of it; but the fascination with Salem is old stuff in England.

Consider the case of the witch's bud. On August 21, 1902, an inhabitant of Theydon-Bois, Essex, England wrote to the former mayor of Salem:

> Ex Mayor Mr. Rantoul
> Dear Sir.
>
> A mutual friend, Profr [*sic*] Williams Jackson of New York University, gave me your address, and I venture to ask you if you can elucidate the mystery of the enclosed twig? It is said to have been, with many others, cut off a bush in Salem, Mass: growing on the spot where the last witches were burned in yr [*sic*] town! You will observe each bud is a witch's head. Can these have been specially produced, or is it a fact that the bushes on this spot grow in this manner?
>
> I shall be very much obliged if you will investigate the matter; being on the spot you will probably know at once if they are genuine? Apologising for giving you this trouble,
>
> I remain ys [*sic*] truly
> M. West[32]

That one should be interested in such a curiosity is less noteworthy than the fact of the interest coming from England. According to a document in the holdings of the Essex Institute, these buds were being sold on the streets of London "as growing on Gallows Hill in Salem, where, in 1692, the Witches were executed."[33] So there was reason for interest; but why sell buds from Salem on the streets of London? In a letter to Professor Jackson dated December 15, 1902, Professor B. L. Robinson of Harvard University – to whom, apparently, the communication had been passed from Mr. Rantoul – explains that the bud is a natural phenomenon from a native poplar, and that its facial features are explicable in biological terms. He gets into the spirit of things by wondering why more folklore has not developed out of this unusual biological specimen, which, he makes clear, is not restricted to Salem. In his patient and clinical reply, Robinson does not address the historiographic questions raised by this British fascination with American "witchcraft"; but he knows his history well enough gently to make the point, to correct the misconception, about the burnings at Salem.[34]

Burned or not, the "witches" of Salem cross more than one ocean as a metaphor for persecution. Take the tragic case of Lindy Chamberlain, an Australian woman who claimed her baby was killed by a wild animal only to find herself arrested for the baby's murder. The Australian and British press were mesmerized by the case, and the movie *A Cry in the Dark* grew from it.[35] Lindy Chamberlain, in jail proclaiming her innocence, compared her plight to the Salem witches.[36]

From a defense against claims of child abuse, to an appeal for justice from an Australian woman, Salem offers the language for protestations of innocence. Why this tragedy and not others? One reason rests simply with the relative magnitude of the Massachusetts Bay witch-hunt. That is, although in absolute numbers seventeenth-century England surpasses the colony in witchcraft indictments, Massachusetts Bay remains unmatched in that century in posing the full power of the state against its citizenry in the several months of one year.[37] England may have had more witchcraft cases, but it had had no concerted witch-hunt throughout the country as Massachusetts Bay had throughout the colony.

Another reason for the fascination with the Salem trials has less to do with statistical data for witchcraft cases than with imaginative constructions of America: the Western myth that a tired civilization could be restored in the "New World," that infinite possibility and individual freedom would be found on the shores of the new continent. In Caroline Chesebro's novel *Victoria* (1856), this parable of the promise of America and its inability to fulfill it gets played out in a story of unrequited love leading to witchcraft accusation and death; but within the framework of what would become an American tradition, the sexualization of Salem's story, Chesebro' offers something of the model from which the enigma of Salem's hold can be interpreted. Early in the novel, a ship crosses the ocean from England to New England, and Chesebro' writes:

> In this land to which we go, everything noble and great, in development, is to be anticipated. Religious freedom will bring all true freedom in its train. A higher life is surely possible here where there will be no room and no occasion for such temporizing and expediency as abound elsewhere, in older states and among more luxurious people.[38]

The mission of the Puritans to find their own religious hegemony notwithstanding, the power of this other myth, of America founded in religious freedom, has grown over the centuries. Historians trying to change this popular perception have no better chance of doing so than did King Canute in stopping the ocean's tide. Yet as Chesebro' plays out her tale of witchcraft persecution, we see that from the beginning she knew that the promise of America stated at the outset of her novel would not be fulfilled within it. Her story, though not tied to any historical characters or even to Salem, set as it is earlier in the century, still recapitulates our myth of Salem's story. The promise not kept came, paradoxically, to represent the triumph of America. In the final lines of the novel, Chesebro' writes:

> Not shipwrecked did they come to port.
> Victors they hailed the shore.
> And they possess the Land.[39]

No character in this novel is named Victoria; the title refers to this victory of possession, this triumph over the land, and implicitly over those who previously possessed it. The story of witchcraft within it, of the injustice, offers the test of faith and poses the question of whether the original journey held a true promise in a land that executed the innocent. Our national myth of Salem isolates the flaws in a culture that in another myth promised human perfectibility. At the same time the myth of Salem sanitizes the image of a perfected New World by placing the disruption distantly and narrowly, three hundred years ago, in one town with a population of fewer than two thousand people.[40] The failure of America to live up to the dream Europe imagined for it becomes contained in dark Tituba's voodoo-inspired hysteria of young girls in the town of Salem, in the abiding faith that a threshold of superstition had been crossed in 1692.

Of the many motifs that comprise our myth of Salem, one of the most enduring concerns this notion of transition from ignorance to knowledge, as Salem's story parallels the discovery of knowledge in the Garden of Eden, also at a price. In Marion Starkey's modern account, we see the articulation of this transition:

> During the witchcraft, and to some extent through the witchcraft, thinking people in Massachusetts passed over the watershed that divides the mystery and magic of late medieval thinking from the more rational climate of opinion referred to as "the Enlightenment."[41]

Starkey's observation echoes a view persistently expressed throughout the nineteenth and twentieth centuries, of Salem even redeeming the world from superstition by awakening people to the horror and danger of it. At the same time, her language furthers the paradox that has so often resided within this view of escape into enlightenment; for the journey she describes has béen "through the witchcraft," as if witchcraft had indeed been at the root of what happened in 1692. In our "enlightenment" we have held closely to this association of Salem with witchcraft.

The matter here concerns something other than overt claims for actual witchcraft at Salem, whether represented crudely by Montague Summers, romantically by Margaret Murray, or with the sophistication of Chadwick Hansen. At issue is the paradox of rational explanations intertwined with a vocabulary that, intentionally or not, implicitly affirms the victims of the trials as witches. Just as Marion Starkey's words suggest the presence of witchcraft at Salem, as did Stuart Bell's reference to Bridget Bishop as "the first of the Salem witches to be hanged," so too do the words of some of the best scholars who have addressed the subject.

George Lincoln Burr describes Bridget Bishop as "the first witch to be tried," and Richard Weisman writes of Abigail Williams, Elizabeth (Betty) Parris, and "four other bewitched females."[42] Carol F. Karlsen, disputing Paul Boyer and Stephen Nissenbaum's argument about women as economically benefiting from new conditions, writes that "Some witches clearly were, but most were not."[43] Boyer and Nissenbaum themselves refer to "five condemned witches,"[44] and John Demos, in the title of a table pertaining to a group of women accused in 1692, writes "Age of witches."[45] Numerous other examples could be cited from lesser scholars. The point here is not to argue that Burr, Weisman, Karlsen, Boyer and Nissenbaum, or Demos assumed these people actually to be "bewitched" or "witches"; rather, it is to show how powerfully and persistently the myth of witchcraft at Salem endures, how it invades the discourse not merely of popularizers but of learned scholars. As Perry Miller understood, out of the blip in New England history has emerged a myth of witchcraft too powerful to be subdued by scholarship; one that, in a surprising number of instances, instead subdues the scholars.

III

In 1992, the town of Salem observed the tercentenary of the Salem witch trials. Among the many events in Salem that year, the memorial was dedicated, Professor Joseph Flibbert of Salem State College organized a conference that brought to the town an unprecedented array of scholars to assess the trials and related topics of "witchcraft," and the First Church in Salem on September 20 readmitted to church membership Giles Corey and Rebecca Nurse.

That year also brought another anniversary, as the United States of America observed the five hundredth anniversary of Christopher Columbus's voyage of discovery. What had for years been simply a government holiday honoring what schoolchildren learned as the discovery of America became an occasion for bitter arguments over the definition of Columbus as a heroic voyager, the father of civilization in the New World, or as the brutal subjugator and murderer of the indigenous population he encountered.

The Columbus myth and the Puritan myth, in which the Salem trials are subsumed, have in common the idea of discovery, of claiming for civilization a triumph over the wilderness and the "savages" who occupied it, a chance to gain wealth and serve God. The "age of discovery," begun in our "New World" myth by Columbus, led to images of an idealized land, to what Edmundo O'Gorman called *The Invention of America*.[46] In this invented world Western civilization would be reborn, revitalized. Wealth would appear in abundance, and the failures of Europe would be undone.

This European notion of a new world where old disorders are reconciled gained one of its most memorable expressions in the utterance of Shakespeare's Miranda in *The Tempest:*

> Oh, wonder!
> How many goodly creatures are there here!
> How beauteous mankind is! Oh, brave new world,
> That has such people in't![47]

By this point in the play the witchcraft in this brave new world – for witchcraft is real in Shakespeare's *Tempest* – has been conquered, and harmony reigns.

Shakespeare knew of witchcraft as a concept in England. What he imagined would happen in the "brave new world" we can only guess; but the "witches" of that world have not yet been wholly subjugated, the world of harmony has not emerged. In a national fable of America, we have gathered this disorder and placed it in Salem. Those were the superstitious days, and in our myth we have contained the monster within us. Salem's story is now fit for our cartoons and sexual fantasies – even if at times we fear that not all the witches have been burned, and that those who lit the torches have not been wholly barred from our age of "enlightenment."

Appendix
Letter of William Phips to George Corwin, April 26, 1693

[*Note:* The condition of the manuscript has resulted in a few words being lost and in some being too faint for certain identification. Where I have been unable to identify a word or make a comfortable guess, I have placed a question mark with no words in brackets. Where I have made a comfortable guess, I have put the word with a question mark in brackets. The manuscript has almost no punctuation, and I have silently added some. I have similarly normalized a few words, and have expanded some standard abbreviations and silently translated a few Latin forms.

The handwriting in this letter differs from a letter signed by Phips and dated February 21, 1692/3, which is in the holdings of the Colonial Williamsburg Foundation Library; both, however, carry the identifiable signature of William Phips. I am grateful to the Colonial Williamsburg Foundation for allowing me to examine the letter of February 21, and to the American Antiquarian Society for permission to publish below the letter from Phips to Corwin.]

By his Excellency Sir William Phips Knight Captain General & Governor in chief of their Majesties Province of the Massachusetts-Bay in New England to Captain George Corwin High Sheriff of the County of Essex:

Whereas Philip English late of Salem Merchant did by his Petition bearing unto the second of March last past set forth that you the sd George Corwin in the Month of August last did illegally seize into your hands the Goods, Chattles, Merchandize belonging to the sd Philip English and others, praying that you the sd George Corwin might be ordered to appear before me and bring a true Inventory of the same. Whereupon I then issued out my Precept commanding you to appear before me on the sixth day of the sd March and to bring with you a true Inventory of the same in

each particular Specie in full Quantity and Quality to the [whi?]ch precept; you the sd George Corwin did accordingly Appear and did on the
[sd?] day of the said Month oblidge yourself by promises all the Goods,
Chattles &c so seized from the sd Philip English to restore them unto him
the sd Philip English or his order upon demand. These are therefore in
their Majesty's Name to will and require you the sd George Corwin upon
sight hereof to deliver or cause to be delivered all & singularly the Goods,
Chattles [?] &c & Personal Wares, Merchandize, ketch, Sloop or anything
to them in any [wise?] appertaining or belonging with all the Produce,
Issues, and Profits [therein?] by you received or in any wise from the sd
premises accruing or arising by you the sd George Corwin or your Order
so seized – taken or received from the sd Philip English or his assigns (by
virtue or pretense of any Order or colour whatsoever) unto the said Philip
English or his order in their particular Species in full Quantity and Quality
And hereof fail you not as you will Answer the contrary at your Peril.
Given [?] my hand & seale this 26th day of April, the year of our Lord
1693 and in the fifth year [of the reign of William and Mary?].

William Phips

Notes

Introduction

1. Nathaniel Hawthorne, *The Snow-Image and Uncollected Tales*, ed. William Charvat, Roy Harvey Pearce, and Claude M. Simpson (Columbus: Ohio State University Press, 1974), p. 279.
2. Surviving court records usually qualify a person's age, so that someone might be described as "aged about 18" rather than as "18." To avoid consistent qualifications in the text, I am generally omitting these age qualifications. Unless otherwise indicated, ages in the text are based on court records as found in *The Salem Witchcraft Papers: Verbatim Transcripts of the Legal Documents of the Salem Witchcraft Outbreak of 1692*, ed. Paul Boyer and Stephen Nissenbaum, 3 vols. (New York: DaCapo Press, 1977). The Reverend John Hale gives the age of Abigail Williams as 11 and Elizabeth Parris as 9: "A Modest Inquiry into the Nature of Witchcraft" (1702), partially reprinted in *Narratives of the Witchcraft Cases 1648–1706*, ed. George Lincoln Burr (New York: Charles Scribner's Sons, 1914), pp. 395–432, cited p. 413.

   Subsequent references to *The Salem Witchcraft Papers* will be cited parenthetically in the text as *SWP*.
3. Rev. John Hale, "A Modest Inquiry," in Burr, *Narratives*, p. 413. Cotton Mather indicates 1688 as the year of the Goodwin episode. See "Memorable Providences, relating to Witchcrafts and Possessions" (1689) in Burr, *Narratives*, pp. 89–144, cited p. 100. Hale may have confused the 1689 publication date of "Memorable Providences" with the date of the occurrence.
4. C. Mather, "Memorable Providences," in Burr, *Narratives*, p. 100.

5. Ibid., p. 101.
6. Excellent studies offering backgrounds on the subject of New England witchcraft include John Demos, *Entertaining Satan: Witchcraft and the Culture of Early New England* (Oxford: Oxford University Press, 1982); Richard Godbeer, *The Devil's Dominion: Magic and Religion in Early New England* (Cambridge: Cambridge University Press, 1992); Carol F. Karlsen, *The Devil in the Shape of a Woman* (New York: W. W. Norton, 1987); and Richard Weisman, *Witchcraft, Magic, and Religion in 17th-Century Massachusetts* (Amherst: University of Massachusetts Press, 1984). For selected documents from some of the cases, see *Witch-Hunting in Seventeenth-Century New England: A Documentary History 1638–1692,* ed. David D. Hall (Boston: Northeastern University Press, 1991).
7. This and the above quotation are from *The History of the Colony and Province of Massachusetts-Bay* (1764), 3 vols., ed. Lawrence Shaw Mayo (Cambridge, Mass.: Harvard University Press, 1936), vol. II, pp. 17–18. I have used 1764 as the original date of publication, but the three-volume work did not see complete publication until 1828. For a discussion of the textual history, see Mayo's introduction, I, vi–vii.
8. Hale, "A Modest Inquiry," in Burr, *Narratives,* pp. 414–15.
9. Godbeer, *The Devil's Dominion,* pp. 238–42, lists 156 known cases. It is probable that other cases occurred with records of them not surviving. Godbeer lists four who died in prison, including Lydia Dustin, who was acquitted in her 1693 trial and ordered released once she paid her jail bills – which, apparently, she could not do; thus she died in prison on March 10, 1693 (*SWP* III: 958). Others may also have died in prison without the records surviving.
10. Paul Boyer and Stephen Nissenbaum, *Salem Possessed: The Social Origins of Witchcraft* (Cambridge, Mass.: Harvard University Press, 1974).
11. For an argument against the village quarrel view see Larry Gragg, *The Salem Witch Crisis* (New York: Praeger, 1992), p. 142. Gragg points to the Andover aspect of the witchcraft episode even though the community "was notable for its harmony."
12. Nathaniel Hawthorne, *The Scarlet Letter* (1850), ed. William Charvat, Roy Harvey Pearce, and Claude M. Simpson (Columbus: Ohio State University Press, 1962), p. 9.
13. Mary Wilkins Freeman, *Giles Corey, Yeoman* (New York: Harper, 1893); J. W. DeForest, *Witching Times* (1856), ed. Alfred Appel, Jr. (New Haven: College and University Press, 1967); and Henry Wadsworth Longfellow, *Giles Corey of the Salem Farms,* in *The New-England Tragedies* (Boston: Ticknor & Fields, 1868), pp. 97–179.
14. *Salem-Village Witchcraft: A Documentary Record of Local Conflict in Colonial New England,* ed. Paul Boyer and Stephen Nissenbaum (Belmont, Calif.: Wadsworth Publ., 1972).
15. Weisman, *Witchcraft, Magic, and Religion,* p. 112, for example.

1. Dark Eve

1. James F. Droney, "The Witches of Salem," *Boston* (Boston: Greater Chamber of Commerce, October 1963), pp. 42–6, 65, 92–3, at p. 46.
2. Charles W. Upham, *Salem Witchcraft; with An Account of Salem Village, and a History of Opinions on Witchcraft and Kindred Subjects* (1867), 2 vols.; reprinted (Williamstown, Mass.: Corner House Publ., 1971).
3. Ibid., II, pp. 2–3.
4. Marion L. Starkey, *The Devil in Massachusetts: A Modern Enquiry into the Salem Witch Trials* (New York: Alfred A. Knopf, 1949); 2d ed. (1950), pp. 10–11, 15.
5. Paul Boyer and Stephen Nissenbaum, *Salem Possessed: The Social Origins of Witchcraft* (Cambridge, Mass.: Harvard University Press, 1974), p. 181.
6. Kai Erikson, *Wayward Puritans: A Study in the Sociology of Deviance* (New York: John Wiley and Sons, 1966), p. 141.
7. Chadwick Hansen, *Witchcraft at Salem* (New York: George Braziller, 1969), p. 31.
8. Selma R. Williams and Pamela J. Williams, *Riding the Night Mare: Women & Witchcraft* (New York: Atheneum, 1978), p. 147.
9. Katherine W. Richardson, *The Salem Witchcraft Trials* (Salem, Mass.: Essex Institute, 1983), p. 6.
10. J. W. Hanson, *History of the Town of Danvers from its Earliest Settlements to the Year 1848* (Danvers, Mass., 1848) is silent on the myth that Upham would codify.
11. *Three Sovereigns for Sarah: A True Story,* dir. Philip Leacock (PBS, 1985), 152 min.; originally presented as a three-episode series on "American Playhouse."
12. "Witch Trials Began as Prank," *Press & Sun Bulletin* (Binghamton, N.Y.), October 28, 1990, p. 140.
13. *Daily News* (New York), September 17, 1991, p. 20; *Newsweek,* August 31, 1992, p. 65; *Smithsonian,* vol. 23, no. 1 (April 1992), p. 118; *Harvard Magazine,* vol. 94, no. 4 (March–April 1992), p. 46.
14. Enders A. Robinson, *The Devil Discovered: Salem Witchcraft 1692* (New York: Hippocrene Books, 1991), p. 134; Stuart Bell, M.P., *When Salem Came to the Boro* (London: Pan Books, 1988), p. 4.
15. Chadwick Hansen, "The Metamorphosis of Tituba, or Why American Intellectuals Can't Tell an Indian Witch from a Negro," *New England Quarterly,* vol. 47, no. 1 (March 1974), pp. 3–12. For a more recent and intriguing essay on the possible origins of Tituba, see Elaine G. Breslaw, "The Salem Witch from Barbados: In Search of Tituba's Roots," *Essex Institute Historical Collections,* vol. 128 (October 1992), pp. 217–38. Breslaw speculates on a possible identification of Tituba, one that would indicate her age in 1692 as "between twenty-five and thirty years old" (p. 224).

16. Carolus M. Cobb, "The Medical Aspect of Salem Witchcraft," typescript of talk delivered to Rebecca Nurse Memorial Association, August 6, 1910, p. 9, Essex Institute, Salem, Mass. I am grateful to the Essex Institute and to Jane E. Ward, Curator of Manuscripts, for permission to quote from this typescript.

17. Sidney Perley, *The History of Salem Massachusetts* (Salem, Mass.: privately published, 1924), III, p. 255.

18. Regarding the issue of some *Salem Witchcraft Paper* documents being trial documents, in spite of prevailing beliefs that no trial records survive, see Chapter 7, pp. 137–8

19. These works are reprinted to varying extents in *Narratives of the Witchcraft Cases 1648–1706*, ed. George Lincoln Burr (New York: Charles Scribner's Sons, 1914), as follows: Cotton Mather, "The Wonders of the Invisible World" (1693), pp. 203–52; Robert Calef, "More Wonders of the Invisible World" (1700), pp. 289–394. Rev. John Hale, "A Modest Inquiry into the Nature of Witchcraft" (1702), pp. 395–432.

20. Thomas Hutchinson, *The History of the Colony and Province of Massachusetts-Bay* (1764), 3 vols., ed. Laurence Shaw Mayo (Cambridge, Mass.: Harvard University Press, 1936).

21. Ann Putnam's age has variously been given by commentators as 12 or 13. I am following Deodat Lawson's indication that she was 12. Lawson, "A Brief and True Narrative" (1692), in Burr, *Narratives*, p. 155.

22. More specifically, Elizabeth Hubbard was the niece of Griggs's wife Elizabeth. See H. Minot Pitman, "Early Griggs Families of Massachusetts," *New England Historical and Genealogical Register*, vol. 123 (July 1969), p. 172.

23. In connection with the Salem witch trials, David D. Hall writes about folk legends of "shape-shifting black dogs." See *Worlds of Wonder, Days of Judgment: Popular Religious Belief in Early New England* (New York: Alfred A. Knopf, 1989), p. 88. Perhaps the white dog is connected to this motif.

24. Hale, "A Modest Inquiry," in Burr, *Narratives*, pp. 413–14.

25. Shirley Jackson, *The Witchcraft of Salem Village* (New York: Random House, 1956), p. 87.

26. On Osborne's age, see Carol F. Karlsen, *The Devil in the Shape of a Woman* (New York: W. W. Norton, 1987), p. 243. For land disputes see Boyer and Nissenbaum, *Salem Possessed*, p. 193, which also provides details of Sarah Osborne's marriage to her servant: Various commentators have felt that this marriage made Sarah Osborne vulnerable to accusations of witchcraft. For church attendance of Sarah Good and Sarah Osborne, see *SWP* II: 360, 611.

27. Calef, "More Wonders," in Burr, *Narratives*, p. 343.

28. Hale, "A Modest Inquiry," in Burr, *Narratives*, p. 415.

29. Ann Petry, *Tituba of Salem Village* (New York: Harper Trophy, 1964), p. 12.

30. Maryse Condé, *I, Tituba, Black Witch of Salem,* trans. Richard Philcox (Charlottesville: University Press of Virginia, 1992), particularly p. 93.

31. Hale, "A Modest Inquiry," in Burr, *Narratives,* p. 415.

32. John Webster, *The Displaying of Supposed Witchcraft, Wherein is affirmed that there are many sorts of Deceivers and Imposters, and Divers persons under a passive Delusion of Melancholy and Fancy* (London, 1677). For the debate between Webster and Joseph Glanvill, an important source for defenders of the Salem episode, see Thomas Harmon Jobe, "The Devil in Restoration Science: The Glanvill–Webster Witchcraft Debate," *Isis,* vol. 72 (1981), pp. 343–56.

33. *The Complete Works of Thomas Shadwell,* vol. 4, ed. Montague Summers (London: Fortune Press, 1927), p. 101.

34. Calef, "More Wonders," in Burr, *Narratives,* p. 342.

35. Hale, "A Modest Inquiry," in Burr, *Narratives,* pp. 413–14.

36. Transcribed by William Thaddeus Harris, *New England Historical and Genealogical Register,* vol. 11 (April 1857), p. 133. For a modern printing of this episode, see *Salem-Village Witchcraft: A Documentary Record of Local Conflict in Colonial New England,* ed. Paul Boyer and Stephen Nissenbaum (Belmont, Calif.: Wadsworth Publ., 1972), p. 278. The reference to Sibley as "sister" is congregational.

37. Rossell Hope Robbins, *The Encyclopedia of Witchcraft and Demonology* (New York: Crown Publ., 1959), p. 431.

38. Samuel Willard, *Some Miscelliny Observations On Our Present Debates Respecting Witchcrafts, in a Dialogue between S & B,* pseudonymously by "P. E. and J. A." (Philadelphia, 1692), p. 7.

39. William Perkins, *A Discourse of the Damned Art of Witchcraft* (Cambridge: Perkins, 1608); Richard Bernard, *A Guide to Grand-Jury-Men . . . in Cases of Witchcraft* (London, 1627).

40. Exodus 22:18.

41. Boyer and Nissenbaum, *Salem Possessed,* p. 6.

42. For a valuable discussion of Massachusetts Bay government during the period of the revoked charter, see T. H. Breen, *Puritans and Adventurers* (New York: Oxford University Press, 1980), pp. 81–105.

43. David Konig, *Law and Society in Puritan Massachusetts: Essex County, 1629–1692* (Chapel Hill: University of North Carolina Press, 1979), p. 168.

44. The view that Salem went wrong because Phips replaced Bradstreet is not an original one, but it is no less persuasive for that. See Upham, *Salem Witchcraft,* I, p. 451.

45. For the establishment of the court see Thomas Hutchinson, *The Witchcraft Delusion of 1692,* notes by William Frederick Poole (Boston: privately printed, 1870), p. 32. Hutchinson identifies the original court members as William Stoughton, John Richards, Nathaniel Saltonstall, Wait Winthrop, Bartholomew Gedney, Samuel Sewell, John Ha-

thorne, Jonathan Corwin, and Peter Sergeant. Burr, *Narratives*, pp. 185, 355, says that Corwin took Nathaniel Saltonstall's place when he resigned, but the original court included both. Burr seems to be following Upham, *Salem Witchcraft*, II, p. 251.

46. In his listing of witchcraft cases in Massachusetts Bay prior to the Salem witch trials, Richard Weisman identifies four certain executions and one probable execution. See Richard Weisman, *Witchcraft, Magic, and Religion in 17th-Century Massachusetts* (Amherst: University of Massachusetts Press, 1984), pp. 191–203.

47. Joseph B. Felt, *Annals of Salem* (Salem, Mass.: W. & S. B. Ives, 1845; 2d ed., Boston: James Munroe & Co., 1849), II, p. 478. In a note at the end of her novel, *Tituba of Salem Village* (p. 254), Ann Petry asserts that Tituba was sold to a weaver named Samuel Conklin, who subsequently purchased John Indian. I have found no primary source to confirm either Felt or Petry. However, in his first edition of *Annals of Salem,* Felt makes no reference to the sale of Tituba. Presumably he found some evidence after the first edition and prior to the second. I can make no guess as to how good this evidence is.

2. The girls of Salem

1. Thomas Hutchinson, *The History of the Colony and Province of Massachusetts-Bay* (1764), 3 vols., ed. Laurence Shaw Mayo (Cambridge, Mass.: Harvard University Press, 1936), II, pp. 46–7. For an earlier account of the episode see Daniel Neal, *History of New-England* (London, 1720), 2 vols., I, pp. 495–541.

2. Hutchinson, *History,* II, p. 47. For Hutchinson's source see *SWP* III, p. 1016. The first complaint to appear in print about the character of the accusers appears in Samuel Willard, *Some Miscelliny Observations On Our Present Debates Respecting Witchcrafts, in a Dialogue between S & B,* pseudonymously by "P. E. and J. A." (Philadelphia, 1692), pp. 7–8. For a similar view by Cotton Mather after the trials had ended, see his *The Life of Sir William Phips* (1697), ed. Mark Van Doren (New York: Covici–Friede Inc., 1929), p. 145. Enders A. Robinson, *The Devil Discovered: Salem Witchcraft 1692* (New York: Hippocrene Books, 1991), p. 249, offers without citation an account of what later happened to some of the accusers, a description generally at variance with the view of them as "profligate." Susannah Sheldon, described on May 8, 1694, as "a person of Evill fame," had some legal difficulties in Providence, Rhode Island: *The Early Records of the Town of Providence,* ed. Horatio Rogers, George M. Carpenter, and Edward Field, vol. 10 (Providence, R.I.: Snow and Farnham, 1896), pp. 13–14. I cannot confirm that she is the same Susannah Sheldon from the "circle of girls," but the record does refer to her as having come to Providence from elsewhere.

3. Hutchinson, *History,* II, p. 47.
4. Charles W. Upham, *Salem Witchcraft; with An Account of Salem Village, and a History of Opinions on Witchcraft and Kindred Subjects* (1867), 2 vols.; reprinted (Williamstown, Mass.: Corner House Publ., 1971), II, p. 2.
5. Ibid., p. 5.
6. Alison Lurie, *Imaginary Friends* (New York: Avon Books, 1967), p. 66.
7. Arthur Miller, "Again They Drink from the Cup of Suspicion," *New York Times,* Sunday, November 26, 1989, pp. 5, 36, at p. 36.
8. James F. Droney, "The Witches of Salem," *Boston* (Boston: Greater Chamber of Commerce, October 1963), pp. 42–6, 65, 92–3, at p. 65.
9. Marion L. Starkey, *The Devil in Massachusetts: A Modern Enquiry into the Salem Witch Trials* (New York: Alfred A. Knopf, 1949); 2d ed. (1950), p. 97.
10. "Pediatric Aspects of the Salem Witchcraft Tragedy," *American Journal of Diseases of Children,* vol. 65 (May 1943), reprinted in *Witches and Historians: Interpretations of Salem,* ed. Marc Mappen (Huntington, N.Y.: Robert E. Krieger Publ., 1980), p. 63.
11. Chadwick Hansen, *Witchcraft at Salem* (New York: George Braziller, 1969), p. x.
12. John Demos, "Underlying Themes in the Witchcraft of Seventeenth-Century New England," *American Historical Review,* vol. 75 (June, 1970), pp. 1311–26.
13. Marion L. Starkey, *The Devil in Massachusetts,* p. 13, had argued a tension between the psychological and sociological in seeing "these girls . . . with repressed vitality, with all manner of cravings and urges for which village life afforded no outlet." Her view was incorporated into the more sophisticated thesis of Lyle Koehler in his analysis of women and power in seventeenth-century New England, *A Search for Power* (Urbana: University of Illinois Press, 1980), p. 396. See Koehler generally, pp. 383–417.
14. John Demos, *Entertaining Satan: Witchcraft and the Culture of Early New England* (Oxford: Oxford University Press, 1982).
15. Paul Boyer and Stephen Nissenbaum, *Salem Possessed: The Social Origins of Witchcraft* (Cambridge, Mass.: Harvard University Press, 1974).
16. Richard Weisman, *Witchcraft, Magic, and Religion in 17th-Century Massachusetts* (Amherst: University of Massachusetts Press, 1984).
17. Carol F. Karlsen, *The Devil in the Shape of a Woman* (New York: W. W. Norton, 1987).
18. The social model has become so pervasive that James E. Kences asserts that the "afflicted" accusers "are no longer accused of fraud." "Some Unexplored Relationships of Essex County Witchcraft to the Indian Wars of 1675 and 1689," *Essex Institute Historical Collections,* vol. 120 (July 1984), p. 211.

19. Linnda Caporael, "Ergotism: The Satan Loosed in Salem?" *Science,* vol. 192, no. 4234 (April 2, 1976), p. 25.
20. Nicholas P. Spanos and Jack Gottlieb, "Ergotism and the Salem Village Witch Trials," *Science,* vol. 194, no. 4272 (December 24, 1976), p. 1390.
21. Mary K. Matossian, "Ergot and the Salem Witchcraft Affair," *American Scientist* (July–August 1982), p. 356.
22. For Brattle as a scientist, see Rick Kennedy, "Thomas Brattle and the Scientific Provincialism of New England, 1680–1713," *New England Quarterly,* vol. 63, no. 4 (December 1990), pp. 584–600. For Brattle's observations on the witch trials and the health of the accusers, see Chapters 4 and 9 of the present volume.
23. Walter Sullivan, "New Study Backs Thesis on Witches," *New York Times,* August 29, 1982, p. 30.
24. Gerald C. Davidson and John M. Neale, *Abnormal Psychology: An Experimental Clinical Approach,* 4th ed. (New York: John Wiley & Sons, 1986).
25. Spanos and Gottlieb, "Ergotism," p. 1391.
26. Ibid., p. 1392.
27. I wish to emphasize that in pointing to this slip by Boyer and Nissenbaum I in no way mean to diminish their extraordinary contributions to the scholarship on Salem; indeed, my own work is heavily indebted to them. I cite them only to emphasize the strength of the myth of the accusers as "girls" – a myth strong enough to have caught even people of such eminence using this habituated description.
28. Upham, *Salem Witchcraft,* II, p. 510.
29. The association of pins with witchcraft cases was not an invention of the Salem accusers. We get comments on the subject from, for example, Joseph Glanvill, who strongly believed in witchcraft activity, and from Reginald Scot, who expressed great skepticism on the subject. Glanvill, *Saducismus Triumphatus* (London, 1681), p. 2; Scot, *The Discoverie of Witchcraft* (1584), intro. Hugh Ross Williamson (Carbondale, Ill.: Southern Illinois University Press, 1964), p.124. The concept of connecting pins with affliction was old in Scot's day.
30. In 1693 the sermon was reprinted in Boston and London as "Christ's Fidelity the Only Shield against Satan's Malignity." For a discussion of the textual history see *Narratives of the Witchcraft Cases 1648–1706,* ed. George Lincoln Burr (New York: Charles Scribner's Sons, 1914), pp. 147–9. The above citation is from the Appendix to "Christ's Fidelity," in Upham, *Salem Witchcraft,* II, p. 530. Upham modernized punctuation and capitalization but was otherwise faithful to the text.
31. John Webster, *The Displaying of Supposed Witchcraft, Wherein is affirmed that there are many sorts of Deceivers and Imposters, and Divers persons under a passive Delusion of Melancholy and Fancy* (London, 1677), p. 272.

32. "Former Page Admits Homosexual Charges Were Nothing but Lies," *Binghamton Evening Press,* August 28, 1982, p. 1A; "2 Minn. Youngsters Recant Testimony on Sexual Abuse," *Binghamton Sunday Press,* December 16, 1984, p. 5F. Both stories are from the Associated Press.

33. Herman Melville, *Billy Budd,* ed. Harrison Hayford and Merton M. Sealts, Jr. (Chicago: University of Chicago Press, 1962), p. 108; *The Confidence-Man,* vol. 10 in *The Complete Writings of Herman Melville,* gen. ed. Harrison Hayford, Hershel Parker, and G. Thomas Tanselle (Evanston, Ill.: Northwestern University Press / Chicago: Newberry Library, 1984), p. 32.

34. Robert Calef says that she was at the examination of Martha Corey on March 21; he goes on to say that she was not only one of the original accusers but was "also [among] the chief in these Accusations"; "More Wonders of the Invisible World" (1700), in Burr, *Narratives,* pp. 289–394, cited p. 344. It is impossible to say if Calef is mistaken as to whether Betty was at the examination on March 21, but he is certainly mistaken in lumping her with Ann Putnam and Abigail Williams as "chief" accusers, except perhaps in the very early stages. Calef also has a problem in chronology at the outset of the episode, in that he has Tituba complained against on or after March 11, when in fact she was arrested February 29 (Burr, p. 342; *SWP* III: 745). The point here is not to discredit Calef, who is a major source of information about the episode, but to offer a reminder that he is not relying on his own observations for everything he reports.

35. In her testimony against Martha Corey and Rebecca Nurse, Anne Sr. is described as "agged about 30 years" (*SWP* II: 603). However, she was apparently under 30, since the record of her admission into the church on June 4, 1691, describes her as *"An. Aetat 27."* See *Salem-Village Witchcraft: A Documentary Record of Local Conflict in Colonial New England,* ed. Paul Boyer and Stephen Nissenbaum (Belmont, Calif.: Wadsworth Publ., 1972), p. 274.

36. Her husband, Joseph Pope, was 41 years old (*SWP* II: 683).

37. Deodat Lawson, "A Brief and True Narrative of Witchcraft at Salem Village" (Boston, 1692), in Burr, *Narratives,* pp. 145–64, cited p. 155. This is the April 1692 version of his sermon "A Brief and True Narrative of Some Remarkable Passages," mentioned earlier; see n. 30.

38. Weisman, *Witchcraft, Magic, and Religion,* p. 17.

39. See the letter to John Richards, May 31, 1692, particularly p. 40, in *Selected Letters of Cotton Mather,* ed. Kenneth Silverman (Baton Rouge: Louisiana State University Press, 1971). Silverman attributes the letter to Mather, although it is not in his hand.

40. See "Vital Records of Topsfield, Massachusetts, to the End of the Year 1849," *Historical Collections of the Topsfield Historical Society,* vol. 9 (Topsfield, Mass.: The Society, 1903), p. 55. Abigail was the step-

daughter of Deliverance; I am grateful to David L. Greene for pointing this out to me.

41. A few of the indictments, almost all from the Andover cases, charge covenanting with the devil rather than afflicting on the day of the examination. Even in the Andover cases, however, the indictments charging a covenant with the devil normally supplement the basic charge of afflicting the accuser on the day of an examination.

42. John Proctor was indicted for afflicting Mary Warren on March 26. This was not the day of Proctor's examination, and the dating in this indictment offers an exception to the standard practice of having the affliction occur on the day of the examination.

43. For a discussion of the dates and circumstances surrounding the accusation of John Proctor, see Chapter 6.

44. Ann Rinaldi, *A Break with Charity* (San Diego: Harcourt Brace Jovanovich, 1992), pp. 116–17.

45. This estimate of her age is based on Carol F. Karlsen's evidence that she was 37 in 1709; *The Devil in the Shape of a Woman*, p. 228.

46. Linnda Caporael says that Sarah Churchill "testified in only two cases" ("Ergotism," p. 24), but such an assertion could only be valid under a limited definition of testimony. Sarah Churchill was involved in the cases of Ann Pudeator, Bridget Bishop, George Jacobs, Sr., Jane Lilly, Alice Parker, Mary Parker, William Proctor, and John Willard.

47. I have modernized the language here because of the passage's difficulty in the original.

48. For her age see Sidney Perley, *The History of Salem Massachusetts* (Salem, Mass.: privately published, 1924), III, pp. 284, 109–10.

49. Calef writes that "she had an Imposthume [abscess] in her head, which was her Escape" ("More Wonders," in Burr, *Narratives,* p. 366); why illness would prevent execution is hard to say, and it is difficult to be certain that Calef's reason is accurate. Although Margaret could not have anticipated it, in the end the authorities were not executing anyone as young as she was. Indeed, it is probable that nobody younger than 38 was executed. I have not succeeded in tracking down all the ages of the executed, but the generalization is not likely to be far off. In view of this, it seems unlikely that the "Imposthume" was the actual reason for Margaret's survival.

3. Boys and girls together

1. Chadwick Hansen, intro. to Robert Calef, "More Wonders of the Invisible World" (1700); reprinted (Bainbridge, N.Y.: York Mail-Print, Inc., 1972), p. xv, n. 4.

2. Calef, "More Wonders, " largely reprinted in *Narratives of the Witchcraft Cases 1648–1706,* ed. George Lincoln Burr (New York: Charles Scribner's Sons, 1914), pp. 289–394, cited pp. 371–2.

3. Reverend John Hale, "A Modest Inquiry into the Nature of Witch-craft" (1702), partially reprinted in Burr, *Narrative*, pp. 395–432, cited p. 423.

4. Thomas Hutchinson argues that all the proceedings were illegal. He reasons that the General Court had passed a law regarding witchcraft "in the words of the statute of James the first," which "was disallowed by the King." His point is that if James's statute had applied, there would have been no reason to pass the law; if it had not applied, he knew of no law to justify the execution of people as witches. Hutchinson, *The History of the Colony and Province of Massachusetts-Bay* (1764), ed. Laurence Shaw Mayo (Cambridge, Mass.: Harvard University Press, 1936), II, p. 45.

5. Calef, "More Wonders, " in Burr, *Narratives*, p. 372.

6. Charles W. Upham, *Salem Witchcraft; with An Account of Salem Village, and a History of Opinions on Witchcraft and Kindred Subjects* (1867), 2 vols.; reprinted (Williamstown, Mass.: Corner House Publ., 1971), II, p. 460. A daughter of Dane, Elizabeth Faulkner, was sentenced to death. Another daughter, according to Upham, Elizabeth Johnson, Sr., mother of Elizabeth Jr., was also among the accused. The relationship between Abigail Faulkner and Elizabeth Johnson, Jr., is confusing, however: In the court records, Elizabeth Johnson is described as a cousin of Abigail Faulkner, although reference is made to Faulkner's "sister Jonson" (*SWP* I: 328). Perhaps they were half sisters.

7. Martha Sprague sometimes appears in documentation as Martha Tyler. I have not been able to determine why this is so, but she is not the same Martha Tyler who, as a confessor, was interviewed in prison in an interview attributed to Increase Mather; see *SWP* III: 777–8. Upham, *Salem Witchcraft*, II, p. 404, is the source of this attribution, but Upham is not positive about the identification, referring to the interview as "a document of which he [Mather] is supposed to have been the author."

8. In 1634 the Robinson case prompted a play with comic aspects about witchcraft: Thomas Heywood and Richard Brome's *The Late Lancashire Witches*. For an account of the Robinson fraud, important because it was printed close to the time of the Salem witch trials, see John Webster, *The Displaying of Supposed Witchcraft, Wherein is affirmed that there are many sorts of Deceivers and Imposters, and Divers persons under a passive Delusion of Melancholy and Fancy* (London, 1677), pp. 276–8. For the other cases, see Rossell Hope Robbins, *The Encyclopedia of Witchcraft and Demonology* (New York: Crown Publ., 1959), s.v. "Leicester Boy," "Burton Boy," "Bilson Boy," and "Pendle Swindle."

9. Calef, "More Wonders," in Burr, *Narratives*, p. 348. The person is not named, but it is almost certainly John Indian; there are simply no other candidates for the role here.

10. The Reverend Deodat Lawson, former minister at Salem Village, in his sermon at Salem Village on March 25, 1692, had urged parishioners to

"put on the whole armor of God" in the fight against Satan. Lawson, "Christ's Fidelity the Only Shield Against Satan's Malignity," in *Salem-Village Witchcraft: A Documentary Record of Local Conflict in Colonial New England*, ed. Paul Boyer and Stephen Nissenbaum (Belmont, Calif.: Wadsworth Publ., 1972), p. 127. Both Louder and Gray used this expression; perhaps they had attended the sermon.

11. Nicholas P. Spanos and Jack Gottlieb, in their masterful refutation of ergot poisoning as a plausible explanation of what happened in Salem, suggest that two bedroom cases – those of Stephen Bittford and Benjamin Gould – "consisted primarily of what were probably dreams or hypnagogic experiences." The authors give no indication of why they do not consider perjured testimony a possibility. Nicholas P. Spanos and Jack Gottlieb, "Ergotism and the Salem Village Witch Trials," *Science*, vol. 194, no. 4272 (December 24, 1976), p. 1393. Persis W. McMillen associates the bedroom encounters with "the medieval idea of the succubus"; *Currents of Malice: Mary Towne Esty and Her Family in Salem Witchcraft* (Portsmouth, N.H.: Peter E. Randall, 1990), p. 379.

12. Reginald Scot, *The Discoverie of Witchcraft*, intro. Hugh Ross Williamson (Carbondale, Ill.: Southern Illinois University Press, 1964), p. 87.

13. Calef, "More Wonders," in Burr, *Narratives*, p. 356.

14. Stacy had complained against her in 1688, but not for such activity as this. The charge was theft, stealing brass. See Boyer and Nissenbaum, *Salem-Village Witchcraft*, pp. 159–62.

15. Proctor accurately repeats Andrew's confession to having been a witch for about a month; Richard, however, claimed to have been a witch since the previous January.

16. Larry Gragg, in *A Quest for Security: The Life of Samuel Parris, 1653–1720* (Westport, Conn.: Greenwood Press, 1990), p. 137, interprets Richard's reference to Elizabeth Parris as indicating that Mrs. Parris had become afflicted.

17. For the DeRich–Proctor–Basset family relationship, see Paul Boyer and Stephen Nissenbaum, *Salem Possessed: The Social Origins of Witchcraft* (Cambridge, Mass.: Harvard University Press, 1974), p. 184.

18. This testimony is undated, although probably given around August 4. I have assumed that the reference to "Corey" is to Giles rather than his wife Martha, since DeRich testified elsewhere against Giles. *SWP* I: 245.

19. This apparently means that he attempted to get them to recant their confessions. It is not clear whether this charge is based on some actual activity by Willard, perhaps successful in the case of Margaret, or represents the charge of spectral activity. The first warrant for Willard's arrest is dated May 10, but because he was in hiding before being apprehended he was not examined until May 18. He may have had contact with Margaret in jail.

20. "Andros" may be a misspelling for "Andrews" in the deposition.
21. Such use of folk magic is consistent with the image of folk belief in magic described by David D. Hall, *Worlds of Wonder, Days of Judgment: Popular Religious Belief in Early New England* (New York: Alfred A. Knopf, 1989).

4. June 10, 1692

1. Henry Wadsworth Longfellow, *Giles Corey of the Salem Farms,* in *The New-England Tragedies* (Boston: Ticknor & Fields, 1868), pp. 97–179, cited p. 142.
2. Robert Calef, "More Wonders of the Invisible World" (1700), largely reprinted in *Narratives of the Witchcraft Cases 1648–1706,* ed. George Lincoln Burr (New York: Charles Scribner's Sons, 1914), pp. 289–394, cited p. 349.
3. See the bill of John Arnold indicating that Sarah Good and Sarah Osborne were in chains on March 9; *SWP* III: 953.
4. Samuel Willard cites defenders of the trials as observing that the accused must "pass through two Juries, where he will have the liberty to Vindicate his Innocence openly." Willard, *Some Miscelliny Observations On Our Present Debates Respecting Witchcrafts, in a Dialogue between S & B,* pseudonymously by "P. E. and J. A." (Philadelphia, 1692), p. 3.
5. Willard, *Some Miscelliny Observations,* p. 9.
6. Sir William Phips, letter of February 21, 1693, to the Earl of Nottingham in London, in Burr, *Narratives,* pp. 198–202, cited p. 199.
7. "Letter of Thomas Brattle, F.R.S.," in Burr, *Narratives,* pp. 165–90, cited pp. 188–9.
8. Boyer and Nissenbaum indicate that Saltonstall resigned between June 10 and June 15. I have no reason to doubt them, although I have not been able to confirm the date. See *Salem-Village Witchcraft: A Documentary Record of Local Conflict in Colonial New England,* ed. Paul Boyer and Stephen Nissenbaum (Belmont, Calif.: Wadsworth Publ., 1972), p. 117. Tradition and speculation have generally placed the resignation around the time cited by Boyer and Nissenbaum; however, Daniel Neal, *History of New-England* (London, 1720), I, p. 502, includes Saltonstall as a judge at the trial of George Burroughs on August 5. Whether Neal knew something on this point unavailable to later historians cannot be determined, and the date of Saltonstall's resignation remains uncertain.
9. Cotton Mather, *The Life of Sir William Phips* (1697), ed. Mark Van Doren (New York: Covici–Friede, 1929), p. 145. See also *The Diary of Cotton Mather,* 2 vols., preface by Worthington Chauncey Ford, 1911; reprinted (New York: Frederick Ungar Publ., n.d.), I, p. 151. By this

time, indications of past support for the trials had become an embarrassment, and probably for that reason Mather omitted printing here three of the sections in the "Return of Several Ministers." These included Sec. I, showing sympathy for the afflicted; Sec. II, appreciation to the authorities for their efforts in discovering witchcraft; and Sec. VIII, which called for "vigorous prosecution" of witchcraft. What remained in Mather's reprinting was the call for moderation and the implicit criticism of the proceedings.

10. Boyer and Nissenbaum, *Salem-Village Witchcraft*, pp. 117–18.
11. George H. Moore, *Notes on the History of Massachusetts; With Illustrative Documents* (Worcester, Mass.: 1883), in *Proceedings of the American Antiquarian Society*, n.s., vol. I, p. 171.
12. Calef, "More Wonders," in Burr, *Narratives*, p. 359. See also Joseph B. Felt, *Annals of Salem* (Salem, Mass.: W. & S. B. Ives, 1846; Boston: James Munroe & Co., 2d ed., 1849), II, p. 479.
13. Samuel G. Drake, *The Witchcraft Delusion in New England*, 3 vols. (1866); reprinted (New York: Burt Franklin, 1970), III, p. 137.
14. See Chapters 7 and 9.
15. David L. Greene, "Salem Witches I: Bridget Bishop," *American Genealogist*, vol. 57, no. 3 (July 1981), pp. 129–38, cited pp. 130–1. Greene also published "Bridget Bishop Correction," *American Genealogist*, vol. 58, no. 3 (July 1982), p. 163: The editor had inadvertently omitted a paragraph in the original essay. See also Boyer and Nissenbaum, *Salem-Village Witchcraft*, pp. 157–8.
16. Charles W. Upham, *Salem Witchcraft; with An Account of Salem Village, and a History of Opinions on Witchcraft and Kindred Subjects* (1867), 2 vols.; reprinted (Williamstown, Mass.: Corner House Publ., 1971), I, p. 192.
17. For Greene's argument, see his "Salem Witches I: Bridget Bishop" and the later correction (see n. 15 above). My own reading of *The Salem Witchcraft Papers* has persuaded me on additional grounds that Greene's overwhelming case is surely right. Many fine scholars have perpetuated the misidentification. Unusual for not making the mistake is Carol F. Karlsen, *The Devil in the Shape of a Woman* (New York: W. W. Norton, 1987). The most prominent scholars to make the error, and in modern times the most influential, are Paul Boyer and Stephen Nissenbaum, *Salem Possessed: The Social Origins of Witchcraft* (Cambridge, Mass.: Harvard University Press, 1974), pp. 192–3; this work, of course, was written before Greene's discovery. Recently, Enders A. Robinson has accurately used Greene; Robinson, *The Devil Discovered: Salem Witchcraft 1692* (New York: Hippocrene Books, 1991), pp. 307–8. Richard Godbeer, *The Devil's Dominion: Magic and Religion in Early New England* (Cambridge: Cambridge University Press, 1992), pp. 201, 238, avoids the main elements of the myth, although he continues the tradition of misplacing her as a Salem Village resident.

18. Upham, *Salem Witchcraft*, I, pp. 192–3.
19. Greene, "Salem Witches I," p. 133.
20. The idea that there was an illegal tavern comes essentially from Upham, *Salem Witchcraft* (I, pp. 192–3), whose confused account leaves us with no solid evidence that such a tavern actually existed. The evidence for it comes from Hale's testimony, which refers to late-night drinking and perhaps implies an illegal tavern, but is ambiguous on this.
21. Greene, "Salem Witches I," p. 134.
22. Ibid., p. 135. In another instance, Hale, quarreling with Thomas Maule over witchcraft, among other theological matters, refers to "*B.B.,*" no doubt Bridget Bishop, as a person who Maule had believed was a witch. There is no connection in this passage to Hale's testimony in 1692. See "A Modest Inquiry into the Nature of Witchcraft" (1702), intro. Richard Trask (Bainbridge, N.Y.: York Mail-Print, Inc., 1973), pp. 155–6.
23. Marion L. Starkey, *The Devil in Massachusetts: A Modern Enquiry into the Salem Witch Trials* (New York: Alfred A. Knopf, 1949); 2d ed. (1950), p. 154.
24. Montague Summers, *The Geography of Witchcraft* (London: Routledge & Kegan Paul, 1927), p. 307.
25. Boyer and Nissenbaum mistakenly identify the person here as Mary Parker rather than Alice Parker. Mary Parker was from Andover, but the Goodwife Parker referred to by Shattuck was from Salem, and that was Alice. Mary Parker was a widow (*SWP* II: 630), whereas the woman accused by Shattuck was the wife of John Parker, a mariner (*SWP* II: 635). All the evidence suggests Alice, and none suggests Mary. See Chapter 8, n. 37, for further explication.
26. For her age see John Demos, *Entertaining Satan: Witchcraft and the Culture of Early New England* (Oxford: Oxford University Press, 1982), p. 66. Karlsen, *The Devil in the Shape of a Woman*, p. 93, also gives her age as 67. David L. Greene, "Salem Witches III: Susanna Martin," *American Genealogist*, vol. 58, no. 4 (October 1982), pp. 193–205, cited p. 193, says that she was probably born between 1620 and 1625.
27. See, for example, the consistent marks of Joshua Conant: *SWP* I: 336, 460, 512, 620.
28. At the top of *SWP* I: 107, where the names of Susannah Martin and Sarah Good appear as women being examined, Sarah Good's name is written as "Sara" rather than as "Sarah" as it actually appears in the court record. The dropping of an "h" in transcription is not in itself significant, but as this error occurs in connection with other transcription errors it warrants a cautionary note. As valuable as the transcriptions in *The Salem Witchcraft Papers* are, they cannot be read as if in all cases they are reliable.

I am grateful to the staff of the Essex Institute in Salem, Massachusetts, for their courtesy and helpfulness.

29. Chadwick Hansen, *Witchcraft at Salem* (New York: George Braziller, 1969). Hansen's overall description of the witchcraft episode of 1692 is the most comprehensive and generally most reliable one in print. However, his thesis regarding the definition and practice of witchcraft as applied to 1692 – especially his identification of specific people as witches – strikes me as exceptionally weak, as does his broad assumption that the accusers were hysterical. I do not doubt that "cunning folk" in the colony traded on fears of witchcraft; I simply believe that the people he has identified as witches are selected by him with wholly inadequate evidence. I also do not rule out the possibility that hysteria among some accusers existed; but I believe that Hansen has, on the whole, been fooled by the main accusers.

30. David D. Hall, "Witchcraft and the Limits of Interpretation," *New England Quarterly,* vol. 59, no. 2 (June 1985), p. 265.

31. Boyer and Nissenbaum, *Salem-Village Witchcraft,* p. xi.

32. For example, Selma R. Williams and Pamela J. Williams, *Riding the Night Mare: Women & Witchcraft* (New York: Atheneum, 1978), p. 192, where Wilmot Reed is described as a witch. Reed was one of the women Hansen identified as such. For the *New York Times,* see Mary Cantwell's "The Editorial Notebook" (October 5, 1982), p. 30. For the *New York Review of Books,* see Lawrence Stone, "The Disenchantment of the World" (December 2, 1971), p. 20.

33. John Demos, "Underlying Themes in the Witchcraft of Seventeenth-Century New England," *American Historical Review,* vol. 75 (June 1970), p. 1312.

34. Summers, *The Geography of Witchcraft.* See also his *The History of Witchcraft and Demonology* (London: Routledge & Kegan Paul, 1926).

35. Hansen, *Witchcraft at Salem,* p. 65.

36. Ibid., p. 66.

37. Ibid., p. 67.

38. Ibid., p. 70.

39. See Chapter 8 for Samuel Shattuck's role in the Alice Parker case and for clarification of her identity.

40. Greene, "Salem Witches I," p. 135.

41. Caroline E. Upham, *Salem Witchcraft in Outline* (Salem, Mass.: Salem Press, 1891), p. 94.

42. Starkey, *The Devil in Massachusetts,* p. 99.

43. Summers, in *Geography of Witchcraft,* pp. 346–9, writes about a secret coven of witches that included Bridget Bishop. For details of Bridget Bishop's life I am heavily indebted to Greene, "Salem Witches I" and to Boyer and Nissenbaum, *Salem-Village Witchcraft,* pp. 154–8.

44. The estimate of her age is made by John Demos, *Entertaining Satan,* p. 66.

45. Greene, "Salem Witches I," p. 129.

46. Ibid., p. 130.

47. Boyer and Nissenbaum, *Salem-Village Witchcraft*, pp. 157–8; there, "Wonn" is glossed as "Juan."
48. Karlsen, *The Devil in the Shape of a Woman*, pp. 77ff; also p. 75. For Bridget Bishop's legal difficulties, see Greene, "Salem Witches I," pp. 129–30. For other profiles of women more likely than others to be accused as witches, see John Demos, *Entertaining Satan*, pp. 57ff.
49. Boyer and Nissenbaum, *Salem-Village Witchcraft*, p. 157.
50. Greene, "Salem Witches I," p. 131. Greene indicates that the marriage occurred on or before 1687.
51. Boyer and Nissenbaum, *Salem-Village Witchcraft*, p. 162.
52. Karlsen makes this connection in *The Devil in the Shape of a Woman*, p. 38.
53. Exactly what was implied by the attainders remains unclear. Stoughton apparently authorized property seizures as Phips claimed in February 1693 (*SWP* III: 865). For a discussion of the seizure of estates, see Chapter 9, §III; for the view of Phips regarding the legality of such seizures see the Appendix. Attainders can influence rights of inheritance. They may also imply forfeiture of estates but do not always carry that implication.
54. Boyer and Nissenbaum, *Salem-Village Witchcraft*, pp. 51–2; *SWP* III: 1015–17.
55. Stanley Eames, "Legislative Group Favors Clearing Salem Witches," *Boston Herald*, February 14, 1957, p. 38.
56. Hansen, *Witchcraft at Salem*, p. 219.

5. July 19, 1692

1. Willam Weber, "Vandals Haunt Witch Cemetery," *Marblehead Messenger*, July 19, 1973, p. 16.
2. Robert Calef, "More Wonders of the Invisible World" (1700), largely reprinted in *Narratives of the Witchcraft Cases 1648–1706*, ed. George Lincoln Burr (New York: Charles Scribner's Sons, 1914), pp. 289–394, cited p. 358.
3. Nathaniel Hawthorne, *The House of the Seven Gables* (1851), ed. William Charvat, Roy Harvey Pearce, and Claude M. Simpson (Columbus: Ohio State University Press, 1965), p. 8. For an interpretation of Hawthorne's use of a male to utter the words of Sarah Good, see Louise DeSalvo, *Nathaniel Hawthorne* (Atlantic Highlands, N.J.: Humanities Press, 1987), p. 80.
4. The story first appeared in Thomas Hutchinson, *The History of the Colony and Province of Massachusetts-Bay* (1764), ed. Laurence Shaw Mayo (Cambridge, Mass.: Harvard University Press, 1936), II, p. 41.
5. Hawthorne's reference in *The Scarlet Letter* to "the martyrdom of the witches," expresses a view more consistent with that of his archenemy, Charles W. Upham.

6. Hutchinson, *History*, II, p. 20.
7. Winfield Nevins, *Witchcraft in Salem Village* (Salem, Mass.: North Shore Publ. / Boston, Mass.: Lee and Shepard, 1892), p. 54.
8. William Nelson Gemmill, *The Salem Witch Trials: A Chapter of New England History* (Chicago: A. C. McClurg & Co., 1924), p. 97.
9. Kai Erikson, *Wayward Puritans: A Study in the Sociology of Deviance* (New York: John Wiley and Sons, 1966), p. 143.
10. Chadwick Hansen, *Witchcraft at Salem* (New York: George Braziller, 1969), p. 32.
11. Arlin Turner, *Nathaniel Hawthorne. A Biography* (New York: Oxford University Press, 1980), p. 74.
12. My calculation of her age here is based on a petition by her brothers regarding the estate of their father, John Solart. She is referred to as being 28 in 1682, which was ten years before her execution. *Salem-Village Witchcraft: A Documentary Record of Local Conflict in Colonial New England*, ed. Paul Boyer and Stephen Nissenbaum (Belmont, Calif.: Wadsworth Publ., 1972), p. 142.
13. Erikson, *Wayward Puritans*, pp. 143–4.
14. Hansen, *Witchcraft at Salem*, pp. 32–3, 217.
15. Gemmill, *The Salem Witch Trials*, p. 98.
16. Nevins, *Witchcraft in Salem Village*, p. 54.
17. Hutchinson, *History*, II, p. 20.
18. Selma R. Williams and Pamela J. Williams, *Riding the Night Mare: Women & Witchcraft* (New York: Atheneum, 1978), p. 153. The source for Sarah Good as looking old in her own time is probably Marion L. Starkey, *The Devil in Massachusetts: A Modern Enquiry into the Salem Witch Trials* (New York: Alfred A. Knopf, 1949); 2d ed. (1950), p. 34. Starkey's book is often cited as the best general introduction to the Salem witch trials. Of Sarah Good, Starkey writes: "Hard times had toughened Sarah. She was a powerful hag. . . . Withal, her matted hair was so gray, her face so seamed and leathery that people seeing her alone estimated her age at seventy. Actually she was much younger; one child, Dorcas, was still under six, and she was even now carrying another." There is no historical basis for the description of Sarah Good as looking old, nor for the color of her hair or the texture of her skin.
19. Arthur Miller, *The Crucible*, in *The Portable Arthur Miller*, ed. and intro. Harold Clurman (Penguin Books, 1977), Act 2, p. 192.
20. James F. Droney, "The Witches of Salem," *Boston* (Boston: Greater Chamber of Commerce, October 1963), pp. 42–6, 65, 92–3, at pp. 44–5.
21. For the connection to Poole, see Paul Boyer and Stephen Nissenbaum, *Salem Possessed: The Social Origins of Witchcraft* (Cambridge, Mass.: Harvard University Press, 1974), p. 204.
22. The indictment against Sarah Good for afflicting Sarah Bibber is unusual in that she is accused of afflicting on May 2, which was not the

day of her examination. The indictments for afflicting Elizabeth Hubbard and Ann Putnam, Jr., are consistent with the normal pattern in that the day of affliction is the same as the day of the examination, March 1 (*SWP* II: 365–7).

23. Abbott Lowell Cummings, *The Framed Houses of Massachusetts Bay, 1625–1725* (Cambridge, Mass.: Harvard University Press, 1979), p. 123.
24. See Boyer and Nissenbaum, *Salem Possessed*, p. 116 for discussion of the petition in support of Rebecca Nurse.
25. Charles W. Upham, *Salem Witchcraft; with An Account of Salem Village, and a History of Opinions on Witchcraft and Kindred Subjects* (1867), 2 vols.; reprinted (Williamstown, Mass.: Corner House Publ., 1971), pp. 187–8.
26. Reverend A. P. Putnam, "Address at the dedication of a tablet in honor of forty friends of Rebecca Nurse, of Salem Village" (Boston: Thomas Todd, Printer, 1894), Introduction and p. 37.
27. Starkey, *The Devil in Massachusetts*, p. 192.
28. Upham, *Salem Witchcraft*, II, pp. 291–2.
29. Hansen, *Witchcraft at Salem*, p. 131.
30. Droney, "The Witches of Salem," p. 65.
31. See Chapter 4, §I.
32. Calef, "More Wonders," in Burr, *Narratives*, p. 358.
33. Montague Summers, *The Geography of Witchcraft* (London: Routledge & Kegan Paul, 1927), p. 325. The embellishment of Summers grows from nineteenth-century versions, as the one created by Caroline E. Upham, daughter-in-law of Charles W. Upham: "The demented people, trampling reason under foot in their fury, so intimidated the judges that the favorable verdict was withdrawn, and Rebecca Nurse condemned to die by the grossest perversion of justice in the annals of our country"; Caroline E. Upham, *Salem Witchcraft in Outline* (Salem, Mass.: Salem Press, 1891), p. 76.
34. Calef, "More Wonders," in Burr, *Narratives*, p. 358.
35. Ibid., p. 360. According to Calef, "she was sent out of the Court, and it was told about she was mistaken in the person." Samuel Willard believed in witchcraft, as attested to by his comments in "The Boston Ministers 'To the Reader'" – the preface, written with three others, to Cotton Mather's "Memorable Providences, relating to Witchcrafts and Possessions" (1689) (see Burr, *Narratives*, pp. 95–6); but in his pseudonymously authored *Some Miscelliny Observations On Our Present Debates Respecting Witchcrafts, in a Dialogue between S & B*, by "P. E. and J. A." (Philadelphia, 1692), Willard expressed his clear dissatisfaction with the judicial proceedings of 1692.
36. Calef, "More Wonders," in Burr, *Narratives*, pp. 357–8.
37. Ibid., p. 358.
38. Ibid., p. 359.

39. David L. Greene, "Salem Witches III: Susanna Martin,"*American Genealogist,* vol. 58, no. 4 (October 1982), p. 195; Carol F. Karlsen, *The Devil in the Shape of a Woman* (New York: W. W. Norton, 1987), p. 91.

40. For biographical information on Susannah Martin, see Karlsen, *The Devil in the Shape of a Woman,* pp. 89–95.

41. William Carlos Williams, *In the American Grain* (New York: Albert & Charles Boni, 1925), pp. 92–100.

42. C. E. Upham, *Salem Witchcraft in Outline,* p. 142.

43. 1 Samuel 28. Although the word "witch" does not appear in scripture here, a woman generally described as "the Witch of Endor" responds to the appeal of Saul, and raises the dead Samuel or the shape of Samuel, depending on the interpretation. The Puritans assumed this to be a demonic episode, and Susannah Martin is arguing that if such a one as Saul could be fooled by a shape, others could too.

44. See Karlsen, *The Devil in the Shape of a Woman,* p. 93, regarding the 1686 death of George Martin. Her age, according to correspondence from David L. Greene, has been determined in "the Bishop's Transcripts of the Olney, Buckinghamshire, parish register, under [September] 1621," the year of her baptism. As of this writing, this information is scheduled to appear in an issue of *American Genealogist.*

45. For the roots of tales concerning demonic dogs and women staying dry in the rain, see David D. Hall, *Worlds of Wonder, Days of Judgment: Popular Religious Belief in Early New England* (New York: Alfred A. Knopf, 1989), p. 88.

46. Clifford Lindsey Alderman, *A Cauldron of Witches* (Great Britain: Bailey Brothers and Swinfen Ltd., 1971), p. 157. Popular representations of Salem "witches" tend to depict them either as old hags or as young and sexy. The cover of Alderman's book favors the latter, with two attractive young women, one blond, one dark, dancing in front of a pot over a fire. The devil hovers over them.

47. In an undated document Boyer and Nissenbaum list Sarah Wilds as a witness against Sarah Good (*SWP* II: 364). The attribution is based on a document that, according to Boyer and Nissenbaum, was probably a memo rather than an official court record. The four witnesses named include Sarah Wilds; John and Joseph Andrews, two men who testified against her; and William Perkins, whose identity is not clear, although he may be related to A. Z. Perkins, who testified against Wilds. I am suggesting that the document actually conflates a reference to Sarah Good with three witnesses against Sarah Wilds. There is no other evidence to indicate that Wilds cooperated with the authorities in naming people as witches.

48. The recorded testimony is confusing in that the names of "Mary" and "Sarah" appear to be used interchangeably to identify the Goody Red-

dington involved in the controversy. Sarah Reddington was the widow of John Reddington, who died in 1690, the very year in which she had married him. She remarried in 1691. John Reddington's previous wife had been Mary Reddington, and it was she who had claimed years before to have been bewitched by Sarah Wilds. Since the controversy predated Sarah's marriage to John, the wife of John Reddington accused in the garbled testimony had to have been Mary Reddington. See David L. Greene "Sarah, Widow of John Witt of Lynn, John Red(d)ington of Topsfield, and Edward Bragg of Ipswich, Massachusetts," *New England Historical and Genealogical Register,* vol. 141 (January 1987), pp. 19–21.

49. Upham, *Salem Witchcraft,* II, p. 219.
50. Ibid., pp. 221–2.
51. Ibid, p. 222.

6. August 19, 1692

1. "Letter of Thomas Brattle, F.R.S.," in *Narratives of the Witchcraft Cases 1648–1706,* ed. George Lincoln Burr (New York: Charles Scribner's Sons, 1914), pp. 165–90, cited p. 177.
2. See John Demos, *Entertaining Satan: Witchcraft and the Culture of Early New England* (New York: Oxford University Press, 1982), pp. 401–9, for a list of New England witchcraft cases and their dispositions. One case does exist of a man hanged for witchcraft in New England, although not in Massachusetts Bay. Regarding this case, that of Nathaniel Greensmith in 1662 or 1663, see Demos, pp. 352, 405. For a record of witchcraft cases in Massachusetts and their dispositions, see also Richard Weisman, *Witchcraft, Magic, and Religion in 17th-Century Massachusetts* (Amherst: University of Massachusetts Press, 1984), pp. 192–203.
3. Kenneth Silverman, ed., *Selected Letters of Cotton Mather* (Baton Rouge: Louisiana State University Press, 1971), p. xviii.
4. *The Diary of Samuel Sewall 1674–1729,* vol. I, in *Collections of the Massachusetts Historical Society,* vol. v, 5th ser. (Cambridge, 1878), p. 363.
5. For a traditional account of this see Marion L. Starkey, *The Devil in Massachusetts: A Modern Enquiry into the Salem Witch Trials* (New York: Alfred A. Knopf, 1949); 2d ed. (1950), pp. 78–9. Little reason exists to doubt the accuracy of this tradition that Cloyce was accused because of her reaction to her sister's situation.
6. A deposition appears in *The Salem Witchcraft Papers* (I: 535) in connection with a man named John Lee, whose name appears nowhere else in the surviving records connected with the trials. The editors, Boyer and Nissenbaum, suggest April 11 as the date of his deposition, but this is an error carried over from the earlier WPA typescript. No depositions

in connection with the Salem witch trials have such an early date, but that is not the only evidence that an error was made. The actual surviving manuscript of the John Lee case simply gives no date at all: The WPA compilers had pasted it on a board below an unrelated matter, in a different hand, connected with John Proctor, where the date is unambiguously April 11. Someone seeing the John Lee case below it mistakenly made a connection. I am grateful to the staff at the Essex Institute for helping me track down the origin of the error.

7. Thomas Brattle, "Letter," in Burr, *Narratives,* p. 184.
8. Starkey, *The Devil in Massachusetts,* pp. 183–4.
9. Abigail's recorded comment on April 11 in reference to John Proctor was that "you can pinch as well as your wife & more to that purpose" (*SWP* II: 677). On April 6 she complaine ⸢ ⸥bout him afflicting her that night. Her complaints were recorded by Parris.
10. Charles W. Upham, *Salem Witchcraft; with An Account of Salem Village, and a History of Opinions on Witchcraft and Kindred Subjects* (1867), 2 vols.; reprinted (Williamstown, Mass.: Corner House Publ., 1971), II, pp. 106–9.
11. Sewall, *Diary,* I, p. 358. Sewall notes the presence of Nicholas Noyes and John Higginson, who offered prayers at the beginning and end of the hearing.
12. The transcription of Corey's examination does not appear in *The Salem Witchcraft Papers;* for that examination on April 19, see Samuel G. Drake, *The Witchcraft Delusion in New England,* 3 vols. (1866); reprinted (New York: Burt Franklin, 1970), III, pp. 169–73.
13. For the family connections see Paul Boyer and Stephen Nissenbaum, *Salem Possessed: The Social Origins of Witchcraft* (Cambridge, Mass.: Harvard University Press, 1974), p. 184.
14. See 1 Samuel 28 for the Witch of Endor; see also Chapter 5, n. 43. Ironically, John Webster, perhaps the most famous seventeenth-century theological skeptic on witchcraft, rejected the basis for a defense on this biblical precedent, arguing that the "Woman of Endor," as he took pains to call her, was a fraud who never did raise Samuel, body or soul. See Webster, *The Displaying of Supposed Witchcraft, Wherein is affirmed that there are many sorts of Deceivers and Imposters, and Divers persons under a passive Delusion of Melancholy and Fancy* (London, 1677), pp. 165ff.
15. See Chapter 3, p. 61.
16. Sidney Perley, *The History of Salem Massachusetts* (Salem, Mass.: privately published, 1924), I, p. 23. Upham, in *Salem Witchcraft,* II, p. 312, writes that she "gave birth to a child, about a fortnight after [Proctor's] execution," a date clearly inconsistent with Perley's. Neither provides supporting evidence.
17. For her subsequent identification as Elizabeth Richards, see *SWP* III: 1035, 1039.

18. John Proctor's will survives (Essex County Probate no. 22851). For a slightly inaccurate transcription, see Leland H. Procter, *John Proctor of Ipswich and Some of His Descendants* (Springfield, Mass.: Springfield City Library, 1985), p. 9.

19. Cited in Robert Croll Stevens and Jane Eleanor (Knauss) Stevens, *Ancestry of the Children of Robert Croll Stevens and Jane Eleanor (Knauss) Stevens,* vol. 1 (Pittsford, N.Y., 1982), p. 44.8.

20. For a discussion of legal aspects connected with the will and the quarrel over it, see "December Meeting, 1884," *Proceedings of the Massachusetts Historical Society,* 2d ser., vol. 1 (1884–5), pp. 344–6.

21. Robert Calef, "More Wonders of the Invisible World" (1700), in Burr, *Narratives,* pp. 289–394, cited p. 364. For Proctor's age, see Boyer and Nissenbaum, *Salem Possessed,* p. 200.

22. For the connection of Aaron Wey to the Wilkins family, see David L. Greene, "Bray Wilkins of Salem Village MA and His Children," *American Genealogist,* vol. 60, no. 1 (January 1984), pp. 1–18, cited pp. 4–5. In my understanding of the Wilkins family, and of Willard's place in it, I have benefited greatly from Greene's research.

23. Calef, "More Wonders," in Burr, *Narratives,* p. 361.

24. For the age of Daniel Wilkins see David L. Greene, "Bray Wilkins of Salem Village MA and His Children" [pt. 2], *American Genealogist,* vol. 60, no. 2 (April 1984), pp. 101–13, esp. p. 105, and *New England Historical and Genealogical Register,* vol. 13 (January 1859), p. 56, where the date of his death is indicated as May 16 by bewitchment. Greene takes issue with Boyer and Nissenbaum as to the identity of Willard's wife. He argues (pp. 111–13) that the wife, Margaret, was the daughter of Thomas Wilkins, thereby explaining why Thomas Wilkins did not join the general family attack on Willard. Boyer and Nissenbaum, *Salem Possessed,* p. 195, on the other hand, identify Margaret as the daughter of Philip and Margaret Knight.

25. Greene, "Bray Wilkins" [pt. 1], p. 3.

26. See Chapter 2, §III.

27. "The Return of Several Ministers," in *Salem-Village Witchcraft: A Documentary Record of Local Conflict in Colonial New England,* ed. Paul Boyer and Stephen Nissenbaum (Belmont, Calif.: Wadsworth Publ., 1972), p. 118. In using the word "man," they also meant to include women.

28. See Chapter 2, §V.

29. Upham, *Salem Witchcraft,* II, pp. 353–4.

30. David L. Greene, "Salem Witches II: George Jacobs," *American Genealogist,* vol. 58, no. 2 (April 1982), pp. 65–76, cited p. 73. This valuable essay on Jacobs unfortunately contains a number of editorial errors that were beyond the control of Greene. He has very kindly sent me a corrected copy of the published essay. This and subsequent citations of the printed essay are unaffected by the errors unless specifically indicated.

31. One other indictment survives, an anomaly in that it does not follow the formula, naming no victim; instead, it accuses her of making a covenant with the devil. The jury rejected this indictment, presumably in January (*SWP* II: 494).

32. Greene, "Salem Witches II," p. 73. On Nov. 30, 1699, Margaret had married a man named John Foster. Whether this is the same John Foster who was summoned on August 4 to testify against George Jacobs, Sr., is uncertain (*SWP* II: 479). We have no record of why he was called or whether he came.

33. George Jacobs, Jr., was giving rough calculations; that is, Margaret was examined May 11, and Rebecca May 18. Margaret, in seven months would have been released in December instead of January, which was presumably not the case.

34. Greene, "Salem Witches II," p. 69. Greene points out broader motives for the changing of the will, but nevertheless sees the bequest to Margaret as "a gesture of forgiveness." Scholars checking this citation will note that Greene does not mention Margaret as the recipient of the ten pounds. The omission results from one of the editorial errors mentioned in n. 30.

35. Upham, *Salem Witchcraft*, II, p. 319.

36. For the origin of the tradition in print, see "Salem Witches II," pp. 70–1.

37. Ibid., p. 71. The chances that they belonged to George Jacobs, Sr., are slim, since the notion that they did is based on a tradition finding print in 1859 that George Jacobs, Jr., after witnessing the execution of his father, brought the remains of the elder Jacobs home for burial. The trouble with the story is that George Jacobs, Jr., was in hiding for his life, having left his wife and children to the judicial system. He was hardly likely to be present at a public execution. On this and other grounds, David L. Greene has argued persuasively against the accuracy of the tradition.

38. Ibid., pp. 71–2.

39. Cotton Mather, "The Wonders of the Invisible World" (1693), largely reprinted in Burr, *Narratives,* pp. 203–52, cited p. 244.

40. Montague Summers, *The History of Witchcraft and Demonology* (London: Routledge & Kegan Paul, 1926); reprinted (New Hyde Park, N.Y.: University Books, 1956), p. 124. The reprint edition has an unfriendly foreword by Felix Morrow. DeForest's novel first appeared in *Putnam's Magazine* (vols. 8–9, 1856–7).

41. For a brief, valuable description of some of the known facts and speculations about her life, see Carol F. Karlsen, *The Devil in the Shape of a Woman* (New York: W. W. Norton, 1987), pp. 98–101.

42. Boyer and Nissenbaum, *Salem-Village Witchcraft,* p. 298.

7. George Burroughs and the Mathers

1. *The Diary of Cotton Mather,* 2 vols., preface by Worthington Chauncey Ford, 1911; reprinted (New York: Frederick Ungar Publ., n.d.), I, p. 142.
2. For Burroughs conducting a ministry in Wells, see Charles W. Upham, *Salem Witchcraft; with An Account of Salem Village, and a History of Opinions on Witchcraft and Kindred Subjects* (1867), 2 vols.; reprinted (Williamstown, Mass.: Corner House Publ., 1971), II, p. 149.
3. Paul Boyer and Stephen Nissenbaum, *Salem Possessed: The Social Origins of Witchcraft* (Cambridge, Mass.: Harvard University Press, 1974. A letter dated April 21 from Thomas Putnam to Hathorne and Corwin, referring to "a wheel within a wheel," was first cited by Upham in *Salem Witchcraft,* II, pp. 139–40, 150, as connected to the impending accusation against Burroughs. Boyer and Nissenbaum, p. 6, make the same connection, and the letter is printed in *The Salem Witchcraft Papers* (I: 165–6) as applying to Burroughs. While this letter may indeed refer to Putnam alerting Hathorne and Corwin of the impending charge against Burroughs, no good evidence supports the claim. Burroughs was formally complained against on April 30, along with several other people (*SWP* I: 151), and I can find nothing to confirm the connection of this letter to the charge against Burroughs. The letter remains significant, however, in offering evidence of close communication between Putnam and the magistrates. It remains impossible to prove that Thomas Putnam or Samuel Parris "orchestrated" the accusations, as various writers have over the years indicated; but it also remains hard to believe that Putnam was not, to put the best construction on it, at least inadvertently providing names to the accusers. The same may also apply to Parris.
4. See Chapter 5, §II and n. 35.
5. Dane's daughter and granddaughter, Elizabeth Johnson, Sr. and Jr,. were accused, as was his daughter, Abigail Faulkner, and his daughter-in-law, Deliverance Dane. For Dane's accusation see *SWP* II: 616; for Elizabeth Johnson and her daughter, see *SWP* III: 883; for Abigail Faulkner's family connection, see Carol F. Karlsen, *The Devil in the Shape of a Woman* (New York: W. W. Norton, 1987), p. 218; and for Deliverance Dane's relationship, see Richard Weisman, *Witchcraft, Magic, and Religion in 17th-Century Massachusetts* (Amherst: University of Massachusetts Press, 1984), p. 245, n .43.
6. A notable exception appears in *So Dreadful a Judgment: Puritan Responses to King Philip's War, 1676–1677,* ed. Richard Slotkin and James K. Folsom (Middletown, Conn.: Wesleyan University Press, 1978), p. 76. Slotkin and Folsom refer without elaboration to "the condemnation of religious dissidents like the Reverend George Burroughs. . . ."

7. George H. Moore, *Notes on the History of Witchcraft in Massachusetts; With Illustrative Documents* (Worcester, Mass.: 1883), in *Proceedings of the American Antiquarian Society*, n.s., vol. II, p. 171.

8. My understanding of the relationship between the Baptists and the Puritans is heavily indebted to the extraordinary study of William G. McLoughlin, *New England Dissent 1630–1883: The Baptists and the Separation of Church and State*, 2 vols. (Cambridge, Mass.: Harvard University Press, 1971). If I have made incorrect inferences, the fault is mine and not his. For a more recent and valuable study see Carla Gardina Pestana, *Quakers and Baptists in Colonial Massachusetts* (Cambridge: Cambridge University Press, 1991).

   I have also benefited from discussions with Norman Burns on the issue of religious dissent and from the research of my students, David Callaway and Everett Wilson. The possibility of a link between Burroughs and the Baptists as a cause of persecution was first suggested to me by Callaway. Again, any mistakes are mine.

9. For a discussion of the serious implications of the Baptist theology for the Puritan establishment, see McLoughlin, *New England Dissent*, pp. 28–48.

10. *Massachusetts Province Laws 1692–1699*, ed. note by John D. Cushing (Wilmington, Del.: Michael Glazier, Inc., 1978), p. 11.

11. "Letter of Thomas Brattle, F.R.S.," in *Narratives of the Witchcraft Cases 1648–1706*, ed. George Lincoln Burr (New York: Charles Scribner's Sons, 1914), pp. 165–90, cited p. 189.

12. Samuel Willard, *A Compleat Body of Divinity* (Boston: Green & S. Kneeland for B. Eliot & D. Henchman, 1726); reprinted with an introduction by Edward M. Griffin (New York and London: Johnson Reprint Corp., 1969), p. 855.

13. Cotton Mather, "The Wonders of the Invisible World" (1693), largely reprinted in Burr, *Narratives*, pp. 203–52, cited p. 217.

14. Letter to John Foster, August 17, 1692, in *Selected Letters of Cotton Mather*, ed. Kenneth Silverman (Baton Rouge: Louisiana State University Press, 1971), p. 41.

15. *Diary of Cotton Mather*, I, p. 142. In his letter of July 23, John Proctor identifies two of the five confessors as Richard and Andrew Carrier (*SWP* II: 689). The other three are almost certainly Ann Foster, her daughter, Mary Lacey, Sr., and her granddaughter, Mary Lacey, Jr.

16. Increase Mather, *Cases of Conscience Concerning evil Spirits Personating Man, Witchcrafts, infallible Proofs of Guilt in such as are accused with that Crime. All Considered according to the Scriptures, History, Experience, and the Judgment of many Learned men* (Boston, 1692). The book was also printed in London in 1693. For the circumstances and dating of the publication of *Cases*, see Stephen Foster, *The Long Argument: English Puritanism and the Shaping of New England Culture, 1570–1700* (Chapel Hill: University of North Carolina Press, 1991), p. 262.

17. William Hubbard, Samuel Phillips, Charles Morton, James Allen, Michael Wigglesworth, Samuel Whiting, Sr., Samuel Willard, John Baily, Jabez Fox, Joseph Gerrish, Samuel Angier, John Wise, Joseph Capen, and Nehemiah Walter. Among other points, they asserted that witchcraft cases need to be treated with the same scrupulousness as regular criminal cases. They are all identified as ministers by Cotton Mather, *Selected Letters of Cotton Mather,* p. 45.

18. For valuable comment on Mather's general ambivalence, see Michael G. Hall, *The Last American Puritan: The Life of Increase Mather* (Middletown, Conn.: Wesleyan University Press, 1988), p. 261.

19. I. Mather, *Cases of Conscience,* p. 66.

20. Ibid., p. 67.

21. Ibid., p. 34.

22. Hall, *The Last American Puritan,* p. 172.

23. Richard Bernard, *A Guide to Grand-Jury-Men . . . in Cases of Witchcraft* (London, 1627); cited in I. Mather, *Cases of Conscience,* pp. 31–2. On August 1, 1692, a group of elders, including Increase Mather, had met in Cambridge and discussed whether the devil could represent an innocent person in tormenting someone. Although they said he could, they conceded, perhaps out of deference to the civil authorities, *"that such things are rare and extraordinary, especially when such Matters come before Civil Judicatures"* (Mather's emphasis).

24. Heinrich Kramer and James Sprenger, *The Malleus Maleficarum* (ca. 1486); reprinted (London: John Rodker, 1928; New York: Dover, 1971), trans. Montague Summers.

25. I. Mather, *Cases of Conscience,* p. 62.

26. Ibid., pp. 70–1. The comment on "Wonders" came in a later published version of *Cases;* however, Increase surely had known what would be in Cotton's book when he presented *Cases* in early October.

27. For example, compare Cotton Mather's account of Samuel Shattuck's testimony against Bridget Bishop at her trial on June 2 ("Wonders," in Burr, *Narratives,* pp. 225–6) with that in *The Salem Witchcraft Papers* (I: 97–9).

28. For example, the depositional evidence indicating the strength of Burroughs in lifting a barrel of molasses is mentioned in both "Wonders" (Burr, *Narratives,* p. 220) and *The Salem Witchcraft Papers* (I: 160). A reference in *The Salem Witchcraft Papers* to evidence in the "Tryall besides the written Evidences" probably implies inclusion of grand jury testimony (*SWP* I: 178).

29. For an excellent analysis, if one overlooks the hyperbole, of Deliverance Hobbs changing her testimony to suit the needs of the authorities, see Upham, *Salem Witchcraft,* II, pp. 161–2. Although Upham is persuasive in the case that he makes, I cannot confirm the exact dating he uses; he may have had access to additional documentation. The changing of her testimony, however, can be confirmed (see *SWP* II: 419–23).

John Hale inadvertently reveals Deliverance Hobbs's cooperation with the authorities as he relates an anecdote regarding this confessor who told of Burroughs's preaching at the witch meeting. Hale describes, in an event apparently unrelated to the Burroughs case, how someone with a rapier had tried to defend an "afflicted person." Although seeing no shape himself, the man, guided by the accuser, had attacked a specter, hitting it twice. Thereafter, Deliverance Hobbs had confessed to being the specter and showed the wounds, which had corresponded exactly to where the "afflicted person" had said they were. Thus either her shape really had been wounded, or she had colluded with the authorities to identify a "newly healed" wound on her side and a smaller one near her eye as being inflicted "by a Sword or Rapier." Hale, "A Modest Inquiry into the Nature of Witchcraft" (1702), largely reprinted in Burr, *Narratives*, pp. 395–432, cited p. 417.

30. John Neal, *Rachel Dyer: A North American Story* (Portland: Shirley & Hyde, 1828); reprinted (Gainesville, Fla.: Scholars' Facsimiles & Reprints, 1964), with intro. by John D. Seelye; see, e.g., p. 177.

31. C. Mather, "Wonders," in Burr, *Narratives,* p. 219–20.

32. Marion L. Starkey, *The Devil in Massachusetts: A Modern Enquiry into the Salem Witch Trials* (New York: Alfred A. Knopf, 1949); 2d ed. (1950), p. 115.

33. Chadwick Hansen, *Witchcraft at Salem* (New York: George Braziller, 1969), p. 77.

34. Upham, *Salem Witchcraft,* II, p. 300, identifies Greenslit's relation to Ann Pudeator. See also Sybil Noyes, Charles Thornton Libby, and Walker Goodwin Davis, *Genealogical Dictionary of Maine and New Hampshire* (Baltimore: Genealogical Publishing Co., 1972), p. 289. In "Wonders," Cotton Mather refers to a witness who had been persuaded not to testify at the trial of Burroughs but who subsequently had given testimony (in Burr, *Narratives*, p. 220). Perhaps this is Greenslit.

Upham claims that "many of the depositions, how many we cannot tell, were procured after the trials were over, and surreptitiously foisted in among the papers to bolster up the proceedings" (*Salem Witchcraft,* II, pp. 297–8). I do not know how he reached this conclusion.

35. I. Mather, *Cases of Conscience,* "Postscript," p. 70.

36. Cotton Mather is ambiguous as to whether people testifying to the strength of Burroughs did so from personal observation or not, but most of what he describes ("Wonders," in Burr, *Narratives*, pp. 219–20) seems to be testimony appearing in *The Salem Witchcraft Papers,* where Greenslit's is the only personal observation of Burroughs's strength to appear. Mather, of course, is not offering his eyewitness account of the trial, since he did not attend it; but he did study records provided him. At first, it appears as if he is reporting boasts by Burroughs; but his reference to testimony by Burroughs that an *Indian* had performed feats of strength – along with Mather's report of "Spectators" not having seen

this Indian – makes it appear as if someone had seen *Burroughs* perform such feats. However, nothing of this survives in the record, and it may be that the account refers to events after the trial.

37. Upham, *Salem Witchcraft,* II, p. 303.
38. For Mather's observations see "Wonders," in Burr, *Narratives,* pp. 215–22.
39. I. Mather, *Cases of Conscience,* "Postscript," p. 70.
40. *The Autobiography of Increase Mather,* ed. M. G. Hall, *Proceedings of the American Antiquarian Society,* vol. 71 (October 1961), pp. 271–360, cited p. 334.
41. *Diary of Cotton Mather,* I, p. 156.
42. Ibid., p. 171.
43. Ibid., p. 173. For the Margaret Rule story and Mather's controversy with Robert Calef in connection with this, see ibid., pp. 172–3, and Robert Calef, "More Wonders of the Invisible World" (1700), in Burr, *Narratives,* pp. 289–394, cited pp. 307ff.
44. *Diary of Cotton Mather,* I, pp. 151–2.
45. *Selected Letters of Cotton Mather,* p. 42.
46. Kenneth Silverman does not print this part of the letter in his *Selected Letters of Cotton Mather.* My citation is from *Transactions of the Literary and Historical Society of Quebec* (1831), vol. III, 1st ser., pp. 313–16, at p. 316.
47. For skepticism see David Levin, *Cotton Mather: The Young Life of the Lord's Remembrancer, 1663–1703* (Cambridge, Mass.: Harvard University Press, 1978), p. 215, and Stephen Foster, *The Long Argument,* pp. 259–60.
48. Calef, "More Wonders," in Burr, *Narratives,* pp. 360–1.
49. *The Diary of Samuel Sewall 1674–1729,* vol. I, in *Collections of the Massachusetts Historical Society,* vol. v, 5th ser., p. 363. David Levin suggests that it may have been Increase rather than Cotton to whom Sewall refers in saying that these individuals died by a righteous sentence. Levin, *Cotton Mather: The Young Life,* p. 215).
50. McLoughlin, *New England Dissent,* I, p. 64.
51. Ibid., I, p. 125.
52. C. Mather, "Wonders," in Burr, *Narratives,* p. 218.
53. Cotton Mather on religious tolerance, as on almost any issue, is not a matter for simple presentation. On May 14, 1692, the day his father arrived with the new charter, Cotton Mather offered a strong defense against religious persecution and claimed that he himself was persecuted for expressing such views. See his entry for May 14, 1692, *Diary of Cotton Mather,* I, p. 149. Perry Miller has seen this stance, however, "as a political device," even though New England was moving toward the very tolerance he really opposed. Miller, *The New England Mind: From Colony to Province* (Boston: Beacon Press, 1953, 1966), p. 167. For a valuable discussion of the point, see McLoughlin, *New England Dissent,*

I, pp. 108–10. Mather's response to the George Burroughs case seems to support the analysis offered by Miller. For Mather's contempt for the Baptists, as well as for Samuel Willard's hostility to them, see *New England Dissent*, I, p. 109, n. 42.

54. "Memorable Providences, relating to Witchcrafts and Possessions" (1689) in Burr, *Narratives*, pp. 89–144, cited p. 103.

55. *Selected Letters of Cotton Mather*, p. 38.

56. Miller, *The New England Mind*, p. 194.

57. C. Mather, "Wonders," in Burr, *Narratives*, pp. 250–1.

58. Miller, *The New England Mind*, p. 204.

59. C. Mather, "Wonders," in Burr, *Narratives*, p. 215. That Mather approached this task kicking and screaming is hard to believe. In his refusal to endorse the argument his father had made on October 3 in *Cases of Conscience*, he claimed on October 20 that "such a discourse going alone would not only enable our witch-advocates very learnedly to cavil and nibble at the late proceedings against the witches, considered in parcels, while things as they lay in bulk, with their whole dependences, were not exposed. . . ." (*Selected Letters of Cotton Mather*, p. 45).

60. *The Autobiography of Increase Mather*, p. 344. Mather writes, "I doubt that innocent blood was shed," but the context makes clear that he uses "doubt" as synonymous with "dread" or "fear." See *The Oxford English Dictionary*, s.v. Mather's entry is dated May 14; though not written, "1692" is implicit in the order of the entry and the reference to his homecoming that day. However, he writes at the same time about his having "published my Cases of Conscience," which helped prevent "shedding of more Innocent blood." Thus, Mather must have recorded all or part of his May 14 entry well after that date.

61. Durward Grinstead, *Elva* (New York: Covici-Friede, 1929). In 1934, Grinstead shared in the screenwriting of the movie *Maid of Salem* (dir. Frank Lloyd, released 1937), which starred Claudette Colbert and Fred MacMurray. The film is not about the Burroughs story, nor particularly about any real person, but aspects of it show some research into actual events at Salem. Rebecca Nurse is portrayed as a saintly woman doomed to the gallows.

62. For Burroughs in *Rachel Dyer* as a figure of civilization and wilderness, see William J. Scheick, *The Half-Blood: A Cultural Symbol in 19th-Century American Fiction* (Lexington: University of Kentucky Press, 1979), pp. 60–7.

63. The term "half-blood" is from Scheick, *The Half-Blood*. In Neal's *Rachel Dyer*, Burroughs is biologically white but, having lived among the "savages," identifies with both cultures.

64. The standard biographical sketch on Burroughs appears in John Langdon Sibley, *Biographical Sketches of Graduates of Harvard University*, vol. II (Cambridge: Charles William Sever, 1881), pp. 323–34. See also

David L. Greene, "The Third Wife of the Rev. George Burroughs," *American Genealogist*, vol. 56, no. 1 (1980), pp. 43–5.

65. Upham, *Salem Witchcraft*, II, p. 535.
66. Hale, "A Modest Inquiry," in Burr, *Narratives*, p. 421.
67. C. Mather, "Wonders," in Burr, *Narratives*, p. 222. Daniel Neal's two-volume *History of New-England* (London, 1720), containing the first eighteenth-century account of the trials, repeats Mather's version of Burroughs on the powers of witches (I, p. 506).
68. C. Mather, "Wonders," in Burr, *Narratives*, p. 222.

8. September 22, 1692

1. Robert Calef, "More Wonders of the Invisible World" (1700), largely reprinted in *Narratives of the Witchcraft Cases 1648–1706*, ed. George Lincoln Burr (New York: Charles Scribner's Sons, 1914), pp. 289–394, cited p. 369.
2. See, for example, the narrative of Martha Tyler (*SWP* II: 777).
3. Cotton Mather, *Magnalia Christi Americana* (1702), reprinted with introduction and notes by the Rev. Thomas Robbins (Hartford, Conn.: Silas Andrus & Son, 1853), vol. 2, p. 476.
4. Evidence for Mary Bradbury's escape appears in *SWP* III: 981.
5. For the age of Mercy Wardwell, see Carol F. Karlsen, *The Devil in the Shape of a Woman* (New York: W. W. Norton, 1987), p. 105.
6. Karlsen, *The Devil in the Shape of a Woman,* p. 127, reads the passage differently, with her point being that Mercy feared she would not have a young man who would love her and so took the devil. Karlsen writes that Mercy testified that "people told her that 'she should Never hath such a Young Man who loved her,'" making it appear as if Mercy is responding to a generalized concern about having *any* appropriate suitor. Mercy's account makes it clear, however, that she is referring to a specific man who threatens to drown himself, with Mercy doing the rejecting.
7. Both William Barker, Sr., and William Barker, Jr., were among the accused; it is not clear which of the two Mercy Wardwell named here.
8. The qualification about all being confessors stems from the case of "Goody Lawrence," accused by Sarah Wardwell. She appears nowhere else in *The Salem Witchcraft Papers*, and I cannot confirm that she confessed. I am guessing that she did because of Sarah's approach to the whole issue of whom she seemed willing to name.
9. Charles W. Upham, *Salem Witchcraft; with An Account of Salem Village, and a History of Opinions on Witchcraft and Kindred Subjects* (1867), 2 vols.; reprinted (Williamstown, Mass.: Corner House Publ., 1971), p. 349, identifies the other two as Elizabeth Johnson, Jr., and Mary Post. For Sarah Wardwell's condemnation, see *SWP* III: 1006. Both Chadwick Hansen and Marion Starkey have asserted that Sarah Ward-

well held to her confession in January. I do not know on what basis they make this claim. In a letter dated February 21, 1693, Phips explains to the Earl of Nottingham why he gave his reprieve to Sarah Wardwell and the two others convicted in January. He writes that "I was enformed by the Kings Attorny Generall that some of the cleared and the condemned were under the same circumstances or that there was the same reason to clear the three condemned as the rest according to his Judgment" (*SWP* III: 865). It seems highly unlikely that someone still confessing would be in "the same circumstances" as the others. Chadwick Hansen, *Witchcraft at Salem* (New York: George Braziller, 1969), p. 95; Marion L. Starkey, *The Devil in Massachusetts: A Modern Enquiry into the Salem Witch Trials* (New York: Alfred A. Knopf, 1949); 2d ed. (1950), p. 235.

Phips also gave reprieves for five others who had been under sentence of death from the earlier Court of Oyer and Terminer (*SWP* III: 865).

10. I am assuming that the transcriber erroneously recorded the first names of Lilly and Taylor, recorded in Wardwell's accusation as Mary Lilly and Hannah Taylor – names that appear nowhere else, whereas the story of Wardwell, Jane Lilly, and Mary Taylor continues.

11. William Hooper was almost certainly the brother of Wardwell's wife Sarah. For identification of her as from the Hooper family, see Karlsen, *The Devil in the Shape of a Woman*, p. 105. Wardwell refers to him as "his bro[ther] Hooper" (*SWP* III: 741).

12. *The Diary of Samuel Sewall 1674–1729*, vol. I, in *Collections of the Massachusetts Historical Society*, vol. v, 5th ser. (Cambridge, 1878), p. 365.

13. For the names and dates of those condemned in September, see Calef, "More Wonders," in Burr, *Narratives*, p. 366.

14. See Chapter 7, §II.

15. "Vital Records of Topsfield, Massachusetts, to the End of the Year 1849," *Historical Collections of the Topsfield Historical Society*, vol. 9 (Topsfield, Mass.: The Society, 1903), p. 55.

16. Calef, "More Wonders," in Burr, *Narratives*, p. 367.

17. The accounts of Samuel Sewall and Robert Calef differ as to the exact date of the pressing death: Sewall records it as September 19 (*Diary*, p. 364); Calef has it as September 16 ("More Wonders," in Burr, *Narratives*, p. 366). A possible explanation for this apparent discrepancy is that the process of pressing may have begun on the 16th, with Corey surviving until the 19th, although Sewall's description seems to suggest an execution limited to one day. Calef, of course, could simply have been wrong on his date, as he was on others in the proceedings.

18. The examination of Giles Corey does not appear in *The Salem Witchcraft Papers*. The citations here of this examination are from Samuel G. Drake, *The Witchcraft Delusion in New England*, 3 vols. (1866); reprinted (New York: Burt Franklin, 1970), III, pp. 169–73.

19. See Chapter 3, §II.
20. For a representative account see Starkey, *The Devil in Massachusetts,* p. 209.
21. Sewall, *Diary,* I, p. 364.
22. Calef, "More Wonders," in Burr, *Narratives,* p. 367.
23. Rossell Hope Robbins describes the punishment as historically used: "By English law, an accused had to place himself 'on God and the country,' that is, plead Guilty or Not Guilty. For 'standing mute,' the penalty was *peine forte et dure* – slow crushing with heavier and heavier iron weights until the naked victim agreed to plead, or died." Since Corey had probably entered a plea, the Court of Oyer and Terminer seems to have been offering its own variation of *peine forte et dure.* Robbins observes that this punishment was illegal in the colony under the 1641 *Body of Liberties.* Robbins, *The Encyclopedia of Witchcraft and Demonology* (New York: Crown Publ., 1959), pp. 109–10.
24. Sewall, *Diary,* I, p. 364.
25. The petition was by John Moulton, husband of Corey's daughter, Elizabeth. The marriage to Martha was not Corey's first, and I do not know whether Elizabeth was also Martha's daughter (*SWP* III: 986, 1019). For Corey's marital history see Karlsen, *The Devil in the Shape of a Woman,* p. 107.
26. Upham, *Salem Witchcraft,* II, p. 337. For an excellent refutation of this tradition, as well as for other aspects of the Corey case, see David C. Brown, "The Case of Giles Corey," *Essex Institute Historical Collections,* vol. 121 (October 1985), pp. 282–99. See also Sidney Perley, *The History of Salem Massachusetts* (Salem, Mass.: privately published, 1924), III, pp. 288–9.
27. Henry Wadsworth Longfellow, *Giles Corey of the Salem Farms,* in *The New-England Tragedies* (Boston: Ticknor & Fields, 1868), pp. 97–179, cited p. 176.
28. John Demos, *Entertaining Satan: Witchcraft and the Culture of Early New England* (Oxford: Oxford University Press, 1982), p. x. I see a distinction here between the phenomenon described by Demos and the ambivalence of some scholars as to whether people were actually practicing witchcraft.
29. William Carlos Williams, *Tituba's Children,* in *Many Loves and Other Plays* (Norfolk, Conn.: New Directions Books, 1961), pp. 225–300, cited p. 281; Rep. Thaddeus Buczko, cited in John Beresford Hatch, *Salem Witchcraft – Fact or Fiction?* (Salem, Mass.: J. B. Hatch, 1963), p. 7; Nicholas Van Slyck, "Salem Evening News," December 31, 1975; Montague Summers, *The History of Witchcraft and Demonology* (London: Routledge & Kegan Paul, 1926); reprinted (New Hyde Park, N.Y.: University Books, 1956), p. 310.
30. Mary Wilkins Freeman, *Giles Corey, Yeoman* (New York: Harper, 1893).

31. Cotton Mather, "The Wonders of the Invisible World" (1693), largely reprinted in Burr, *Narratives*, pp. 203–52, cited p. 250. The letter refers to the impending pressing to death of Corey and was therefore written around the middle of September. Sewall recorded his learning of the contents on September 20; *Diary*, I, p. 364.

32. For a discussion of this case, see Upham, *Salem Witchcraft*, I, pp. 185–6, and Perley, *The History of Salem Massachusetts*, vol. 3, pp. 106–7.

33. *The Records of the First Church in Salem Massachusetts*, ed. Richard D. Pierce (Salem, Mass.: Essex Institute, 1974), p. 173.

34. *Salem-Village Witchcraft: A Documentary Record of Local Conflict in Colonial New England*, ed. Paul Boyer and Stephen Nissenbaum (Belmont, Calif.: Wadsworth Publ., 1972), p. 280. For a discussion of her subsequent reinstatement in the church, see Boyer and Nissenbaum, *Salem Possessed: The Social Origins of Witchcraft* (Cambridge, Mass.: Harvard University Press, 1974), p. 219.

35. Calef, "More Wonders," in Burr, *Narratives*, p. 367.

36. Carol F. Karlsen writes, "I suspect that the Alice Parker who was executed was in fact Giles Corey's daughter"; for her explanation of this hypothesis, see *The Devil in the Shape of a Woman*, p. 307. David L. Greene, in reviewing Karlsen's book, forcefully challenges this speculation; see Greene, "Reviews of Books, " *New England Historical and Genealogical Register*, vol. 144 (October 1990), pp. 358–60, cited p. 360.

37. For Alden, son of the John Alden of Longfellow's poem, see "Letter of Thomas Brattle, F.R.S.," in Burr, *Narratives*, pp. 165–90, cited p. 170. See Calef, "More Wonders," in Burr, *Narratives*, for Noyes and Hathorne on Martha Corey (p. 344), for Sarah Good (p. 358), for Proctor (361–2); and for Noyes at the September 22 hangings (p. 369). Abigail Somes was a single woman and may have been a target of the accusers to join them, but she did not (*SWP* III: 734, 736).

38. The editors of *The Salem Witchcraft Papers* have tangled the account of Alice Parker with that of Mary Parker; this particular entry appears under the "Mary Parker" section, but is incorrectly placed there. Westgate's testimony was given on June 2, well before Mary Parker's examination, which did not come until the beginning of September (*SWP* II: 633). Mary Parker was a widow from Andover, and her case is related to the later, Andover phase of the episode. Alice Parker was the wife of John Parker, as he is identified in this particular episode. The name Westgate is mentioned early and prominently in the examination of Alice Parker – in fact, in the opening charge from the judiciary that Alice had "cast away Thomas Westgate" (*SWP* II: 623). Mary Warren, at her own examination that day, charged that Alice Parker had told her of casting Westgate away (*SWP* III: 802). Upham, in *Salem Witchcraft*, II, p. 181, correctly associates the Westgate testimony with Alice Parker.

39. This testimony pertains to Alice Parker rather than to Mary Parker as

indicated in *The Salem Witchcraft Papers*. The involvement of Martha Dutch in the case suggests the connection with Alice; and the testimony was given on September 7, just prior to the trial date, September 9, of Alice Parker. The deposition of Bullock was probably used at the trial, but is here for the grand jury. Trial testimony where Mary Parker is mentioned by name indicates that her grand-jury appearance was on September 16. Her trial was held September 17 (Calef, "More Wonders," in Burr, *Narratives*, p. 366).

40. The testimony against Bridget Bishop was given on June 2, but there is no date for the testimony against Alice Parker. This testimony is misidentified in *The Salem Witchcraft Papers* as being against Mary Parker. That it is aimed at Alice is clear from her identification in it as the husband of John Parker, a "Mariner" (*SWP* II: 635). Like Alice Parker, Samuel Shattuck was from Salem, and the testimony makes it clear that the woman being described lived in proximity to him.

41. See Hansen, *Witchcraft at Salem,* pp. 65–6, for the use of Shattuck in support of the idea of Bridget Bishop as a witch. A discussion of this issue occurs above in Chapter 4, §I.

42. For some background on Margaret Scott (Margaret Stevenson prior to marrying Benjamin Scott), see George Brainard Blodgette and Amos Everett Jewett, *Early Settlers of Rowley, Massachusetts* (Rowley, Mass.: Amos Everett Jewett, 1933), pp. 329–30; *The Probate Records of Essex County Massachusetts,* vol. 2 (Salem, Mass.: Essex Institute, 1917), pp. 238–9; and Karlsen, *The Devil in the Shape of a Woman,* pp. 65, 114.

43. Samuel G. Drake, *Annals of Witchcraft in New England and elsewhere in the United States* (1869); reprinted (New York: Benjamin Blom, 1967), p. 198.

44. Win Brooks, "Still No Vindication for Salem's Comely Witch," *American Weekly,* September 29, 1946, pp. 6–7, cited p. 6.

45. Eleanor Early, "Salem 'Witches' Finally Cleared," *Salem News,* May 1, 1957, p. 1.

46. Nathaniel Hawthorne, *Blithedale Romance* (1852), ed. William Charvat, Roy Harvey Pearce, and Claude M. Simpson (Columbus: Ohio State University Press, 1964), p. 214.

47. I am indebted to Marilyn Wienk for calling to my attention a large number of instances where nineteenth-century writers employ the idea of "witchery."

48. *I Married a Witch,* dir. René Clair (Universal, 1942), 76 min.

49. Karlsen, *The Devil in the Shape of a Woman,* p. 142, identifies Ann Pudeator as a midwife.

50. Hansen, *Witchcraft at Salem,* p. 71; he gives no source for Wilmot Reed as "town witch." Those picking up the story of Wilmot Reed as witch after Hansen's book include Selma R. Williams and Pamela J. Williams, *Riding the Night Mare: Women & Witchcraft* (New York: Atheneum, 1978), p. 191. Boyer and Nissenbaum may imply it in *Salem-*

Village Witchcraft (see above, Chapter 4, §I). Prior to Hansen, the notion of actual witchcraft as a factor in 1692 had been pursued primarily by Montague Summers, in his *The Geography of Witchcraft* (London: Routledge & Kegan Paul, 1927) and *History of Witchcraft and Demonology* (1926), as well as by Margaret Murray in *The God of the Witches* (1931), reprinted (New York: Oxford University Press, 1970). Both Summers and Murray depend on depositional testimony for their conclusions; neither is reliable in assessing what occurred in 1692 or a likely source for Boyer and Nissenbaum.

51. Caroline E. Upham, *Salem Witchcraft in Outline* (Salem, Mass.: Salem Press, 1891), p. 99.

52. An enigmatic dating on her examination of April 22 is recorded as "March 24'th." (*SWP* I: 289). I have not been able to make any sense of this entry, but have confirmed that it is accurately transcribed from the original to *The Salem Witchcraft Papers*. Perhaps others will be able to make something of it.

53. Traditionally, the fate of Sarah Cloyce has been presented as something of a mystery, but this has more to do with legend than with court records. For the rejection of the indictment, see *SWP* I: 221–3. I infer the January date from the fact that similar cases leading to rejected indictments were heard then and that the jury foreman, who is identified in the documents, was Robert Payne, who as foreman heard similar January cases. Thus, the evidence for January, though circumstantial, is overwhelming. I infer the September 9 examination from the indictment that accuses her of afflicting Rebecca Towne that day (*SWP* I: 222–3). The speculation that Rebecca was a relative stems from the fact that Sarah Cloyce was a member of a "Towne" family.

   In a letter dated May 24, 1979, Mildred E. Danforth, a descendant of Mary Easty, wrote to Mary M. Ritchie, Assistant Librarian at the Essex Institute in Salem, stating that Sarah Cloyce had escaped from prison and been harbored by Thomas Danforth; the letter is in the holdings of the Essex Institute. I cannot confirm that Sarah Cloyce escaped from prison or that Danforth sheltered her; but if he did it would suggest the extent to which he had come to doubt the justice of the proceedings. I am grateful to Mildred Danforth for her generosity in writing to me in answer to my queries as I sought to explore this issue.

54. *Three Sovereigns for Sarah: A True Story*, dir. Philip Leacock (PBS, 1985), 152 min.; originally presented on "American Playhouse."

55. Calef, "More Wonders," in Burr, *Narratives*, p. 346.

56. Another document, however, shows that she was ordered to Boston jail on May 25 (*SWP* I: 255). I cannot account for the conflicting dates except in speculating that the first jailing was not in Boston, but only appears so as a result of an ambiguity in the court record. The same set of jail dates apply for the Proctors, Rebecca Nurse, Martha Corey, and Dorcas Good.

57. Persis W. McMillen makes a strong case that neither sister was literate; presumably, their petitions were dictated. The handwriting on the two petitions differs. Whether the sisters had any help in composing the petitions is impossible to say. McMillen, *Currents of Malice: Mary Towne Esty and Her Family in Salem Witchcraft* (Portsmouth, N.H.: Peter E. Randall, 1990), pp. 17–18.

58. The story originates with Calef's observation that Mrs. Hale had been accused in October, leading to a change of view by Hale and others regarding the proceedings. See Calef, "More Wonders," in Burr, *Narratives*, pp. 369–70.

59. Brattle, "Letter," in Burr, *Narratives*, pp. 177–8; Upham, *Witchcraft at Salem*, II, p. 345 (where she is not referred to by name; her identification as Mrs. Thacher is clear from Upham's index). Upham feels that Jonathan Corwin's silence at the examinations suggested doubts about the proceedings, even though Corwin was to become a judge on the trial court. Upham speculates that this attitude led to the accusation of Corwin's mother-in-law, Mrs. Thacher. For more on Upham's views of Corwin, see *Witchcraft at Salem*, II, pp. 448, 453.

60. For the end of the court, see Sir William Phips, letter of February 21, 1693, to the Earl of Nottingham, in Burr, *Narratives*, pp. 198–202, cited p. 200. Calef erroneously dates the charge by Mary Herrick as having occurred in October, and almost all commentators have followed suit; but her story is clearly told in November, on the 14th; see Calef, "More Wonders," in Burr, *Narratives*, p. 369.

61. In Marion L. Starkey's account, "The Ghost of Mary Esty," the Mary Herrick story figures prominently in the conversion of Hale and in the ending of the trials; *The Devil in Massachusetts*, pp. 216–18. For a rare refutation of the legend that the accusation against Mrs. Hale helped end the trials, see Chadwick Hansen's introduction to Robert Calef, "More Wonders of the Invisible World" (1700); reprinted (Bainbridge, N.Y.: York Mail-Print, Inc., 1972), p. x.

62. The bracket in "wor[l]d" is not mine, but appears in *The Salem Witchcraft Papers*.

63. Brattle, "Letter," in Burr, *Narratives*, p. 184.

64. Chadwick Hansen is one of the few who has emphasized the point that Mary Easty was appealing for "a fundamental change," but he fails to realize that a change occurred, arguing instead that the court "made no plans to change their procedure" (*Witchcraft at Salem*, p. 152). The obvious change, of course, was in trying confessors.

65. Calef, "More Wonders," in Burr, *Narratives*, pp. 367–8.

9. Assessing an inextricable storm

1. Rev. Michael Wigglesworth, letter to Increase Mather, *Collections of the Massachusetts Historical Society*, vol. 8, 4th ser, p. 646. The letter is dated

"5 month, 22 day," which probably means July 22 (1704) according to old calendar usage.

2. I am agreeing with the editors of *The Salem Witchcraft Papers* that the woman accused here by Mary Warren was Sarah Cole of Lynn even though she is described in the transcription as the wife of Abraham Cole, who was from Salem and whose wife was also named Sarah. The husband of Sarah Cole of Lynn was named John. One possibility is that the examination of Sarah Cole of Lynn belongs with Sarah Cole of Salem, but this is not likely: Sarah of Lynn was arrested October 3, and the examination of her that day seems probable. I believe that the transcriber, who refers to the examination as applying to Sarah Cole of Lynn, simply identified her husband incorrectly. Abraham Cole's wife Sarah was arrested September 15 and probably examined around that time (*SWP* I: 235).

3. For the summoning of accusers to Gloucester, see Robert Calef, "More Wonders of the Invisible World" (1700), largely reprinted in *Narratives of the Witchcraft Cases 1648–1706,* ed. George Lincoln Burr (New York: Charles Scribner's Sons, 1914), pp. 289–394, cited p. 373.

4. Ibid., p. 373.

5. George H. Moore takes the view that the attainders never actually became law. See Moore, *Notes on the History of Witchcraft in Massachusetts,* in *Proceedings of the American Antiquarian Society,* n.s., vol. II (Worcester, Mass., 1883), p. 178.

6. Thomas Hutchinson, *The History of the Colony and Province of Massachusetts-Bay* (1764), ed. Laurence Shaw Mayo (Cambridge, Mass.: Harvard University Press, 1936), II, p. 12.

7. Winfield Nevins, *Witchcraft in Salem Village* (Salem, Mass.: North Shore Publ. / Boston, Mass.: Lee and Shepard, 1892), p. 7.

8. Alfred Appel, Jr., in J. W. DeForest, *Witching Times* (1856), ed. Alfred Appel, Jr. (New Haven: College and University Press, 1967), p. 20; Andrew Lang, *Boston Transcript,* November 6, 1907, reprinted from *London Morning Post.*

9. Richard Weisman, *Witchcraft, Magic, and Religion in 17th-Century Massachusetts* (Amherst: University of Massachusetts Press, 1984), p. 161.

10. "Letter of Thomas Brattle, F.R.S.," in *Narratives of the Witchcraft Cases 1648–1706,* ed. George Lincoln Burr (New York: Charles Scribner's Sons, 1914), pp. 165–90, cited p. 169. Hereafter in this chapter, Brattle's letter will be cited as LTB and page references given in the text.

11. Perry Miller assumes the reference is to "Elisha Cooke's anti-charter party." Miller, *The New England Mind: From Colony to Province* (Boston: Beacon Press; 1953, 1966), p. 196.

12. Boyer and Nissenbaum attribute this account to Alden himself but give no reason for their attribution; it may be correct, but it is hard to confirm (*SWP* I: 52). The account appears in Calef's "More Wonders," and is written in the third person about Alden (in Burr, *Narratives,*

pp. 353–4). Certainly the writer was sympathetic to Alden, and there is precedent for people writing in the third person about themselves. Burr makes the same attribution (p. 170n).

13. Charles W. Upham, *Salem Witchcraft; with An Account of Salem Village, and a History of Opinions on Witchcraft and Kindred Subjects* (1867), 2 vols.; reprinted (Williamstown, Mass.: Corner House Publ., 1971), II, p. 544. The letter appears on pp. 538–44. Upham concludes that because Corwin kept the document, "he appreciated the weight of its arguments. It is not improbable that he expressed himself to that effect to his brethren on the bench, and perhaps to others (*Salem Witchcraft*, II, p. 448). If he did, and there is no real evidence to support the idea, it would suggest that even a condemning judge did not believe in the actions of the court.

14. Paul Boyer and Stephen Nissenbaum, *Salem Possessed: The Social Origins of Witchcraft* (Cambridge, Mass.: Harvard University Press, 1974).

15. Carol F. Karlsen, *The Devil in the Shape of a Woman* (New York: W. W. Norton, 1987).

16. Marion L. Starkey, *The Devil in Massachusetts: A Modern Enquiry into the Salem Witch Trials* (New York: Alfred A. Knopf, 1949); 2d ed. (1950), pp. 182–5, suggests, as have others, that the Reverend Thomas Bernard of Andover was involved in bringing the accusers there, and in organizing tests for finding witches. Robert Calef, identifying him as "The Rev. Thomas Barnard, associate minister at Andover," prints an account by six women who ambiguously link him to tests done on them for identifying witchcraft ("More Wonders," in Burr, *Narratives,* p. 375). The testimony of the women also appears in *SWP* III: 971–2.

17. Joseph B. Felt, *Annals of Salem* (Salem, Mass.: W. & S. B. Ives, 1845; 2d ed., Boston: James Munroe & Co., 1849), II, p. 478.

18. Boyer and Nissenbaum in *Salem Possessed,* p. 203, write that testimony "secured from ministers in Ipswich, Marblehead, and Salem Town . . . may have saved her." The other ministers who spoke for Sarah Buckley were John Higginson and Samuel Cheever, but there is no record of their testimony before January 2; thus, unless they had spoken earlier, their support would not have been a determining factor in her survival.

19. The attribution of Wise as author is from Upham, *Salem Witchcraft*, II, p. 304.

20. Stephen L. Robbins, "Samuel Willard and the Spectres of God's Wrathful Lion," *New England Quarterly*, vol. 60, no. 4 (December 1987), pp. 596–603. See also David C. Brown, "The Salem Witchcraft Trials: Samuel Willard's *Some Miscellany Observations*," *Essex Institute Historical Collections,* vol. 122 (July 1986), pp. 207–17; and Mark A. Peterson, "'Ordinary' Preaching and the Interpretation of the Salem Witchcraft Crisis by the Boston Clergy," *Essex Institute Historical Collections,* vol. 129 (January 1993), pp. 84–102.

21. "December Meeting, 1884," *Proceedings of the Massachusetts Historical Society,* 2d ser., vol. 1 (1884–5), p. 356. The ministers, Henry Selijns, Peter Peiretus, Godfrey Dellius, and Rudolph Varich, responded on October 11 to a series of questions asked on October 5 by Joseph Dudley. In contrast to Brattle, however, these ministers thought that the devil could inflict torments without "wasting of the body, and . . . weakening of . . . spirits," p. 357.

22. Sir William Phips, letter of February 21, 1693, to the Earl of Nottingham, in Burr, *Narratives,* pp. 198–202, cited p. 196.

23. Ibid., pp. 196–7.

24. Ibid., p. 201. For Calef's account of Stoughton at the Charlestown court, see "More Wonders," in Burr, *Narratives,* pp. 382–3.

25. Hutchinson, *History,* II, p. 46.

26. Phips, "Letter," in Burr, *Narratives,* p. 201.

27. Karlsen, *The Devil in the Shape of a Woman,* p. 106.

28. Karlsen's source is Richard B. Morris, *Studies in the History of American Law* (New York: Columbia University Press, 1930); 2d ed. (Philadelphia: Joseph M. Mitchell, 1959), pp. 159–60. Morris, p. 160, refers to a law providing attainder, although he is silent on when in 1692 it occurred. His source is *The Charters and General Laws of the Colony and Province of Massachusetts Bay* (Boston: T. B. Wait, 1814), pp. 735–6. The law to which Morris refers was not passed at the height of the episode, but was proposed in October, according to *The Charters and General Laws,* and passed in December, according to *The Salem Witchcraft Papers* (III: 885). The documents appear in the two sources with different dates for each, although the wording in the two is almost identical. The one in *The Salem Witchcraft Papers* is clearer, however, in indicating that the legislation printed was passed then rather than proposed. Although Morris indicates otherwise, the law does not specifically establish any laws of attainder; however, it does make reference to appropriate punishments for people who have been "lawfully convicted and attainted" (*Charters,* 735; *SWP* III: 885).

29. Moore, *Notes on the History of Witchcraft in Massachusetts,* p. 170.

30. For Phips's views on the seizures, see the Appendix to this volume.

31. Weisman, *Witchcraft, Magic, and Religion,* p. 98.

32. Hutchinson, *History,* I, p. 377.

33. Wigglesworth, "Letter," p. 646.

34. Upham, *Salem Witchcraft,* II, p. 471.

35. Ibid., pp. 471, 252–3.

36. Calef, "More Wonders," in Burr, *Narratives,* p. 361.

37. The pattern of exploiting women with property and without male protectors is consistent with Carol Karlsen's argument in *The Devil in the Shape of a Woman* about the kinds of women most subject to witchcraft accusation.

38. Calef, "More Wonders," in Burr, *Narratives*, p. 370.
39. Julius Goebel, Jr., and T. Raymond Naughton, *Law Enforcement in Colonial New York: A Study in Criminal Procedure (1664–1776)* (New York: Commonwealth Fund, pp. 525, 527. As Goebel and Naughton make clear, the failure to collect money for the Crown extended beyond New York to the other colonies.
40. Michael Dalton, *The Countrey Justice, Containing the Practice of the Justices of Peace out of their Sessions* (1622), reprinted (New York: Arno Press, 1972), p. 11. Dalton's *Country Justice* went through many editions and was the standard source in English law for Justices of the Peace. What they could not take for themselves was not to be taken by sheriffs. For Dalton on this subject as it pertains to sheriffs, see his *Office and Authoritie of Sherifs* (1623), reprinted (Abingdon, Oxon, England: Professional Books Ltd., 1985), esp. pp. 29 and 187.

    Corwin seems not to have shared his booty with his deputy, George Herrick, who appealed for compensation on the grounds that doing his legal work prevented him from earning his regular income and impoverished him (*SWP* III: 880).
41. English continued his claims, and in 1718 the committee considering English's claims recommended that he be awarded "out of the publick Treasury Two hundred Pounds, in full Satisfaction for what he may have sustained & suffered . . . "(*SWP* III: 1044–5).
42. Richard P. Gildrie, *Salem, Massachusetts 1626–1683: A Covenant Community* (Charlottesville: University Press of Virginia, 1975), p. 135.
43. Curwen Family Papers, American Antiquarian Society. I am grateful to Thomas Knoles and the AAS for permission to cite this document and to print it in the Appendix. For assisting me in matters related to the transcription of the letter, I am grateful to Mr. Knoles, Evelyn Rosenthal, Albert Tricomi, and Paul Szarmach.

    David C. Brown, argues that the General Court on December 14, 1692, passed a bill sanctioning the confiscations of the previous summer. He argues that they did so "to prevent legal retribution from overtaking them." "The Case of Giles Corey," *Essex Institute Historical Collections*, vol. 121 (October 1985), pp. 282–99, cited pp. 296–7.
44. Upham, *Salem Witchcraft*, II, pp. 472–3. Kenneth Murdock has noted that the upheaval caused by the trials did not damage Stoughton politically. "Lest one fancy that popular feeling was in advance of the ministers', it is worth while to note that of all the new judges, Stoughton received most votes" in the election of December 7, 1692. Sewall has a diary entry on December 6, 1692, for Stoughton's election as Chief Justice; subsequent entries confirm his continuing electoral strength. In 1695 Stoughton only dropped from first- to third-highest vote-getter, whereas Saltonstall, who had protested the court's conduct, received insufficient votes for election. Elsewhere in his diary, Sewall reveals that

Saltonstall had been accused of afflicting people. Murdock, *Increase Mather: The Foremost American Puritan* (Cambridge, Mass.: Harvard University Press, 1926), p. 303. Sewall, see *The Diary of Samuel Sewall 1674–1729*, vol. I, in *Collections of the Massachusetts Historical Society*, vol. v, 5th ser.), pp. 370, 373–4, 388, 406. Murdock, though accurate in pointing to Stoughton's electoral strength, draws too great an inference in seeing this as a reflection of "popular feeling" about him, since the electorate was limited to a relatively small part of the population.

45. Although I disagree with some of his conclusions, a fine discussion of the legal complexities has recently been offered by David C. Brown in "The Forfeitures at Salem," *William and Mary Quarterly* (January 1993), pp. 85–111.

46. The letter is dated January 17, 1692, but that is because Parris was using the old calendar system, in which the new year did not start until March. Parris's generosity was probably pragmatic rather than altruistic, since he was in the midst of seeking his salary from a community that was reluctant to give it. See Boyer and Nissenbaum, *Salem Possessed*, pp. 69–70, and *Salem-Village Witchcraft: A Documentary Record of Local Conflict in Colonial New England*, ed. Paul Boyer and Stephen Nissenbaum (Belmont, Calif.: Wadsworth Publ., 1972), pp. 255–8, 280–1.

47. "Letter, Samuel Parris to Jonathan Corwin, January 17, 1692/3, Curwen Family Papers, Essex Institute, Salem, Mass." Brackets indicate words that are not absolutely clear in the letter manuscript. For permission to print this letter, I am grateful to the Essex Institute and its Curator of Manuscripts, Jane E. Ward.

48. Sewall, *Diary*, I, p. 388.

49. Ibid., p. 445.

50. Calef, "More Wonders," in Burr, *Narratives*, p. 387.

51. *The Diary of Cotton Mather*, 2 vols., preface by Worthington Chauncey Ford, 1911; reprinted (New York: Frederick Ungar Publ., n.d.), I, p. 216.

52. See Chapter 2, §II.

53. Margaret Murray, *The God of the Witches* (1931), reprinted (New York: Oxford University Press, 1970), p. 67.

54. Herman Melville, *Moby-Dick* (1851), vol. 6 in *The Complete Writings of Herman Melville*, gen. ed. Harrison Hayford, Hershel Parker, and G. Thomas Tanselle (Evanston, Ill.: Northwestern University Press / Chicago: Newberry Library, 1988), p. 12.

10. Salem story

1. John Updike, *Pigeon Feathers and Other Stories* (New York: Alfred A. Knopf, 1962), pp. 187–96, cited p. 188.

2. Margaret Murray, *The God of the Witches* (1931), reprinted (New York: Oxford University Press, 1970).

3. Robert Rosenthal, "Salem's New Witch Weaves a Spell," *Boston Globe,* October 31, 1974, p. 29.

4. See Richard Godbeer, *The Devil's Dominion: Magic and Religion in Early New England* (Cambridge: Cambridge University Press, 1992), pp. 238–42; *Salem-Village Witchcraft: A Documentary Record of Local Conflict in Colonial New England,* ed. Paul Boyer and Stephen Nissenbaum (Belmont, Calif.: Wadsworth Publ., 1972), pp. 376–8; and Richard Weisman, *Witchcraft, Magic, and Religion in 17th-Century Massachusetts* (Amherst: University of Massachusetts Press, 1984), pp. 209–16. David D. Hall estimates that close to two hundred people were accused; *Witch-Hunting in Seventeenth-Century New England: A Documentary History 1638–1692,* ed. David D. Hall (Boston: Northeastern University Press, 1991), p. 4.

5. "The Best of Salem," ed. and publ. Christine Sullivan and Carolyn Tolles (Salem, Mass., 1983).

6. Anne Driscoll, "For Salem, a Reminder of a Dark Past," *New York Times,* Sunday, October 30, 1988, p. 51.

7. *Diary and Autobiography of John Adams,* ed. L. H. Butterfield, vol. 1 (Cambridge, Mass.: Belknap Press of Harvard University Press, 1961); 2d ed. (1962), p. 319.

8. Charles W. Upham, *Salem Witchcraft; with An Account of Salem Village, and a History of Opinions on Witchcraft and Kindred Subjects* (1867), 2 vols.; reprinted (Williamstown, Mass.: Corner House Publ., 1971), II p. 441.

9. Nathaniel Hawthorne, "Alice Doane's Appeal," in *The Snow-Image and Uncollected Tales,* ed. William Charvat, Roy Harvey Pearce, and Claude M. Simpson (Columbus: Ohio State University Press, 1974), p. 280.

10. Upham, *Salem Witchcraft,* II, pp. 379–80.

11. Rev. A. P. Putnam, "Address at the dedication of a tablet in honor of forty friends of Rebecca Nurse, of Salem Village. July 29, 1892" (Boston: Thomas Todd, Printer, 1894), p. 37.

12. In 1867 Upham identified the site based on "tradition" and on an anecdote attributed to a man named John Symonds, born in 1692, whose nurse is said to have seen the hangings from the Symonds' house. See *Salem Witchcraft,* II, pp. 376–7. Upham's identification has been challenged by, among others, Sidney Perley, "Where the Salem 'Witches' Were Hanged," *Historical Collections of the Essex Institute,* vol. 57 (January 1921), pp. 1–18. In 1903, a newspaper account identifies a tablet on a hill identified as "Gallows hill," but the author of the story argues that the hangings occurred at the base of this hill; "Salem Witches Were Not Hung on Gallows Hill," *Boston Record,* June 10, 1903. The location of the executions remains uncertain.

13. Undated clipping under "Witchcraft Miscellany," Essex Institute, Salem, Mass.
14. John Beresford Hatch, *Salem Witchcraft – Fact or Fiction* (Salem, Mass.: privately published, 1963), p. 3.
15. News release, "Salem Witch Memorial Committee Miscellany" (1970), Essex Institute, Salem, Mass.
16. James Dodson, "It's Still Easy to Meet a Witch in Salem," *Yankee,* vol. 50 (October 1986), pp. 106–15, 188–91, 193, cited p. 193; Driscoll, "For Salem, a Reminder of a Dark Past," p. 51.
17. Robert H. Kahn "Ghost Writing," *Binghamton Press & Sun–Bulletin,* October 31, 1991, p. D1.
18. Joseph Perkins, in *The Intelligencer* (Doylestown, Pa.), November 27, 1992, p. A10.
19. "NFL Has Gone Too Far," *Binghamton Evening Press,* September 18, 1984, p. 1B.
20. Jim Borgman, in *Binghamton Evening Press,* July 22, 1981, p. 14A.
21. Jim Castelli, cited in *Binghamton Evening Press,* June 30, 1984, p. 8C.
22. "Policewoman Defends Nude Poses," *Binghamton Evening Press,* December 2, 1982, p. 106 (Associated Press story).
23. Arthur Wade, "Baby Speaks in Voice of Witch Burned at Stake," *Weekly World News,* April 10, 1984, p. 5.
24. Michael Van Walleghen, "The Permanence of Witches," in *The Wichita Poems* (Urbana: University of Illinois Press, 1966), p. 25; Walt Whitman, "Song of Myself," in *The Collected Writings of Walt Whitman,* ed. Gay Wilson Allen and Sculley Bradley (New York: New York University Press, 1965), p. 66.
25. Henry David Thoreau, *Walden, or Life in the Woods* (1854), ed. J. Lyndon Shanley (Princeton, N.J.: Princeton University Press, 1971), pp. 130–1.
26. John Winthrop citation from *The Puritans,* vol. 1, ed. Perry Miller and Thomas H. Johnson (1938); reprinted (New York: Harper & Row, 1963), p. 199.
27. Upham, *Salem Witchcraft,* II, pp. 437–8.
28. See Winthrop D. Jordan, *White Over Black: American Attitudes Toward the Negro 1550–1812* (Chapel Hill: University of North Carolina Press), p. 118.
29. Perry Miller, *The New England Mind: From Colony to Province* (Boston: Beacon Press; 1953, 1966), p. 191.
30. Stuart Bell, M.P., *When Salem Came to the Boro: The True Story of the Cleveland Child Abuse Cases* (London: Pan Books Ltd., 1988), p. 3.
31. Alan Macfarlane, *Witchcraft in Tudor and Stuart England* (London: Routledge & Kegan Paul, 1970), p. 135.
32. ALS, M. West to Robert S. Rantoul, 21 Aug. 1902, M. West Papers, Essex Institute, Salem, Mass. For permission to publish this material, as

well as the material cited in notes 32 and 33, I am grateful to the Essex Institute and to its Curator of Manuscripts, Jane E. Ward. The bud remains at the Essex Institute.

33. Undated typescript, M. West Papers, Essex Institute, Salem, Mass.
34. ALS, Prof. B. L. Robinson to Prof. Jackson, 15 Dec. 1902, M. West Papers, Essex Institute, Salem, Mass.
35. *A Cry in the Dark*, dir. Fred Schepisi (Warner Bros., 1988), 121 min. The story of Lindy Chamberlain had previously been filmed as *Who Killed Baby Azaria?*
36. Alan Attwood, "Back from the Wilderness," *London Sunday Times Magazine*, May 7, 1989, pp. 20–3, cited p. 23.
37. Getting exact statistics for English witchcraft persecutions is complex, but data extrapolated from Macfarlane's *Witchcraft in Tudor and Stuart England* make clear that more indictments occurred in England during a comparable period than in Massachusetts Bay colony. For a list of New England indictments excluding Salem, see John Demos, *Entertaining Satan: Witchcraft and the Culture of Early New England* (Oxford: Oxford University Press, 1982), pp. 401–9.
38. Caroline Chesebro', *Victoria; or, the World Overcome* (New York: Derby and Jackson, 1856), p. 19.
39. Ibid., p. 465.
40. Joseph B. Felt estimates the Salem population in 1690 as 1,680, but some ambiguity exists as to whether or not he includes Salem Village in the count. Felt, *Annals of Salem* (Salem, Mass.: W. & S. B. Ives, 1845; 2d ed., Boston: James Munroe & Co., 1849), II, p. 410.
41. Marion L. Starkey, *The Devil in Massachusetts: A Modern Enquiry into the Salem Witch Trials* (New York: Alfred A. Knopf, 1949); 2d ed. (1950), p. iv.
42. *Narratives of the Witchcraft Cases 1648–1706,* ed. George Lincoln Burr (New York: Charles Scribner's Sons, 1914), p. 223n; Weisman, *Witchcraft, Magic, and Religion,* p. 141.
43. Carol F. Karlsen, *The Devil in the Shape of a Woman* (New York: W. W. Norton, 1987), p. 217.
44. Paul Boyer and Stephen Nissenbaum, *Salem Possessed: The Social Origins of Witchcraft* (Cambridge, Mass.: Harvard University Press, 1974), p. 7.
45. Demos, *Entertaining Satan,* p. 66.
46. Edmundo O'Gorman, *The Invention of America* (Bloomington: Indiana University Press, 1961).
47. William Shakespeare, *The Tempest* (act 5, sc. 1). For the European imagining of America and the connection of *The Tempest* to it, see Leo Marx, *The Machine in the Garden: Technology and the Pastoral Ideal in America* (New York: Oxford University Press, 1967), pp. 34ff.

Index

Continued from the front of the book

Schmitt